PAPER SQUARE GE
THE MATHEMAT

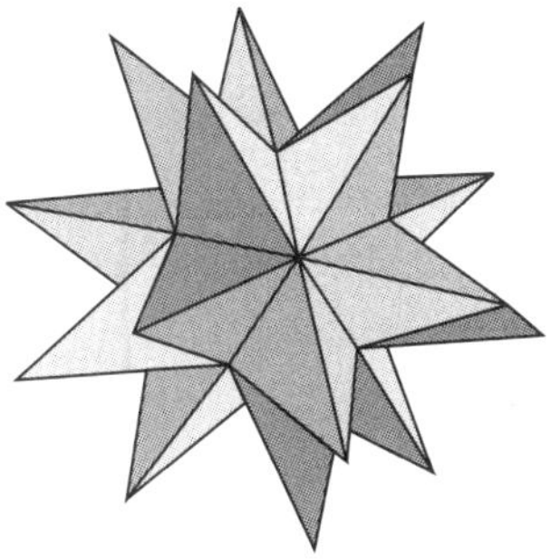

Authors
Michelle Pauls
Tamsen Lomeli

Illustrator
Margo Pocock

Technical Illustrator
Michelle Pauls

Editors
Betty Cordel
Michelle Pauls

Desktop Publishing
Tanya Adams
Tracey Lieder

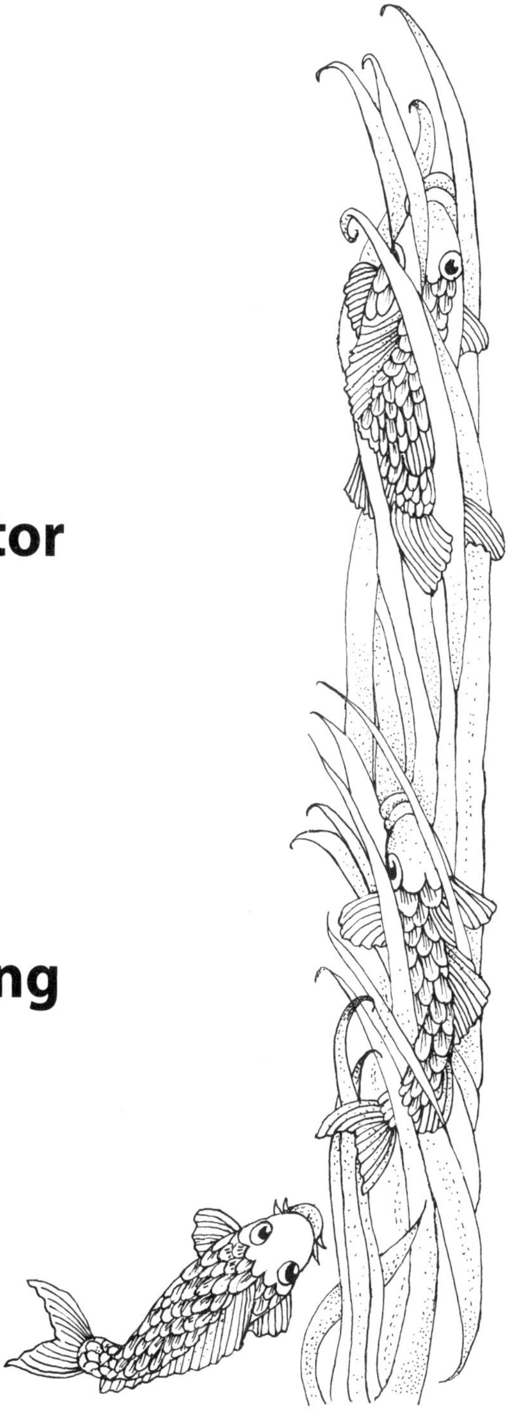

This book contains materials developed by the AIMS Education Foundation. **AIMS** (**A**ctivities **I**ntegrating **M**athematics and **S**cience) began in 1981 with a grant from the National Science Foundation. The non-profit AIMS Education Foundation publishes hands-on instructional materials (books and the quarterly magazine) that integrate curricular disciplines such as mathematics, science, language arts, and social studies. The Foundation sponsors a national program of professional development through which educators may gain both an understanding of the AIMS philosophy and expertise in teaching by integrated, hands-on methods.

Schools, school districts, and other non-profit educational agencies may purchase unlimited duplication rights for AIMS activities for use at one or more school sites. Visit the AIMS website, www.aimsedu.org, for more information or contact AIMS:

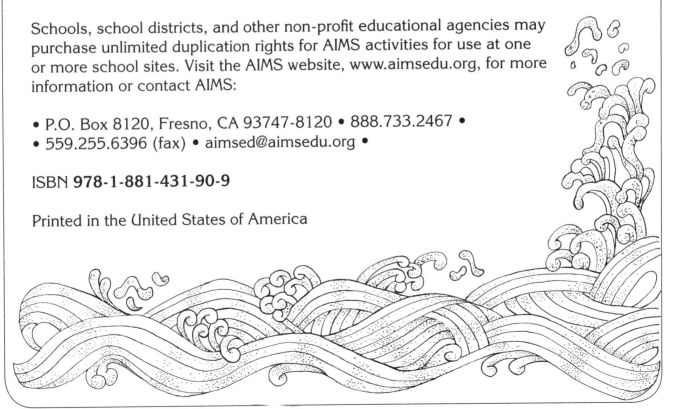

• P.O. Box 8120, Fresno, CA 93747-8120 • 888.733.2467 •
• 559.255.6396 (fax) • aimsed@aimsedu.org •

ISBN **978-1-881-431-90-9**

Printed in the United States of America

I HEAR AND I FORGET

I SEE AND I REMEMBER

I DO AND I UNDERSTAND

—Chinese Proverb

TABLE OF CONTENTS

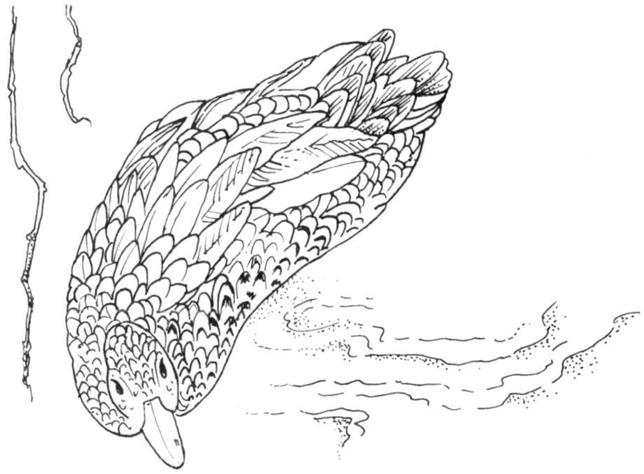

NOTES FROM THE AUTHORS

Origami has never been an area in which I have any special interest or experience. Aside from folding "cootie catchers," my sole exposure to origami as a child was in my father's fifth grade class, where, by exhibiting extraordinary insight or problem-solving skills, you would earn a "Golden Flapping Bird" award. This award was an origami crane that had wings that moved up and down as you pulled on the tail. The coveted prize was received with great pride, but I don't recall any of my classmates ever attempting to learn the design or fold it themselves.

The next time I encountered origami was in September of 1999 when I was given Tamsen Lomeli's masters project and assigned the task of making it into an AIMS publication. I was immediately plunged into a world that I had never before experienced, and found that it was challenging, exciting, and a whole lot of fun. The more I discovered, the more I realized how much more there was to discover. I have never ceased to be amazed at the multitude of things that are possible with just a few squares of paper folded in a certain way.

As the book began to take shape, I became dissatisfied with several of the units that I had found to use, in particular the unit for the dodecahedron and the unit for the stellated octahedron. This dissatisfaction led me to try and design my own units for these shapes, and I discovered that with a little perseverance (and a lot of scratch paper) I was able to develop units with which I was satisfied. It was amazing to me that even with my relative lack of origami experience, I was able to achieve success, not only in folding some fairly complex models, but also in designing some basic units of my own.

Another discovery that I made while embarking on this project was the amazing generosity and helpfulness of the origami community. Through the process of contacting the various designers to obtain permission to use their models, I found a group of people that were genuinely interested and excited about what I was doing and thrilled to have their work be a part of this book. I received invaluable assistance and advice from these fellow enthusiasts and was encouraged by them that the need for a book such as this exists.

I hope *Paper Square Geometry* is as enjoyable for you and your students to use as it was for me to write. Whether you have had experience with origami before, or, like me, are coming to it for the first time as an adult, you should be able to find activities within these pages to challenge and excite you. My hope is that you will use the models presented here to help your students gain an appreciation for the presence of geometry outside the sterile page of proofs and theorems and give them meaningful connections that they will remember for years to come.

-MICHELLE PAULS

On a rainy day 25 years ago, my mother and I sat cross-legged on the floor of the family room amidst tea cups and paper squares, staring intently at the pages of a book. Behind us was an ever-growing pile of crumpled up papers, unsuccessful attempts at folding "the perfect" origami swallow. Hours flew by as we sat folding madly in an attempt to create a paper swallow whose wings would flap when its tail was pulled.

At that time neither my mother or I realized what a great impact this activity, along with many others like it, would have on my attitude toward learning and the course my life would take. As a result of many hands-on experiences, I grew to love learning and value education. A special interest in mathematics and paper folding developed, and I have a great desire to share my love and enthusiasm for mathematics with students using hands-on activities. What began as a mother/daughter, rainy day activity has blossomed over the years into an extremely motivating approach to teaching geometry.

-TAMSEN LOMELI

ABOUT THE CREATORS

Other than origami, what do the people who design origami models do? We asked that question of the people who designed the models we use in this book, and were amazed at the variety of responses. Here is what some of the creators had to say about themselves.

MARC KIRSCHENBAUM

For well over two decades, I have derived great pleasure from origami, the ancient Japanese art of paper folding. Throughout the years, I have managed to design hundreds of original origami works. A number of these works have won awards and have been featured in libraries and museums around the world (most notably the Smithsonian and the American Museum of Natural History). Many of my works can be found in origami periodicals, and I have released a book of my musician origami titled *Paper in Harmony* (ISBN 0-615-11281). By trade, I am an active partner in an executive recruiting firm for computer professionals, located not far from my place of residence in New York City. I am also an active member of OrigamiUSA, a premiere international origami organization. I am currently on the board of directors, and manage the production of many of this organization's publications.

JEANNINE MOSELY

I began folding paper at the age of five when my parents bought me an introductory book on origami. At eight, I became interested in polyhedra when my dad brought home a book of one of Martin Gardner's early collections of his *Mathematical Games* columns. Later, as a mathematics major in college, I brought these two interests together and began trying to fold polyhedra. I developed methods of making the five Platonic solids, each from a single sheet of paper. I folded some other interesting shapes as well. While in graduate school, I began experimenting with modular origami, making complex shapes out of multiple sheets of paper that linked without the use of tape or glue. I created my design for the Stellated Dodecahedra in 1984, shortly after completing my Ph.D. in Electrical Engineering and Computer Science at MIT. Since leaving school, I have worked as a software engineer, designing and implementing algorithms for geometric modeling for the Computer Aided Design industry. I have written software that has been used by customers to design aircraft engines and fuselages, automobiles, custom hip replacement joints, and a revolutionary bicycle that helped its rider win an Olympic medal.

ROBERT NEALE

I was the first president of the Friends of the Origami Center, which was the predecessor of OrigamiUSA. I began folding paper in 1958 and became acquainted with Lillian Oppenheimer, founder of the Origami Center a year later.

My first creation, Thurber Dog, occurred in 1959. In that same year, some of my models were exhibited in the show at Cooper Union Museum for the Arts of Decoration in New York City. In 1964, I delighted many folders and magicians with my "Bunny Bill," a model folded from paper money in which a rabbit pops up out of a top hat. This model combines my interest in origami and magic, which is also evidenced by my subsequent creations.

In 1994 St. Martin's Press published my *Origami, Plain and Simple.* This volume was long awaited, and finally came into being when Thomas Hull prepared diagrams. My book on creating novelties from paper money, with editing by Sam Randlett and diagrams by Earle Oakes, *Folding Money Fooling*, was published in 1997. Another work on my great variety of modular models is in process.

I am a retired professor of psychology and religion and now write books on origami and magic in Burlington, Vermont.

FLORENCE TEMKO

I have always loved crafts, but origami became a passion for me when someone showed me how to make a flapping bird from a square of paper. I shared my new-found hobby with friends and gave hands-on programs in schools and other places. Participants often asked me to write a book with instructions for the things I taught. After about 30 attempts to find a publisher I succeeded in getting a book into print. What a thrill! The editor discovered that I could write clear directions, which was a talent I did not know I had. She encouraged me to write about other crafts that I enjoyed.

That's the story of how I became a professional author. Besides *Paper Pandas and Jumping Frogs—Origami and its Uses,* I have written 43 other how-to books about origami, other paper arts, and world folk crafts with a total of more than 2 1/2 million copies in print. I always test my written directions on other people, to make sure that they are easily understandable.

I have traveled in 31 countries where I have met with paperfolders, weavers, potters, and many other artisans. These encounters have helped me to understand and present multicultural crafts better.

Besides writing books, I continue to give programs in schools, libraries, and museums, including the Metropolitan Museum of Art, and appear on television.

OTHER CREATORS

TOMOKO FUSÈ

Tomoko Fusè is widely regarded as one of the leading minds in the field of unit origami. In 1970 she studied the art of origami with Master Toyoaki Kawai, and has since created countless models of her own. She travels around the world presenting her work at origami conferences and conventions. She has written many books including *Unit Origami, Origami Boxes, Joy of Origami, Joy of Folding Origami*, and *Growing Polyhedrons.* She lives in Nagano Prefecture, Japan.

MITSONOBU SONOBÈ

Mitsonobu Sonobè created the Sonobè unit, which is used to make several of the models in this book. His unit is virtually legendary in its popularity, and has inspired a generation of folders to develop their own so-called "Sonobè variations."

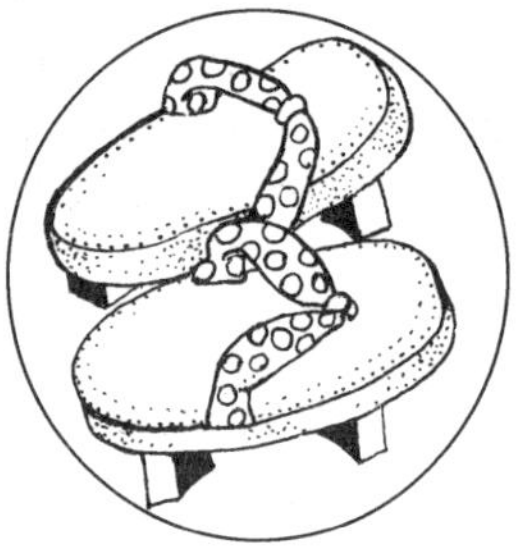

ARTHUR H. STONE

Arthur Stone discovered the flexagon in 1939 while he was a graduate student at Princeton University on a mathematics fellowship. The American-sized paper he received did not fit into his English binder, so he trimmed an inch off the edge to make it fit. When he began to fold the extra strip of paper into various shapes, he discovered the variety of fascinating shapes that we know as flexagons. He resides in the Boston area with his wife Dorothy.

NOTES FROM THE FIELD

Tamsen Lomeli field tested several of the models found in this book with basic math students at a continuation high school. Following are excerpts from her master's project describing the results of this field testing.

The first day of the field testing, students were surprised to see that the textbooks remained on the shelves. After a brief introduction and seeing some sample models, the students quickly involved themselves in the basic box folding lesson *Five-Sided Box.* Many students asked how what they were doing could be called math.

The students worked very well and energetically on all of the unit activities. This author must mention that working well and energetically is not something that normally characterizes this particular group of students. Several students shared that they never knew math could be this interesting. They were genuinely excited about what they were making and learning. Some students continued to fold models outside of class and bring them to display. One student in particular was very talented. One day he brought in a very tiny bird tetrahedron. In the deepest voice imaginable he said, "Mrs. Lomeli, come and look at what I made!" He had the biggest smile on his face. That six foot, five inch tall 18 year old was positively glowing with pride.

With these students being high school students, the geometry taught during the field testing was more in-depth than in the field testing with the junior high students. These high school students had a rudimentary knowledge of basic geometry so they were able to involve themselves more in using logical thinking to prove congruence of figures and establish properties of their models.

It is important to note that the students' response to the unit was so overwhelmingly positive that the school principal stated that the students needed more of these types of learning opportunities. The principal went on to create a math elective class, where the math lessons would be taught by this author using a hands-on, constructivist approach, concentrating on the development of higher order thinking skills. The first week of the class there were only four students, after all, what high school student would want another math class? By the beginning of the second week, 12 more students joined the class, having defected from the physical education class. The word must have spread that something very exciting was happening in the math elective class!

Throughout the field testing, this author was looking for evidence of student growth. Were students developing the ability to think abstractly, reason, discover, understand relationships, and solve problems? Were students in fact developing the tools for mathematical thinking?

By the end of the unit it was clear to see the answer to these questions. Every student who had experienced the unit could assemble any of the models independently, describe their basic properties, and the properties of the two-dimensional shapes they contained, as well as develop a method for finding the surface area of each model. By the time they began folding the last model, most of the students were employing the appropriate geometric terminology and notation to describe the relationships they were seeing. Some of the students were still unclear as to how two or more shapes could be determined to be congruent. Students had little difficulty in classifying the different types of angles. Most students were able to identify an acute angle, right angle, obtuse angle, and straight angle. The area where a significant change in student ability was noticed was in the actual folding of the models. Early on in the unit, some students' models were loosely folded, not precise or compact. Later models such as the 24-sided figure and the triangular box evidenced a great improvement in folding techniques.

It was also interesting to note the complete absence of any discipline issues. Students were so busy using both hands to fold, thinking about the activity, and keeping up with their classmates that there was no opportunity to misbehave. Students that had been identified as sources of possible problems were so engaged in the activities that it didn't occur to them to disrupt the lesson or disturb other students. In several cases, these students were the most excited about the activity and ended up helping other students to complete their models.

It was observed that the students experienced great enjoyment in participating in the field testing of this unit. Many students were so involved in the activities that they continued working even after the bell rang signaling the end of class. A common request students had was for the directions to fold different types of models. Students also continually brought in models of various sizes they had made at home using materials ranging from construction paper to paper napkins. One student brought in a large 24-sided figure made from foil. He referred to it as his "disco ball." It was clear to see that these students had been motivated by the unit and methods used in its presentation.

The students were very proud of what they had accomplished and of all the interesting geometry they had learned. They were honestly surprised at how much they had learned while having so much fun making the origami models.

A BRIEF HISTORY OF ORIGAMI

When most people think of origami, they think of Japan; however, origami actually started in China with the invention of paper sometime in the first century AD. It was not until the sixth century AD, when Buddhist monks carried the secret of paper to Japan, that the art of paper folding began in that country. Because of the initial cost of paper, origami began as a pastime of the wealthy. However, as paper became a more accessible commodity, origami became a widespread practice among people of all classes. For hundreds of years, designs were passed down orally, usually from mother to daughter. This resulted in only the simplest folds surviving from generation to generation.

With the increase of trade in later centuries, origami eventually reached other areas of the world. When the Moors invaded Spain in the eighth century, they carried the secret of origami with them. However, because the Muslim religion prohibits the creation of representational images, their interest in origami was centered in the geometry of the folding process. Even after the Inquisition, which drove the Moors from Spain, paper folding survived in that country, and was taken from there to many other parts of the world.

Despite its long history, the oldest surviving written instructions for origami are in the Japanese book *How to Fold One Thousand Paper Cranes*, which was published in 1797. In 1845, the first collection of origami models, *Window on Midwinter*, was published, also in Japan. The word "origami" itself is also a fairly recent development. It was not until 1880 that the word was coined to describe the art of paper folding. Origami is a combination of the Japanese words *oru* (to fold) and *kami* (paper).

In modern times, the popularity of origami has become worldwide, and there are origami societies, clubs, and organizations across the globe. Modern paper folders are constantly pushing the limits of their imaginations to create paper masterpieces—from completely realistic and anatomically correct insects, to spectacular and complex geometric figures that take 900 units to assemble.

MODEL OF MATHEMATICS

The development of the mathematical experiences in *Paper Square Geometry: The Mathematics of Origami* is consistent with the belief that all learning takes place in four basic environments embodied in the Model of Mathematics. If students are to understand and appreciate their experiences with origami, they must acquire and process knowledge in each of the four environments pictured and described here.

Model of Mathematics

Doing: Real-World Experiences

The circle represents hands-on experiences that are embodied by each of the activities in this book. As students build each origami model, they will connect the geometric principles and properties to real objects and make visual comparisons among their completed models.

Writing: Oral and Written Communication

The triangle represents mathematics in oral and written forms, which students experience by using the language of geometry to represent the concepts and relationships that exist in the folded models and the individual units. As students explore each model, they will make use of the appropriate language and notation to record their discoveries.

Illustrating: Pictorial or Graphic Communication

The square symbolizes the picturing of information which, in this case, involves picturing the three-dimensional models in a two-dimensional form by examining the unfolded units. Students will draw the fold lines that make up individual units and examine the geometric principles and properties that they contain including parallel and perpendicular lines, similar polygons, and congruent polygons.

Thinking: Critical Thinking

The hexagon represents the fourth environment in which there is opportunity to reflect the actions that have been performed and observed. In this setting both the teacher and the learner are engaged in critical thinking, analysis, generalizing, and applications to new settings.

Our best teaching and learning comes from the many connections and translations among these four environments. The model provides a way to design both instruction and evaluation.

NCTM STANDARDS 2000

AIMS is committed to remaining at the cutting edge of providing curriculum materials that are user-friendly, educationally sound, developmentally appropriate, and aligned with the recommendations found in national education reform documents. The following NCTM Standards 2000* are addressed by the activities in *Paper Square Geometry: The Mathematics of Origami.*

Grades 3-5

- ✦ *Identify, compare, and analyze attributes of two- and three-dimensional shapes and develop vocabulary to describe the attributes*
- ✦ *Investigate, describe, and reason about the results of subdividing, combining, and transforming shapes*
- ✦ *Explore congruence and similarity*
- ✦ *Identify and describe line and rotational symmetry in two- and three-dimensional shapes and designs*
- ✦ *Build and draw geometric objects*
- ✦ *Use geometric models to solve problems in other areas of mathematics such as number and measurement*
- ✦ *Develop strategies to determine the surface areas and volumes of rectangular solids*

Grades 6-8

- ✦ *Precisely describe, classify, and understand relationships among types of two- and three-dimensional objects using their defining properties*
- ✦ *Examine the congruence, similarity, and line or rotational symmetry of objects using transformations*

Grades 9-12

- ✦ *Analyze properties and determine attributes of two- and three-dimensional objects*
- ✦ *Explore relationships (including congruence and similarity) among classes of two- and three-dimensional geometric objects, make and test conjectures about them, and solve problems involving them*

* Reprinted with permission from *Principles and Standards for School Mathematics*, 2000 by the National Council of Teachers of Mathematics. All rights reserved.

GENERAL MANAGEMENT

The following questions and answers are designed to help you understand *Paper Square Geometry: The Mathematics of Origami* and how to best use it with your students. Please take the time to carefully read through this section, as there are many important tips that will help you present the material in this book in the most effective way possible.

PRELIMINARY QUESTIONS

Why origami?

A hands-on, discovery-based approach to teaching geometry through origami allows students opportunities to construct their own meaning, discover relationships, and create their own understanding of the imbedded mathematical concepts. When students experience this kind of learning, they are able to retain more of what they have learned. The geometric discoveries students will make and the knowledge they will construct by building three-dimensional geometric models can be applied to many other situations and problems. This approach will also challenge students to enhance their problem-solving skills and discover patterns and relationships.

By using the activities in this book, students will be actively engaged in discovering and understanding geometry concepts through origami. They will gain hands-on experience in using geometry to create three-dimensional models from two-dimensional paper squares and rectangles. The activities in this book will allow students to see geometry in action. They were designed to provide students with different situations in which to take a close look at specific geometric concepts and problems in a concrete fashion. Through the process of folding the individual models, students will increase their spatial awareness, discover and internalize basic geometric concepts, and be presented with meaningful problem-solving situations. These activities will also introduce students to the language of mathematics as they learn to describe their discoveries using appropriate geometric terminology and notation.

In addition to the value of origami as a discovery-based approach, there is the aesthetic quality of the models. Completed origami models make beautiful art projects, and part of the challenge of folding a multi-unit model is determining the color scheme which will produce the most attractive final product. There are also multiple connections that can be made to other subject areas such as social studies, art, and literature.

What if I have never done origami before?

No problem! The activities in this book are user-friendly and come with very specific diagrams and written instructions. Once you have folded a few models, you will begin to develop a folding style that will become quicker and more precise as you gain experience. The models in this book are fairly basic in terms of their folds and assembly, and even a novice should be able to complete them all with a little persistence.

MATERIALS

What kind of paper do the models require?

The models in this book are almost all made from paper squares. There are a few activities that use different sizes and shapes of paper, but the specifics for these are given in the activities. Ideally two-sided paper (paper that has a different color on the front and the back) should be used so that students are able to easily follow the diagrams, which indicate front and back using shading. The most effective paper can vary from model to model. Because most of the models in this book are unit origami, traditional origami paper can sometimes be more difficult to work with because it is typically lightweight and makes flimsier final products. However, in some of the activities, *Origami Squared* and *The Tangram* notably, lightweight paper is an advantage. Colored copy paper is a good weight for many of the models, however, it has the disadvantage of being only one-sided, which can complicate some of the folding instructions. Fadeless® brand paper that many schools have for bulletin boards is a good weight for unit origami models, and has the added benefit of being two-sided. Feel free to experiment with different types of paper to find the best texture, weight, and quality for a particular model.

How important is the size of the paper?

Because so many of the activities ask students to compare two different figures, it is important that all of the models (at least within one section) be made with the same size paper squares. This will preserve the dimensions of the models and make comparisons between two different polyhedra valid. Six-inch squares are the standard in origami, and are a good size for students to begin with, especially if they have had little or no previous folding experience.

Where can I get origami paper?

Two-sided paper squares of a weight suited for a majority of the models in this book can be purchased from AIMS in classroom sets of 480 six-inch squares in 20 colors for $17.95 (order #4130). Any major arts and crafts store or local stationery store should also carry traditional origami paper in a variety of sizes, colors and styles. Additionally, the *Resources* section in the appendix has a long listing of companies, mostly on the Internet, that supply origami paper. Another option is to buy colored copy paper and have it cut into squares at an office supply or copy store, or cut it yourself with an Ellison die-cut or paper cutter.

How many different colors of paper do I need?

Some of the activities have very specific directions as to the number of colors of paper that should be used for that particular model. While these suggestions are not mandatory, they will make it much easier for the students to follow the directions, as well as making a more aesthetic final product. The most colors any single model requires is five, while many require three or four.

Are there other materials needed besides paper?

Many of the activities in this book have students fold an additional unit after they have constructed their model to use for examining the geometric properties and relationships in the fold lines. It is recommended that you use patty paper (which comes pre-cut in squares), or waxed paper for these extra units. Using patty paper or waxed paper allows students to clearly see each fold line, because the creases become white lines when the paper is folded. Waxed paper can also be used on the overhead to show the entire class the crease lines on an unfolded unit because, when placed on an overhead, the creases show up as dark lines against the outline of the square. You can also use a pencil to scratch into the wax to identify angles, line segments, etc. (Patty paper does not work as well on the overhead because it is more opaque than waxed paper, making the creases more difficult to see.) Patty paper can be purchased at restaurant supply stores, or from Key Curriculum Press (see *Resources*). Rulers will also be necessary in many of the activities, and occasionally colored pens or pencils will also be needed.

UNDERSTANDING THE BOOK AND THE ACTIVITIES

How do my students and I read the folding instructions?

A *Glossary of Symbols and Diagrams* has been included to explain the folding instructions. The notation used in this book is generally standard, and can be applied to other origami diagrams outside of this publication, with a few exceptions. Give each student a copy of the *Glossary of Symbols and Diagrams* before they do the first activity, and go over each item as a class, perhaps doing an example of each fold to clarify the process involved. These sheets should be kept by students to refer to as needed in subsequent activities.

What special terminology and concepts will students need to understand for these activities?

A *Glossary of Terms* is provided to give students the mathematical language that they will need to communicate their discoveries as they explore their figures. It also gives them the symbolic language they will need to correctly represent their discoveries using geometric notation. The concept of symmetry has a separate set of activity sheets for students to do so that they become comfortable with the different types of symmetry that they will be asked to identify in the activities. These activity sheets are located in the appendix. Be sure to spend adequate time with all of the terms and symbols so that students have a clear working understanding of their meanings and applications. This is especially important if students have had limited exposure to geometry.

How is this book organized?

This book is organized into six sections: Beginning Folds, Platonic Solids, Stellated Solids, Flexible Origami, Origami Puzzles, and Unit Explorations. An attempt has been made to follow a logical progression and to arrange the activities from least to most difficult; however, this is not always possible. The final section of the book explores three basic origami units: the Sonobè unit, the equilateral triangle unit, and the right triangle unit. These explorations are intended to be done at any time when they fit with the model that the class is folding.

How are the activities organized?

Each activity has a teacher's guide, a set of folding instructions, and an exploration section. The teacher's guide gives information and advice for each specific activity, as well as discussion questions and solutions, if any exist. The folding instructions are not meant to stand alone, but to complement your instruction as you take students through the folding procedure. However, as students encounter the same unit for the second and third time, they will need less and less instruction from you and will be able to rely solely on the written instructions. The exploration section is where students are challenged to look at their models and the individual units in light of geometric properties and principles.

Should the folding and exploration both be done in one day?

Ideally both the folding and exploration would take place in the same period so that the experience is fresh in students' minds; however, this may not be feasible in many cases. For this reason the student sheets have been organized so that the folding and exploration sections are separate and can easily be done on two different days if necessary.

Do I have to do every model in this book for my students to benefit?

Certainly not; students will be able to gain important insight from doing only one or two models. However, the more exposure students have to the ideas in this book, the deeper their understanding of the geometry inherent in the models will become.

How do I choose which models to do with my class?

When choosing which models to do with your students, it is important to look at the "prerequisites" for a given activity. The further along in a section the activity is, the greater the chance that it asks students to make comparisons to a previous activity or model. Be sure that the activities you choose go together and do not ask students to make comparisons to models they have not made or make use of information they do not have.

DOING THE ACTIVITIES WITH YOUR CLASS

How important is accuracy?

Accuracy of folding is critical in origami, especially unit origami. If students are sloppy at the beginning, it can have very frustrating results at later stages when pieces don't fit together as they should. Encourage students to take the time to make their folds correctly, going over some basic folding techniques if necessary. Simple things like lining up edges and making corners meet ensure that pieces will be consistent and fit together well. When following the written instructions, encourage students to check their paper against the diagram for that step. If they do not look the same, a mistake has been made in the folding.

What can I do to help students understand the folding process?

Have a series of papers showing each individual step in the folding process. These models can be labeled and pinned to a bulletin board for students to look at if they get stuck at a certain step. While it may not be practical to do this for every unit, it is certainly feasible, and useful, for the units that are used in several models, such as the Sonobè unit and the equilateral triangle unit.

How should I take the class through the folding process?

There are several different methods for doing origami as a class, each of which has its advantages and disadvantages. If it is the first time students have encountered a particular unit, you will need to go through each step of the folding process as a class. One way to do this is to use a square of waxed paper on the overhead projector. As you do each step in the folding procedure, students can see both the fold line, and the shape of the paper. Another way is to use a large square of paper that you fold and then walk around to show each group. A third possible method is to have aides, student workers, or volunteers learn the folding procedure beforehand and spread themselves throughout the class to help deal with questions as they arise.

How long will it take my students to fold a model?

The amount of time it takes your class to complete an activity will vary widely depending on the difficulty of the model and the experience of the students. At first, even simple models will take an entire class period, but as students gain more experience, they will be able to complete the folding more quickly.

What is the best way for students to work on their folding?

Each class has a different dynamic; however, it is usually works well for students to work together in pairs. This way when students get stuck with a particular fold, they can ask their partners for help before coming to you.

Should each student always fold their own models?

Whenever possible, it is always better for each student to have his or her own model. However, due to the amount of paper and folding required for some of the models, you may find that it is more feasible (and cost-effective) to have students work together in small groups to construct one model rather than each doing their own. When the number of units is greater than 10 or 15 the time (and amount of paper) it takes each student to fold his or her own model can begin to outweigh the benefits. Students can always take a copy of the folding instructions home and make the model outside of class.

Should I do the models myself before I do them with my class?

Yes! *Always* have a completed model of the figure students are trying to assemble available for them to look at. Especially as the models get larger and more complex, the shapes can be difficult to visualize and assemble without a tangible model for referencing. If you have not folded the model yourself, you will also find it very difficult to assist students when they get stuck.

What other things do I need to have prepared in advance?

For each activity where students look at the nature of the folds created by their model, make an overhead transparency of the appropriate diagram or have a waxed paper version of the unit that you have labeled. This will facilitate class discussion and allow students to check their folds for accuracy.

Is there anything else I should know before I use this book with my class?

First: Persevere. You and your students may initially experience frustration as you learn to fold and assemble the models. Keep trying. Look at the diagrams carefully and read the instructions. Always match your paper to the picture at each step along the way. Second: Have fun! Allow yourself to enjoy the creative process that goes on in origami and encourage your students to do the same. You may discover that you have some budding origami enthusiasts or even designers in your class who will use this experience to do many exciting things with paper that you never would have thought were possible.

GLOSSARY OF SYMBOLS AND DIAGRAMS

The following pages explain the symbols, terminology, and diagrams used in this book. Be sure to read them carefully and refer to them as necessary when you are folding your models.

Paper

1. Traditional origami paper comes in squares and is often white on one side, and colored on the other. If you are using two-sided paper for your models, you will need to pay careful attention to how you fold your units. Most of the folds in this book begin with the white side of the paper facing up so that the colored side shows in the completed model. Each diagram has been shaded to indicate front (colored) and back (white). Be sure to pay close attention to which side of the paper is being used or folded at any given time.

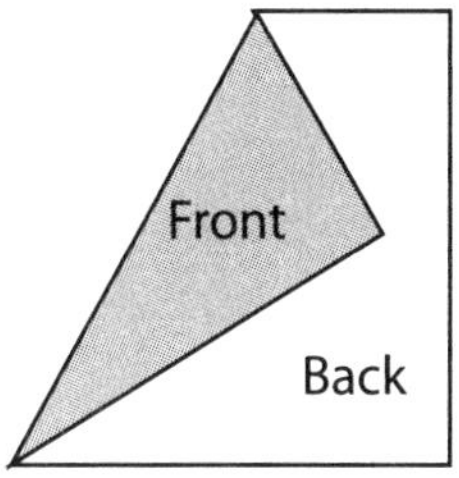

Creases

1. Previous crease lines are indicated by thin lines that do not extend to the edges of the paper. The horizontal and vertical folds in the first diagram result in the paper being divided into four sections, as can be seen by the crease lines in the second diagram.

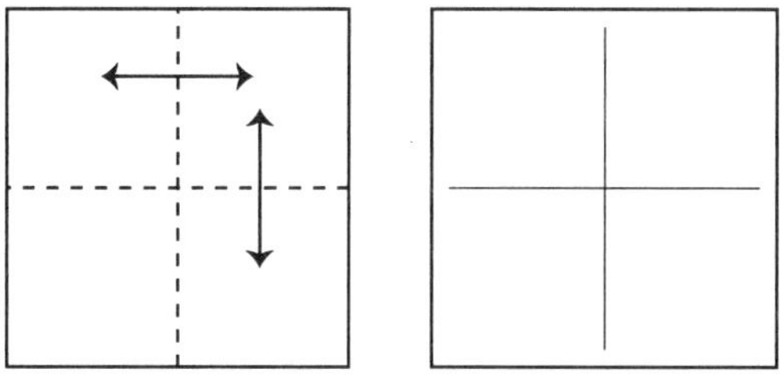

Folds

1. Valley folds are the most common fold you will use in these activities. They are concave creases indicated by a dashed line.

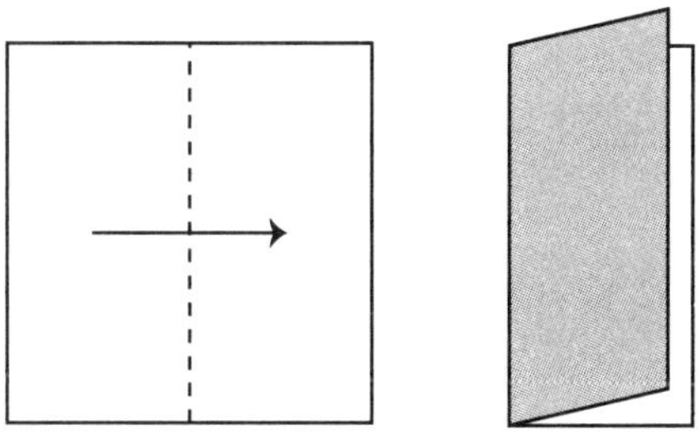

2. Mountain folds are not as common as valley folds in these activities. They occur both by themselves and in combination with valley folds (see Arrows #2). A mountain fold is convex and is indicated by a dash-dot-dot-dash line.

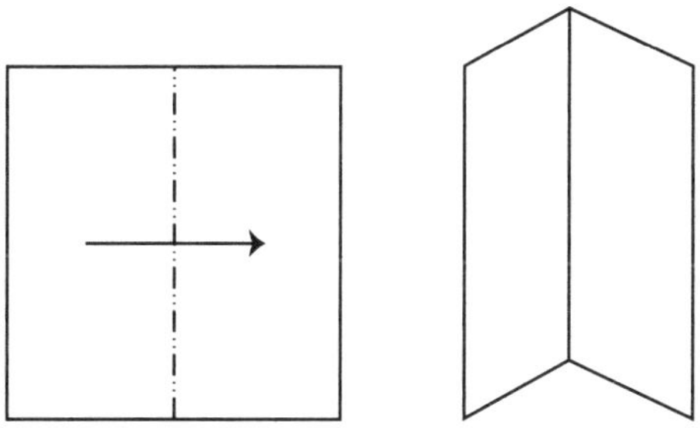

Arrows

1. Arrows indicate the direction in which the paper is to be folded. In the example below, the left side is brought over to the right.

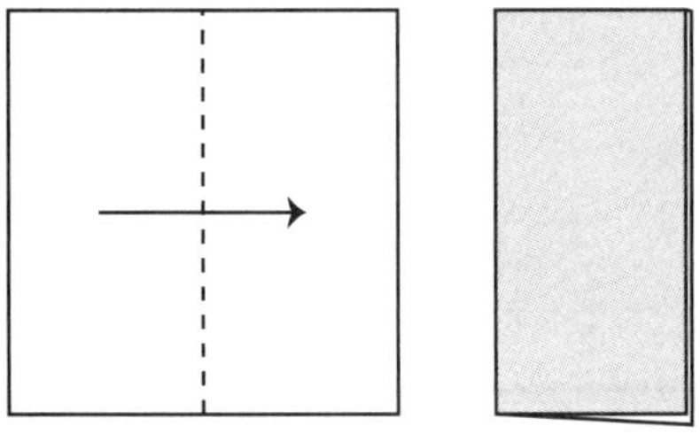

2. A double ended arrow indicates a crease that is to be folded and then opened up. A crease differs from a fold because the paper returns to its previous shape after being folded.

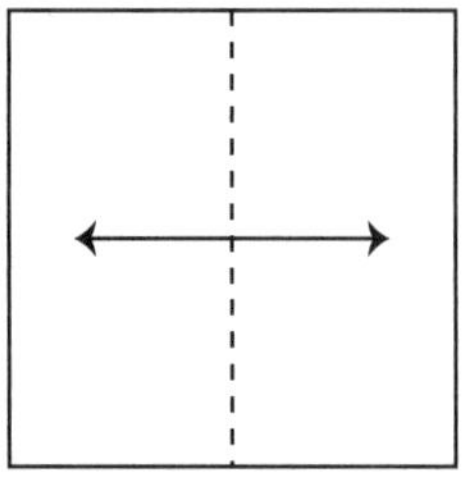

3. A jagged arrow indicates a combination fold where a mountain and a valley fold are both used. In these situations the paper is folded both in (valley) and out (mountain) in the same step.

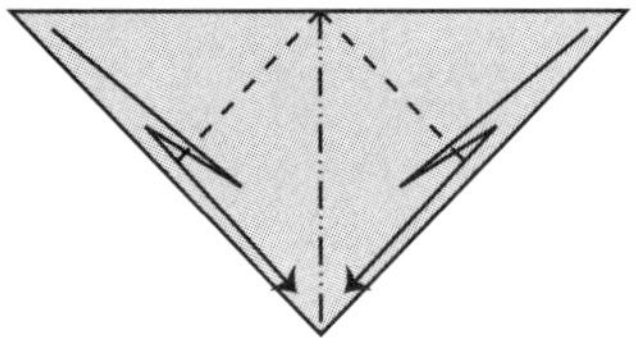

4. An arrow that is partially solid and partially broken indicates that something is inserted at the point where the line becomes broken.

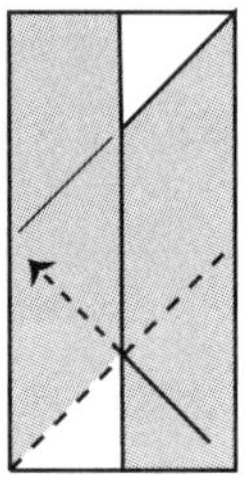

Tips for folding accuracy

1. Always match up corners and edges. Hold the paper in place with one hand, while using the other to make the crease.
2. Make your creases starting at the center of the fold and then moving out towards the corners.
3. Make all creases sharp, running over them with the side of your thumb to reinforce them.
4. Always check your paper against the diagram for that step in the folding process. If your paper doesn't match the picture you see, you have done something wrong.

GLOSSARY OF TERMS

General

- **Congruent:** Having the same size and shape
- **Similar:** Having the same shape, but not necessarily the same size
- **Parallel:** In the same plane, never intersecting
- **Perpendicular:** Intersecting at right angles
- **Line segment:** Part of a line consisting of two endpoints and all of the points in between

Angles

- **Acute angle:** An angle measuring less than 90°
- **Obtuse angle:** An angle measuring greater than 90° but less than 180°
- **Right angle:** An angle measuring 90°
- **Straight angle:** An angle measuring 180°

Geometric Figures

- **Polygon:** A closed, two-dimensional figure formed by joining three or more line segments at their endpoints, such as a triangle, square, hexagon, or octagon
  - **Triangle:** Any three-sided polygon
    - **Scalene Triangle:** A triangle with no two congruent sides
    - **Isosceles Triangle:** A triangle with two congruent sides
    - **Equilateral Triangle:** A triangle with all sides congruent
    - **Acute triangle:** A triangle with three acute angles
    - **Obtuse triangle:** A triangle with one obtuse angle
    - **Right triangle:** A triangle with one right angle
  - **Quadrilateral:** Any four-sided polygon
      - **Trapezoid:** A quadrilateral with only one pair of parallel sides
    - **Parallelogram:** Any quadrilateral that has two pairs of parallel sides
      - **Rectangle:** A parallelogram with four right angles
      - **Square:** A parallelogram with four right angles and four congruent sides

Geometric Solids

- **Polyhedron:** A closed, three-dimensional figure made of polygons, such as a tetrahedron or a cube
  - **Tetrahedron:** A polyhedron having four faces—a regular tetrahedron has four faces that are all equilateral triangles
  - **Cube:** A polyhedron having six faces, each of which is a square
  - **Octahedron:** A polyhedron having eight triangular faces—a regular octahedron has eight faces that are all equilateral triangles
  - **Icosahedron:** A polyhedron having 20 triangular faces—a regular icosahedron has 20 faces that are all equilateral triangles

- **Face:** Any of the polygons that make up a polyhedron
- **Edge:** A line segment along that two faces come together
- **Vertex:** Any point where three or more edges come together

Prefixes for Geometric Figures and Solids

# of Sides/Faces	Prefix	Polygon or Polyhedron
3	tri-	Polygon
4	quad-	Polygon
4	tetra-	Polyhedron
5	penta-	Both
6	hexa-	Both
7	hepta-	Both
8	octa-	Both
9	nona-	Both
10	deca-	Both
12	dodeca-	Both
20	icosa-	Polyhedron

GEOMETRIC NOTATION

In geometry, specific notation is used to identify lines, shapes, angles, properties, etc. The following section explains the notation that you will need as you do the activities in this book. Each of the explanations will use the following figures as examples.

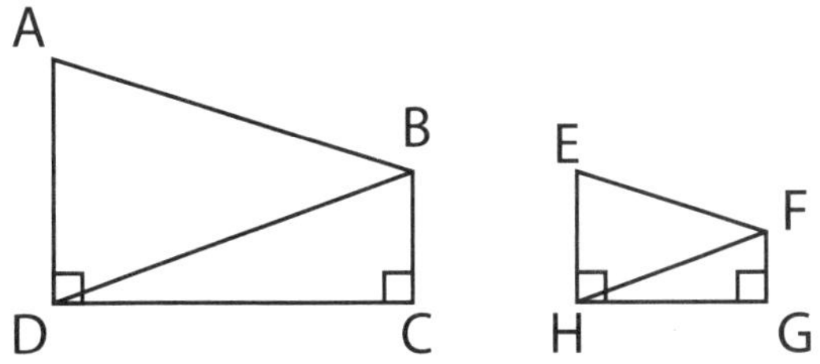

Triangles: In geometric notation a triangle is identified by listing the three points that mark its vertices preceded by a triangle shape. In the figures above there are four triangles: ΔABD, ΔBCD, ΔEFH, and ΔFGH. (The order of the letters is not important, as long as all vertices that make up the triangle are included.)

Quadrilaterals: Likewise, quadrilaterals are identified by listing the four points that mark their vertices preceded by a quadrilateral shape. The figures above would be written:

▱ ABCD and ▱ EFGH

Lines: Line segments are identified by listing the two endpoints that mark the segment with a horizontal line over the two letters. For example, the quadrilaterals above include lines $\overline{AB}$ and $\overline{FH}$.

Angles: Angles are labeled by writing the angle symbol (∠) followed by the letter of the angle. In the diagrams above, $\angle C = 90°$.

Congruent: The symbol ≅ is used to indicate congruence between two lines, angles, figures, etc. In the figures above, angle C is congruent to angle G: $\angle C \cong \angle G$.

Similar: The symbol ~ is used to indicate similarity between two figures. In the diagrams above, the two quadrilaterals are similar: ▱ ABCD ~ ▱ EFGH

Parallel: If two lines are parallel, the lines are listed with two vertical lines in between. For example to say that the line from point A to point D is parallel to the line from point B to point C you would write $\overline{AD} \parallel \overline{BC}$.

Perpendicular: When two lines are perpendicular in a geometric figure, they are marked with a square, as can be seen in the bottom two corners of each figure. The notation for perpendicular lines looks like this: $\overline{AD} \perp \overline{DC}$, $\overline{HG} \perp \overline{FG}$

ORIGAMI MODELS

Five-sided boxes (far left), triangular boxes (top center), bird tetrahedrons (bottom center), rectangular boxes (far right)

Icosahedron (top left), open-faced dodecahedron (top center), octahedron box (top right), regular dodecahedron (center left), regular octahedron (center), octahedron 2 (center right), open-faced cube (bottom left), cubes (bottom center right), tetrahedrons (bottom center),

Great stellated dodecahedron (top left), small stellated dodecahedron (top right), stellated icosahedron (center), 24-sided figure (bottom left), stellated octahedron (bottom center and bottom right)

Ring pinwheel, closed (top left), flexastar, open (top right), ring pinwheel, open (center), flexastar, closed (far right), hexaflexagon (bottom left), rotating tetrahedron (bottom right)

FIVE-SIDED BOX

FOCUS

Students will fold three-dimensional five-sided boxes and identify the geometric properties of their boxes. They will then look at an unfolded unit and determine what relationships exist between the fold lines.

KEY QUESTIONS

What geometric relationships are created by folding the five-sided box model?

What geometric relationships exist in the folded box?

MATH

Properties of geometric shapes
Labeling geometric drawings
Geometric notation
- parallel
- perpendicular
- congruent
- angles

PAPER

One or two squares per model
One square for exploration

ADDITIONAL MATERIALS

Rulers

CREATOR

Unknown

Procedure

1. Hand out the folding instructions (pages three and four) and one paper square to each student.
2. Take students through the folding process step by step. If desired, students can repeat the process with a second square to make a lid for their box, but this is not necessary. (For a good fit, this second square should be just slightly smaller or slightly larger than the original square.)
3. When all students have completed their boxes, have them get into small groups and hand out the remaining student sheets and an additional square of paper to each student.
4. Have students work together to complete the questions and construct the model of their unfolded unit. Students should use rulers for this final section to be sure that their fold lines are drawn as accurately as possible.
5. When all groups have finished, close with a time of class discussion where students share their answers and what they discovered about the geometry inherent in their models.

Discussion

1. What shapes are the sides of the box? [rectangular]
2. What can you say about their relationship to each other? How do you know? [The sides are all congruent, they intersect at right angles, opposite sides are parallel, adjacent sides are perpendicular, etc.]
3. What is the relationship between the length of one side of the box and the height of one side of the box? [The length is twice the height.] How do you know? [Each side can be divided into two congruent squares. Since the side of one square is the height of the rectangular side, the length is twice the height.]
4. What can you say about the relationship between the triangles on the sides of the box? [They are also congruent.]
5. Looking at the side of the box, what can you say about how rectangles can be divided into other shapes?
6. What shape does the bottom of the box appear to be? [square]
7. How can you prove this? (See *Solutions.*)
8. What do you notice about the designs created by the fold lines? [Everything is perfectly symmetrical. The diagonals are all 45° angles, all of the folds are the same distance apart, etc.]
9. Looking at the unfolded unit, which of the fold lines correspond to the base of the box? [Those that form the central square.] ...the sides? [Those that form the four squares around the center.] How do you know?

Extensions

1. Determine the relationship between the size of the original square and the dimensions of the finished box.
2. Have students determine how to make boxes that would fit neatly inside each other and carry out their plan.
3. Use wrapping paper to fold decorative gift boxes for special occasions.

Solutions

Five-Sided Box Exploration

1.a. What are the names of the points where the fold lines meet the outer edges of the square? [midpoints]

b. How do the four smaller squares compare? [They are congruent.]

c. What portion of the larger square is taken up by one smaller square? [one-fourth]

d. Make a statement about the relationship between the two folds made and the results you see. [The folds are perpendicular and divide the paper into four congruent squares.]

2.a. What name would you give the fold line you see in relation to the small square? [diagonal]

b. What can you say about the diagonal of a square and how it divides the square? [It divides the square into two congruent isosceles right triangles.]

3. What shapes are the flaps? [trapezoids]

4. What shape is created by these folds? [rectangle] How do you know? [It has four right angles and two sets of congruent sides.]

6. What shape do you see? [irregular hexagon]

Five-Sided Box Anatomy

The square below shows the lines that students are asked to draw on their squares. The way in which the points are labeled may vary from student to student.

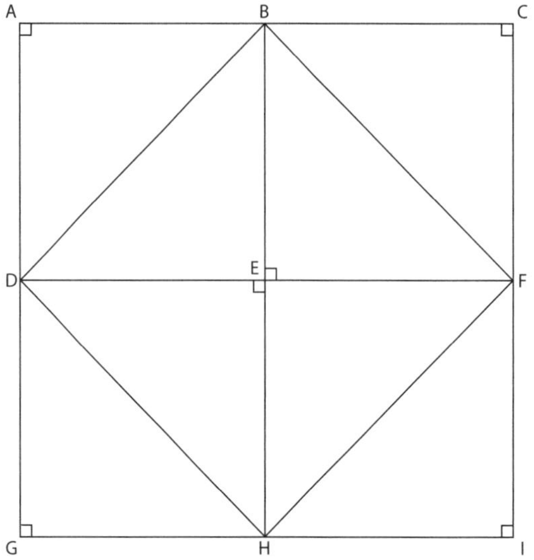

1. Draw in the horizontal and vertical midlines. What types of lines are these? What angles are created at the point of intersection? Label these central angles. [The horizontal and vertical midlines are perpendicular. Ninety-degree angles (marked by the squares) are formed at their intersection.]
2. Draw in the fold lines that connect the midpoints of the sides of your square. What shapes are in each corner? What is their relationship to each other? How do you know? [The lines connecting the midlines create isosceles right triangles in each corner. They all have one 90° angle and two congruent sides.]
4. Use geometric notation to represent the relationship between the large corner triangles. [The relationship between the corner triangles can be written as follows: $\Delta ABD \cong \Delta BCF \cong \Delta DGH \cong \Delta HIF$]
5. Examine the shape in the center of your paper. What does it appear to be? [a square]
6. How can you show this using what you know about the properties of shapes? [We know that line segments BH and DF are perpendicular and intersect at the center of the paper. This means that the paper is divided into four congruent squares. The line segments BF, FH, HD, and DB are all diagonals of these smaller congruent squares. We know that each diagonal is the same length and that the measure of each diagonal is 45° because the lines bisect right angles in congruent squares. Two of these diagonals form each corner of the shape BFHD. Since each diagonal is the same length and 45 + 45 is 90, the shape BFHD must be a square.]

FIVE-SIDED BOX

Folding Instructions

1. Fold the square in half vertically and unfold, and then horizontally and unfold.

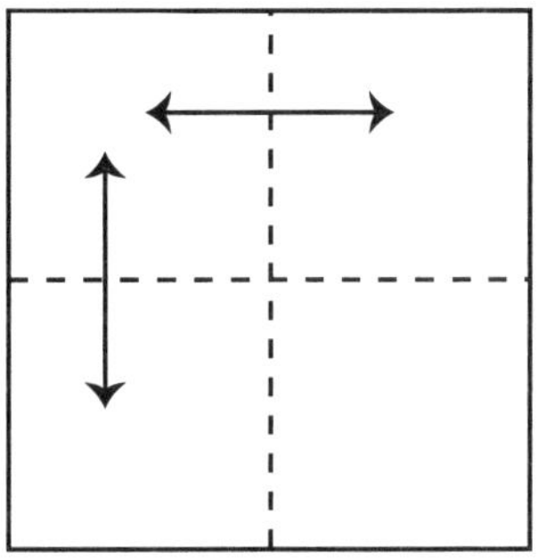

2. Fold each corner of the square in to meet the center.

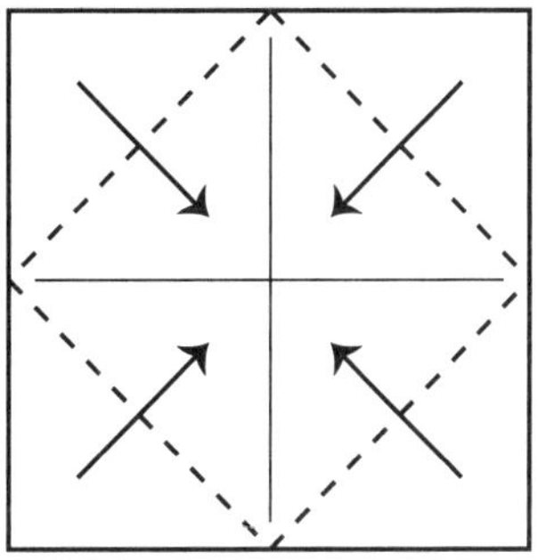

3. Fold each of the original corners under so that they touch the midpoints of their respective sides.

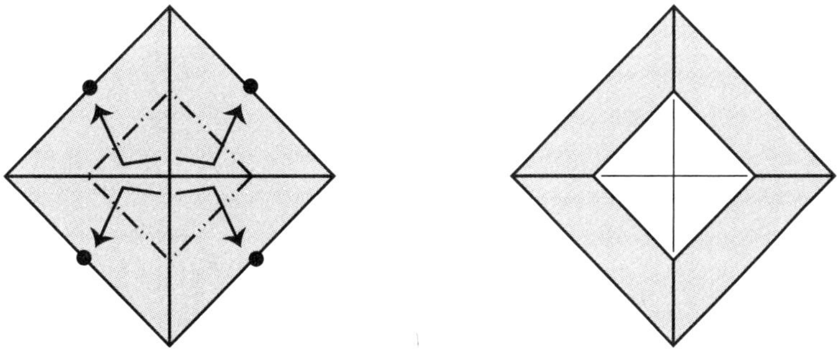

4. Turn the paper over to the back side. Fold the left and right edges in so that they meet in the center of the paper.

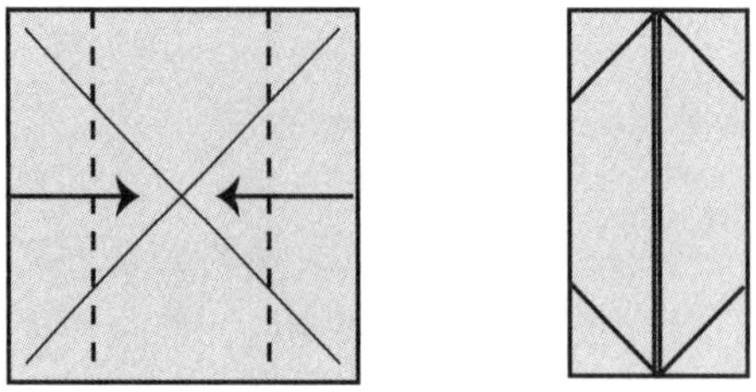

5. a. Fold just the top left flap over to meet the right edge.
   b. Fold the small triangles on the top and bottom in to the midline.
   c. Fold the flap back over along the midline to meet the left edge.

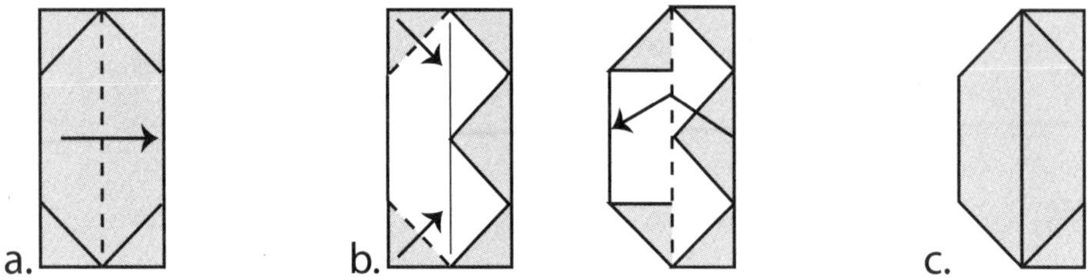

6. Repeat step five in the opposite direction using the top right flap so that the paper looks like the shape below.

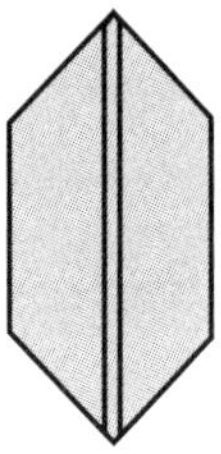

7. Crease where indicated by the dashed lines and pull the sides out while simultaneously pushing the top and bottom in to finish the box.

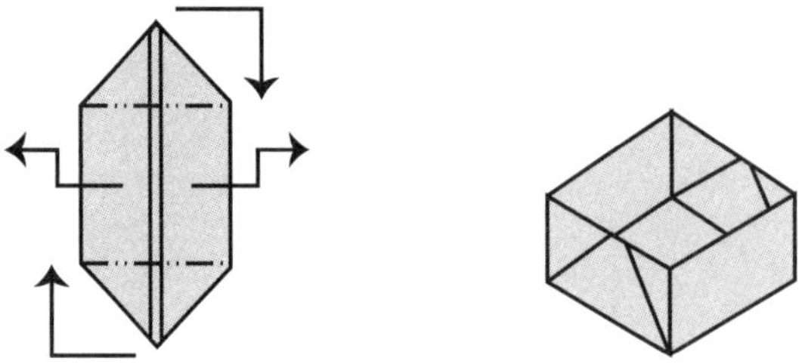

FIVE-SIDED BOX

Exploration

Fold a second five-sided box. As you fold, answer the questions below. Each question is numbered according to the folding instruction with which it corresponds.

1.a. What are the names of the points where the fold lines meet the outer edges of the square?

b. How do the four smaller squares compare?

c. What portion of the larger square is taken up by one smaller square?

d. Make a statement about the relationship between the two folds made and the results you see.

2.a. What name would you give the fold line you see in relation to the small square?

b. What can you say about the diagonal of a square and how it divides the square?

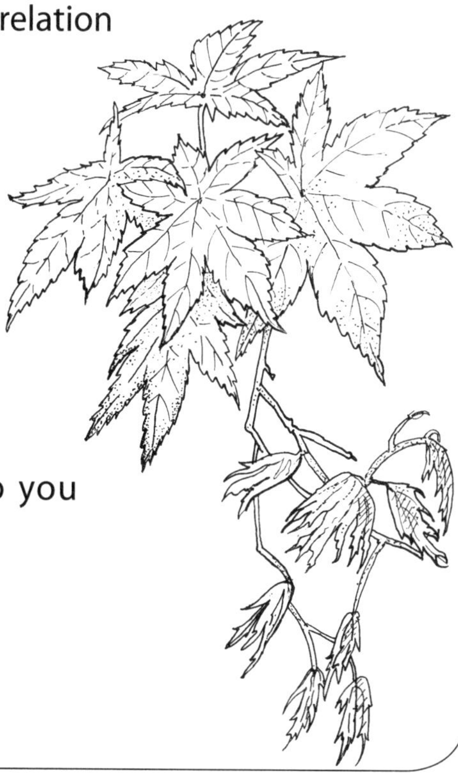

3. What shapes are the flaps?

4. What shape is created by these folds? How do you know?

5. What shape do you see?

FIVE-SIDED BOX

Exploration

Use your completed box to respond to the following questions.

1. What shapes are the sides of the box?

2. What can you say about their relationship to each other? How do you know?

3. What is the relationship between the length of one side of the box and the height of one side of the box?

4. Looking at the side of the box, what can you say about how rectangles can be divided into other shapes?

5. What shape does the bottom of the box appear to be?

FIVE-SIDED BOX Anatomy

Unfold one of your boxes and use it to answer the following questions. A blank square is provided on the next page in which to draw your fold lines.

1. Draw in the horizontal and vertical midlines. What types of lines are these? What angles are created at the point of intersection? Label these central angles.

2. Draw in the fold lines that connect the midpoints of the sides of the square. What shapes are in each corner? What is their relationship to each other? How do you know?

3. Starting with A, use upper-case letters to label the four corners of the square and the points where your drawn lines intersect each other and the sides of the square.

4. Use geometric notation to represent the relationship between the large corner triangles.

5. Examine the shape in the center of the paper. What does it appear to be?

6. How can you "prove" this using what you know about the properties of shapes?

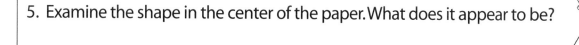

FIVE-SIDED BOX

Anatomy

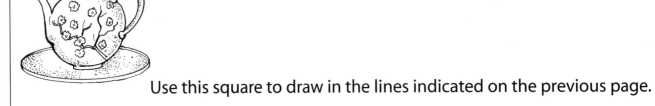

Use this square to draw in the lines indicated on the previous page.

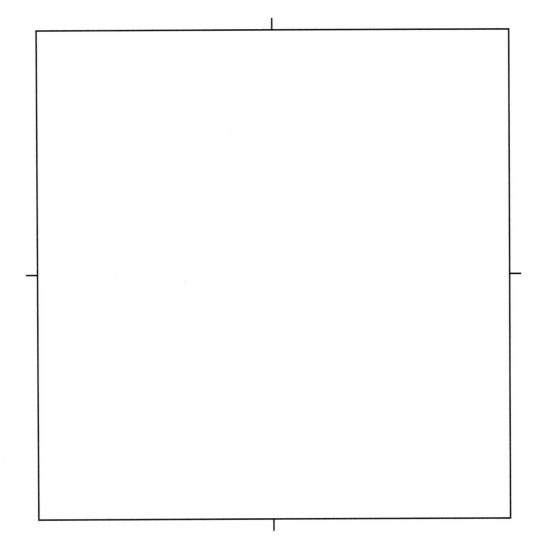

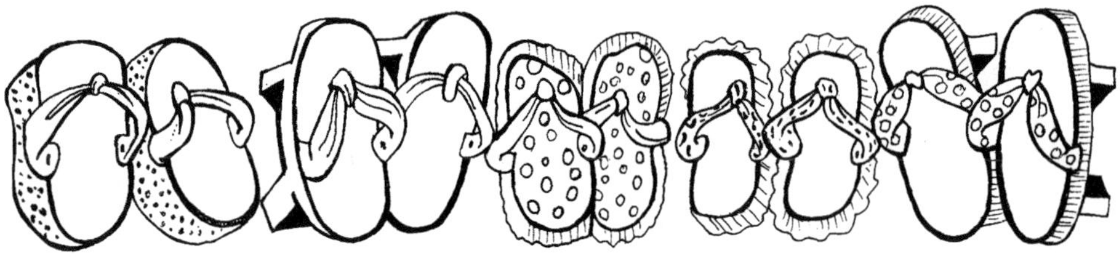

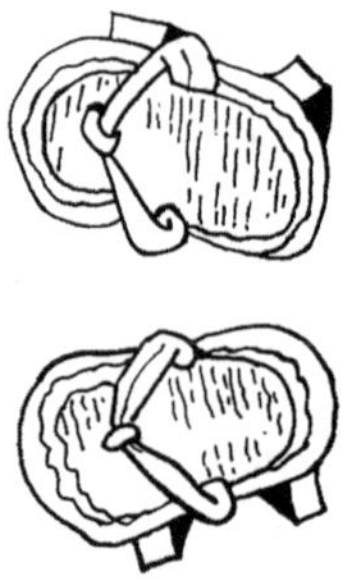

RECTANGULAR BOX

FOCUS

Students will fold a three-dimensional rectangular box and identify geometric relationships between elements of their figures. They will also examine the fold lines of an unfolded unit of the box and identify and label the geometric relationships they see.

KEY QUESTION

What geometric relationships are represented in the folded and unfolded rectangular box?

MATH

Properties of geometric shapes
Labeling geometric drawings
Geometric notation
 parallel
 perpendicular
 congruent
 angles

PAPER

Rectangular pieces, two per model
One for exploration

ADDITIONAL MATERIALS

Rulers

CREATOR

Unknown

Management

1. The paper used for this model must be rectangular in shape; if it is square the resulting box will be square. The dimensions of the rectangle are not important.
2. You may wish to have students make a lid for their rectangular boxes. To do so, they will need a total of four rectangular pieces of paper. For the best fit, two of the pieces should be just slightly smaller or slightly larger than the other two.

Procedure

1. Hand out the folding instructions (pages 11-12) and two rectangular pieces of paper to each student.
2. Guide students through the folding process step by step.
3. Have students fold the second unit and guide them through the assembly process.
4. When each student has successfully assembled his or her rectangular box, hand out the remaining student sheets, additional rectangles, and rulers.
5. Have students work together in small groups to answer the questions and make an accurate diagram of an unfolded unit.
6. When all groups have completed the exploration pages, close with a time of class discussion where students share the properties of their boxes and any other discoveries that they made.

Discussion

1. What shapes are the sides of the box? [rectangular]
2. What can you say about their relationship to each other? [The parallel sides are congruent, they intersect at right angles, etc.] How do you know?
3. What type of angles meet together to form the corners of the box? [90° angles] What assumption can you make about how other box corners might be constructed?
4. What shape does the bottom of the box appear to be? [rectangular] Why do you think so? [It has two sets of parallel sides, four right angles, and two of the sides are longer than the other two.]
5. Using your answers to the above questions, what do you consider to be the properties of a rectangular box? What specific attributes should you look for in determining whether or not a given box is rectangular?

Extensions

1. Determine the relationship between the size of the original pieces of paper and the dimensions of the finished box.
2. Start with rectangles of different sizes and proportions and compare the completed boxes.

Solutions

Rectangular Box Exploration

2.a. What shapes do you see? [rectangles]

b. Are these shapes congruent? [yes] How do you know? [They were made by bisecting a larger rectangle.]

4. What angles are being created by these folds? [right angles]

5. What shapes do the corners form when you fold them up? [isosceles right triangles]

7.a. What angles do you see and where do you see them? [There are right angles where adjacent sides intersect and where all of the sides intersect with the base.]

b. How do you know this is a rectangular box? [The base has two sets of parallel sides, four right angles, and two of the sides are longer than the other two.]

Rectangular Box Anatomy

This is the diagram of an unfolded unit of the rectangular box as students should have drawn it. The answers to the questions on the third exploration sheet are given below.

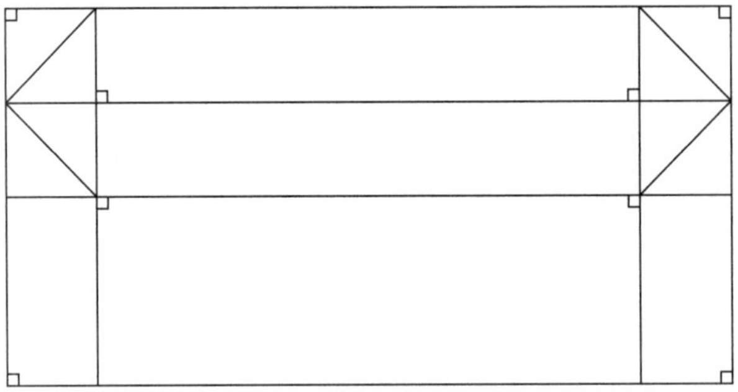

1. Draw in the two horizontal fold lines and the two vertical fold lines. (You will have to use your ruler to determine the proper placement of the vertical lines.) How are these lines related? Use the appropriate geometric notation to label them. [The horizontal and vertical fold lines are perpendicular to each other and should be marked with the right angle sign, as shown above.]
2. Based on your response to the first question, what can you say about the shapes into which the paper is divided? [The paper is divided into a series of rectangles and squares.]
3. How are the squares in the upper right and upper left corners of the unit related? How would you prove that this is true? [The corner squares are congruent. You know that this is true because the vertical fold lines are both the same distance from the sides of the paper, and the top horizontal fold line forms the bottom for both squares.]
4. Consider the four square shapes on the right and left sides of the unit. Draw in the fold lines that they each contain. How do these fold lines divide each square? Are these smaller shapes congruent? How do you know? [These fold lines divide each square into two congruent right isosceles triangles. You know that the triangles are congruent because the fold line bisects the square along its diagonal, dividing it exactly in half.]
5. What shape would the box be if you used the same folding instructions on square papers instead of rectangular ones? Why? [A square box would result because the distance between the two vertical fold lines would be the same as the distance between the horizontal midline and the bottom of the paper. When this is the case, a square box results.]

RECTANGULAR BOX Folding Instructions

1. Begin with a rectangular piece of paper, colored side up, and fold it in half horizontally.

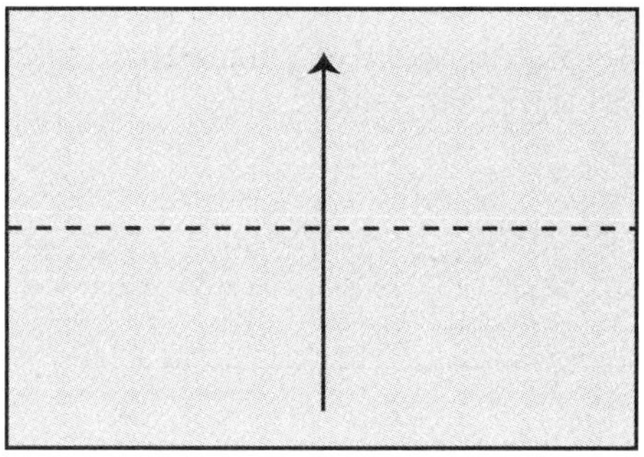

2. Fold the top layer down to meet the bottom of the paper and unfold.

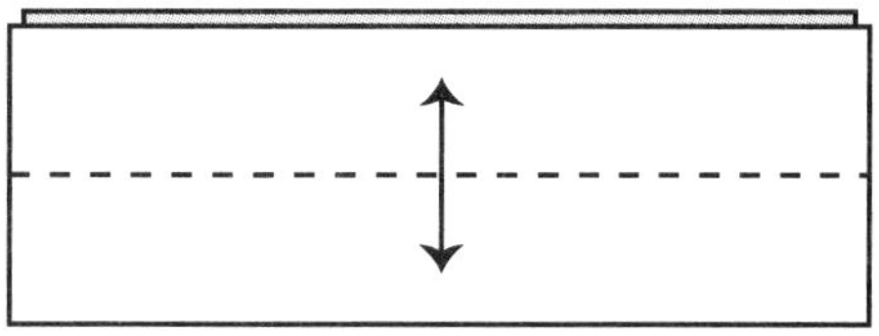

3. Fold the upper left and upper right hand corners of the top flap down to meet the midline, then, leaving the corners down, unfold the entire paper.

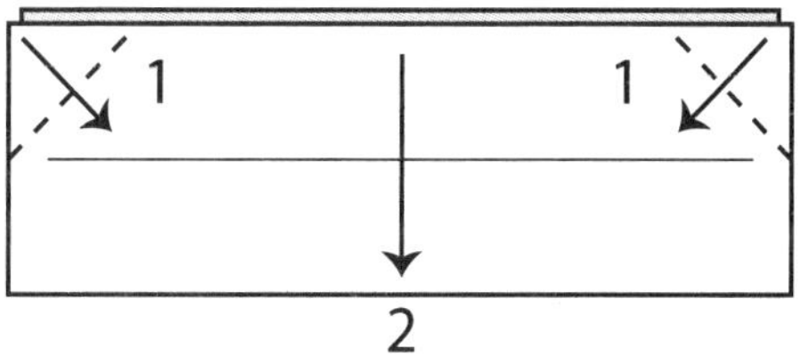

4. Crease the left and right edges where indicated by the dashed lines. Fold the bottom edge up to meet the top edge.

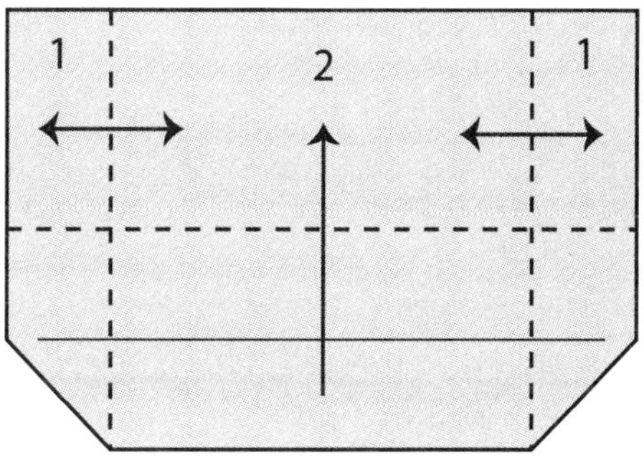

5. Fold the bottom left and right corners up to meet the midline.

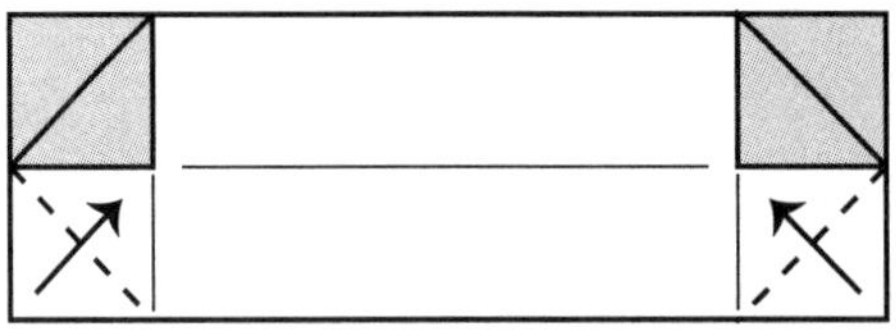

6. Fold the top layer down so that the top edge meets the bottom edge.

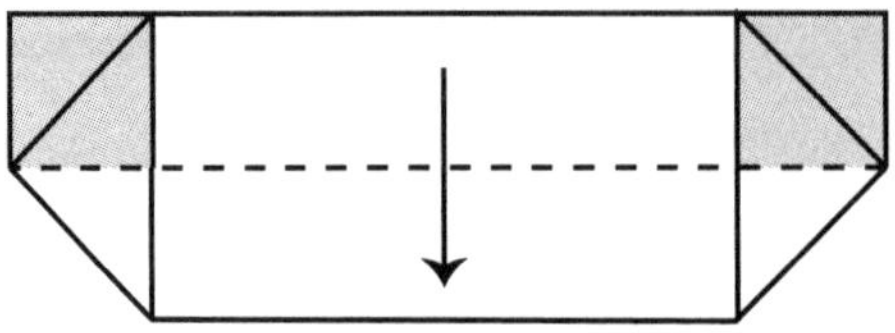

7. Pull the bottom flap and push in the sides where indicated by the dashed lines. Repeat steps one through seven so that you have two rectangular shapes.

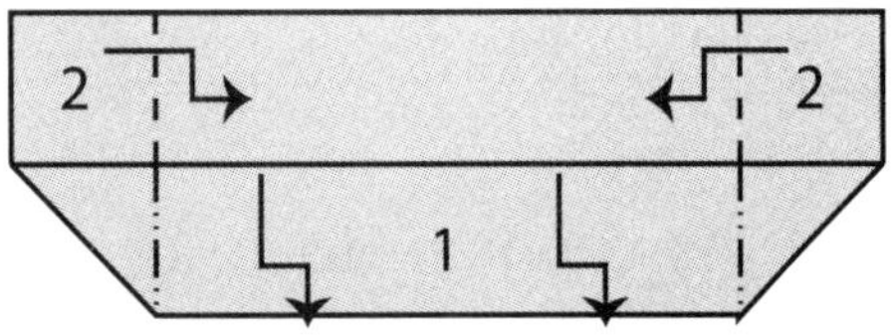

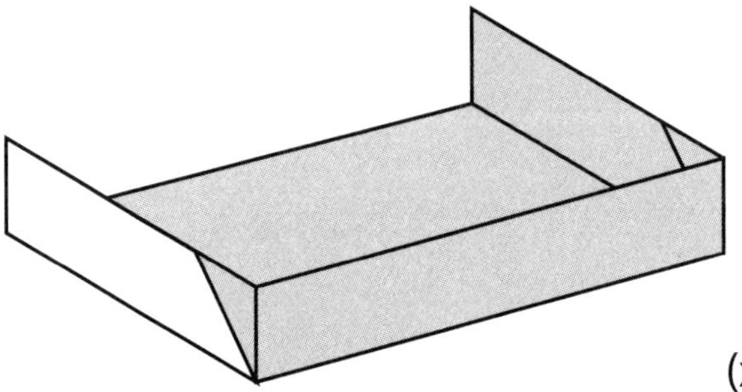

(x 2)

Rectangular Box Assembly

Slide the folded pieces together, tucking the tabs of one piece into the pockets of the other piece.

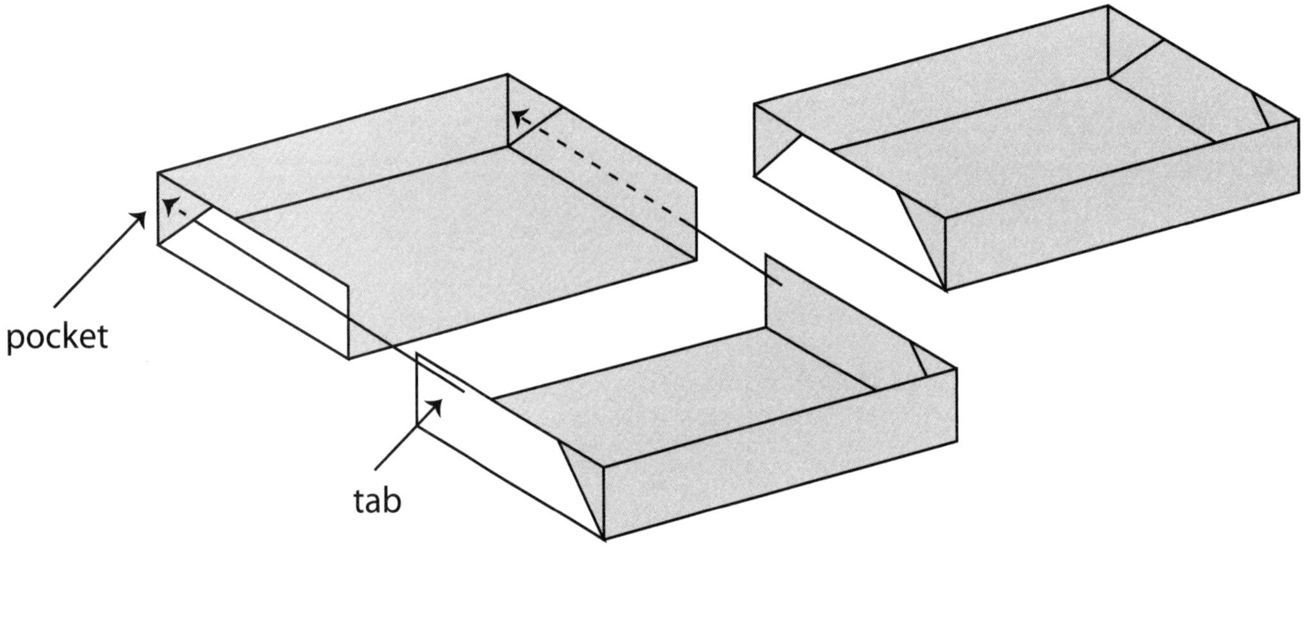

RECTANGULAR BOX Exploration

Fold one unit of the rectangular box. As you fold, answer the questions below. Each question is numbered according to the folding instruction with which it corresponds.

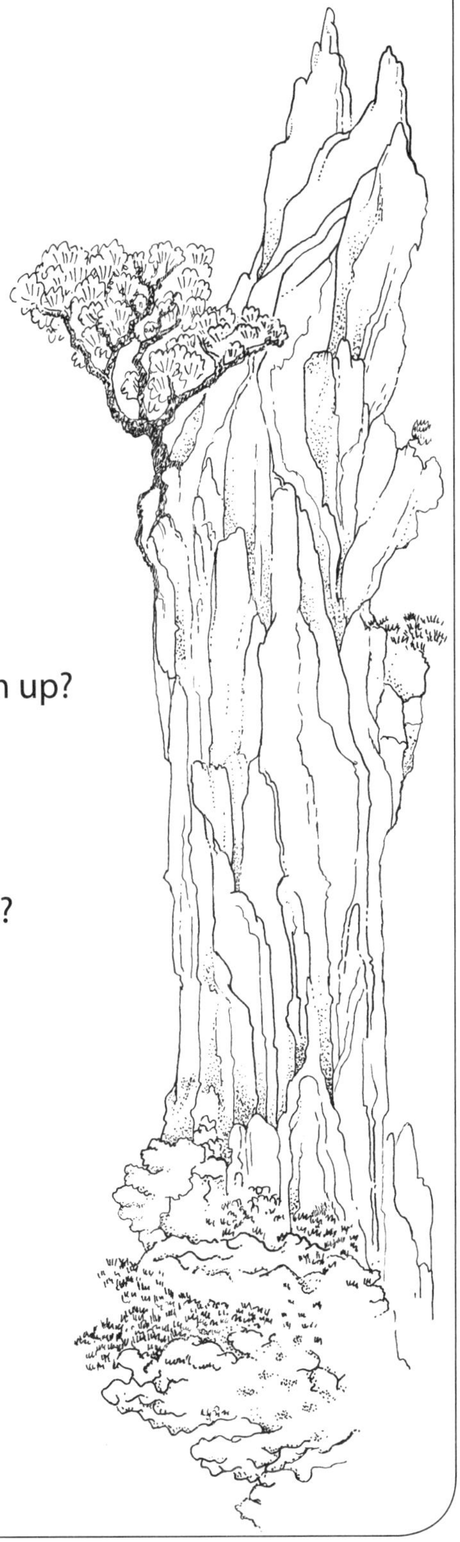

2.a. What shapes do you see?

b. Are these shapes congruent? How do you know?

4. What angles are being created by these folds?

5. What shape do the corners form when you fold them up?

7.a. What angles do you see and where do you see them?

b. How do you know this is a rectangular box?

RECTANGULAR BOX Exploration

Use your rectangular box to respond to the following questions.

1. What shapes are the sides of the box?

2. What can you say about their relationship to each other? How do you know?

3. What type of angles meet together to form the corners of the box? What assumption can you make about how other box corners might be constructed?

4. What shape does the bottom of the box appear to be? Why do you think so?

5. Using your answers to the above questions, what do you consider to be the properties of a rectangular box? What specific attributes should you look for in determining whether or not a given box is rectangular?

RECTANGULAR BOX Anatomy

Use an unfolded rectangular box unit and the blank rectangle on the next page to answer the following questions.

1. Draw in the two horizontal fold lines and the two vertical fold lines. (You will have to use your ruler to determine the proper placement of the vertical lines.) How are these lines related? Use the appropriate geometric notation to label them.

2. Based on your response to the first question, what can you say about the shapes into which the paper is divided?

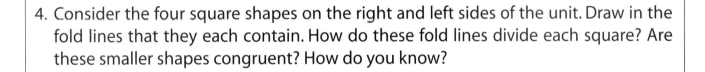

3. How are the squares in the upper right and upper left corners of the unit related? How would you prove that this is true?

4. Consider the four square shapes on the right and left sides of the unit. Draw in the fold lines that they each contain. How do these fold lines divide each square? Are these smaller shapes congruent? How do you know?

5. What shape would the box be if you used the same folding instructions on square papers instead of rectangular ones? Why?

RECTANGULAR BOX Anatomy

Use this rectangle to draw in the appropriate fold lines as indicated on the previous page. The midpoints of each side have been marked to help you.

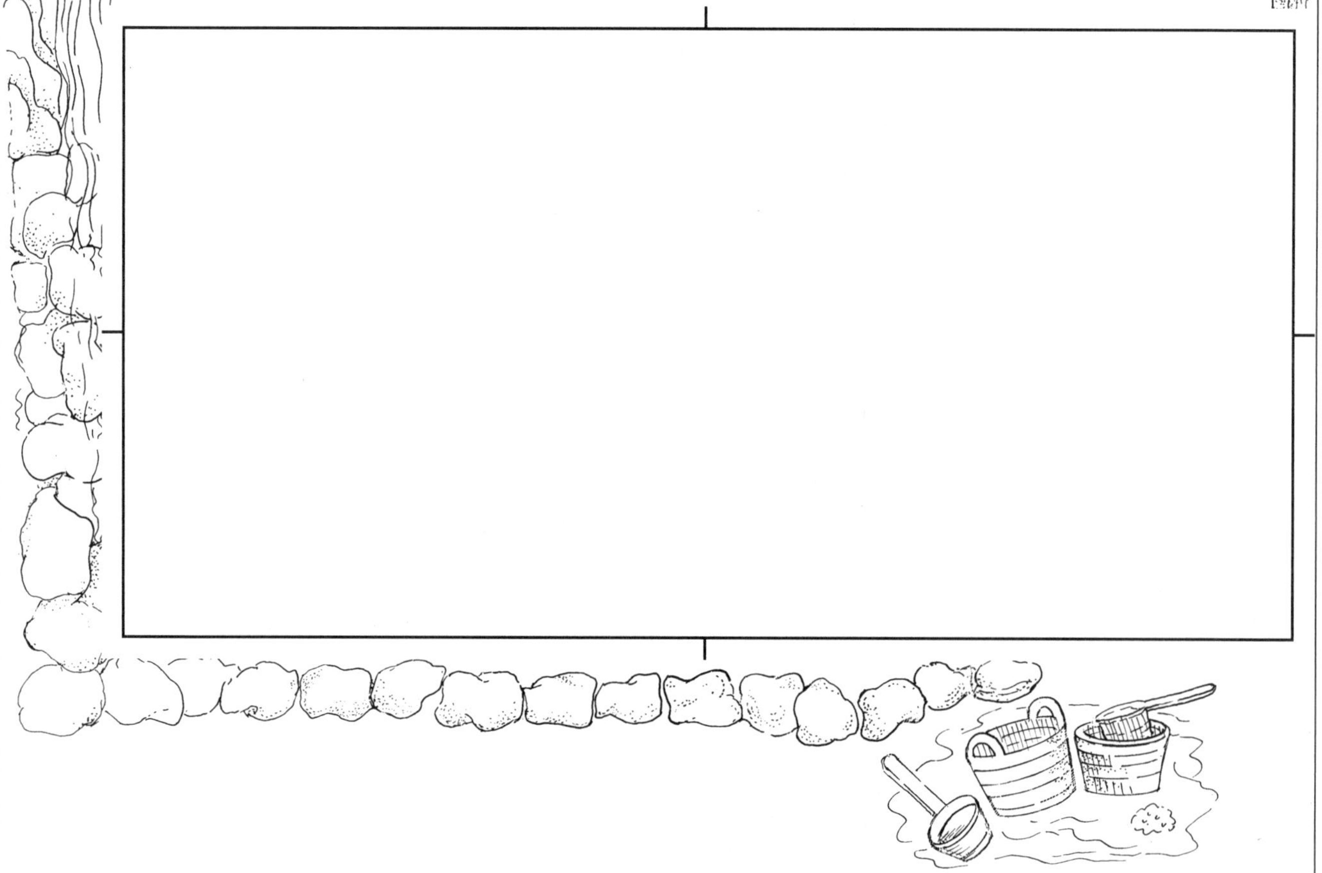

TRIANGULAR BOX

FOCUS

Students will fold a triangular box. They will then use their completed model and an unfolded unit square to identify the geometric shapes created by the folds and properties of both the box and each individual unit.

KEY QUESTIONS

What geometric relationships are represented in the folded triangular box?

What geometric shapes are created by the fold lines in one unit of the triangular box?

MATH

Properties of geometric
- shapes
- angles
- congruence

Geometric notation

INTEGRATED PROCESSES

Observing
Identifying
Comparing and contrasting

PAPER

Three squares per model
One for exploration

CREATOR

Tomoko Fusè

Procedure

1. Hand out the folding instructions (pages 19-22) and three squares of paper to each student. Guide students through the construction of the basic unit for the triangular box.
2. Have students fold their remaining two units and guide them through the assembly of the boxes. Keep in mind that this box can be quite challenging to assemble; students may need more help than usual to put it together.
3. When each student has successfully assembled a box, hand out the final three student sheets and another square of paper to each person.
4. In order to answer the first page of questions, students will need to fold an additional unit, pausing at the indicated places to examine their folds and answer questions about the shape of their paper.
5. Have students work together in small groups to answer these questions and the ones on the following two pages.
6. When all groups are finished, close with a time of class discussion where students share their discoveries and experiences.

Discussion

1. What shapes are the sides of the completed box? [rectangular]
2. What can you say about their relationship to each other? [They are all congruent, they are connected to each other along one edge, etc.] How do you know?
3. What shape is the bottom of the box? [an equilateral triangle] How do you know? [It has three sides that are the same length and three interior angles that are the same.]
4. What can you say about the corner angles of the box? [They are all 60°.] How do you know? [The box is an equilateral triangle, and each interior angle in an equilateral triangle is 60°.]
5. When you looked at the unfolded unit, how many triangles did you discover? (See *Solutions.*)
6. How many rectangles did you discover? (See *Solutions.*)
7. What other shapes did you discover in the unfolded unit? (See *Solutions.*)
8. What else did you discover about the triangular box and the geometry involved in its construction?

Extensions

1. Have students make a second triangular box from slightly smaller or slightly larger paper. This can then be fitted onto the original box as a lid. This makes the box a geometric solid, allowing students to count faces, edges, and vertices.
2. Have students determine the surface area and volume of their boxes using either actual or arbitrary measurements.

Solutions

Triangular Box Exploration

2.a. What shapes do you see? [two rectangles]

b. What is the relationship of the smaller shape to the larger shape? [The smaller rectangle is the same height and one-fourth the width of the larger rectangle.]

3. What type of lines are being created by these folds? [Both parallel and perpendicular lines are created.]

4. What angle is created by this fold in relation to the sides of the paper? [45°] How do you know? [The fold forms an isosceles right triangle, which has one 90° angle and two 45° angles.]

5. What shape does the paper appear to be? [It is a square.] How do you know? [You started with a square, and you folded both the top and left sides in the same amount.]

12. What angle is formed by the corner of the piece? [60°] How do you know? [The corner forms one point of an equilateral triangle, and the measure of each interior angle of an equilateral triangle is 60°.]

Triangular Box Anatomy

This is the diagram of an unfolded unit of the triangular box as students have it on their student sheet. The answers to the questions are given below.

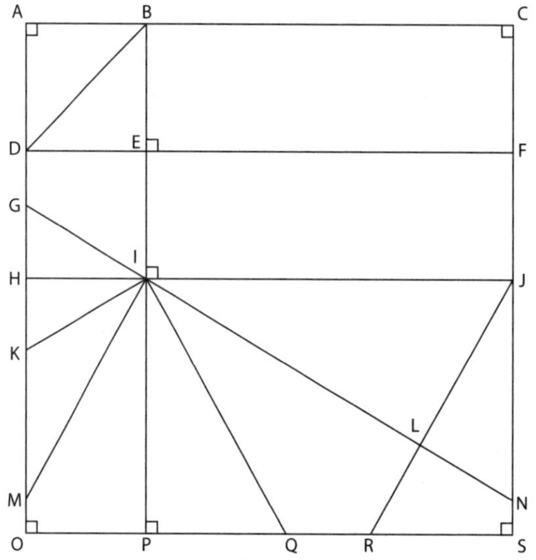

1. How many triangles are made by the folds in the unit? [13] List each one. [ABD, DBE, GIH, GIK, GIM, HIK, HIM, KIM, PIQ, ILJ, INJ, JNL, JSR]
2. What kinds of triangles are they? [There are equilateral, obtuse, isosceles, right isosceles, and right scalene triangles.]
3. How many rectangles are made by the folds in the unit? [There are 17 (remembering that squares are also rectangles.)] List each one. [ACFD, ACJH, ABED, ABIH, ABPO, BCFE, BCJI, BCSP, DFSO, DFJH, DEIH, DEPO, EFJI, EFSP, HJSO, HIPO, IJSP (This does not count the original square, but only those rectangles created by fold lines.)]
4. What other shapes are made? Describe and list several. [There are many other irregular polygons including: DEIG, GIPO, GIQO, HIQO, IJRQ, IJRP, GLRO, DFJLG, EFJRQI, and MILRO.]

TRIANGULAR BOX Folding Instructions

1. Fold the square in half vertically, making only a short crease at the bottom of the paper. Unfold.

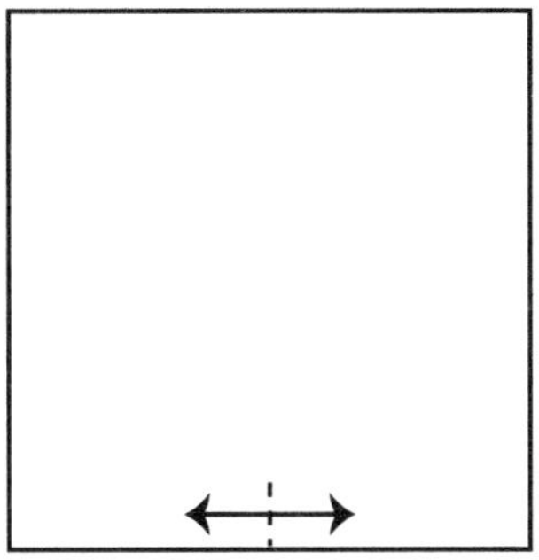

2. Fold the left edge in to the center fold mark, crease, and unfold.

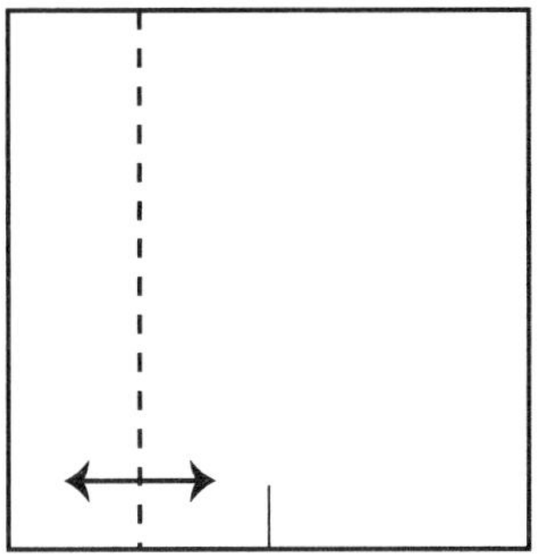

3. a. Fold the square in half horizontally and unfold.
   b. Fold the top edge down so that it meets the horizontal midline.

a. 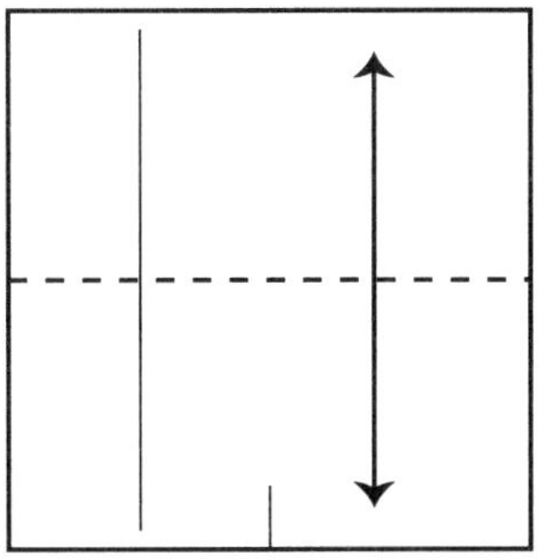

b. 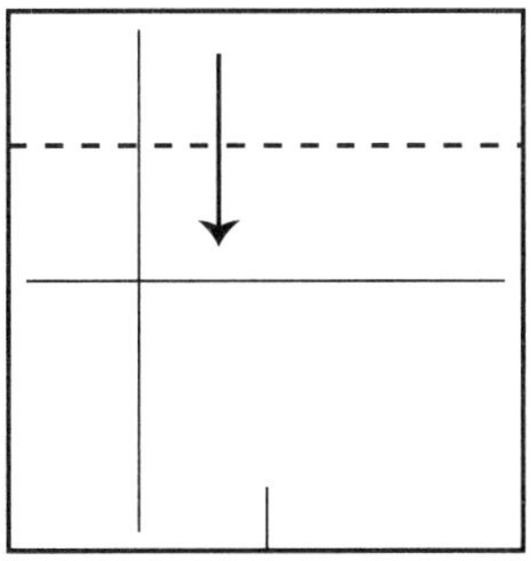

4. Fold the left hand corner of the top flap under as indicated by the dashed line.

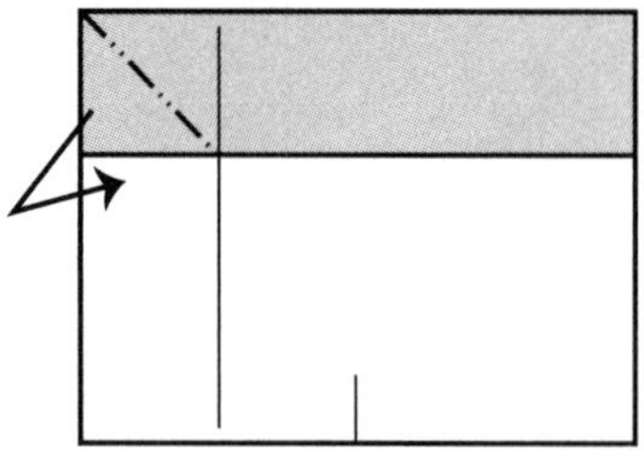

5. Fold the left edge of the paper in along the existing fold line.

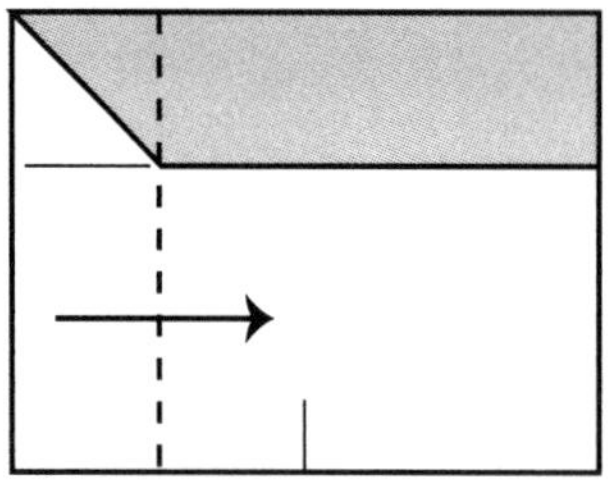

6. Fold the lower left hand corner up to meet the top edge of the paper as indicated by the dashed line.

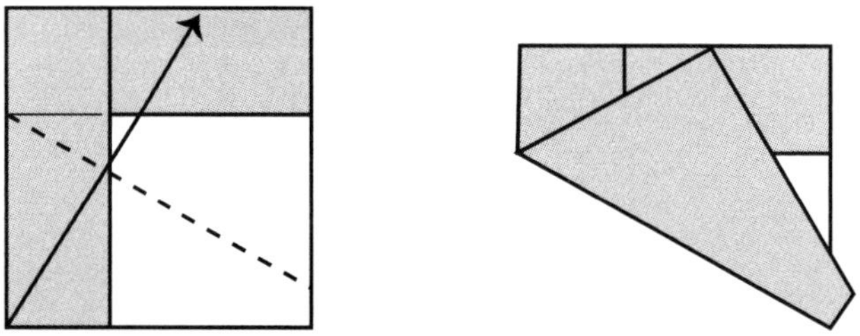

7. Crease the top flap where indicated by the dashed line, then unfold the top flap and the left side.

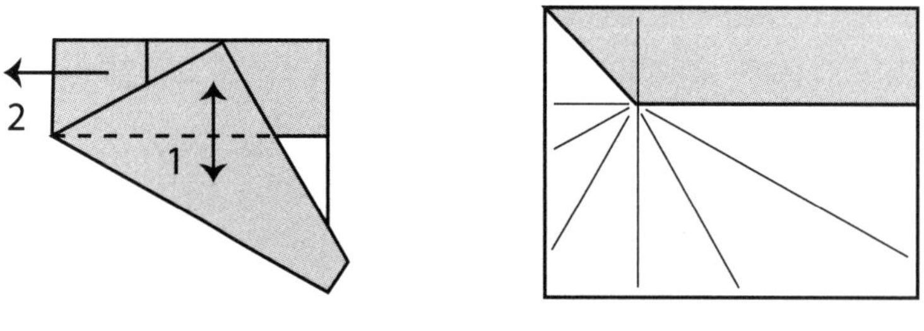

8. Fold the bottom edge of the paper up toward the top edge along the existing crease as indicated.

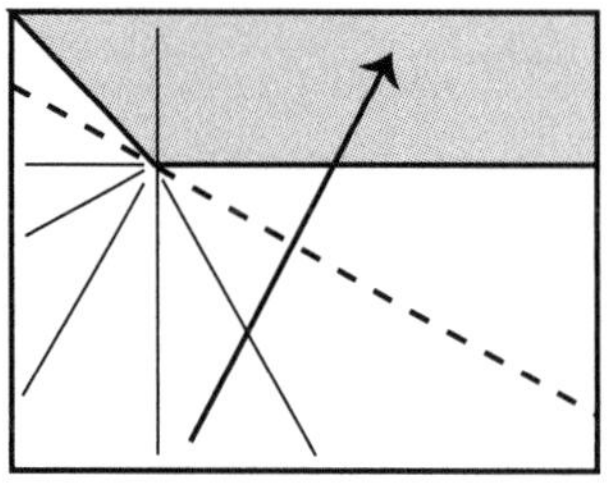

9. Fold the paper so that the two points marked with dots meet. Notice that you are doing a combination mountain/valley fold. You are using pre-existing creases for both folds, but you must reverse the direction of both creases.

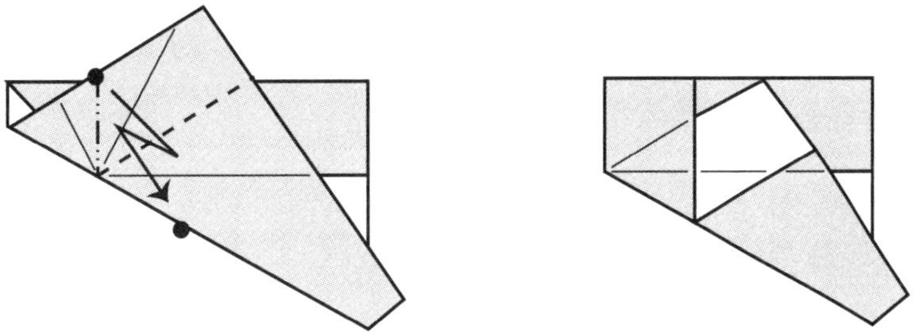

10. Tuck the white flap shown in the figure, underneath the rectangular flap directly behind it.

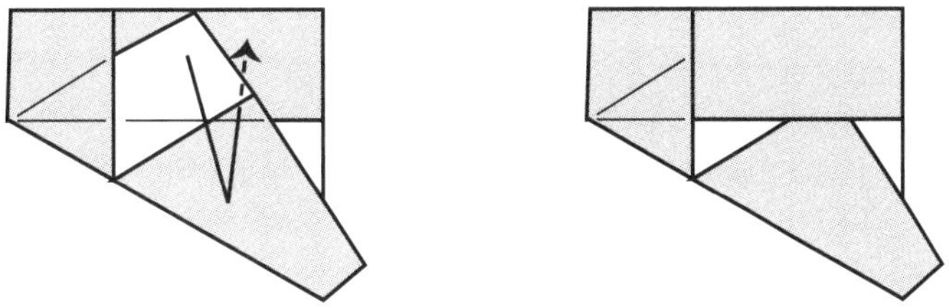

11. Crease the lower right hand portion of the paper as indicated by the dashed line so that the fold line is perpendicular to the lower diagonal edge.

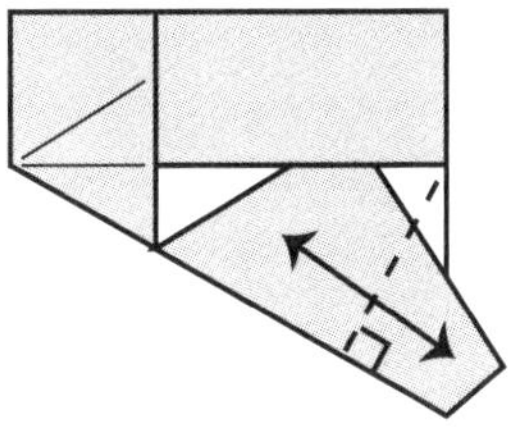

12. Unfold the upper left hand flap while simultaneously lifting the top edge of the paper toward you. This should form one corner of the box. Repeat steps one through 12 two more times so that you have a total of three corner pieces.

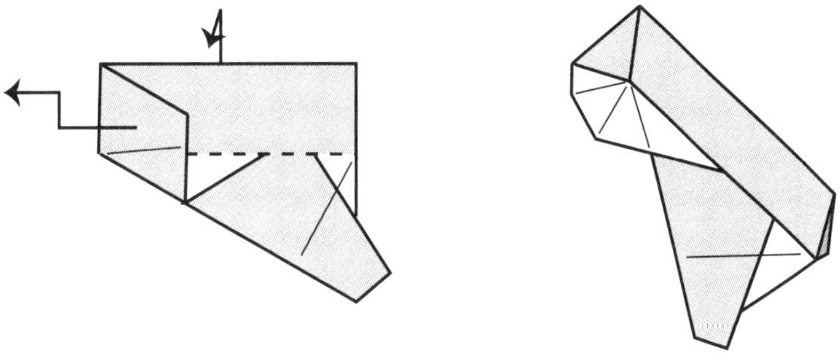

TRIANGULAR BOX Assembly

1. The shorter side of each piece is a pocket. The longer side is a tab. Insert the tab from one piece into the pocket of another, keeping the extra flap from the second piece on the inside, as shown.

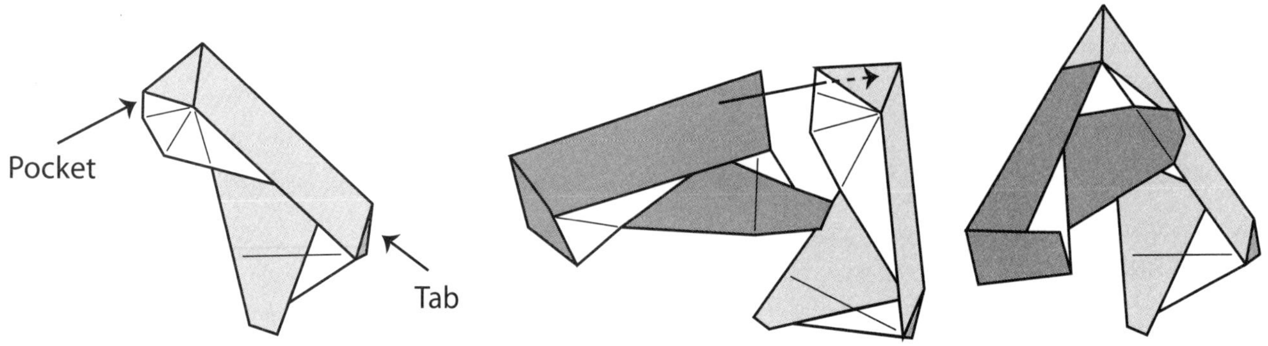

2. Take the extra flap and tuck it under the tab to which it is adjacent.

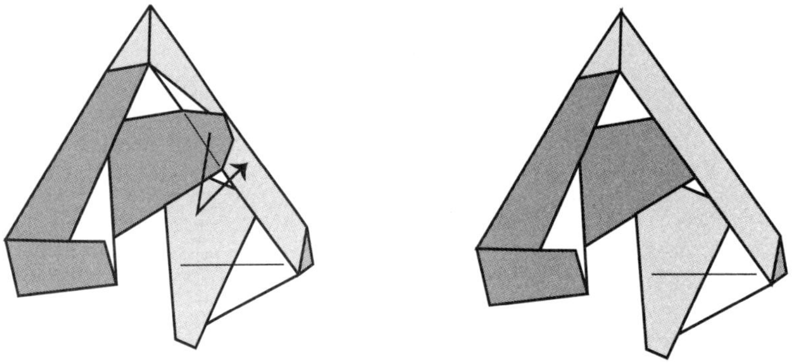

3. Fit the third piece onto the first two by placing the remaining tabs into the remaining pockets. Tuck the two extra flaps under the appropriate tabs to complete the triangular box.

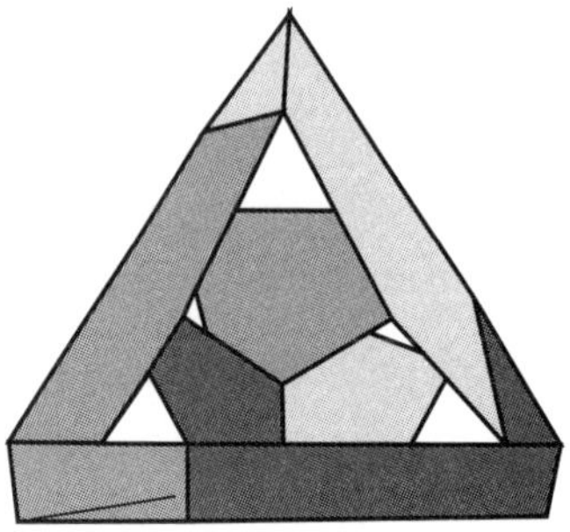

TRIANGULAR BOX Exploration

Fold an additional unit of the triangular box. As you fold, answer the questions below. Each question is numbered according to the folding instruction with which it corresponds.

2.a. What shapes do you see?

b. What is the relationship of the smaller shape to the larger shape?

3. What type of lines are created by these folds?

4. What angle is created by this fold in relation to the sides of the paper? How do you know that?

5. What shape does the paper appear to be? How do you know?

12. What angle is formed by the corner of the piece? How do you know?

TRIANGULAR BOX Exploration

Use your completed triangular box to answer the following questions.

1. What shapes are the sides of the box?

2. What can you say about their relationship to each other? How do you know?

3. What shape does the bottom of the box appear to be? Why do you think so? Be specific.

4. What can you say about the corner angles of the box? How do you know?

5. Using your answers to the above questions, what do you consider to be the properties of the triangular box?

TRIANGULAR BOX Anatomy

Use this drawing of the unfolded unit piece to help answer the questions below. Use the back of your paper to record your responses.

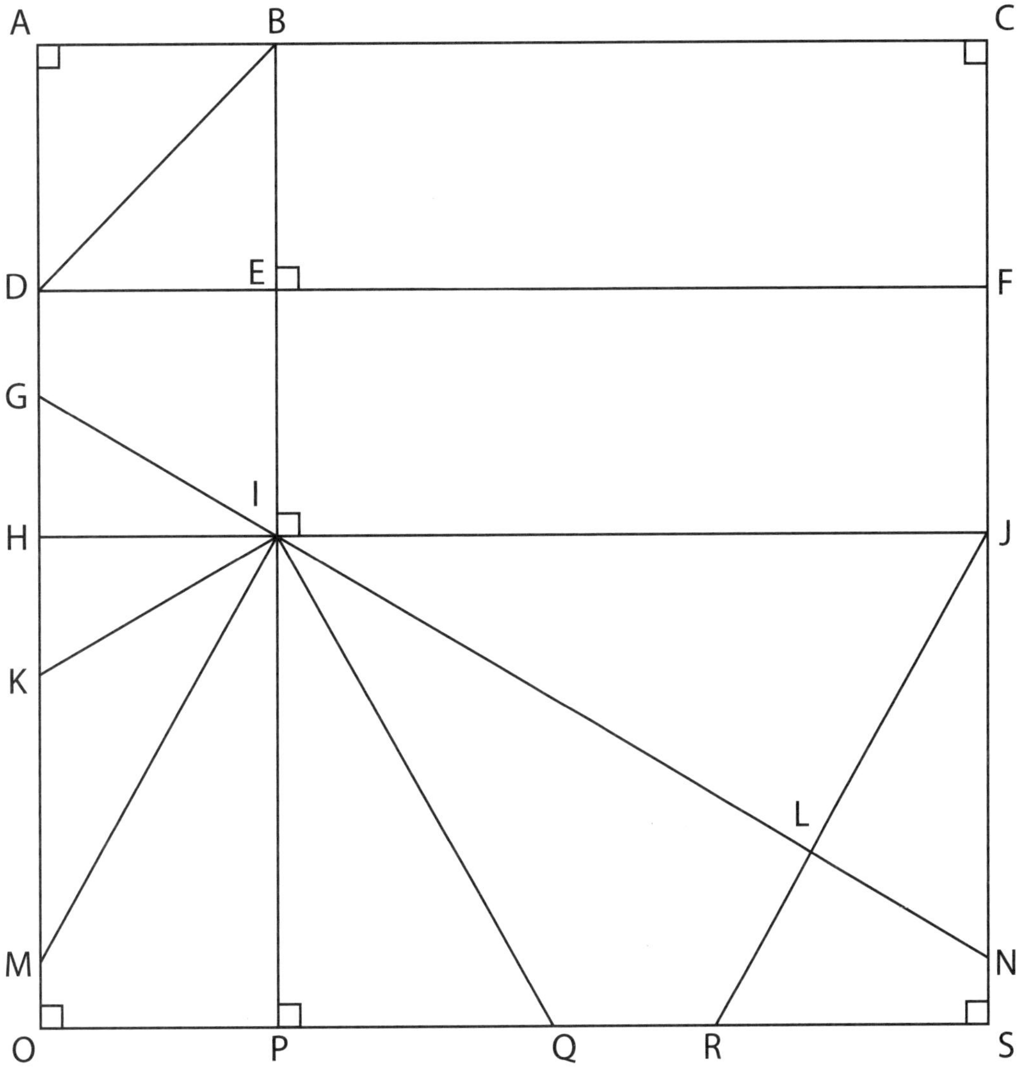

1. How many triangles are made by the folds in the unit? List each one.

2. What kinds of triangles are they?

3. How many rectangles are made by the folds in the unit? List each one.

4. What other shapes are made? Describe and list several.

BIRD TETRAHEDRON

FOCUS

Students will fold a bird tetrahedron and determine the geometric propterties of their model, including the number of faces, edges and vertices, and the surface area.

KEY QUESTION

What are the geometric properties of a completed bird tetrahedron model?

MATH

Properties of polyhedra
- faces
- edges
- vertices

Surface area

PAPER

Three squares per model in three different colors

CREATOR

Mitsonobu Sonobè

Procedure

1. Hand out the folding instructions (pages 27-30) and three paper squares to each student. Bird tetrahedrons are easier to assemble and more aesthetically pleasing if three different colors of paper are used.
2. Go over the folding instructions for one unit of the bird tetrahedron as a class.
3. Have students fold the remaining two units and guide them through the assembly of their bird tetrahedron models.
4. When all students have successfully assembled their models, hand out the remaining student sheets and have students work together in small groups to answer the questions about their models.
5. When all groups have finished, close with a time of class discussion where students share their answers and discoveries.

Discussion

1. What shapes are the faces of the figure? [isosceles right triangles]
2. How many faces, edges, and vertices does the figure have? [faces: six; edges: nine; vertices: five]
3. What does it mean for a polygon to be a tetrahedron? [It must have four faces.]
4. By this definition, is a bird tetrahedron a true tetrahedron? [No.] Why not? [It has six faces, not four.]
5. What would be a more accurate name for the bird tetrahedron? [A hexahedron.]
6. What plan did the group develop for determining the surface area of the model?
7. If the length of the base on one face is three units, and the height is one unit, what is the surface area of the whole figure? [$(\frac{1}{2} \times 3) \times 1 = 1.5$, $1.5 \times 6 = 9$ units^2]

Extensions

1. Have students complete the *Sonobè Unit Exploration.*
2. Have students make a bird tetrahedron using the right triangle unit and compare it to the version made with the Sonobè Unit.

BIRD TETRAHEDRON Folding Instructions

1. Fold the paper in half vertically and unfold.

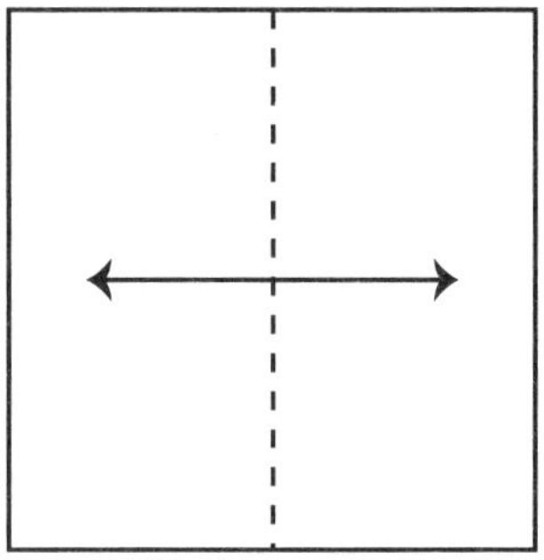

2. Fold the left edge and the right edge in to meet the center crease.

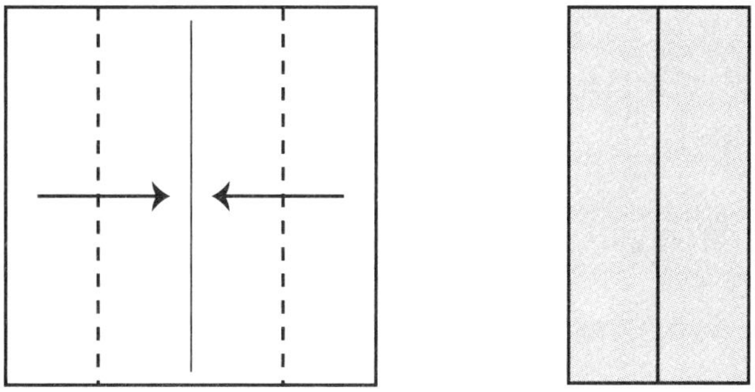

3. Fold as indicated by the dashed lines so that the top left corner meets the right side of the paper and the bottom right corner meets the left side of the paper.

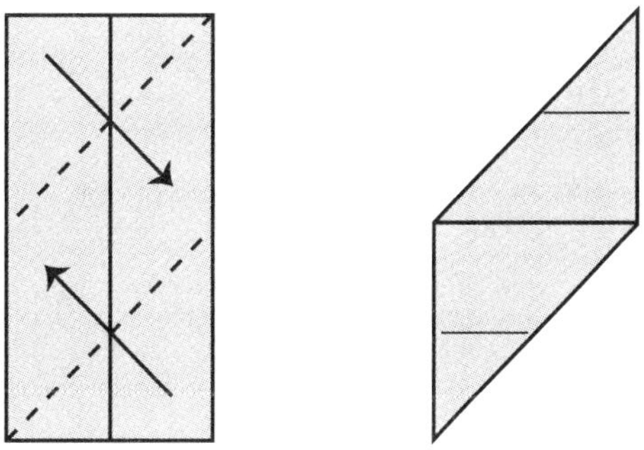

4. Unfold the paper completely. Fold the top right and bottom left corners in along the existing crease lines as shown.

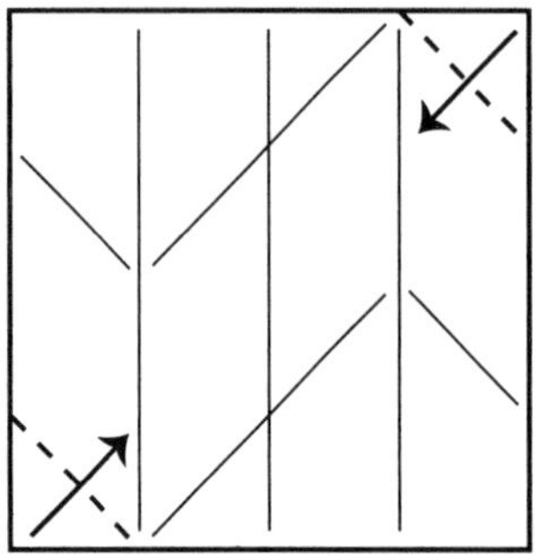

5. Fold the left and right sides of the paper in along the existing crease lines so that the edges meet in the middle.

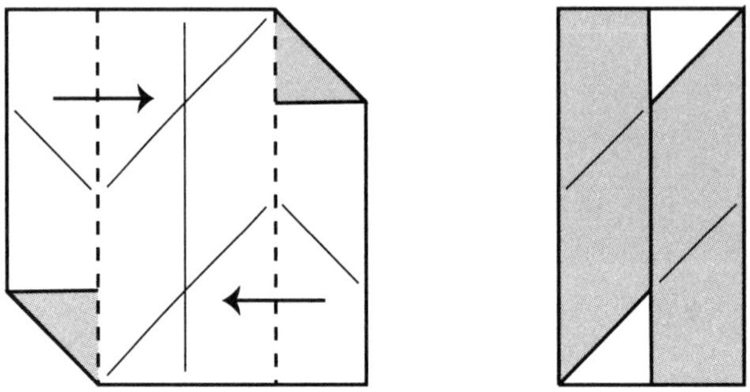

6. Fold the bottom right corner up along the existing crease line, tucking the corner underneath the flap as indicated.

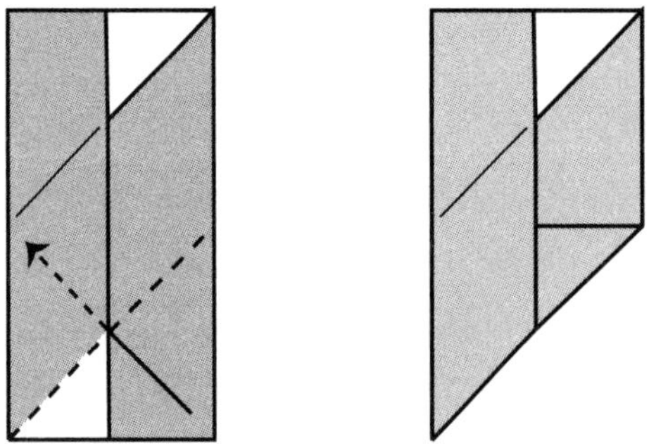

7. Repeat this process with the upper left corner, tucking it under the flap on the right side as indicated.

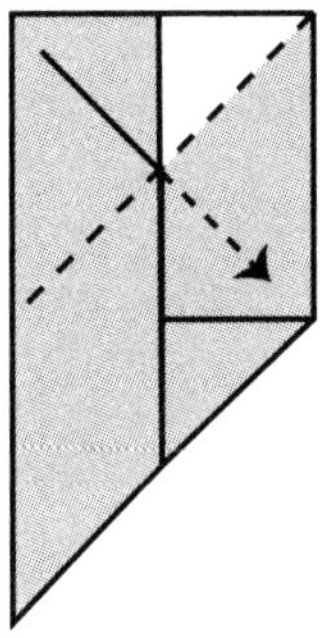

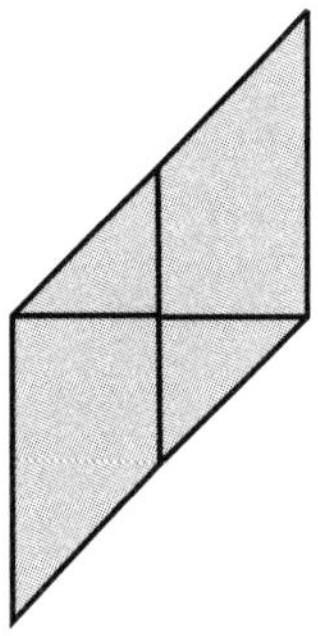

8. Flip the unit over and crease where indicated by the dashed lines.

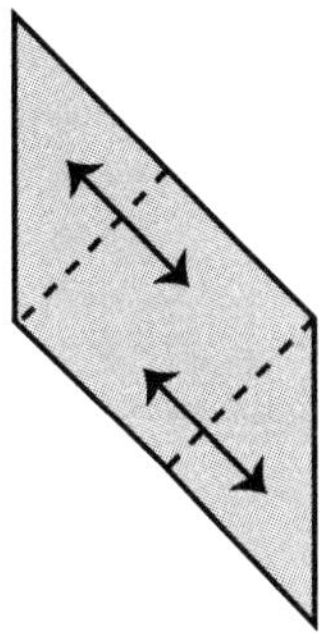

9. Flip the unit back to the front and crease well using a mountain fold along the line indicated. Repeat steps one through nine so that you have a total of three units like the one below.

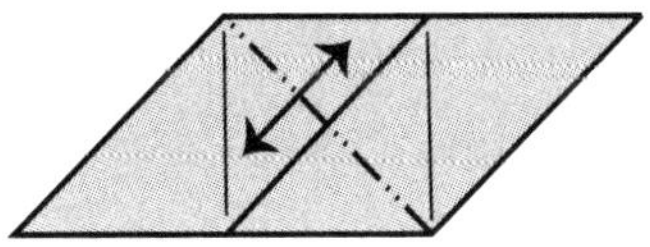

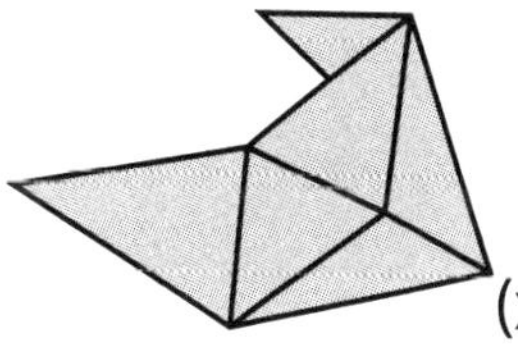

(x 3)

BIRD TETRAHEDRON Assembly

1. Take two of the pieces and fit them together as shown below, with the point of one fitting into the triangular pocket on the side of the other.

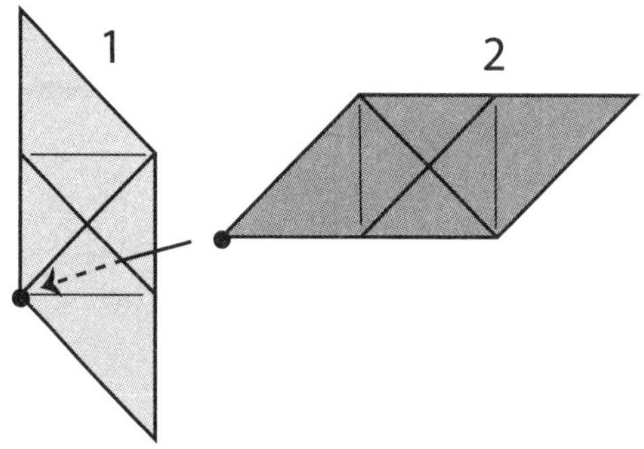

2. Using those same two pieces, put the point of the first one into the triangular pocket on the second one as indicated. To do this, you must crease the pieces where indicated by the dashed lines (using mountain folds).

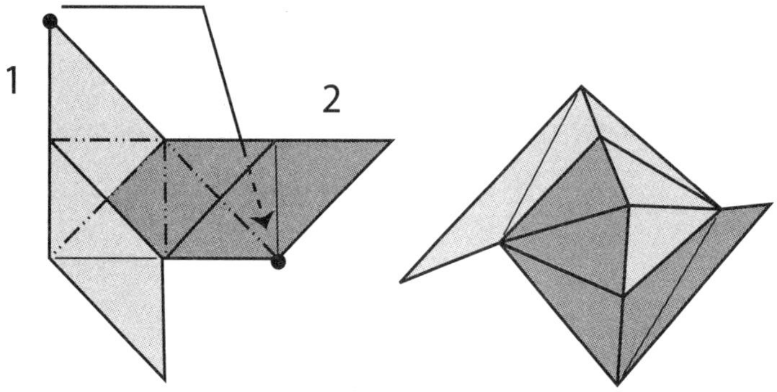

3. Once you have fit the first two pieces together, attach the third piece in the same fashion, placing the points into the two remaining triangular pockets on the sides of the first two pieces. You should now have what is known as a bird tetrahedron.

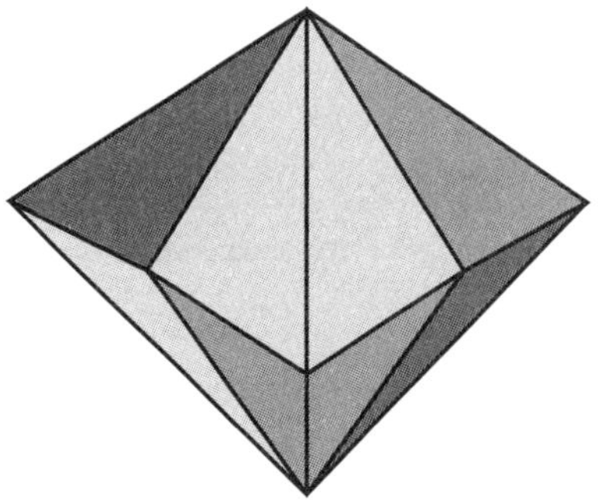

BIRD TETRAHEDRON Exploration

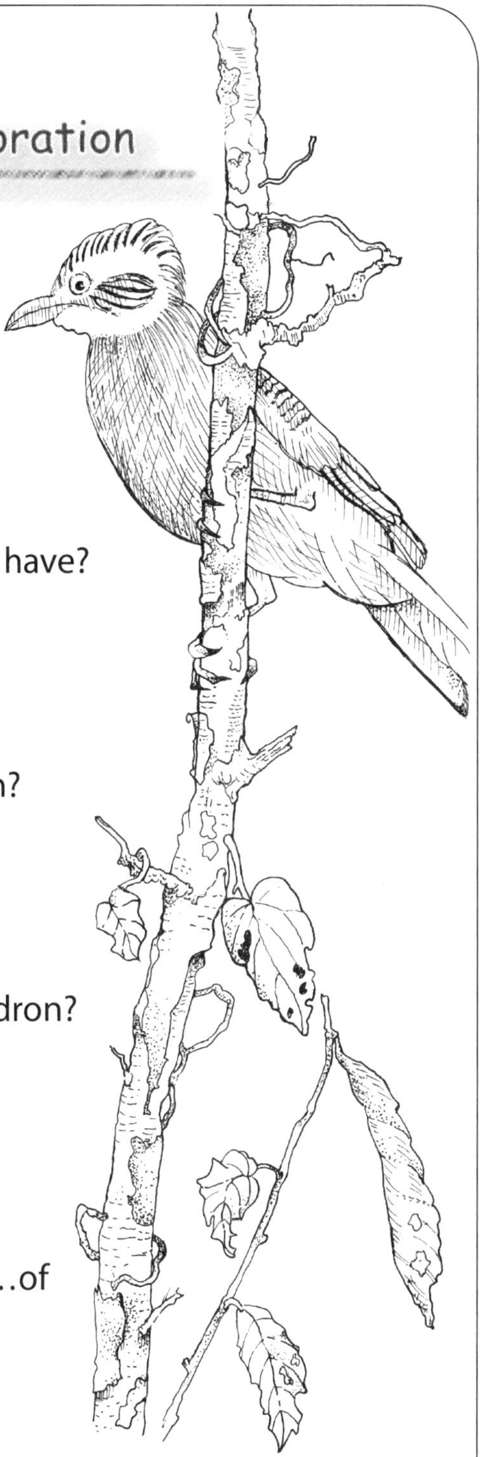

Use your completed bird tetrahedron model to respond to the following questions.

1. What shapes are the faces of the figure?

2. How many faces, edges, and vertices does the figure have?

3. What does it mean for a polygon to be a tetrahedron?

4. By this definition, is a bird tetrahedron a true tetrahedron? Why or why not? If not, what would you call it?

5. How would you find the surface area of one face? ...of the whole figure? Describe your plan.

6. If the length of the base on one face is 3 units, and the height is 1 unit, what is the surface area of the whole figure according to the method you described in question five?

REGULAR TETRAHEDRON

KEY QUESTION

What are the geometric properties of a regular tetrahedron, and how do these compare to those of a bird tetrahedron?

MATH

Properties of polyhedra
- faces
- edges
- vertices

Surface area

INTEGRATED PROCESSES

Observing
Comparing and contrasting
Relating

PAPER

Two squares per model in one or two colors

ADDITIONAL MATERIALS

Bird tetrahedron models

CREATOR

Tomoko Fusè

FOCUS

Students will fold a regular tetrahedron and compare its properties to those of the bird tetrahedron.

Management

1. Because this activity asks students to draw comparisons between the bird tetrahedron and the regular tetrahedron it is very important that both models be made from the same size paper so that the comparisons are valid.

Procedure

1. Hand out the folding instructions (pages 33-37) and two squares of paper to each student. Guide students through the construction of the tetrahedron unit step by step.
2. Have students fold the second unit individually, being sure that they made it a mirror image of the first unit. Take the class through the assembly process, giving assistance as needed.
3. When all students have successfully assembled their tetrahedrons, hand out the remaining student sheet. Students should also have their bird tetrahedron models on hand.
4. Have students work together in small groups to answer the questions and compare the two models.
5. Close with a time of class discussion where students share the discoveries they made about the properties of their tetrahedron and how these relate to the bird tetrahedron.

Discussion

1. How many faces does a regular tetrahedron have? [four] What shape are they? [equilateral triangles]
2. How does this compare to the number and shape of the faces on the bird tetrahedron? [The bird tetrahedron has six faces that are isosceles right triangles.]
3. How many vertices does a regular tetrahedron have? [four] How many edges? [six] How do these values compare to those for the bird tetrahedron? [The bird tetrahedron has five vertices and nine edges.]
4. What was your group's plan for finding the surface area of the tetrahedron?
5. If the base of one face is 3 units and the height is 2.5 units, what is the surface area of the entire tetrahedron? [The surface area of one face is 3.75 units^2, making the surface area of the entire tetrahedron 15 units^2.]
6. How does this surface area compare to the surface area that you calculated for the bird tetrahedron? [The surface area of the bird tetrahedron is nine units^2.]
7. Were you surprised that the polyhedron with more faces had a smaller surface area? Why or why not?
8. How can you explain this apparent paradox? [While the bird tetrahedron has two more faces than the regular tetrahedron, the surface area of each face is more than two units less than the surface area of each face of the tetrahedron. This accounts for the difference in total surface area of the two polyhedra.]

Extensions

1. Have students complete the *Equilateral Triangle Exploration.*
2. Challenge students to construct a square-based pyramid by using two identical tetrahedron units and the flat square unit from the *Tetrahedron Puzzle* activity. This can be compared and contrasted with the tetrahedron.

REGULAR TETRAHEDRON Folding Instructions

1. Fold the square in half vertically and unfold.

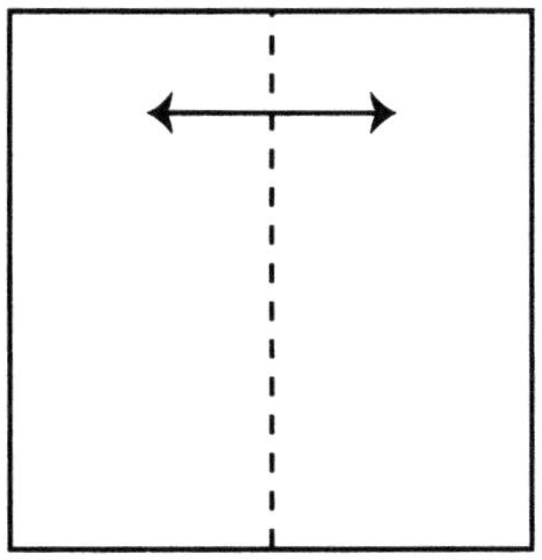

2. Fold from the bottom left corner as indicated by the dashed line so that the bottom right corner touches the midline.

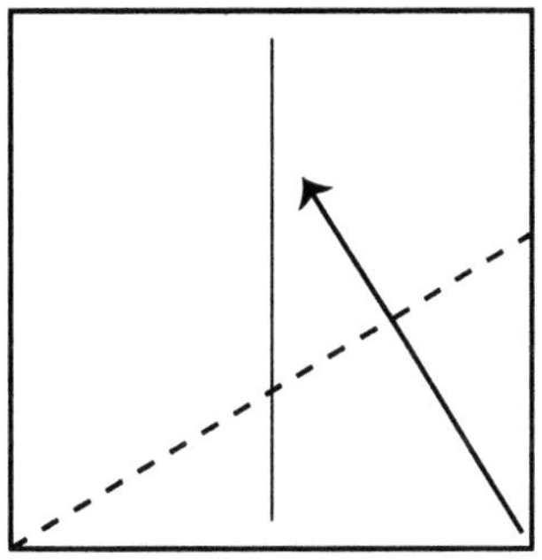

3. Fold the right side over so that the two points marked with dots meet as shown.

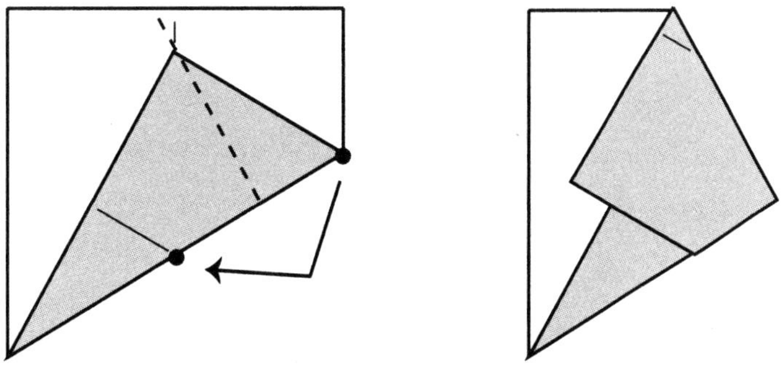

4. Unfold completely and fold the paper horizontally so that the two points marked by dots meet. The horizontal fold should go through the intersection of the two diagonals.

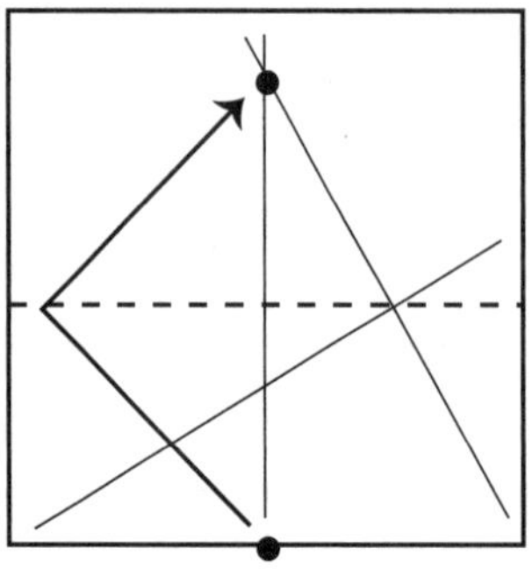

5. a. Fold the top part of the paper down at the point where the bottom edge meets the paper.
   b. Unfold the bottom half, but leave the top part folded down.

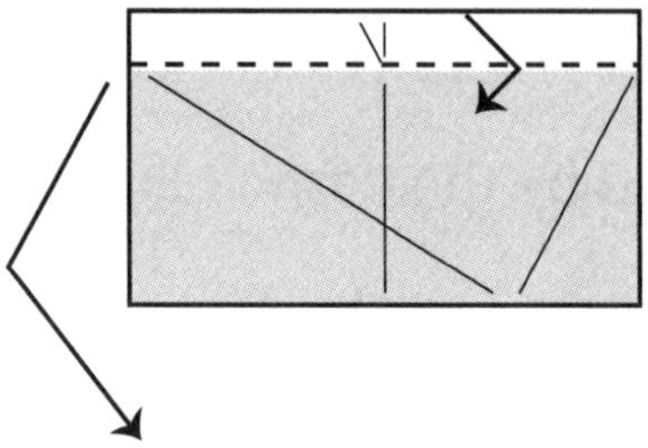

a.

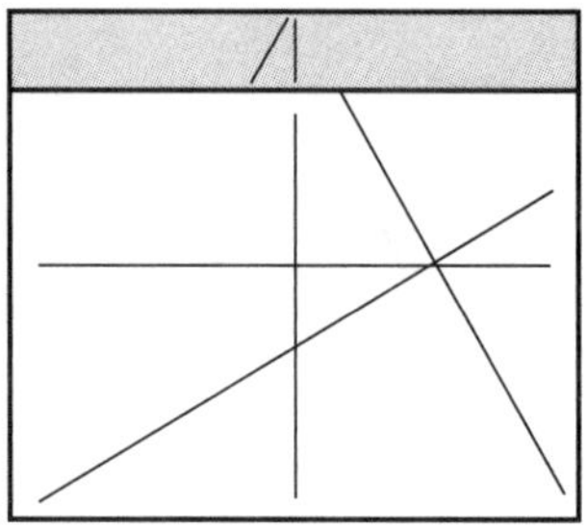

b.

6. Crease as indicated by each of the dashed lines, bringing the corners in to meet the horizontal midline.

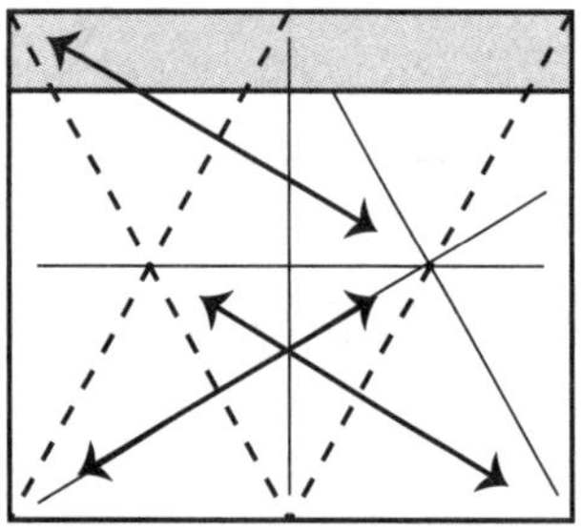

7. Fold the top left and bottom right corners where indicated by the dashed lines so that the corners touch the nearest diagonals. Notice that the two new sides formed are parallel to the nearest diagonals.

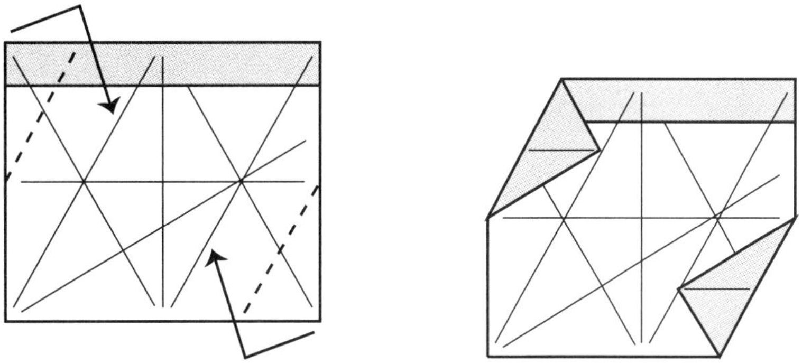

8. Fold again along the diagonals so that the two sides meet in the center.

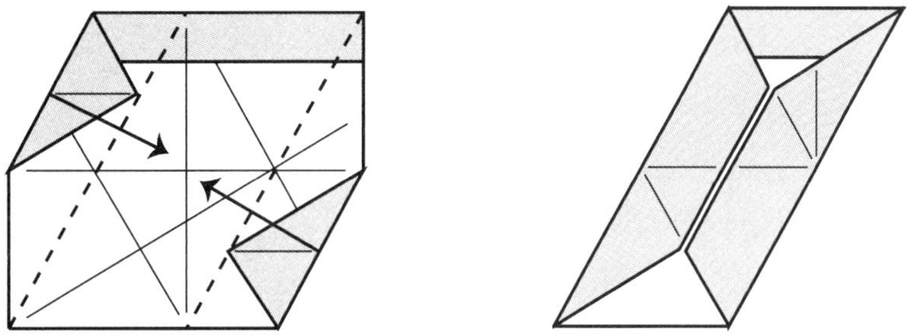

9. Flip the paper over and crease where indicated by the dashed lines.

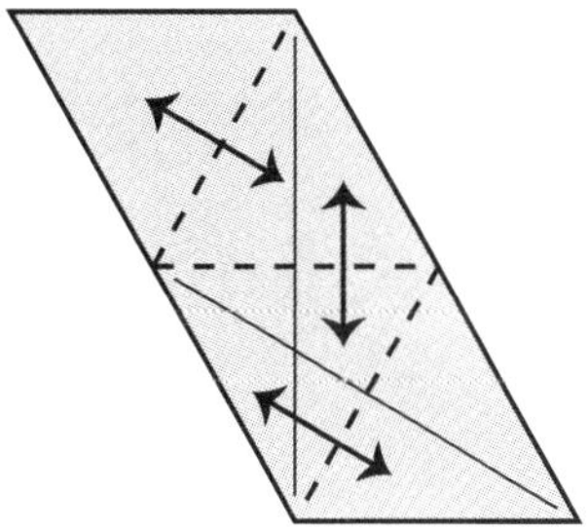

10. Repeat steps one through six with the second square. Steps seven through nine will be done as mirror images.
Fold the top right and bottom left corners where indicated by the dashed lines so that the corners touch the nearest diagonals. Notice that the two new sides formed are parallel to the nearest diagonals.

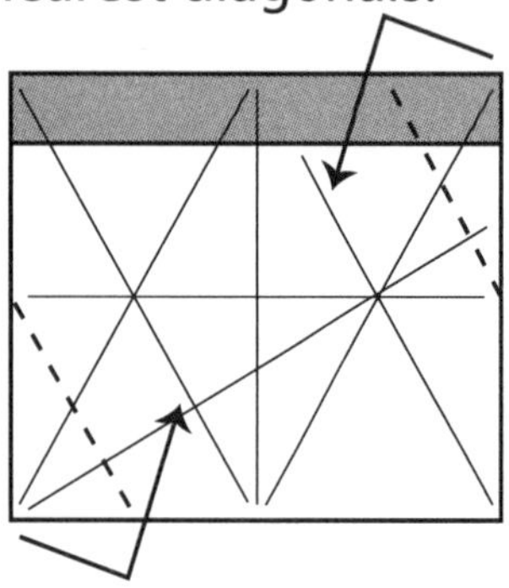

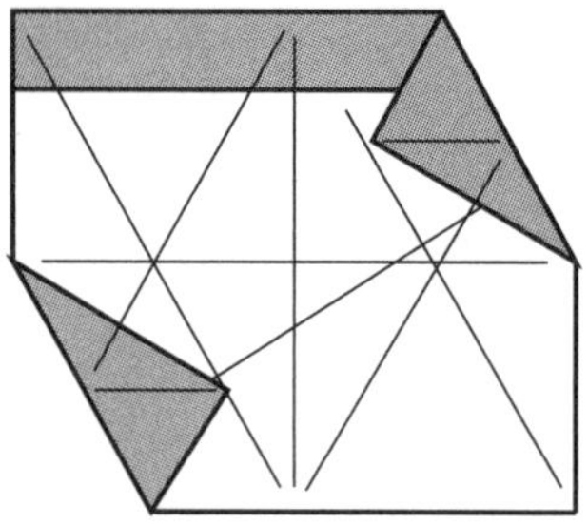

11. Fold again along the diagonals so that the two sides meet in the center.

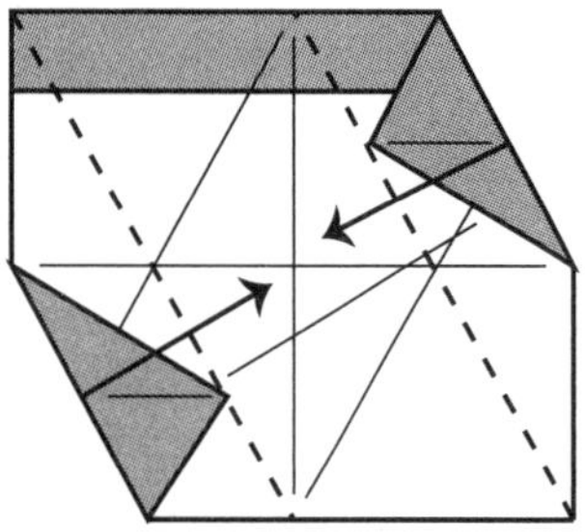

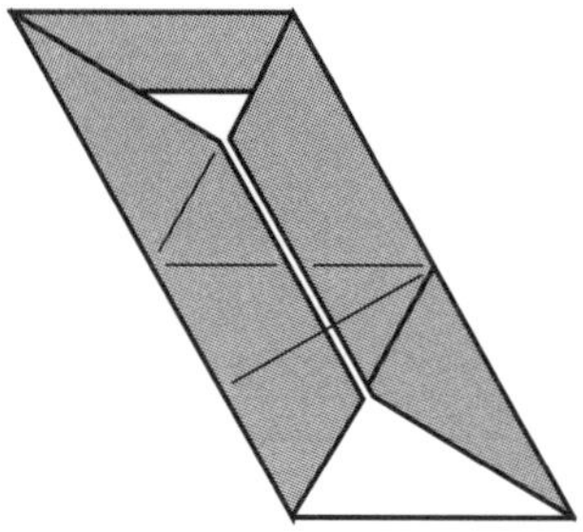

12. Flip the paper over and crease where indicated by the dashed lines.

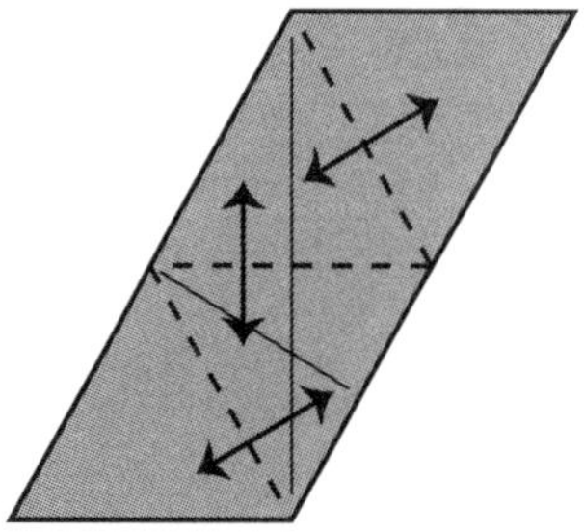

REGULAR TETRAHEDRON Assembly

Connect the pieces as shown, folding the units so that each point is inserted into the indicated pocket. You should be left with a regular tetrahedron.

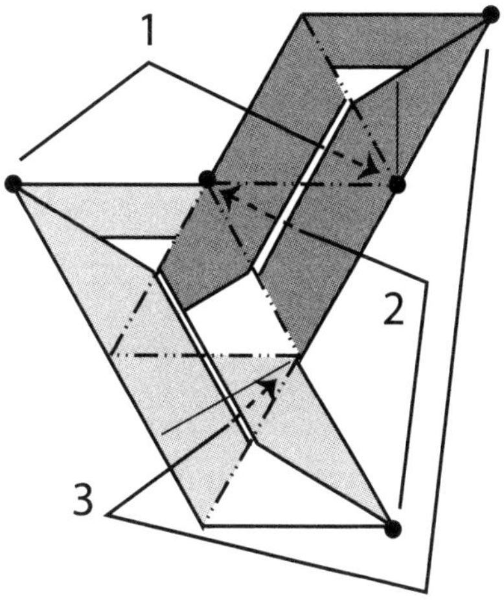

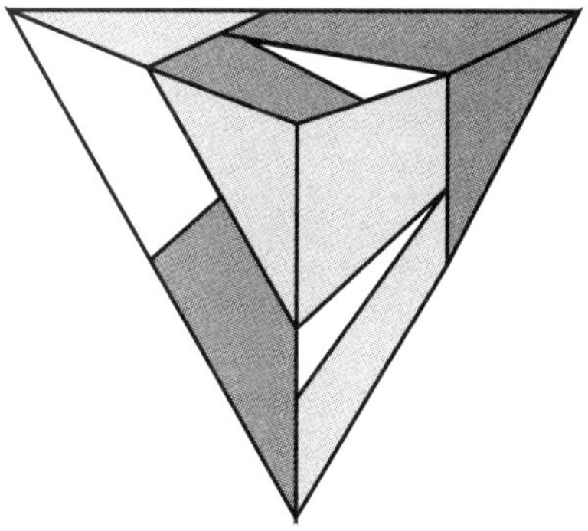

Top view

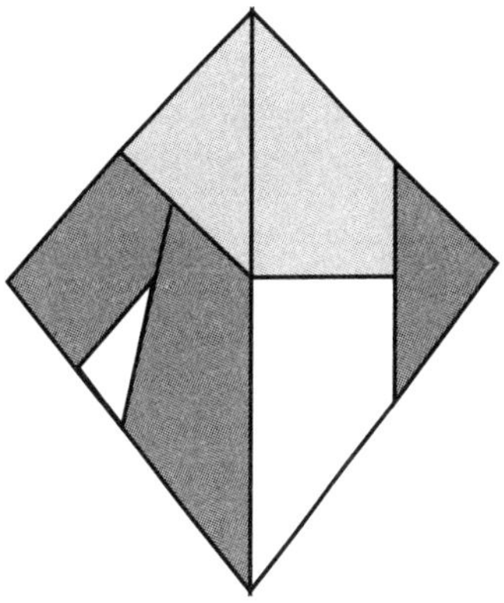

Side view

REGULAR
TETRAHEDRON Exploration

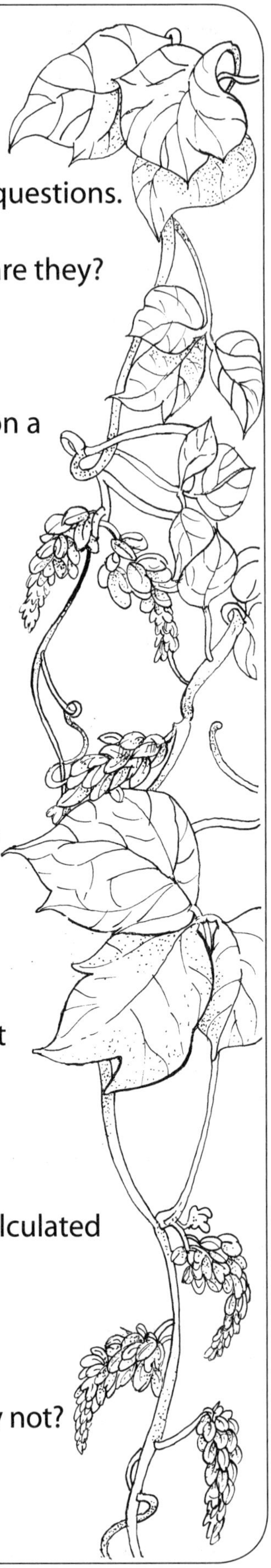

Use your completed tetrahedron model to answer the following questions.

1. How many faces does a regular tetrahedron have? What shape are they?

2. How does this compare to the number and shape of the faces on a bird tetrahedron?

3. How many vertices does a regular tetrahedron have? How many edges? How do these values compare to those for the bird tetrahedron?

4. How would you find the surface area of one face of the tetrahedron? ...of the whole tetrahedron? Describe your plan below.

5. If the base of one face is 3 units and the height is 2.5 units, what is the surface area of the tetrahedron?

6. How does this surface area compare to the surface area you calculated for the bird tetrahedron?

7. Does the difference in these two values surprise you? Why or why not?

CUBE

FOCUS

Students will fold a cube, identify the geometric relationships that are present in the completed model.

KEY QUESTION

What geometric relationships are represented in the folded cube?

MATH

Properties of polyhedra
- congruence
- angles
- parallel
- perpendicular
- faces
- edges
- vertices

Surface area
Symmetry

PAPER

Six squares per model in three different colors

CREATOR

Mitsonobu Sonobè

Management
1. It is best to use three different colors of paper for the cube model. This makes the final assembly much easier because the faces will form "bow ties" with two triangles of one color and two of another.
2. The final question on the exploration sheet asks students to identify the kinds of symmetry they can find in the cube. If your students are not familiar with the concepts of symmetry you may wish to give them the symmetry worksheets included in the appendix, or have them skip that question.

Procedure
1. Hand out the folding instructions (pages 41-44) and six paper squares to each student.
2. Take students through the folding procedure for the basic unit one step at a time. If they have already folded the bird tetrahedron, students should be familiar with the unit.
3. Have students fold the remaining five units, and then guide them through the assembly of their cube.
4. When all students have successfully constructed a cube, have them get into small groups and hand out the remaining student sheet.
5. Have students work together to answer the questions and identify the properties of their cubes.
6. Close with a time of class discussion where students share their discoveries and insights.

Discussion
1. What shape are the sides of the figure? [square]
2. What are four properties of a square? [Various. Four right angles, four congruent sides, two sets of parallel sides, etc.]
3. What can you say about the relationship of the sides of the cube to each other? [They intersect at right angles, they are all congruent, etc.]
4. How many faces, edges, and vertices does your cube have? [faces: six; edges: 12; vertices: 8]
5. How would you determine the surface area of the cube? [Find the surface area of one face and multiply by six.]
6. If the length of one side is two units, what is the surface area of the cube? [24 $units^2$]
7. What kinds of symmetry exist in the cube? [The cube has four planes of bilateral symmetry per face, and three types of rotational symmetry. (See *Solutions* for more detail.)]

Extensions
1. Determine the relationship between the size of the original square and the dimensions of the finished cube.
2. Challenge students to try and make some other cube-related shapes that can be made using the same basic units. Various "colliding" cube models can be made with nine units, 12 units, and 18 units.
3. Make the *Open-Faced Cube* and compare its properties to those of the solid cube. (The *Open-Faced Cube* unit was created by Robert Neale.)
4. If they have not already done so, have students complete the *Sonobè Unit Exploration.*

Solutions

The planes and axes of symmetry that exist in a cube are discussed below.

Types of symmetry in a cube

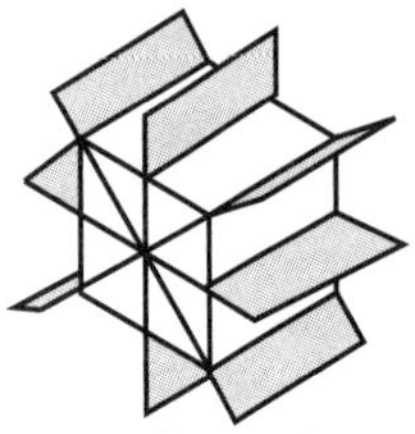

Planes of bilateral symmetry

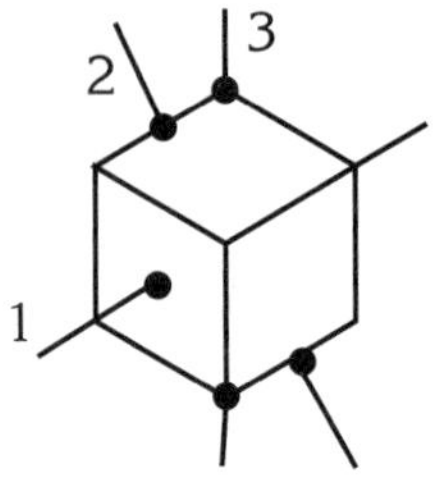

Axes of rotational symmetry

As you can see in the first figure, there are four planes of bilateral symmetry per face of the cube. If you were to slice the cube along any one of these planes, the two halves would be mirror images of each other.

The second figure shows the three different kinds of rotational symmetry that exist in a cube. The axes have been labeled for the purposes of discussion.

1. The first axis goes through the center of two opposite faces. There are three of these axes in a cube (six faces total, one axis for every two faces). These face-to-face axes have 4-fold rotational symmetry. For each 90° the cube is rotated around the axis, it appears to be in the same position.
2. The second axis goes through the center of two opposite edges. There are six of these axes in a cube (12 edges total, one axis for every two edges). These edge-to-edge axes have 2-fold rotational symmetry. For every 180° the cube is rotated around the axis, it appears to be in the same position.
3. The third axis goes through two opposite vertices. There are four of these axes in a cube (eight vertices total, one axis for every two vertices). These vertex-to-vertex axes have 3-fold rotational symmetry. For each 120° the cube is rotated around the axis, it appears to be in the same position.

Open-Faced Cube Exploration

1. Which cube is bigger, the original cube, or the open-faced cube? [The open-faced cube.] How can you explain this? [The way the units are used to construct the cubes differs; the open-faced cube uses a longer portion of each unit to form its edges.]
2. What shape are the openings on each face of the cube? [square] How could you prove this? [Measure the angles and the lengths of the sides.]
3. If you round to the nearest half-centimeter, what is the ratio of one side of the original square of paper to one side of the open-faced cube? [If you use 10 cm squares to construct the units, the side of the open-faced cube is almost exactly 7 cm. This gives a ratio of 10/7.] How does this ratio compare to the ratio for the regular cube? [Assuming the same 10 cm squares, the side of the regular cube is almost exactly 3.5 cm. This gives a ratio of 10/3.5. Notice that this ratio is twice that of the ratio for the open-faced cube.]
4. Based on these ratios, how big would the original squares of paper need to be in order to have the original cube be about the same size as the open-faced cube? [When using the same size paper for both, the finished cube has edges that are almost exactly half the length of those of the open-faced cube. In order for the regular cube to be about the same size, the edges of the original squares would need to be twice as long as those of the open-faced cube. For example, if you used 10 cm squares for the open-faced cube units, you would need to have 20 cm squares for the regular cube units.]
5. How do the sizes of the open-faced cube and the regular cube compare? [The open-faced cube has edges that are almost exactly twice as long as those of the regular cube.] How does this relate to the ratios you discovered above? [The ratio between the regular cube edge-length and the size of the paper is about twice that of the ratio between the open-faced cube edge-length and the size of the paper. This corresponds to the final size of the open-faced cube being twice that of the regular cube.]
6. Use the ratios you discovered to determine the surface area of the open-faced cube if one edge of the regular cube is two units. [As we have discussed, the open-faced cube has edges approximately twice as long as the regular cube. If the regular cube has 2 unit edges and a surface area of 24 units^2, then the open-faced cube would have 4 unit edges and a surface area of 96 units^2. (4 x 4 = 16, 16 x 6 = 96)]

CUBE Folding Instructions

1. Fold the paper in half vertically and unfold.

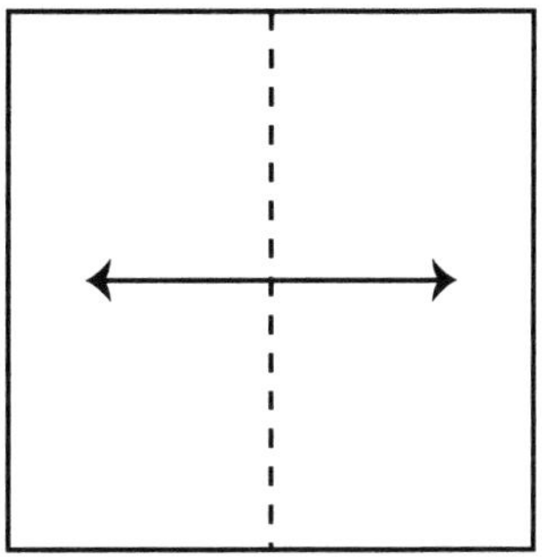

2. Fold the left edge and the right edge in to meet the center crease.

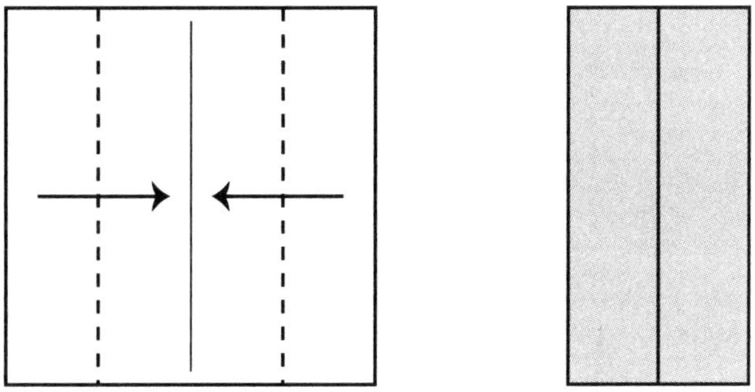

3. Fold as indicated by the dashed lines so that the top left corner meets the right side of the paper and the bottom right corner meets the left side of the paper.

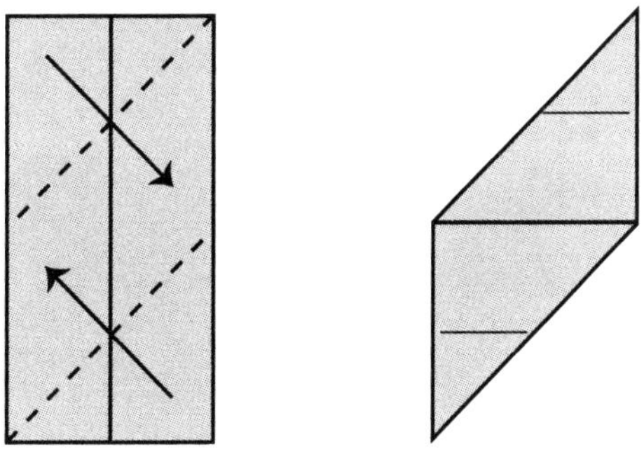

4. Unfold the paper completely. Fold the top right and bottom left corners in along the existing crease lines as shown.

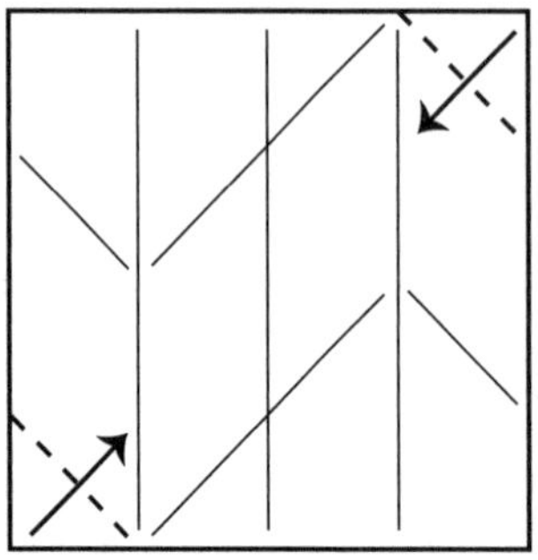

5. Fold the left and right sides of the paper in along the existing crease lines so that the edges meet in the middle.

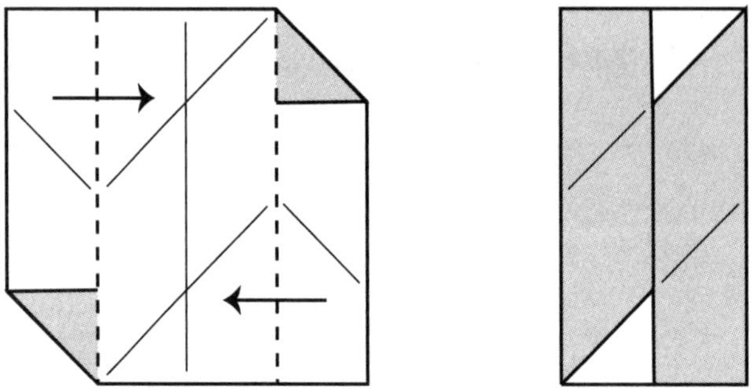

6. Fold the bottom right corner up along the existing crease line, tucking the corner underneath the flap as indicated.

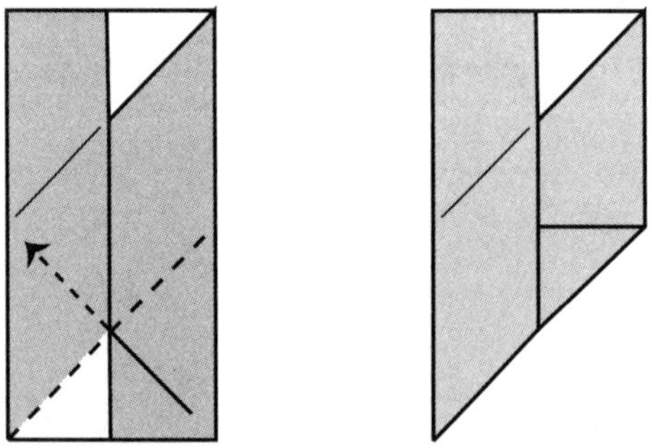

7. Repeat this process with the upper left corner, tucking it under the flap on the right side as indicated.

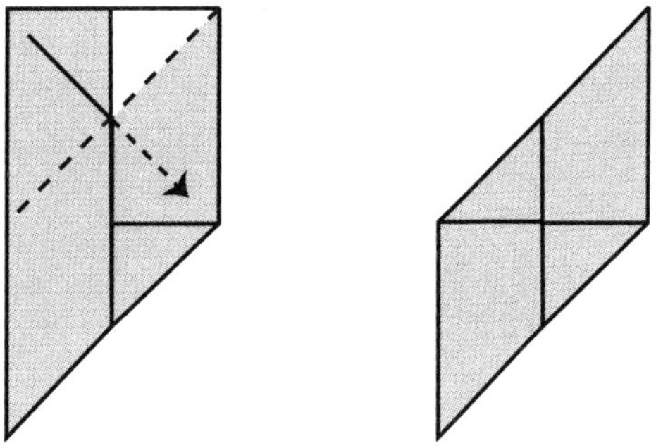

8. Flip the unit over and crease where indicated by the dashed lines. Repeat steps one through eight so that you have a total of six units like the one below.

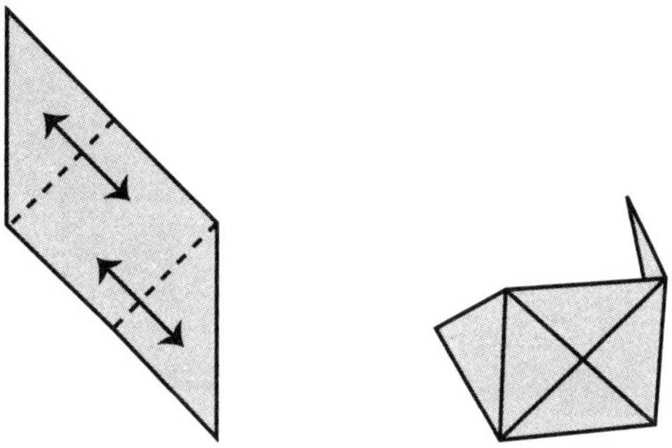

(x 6)

CUBE Assembly

1. Take two units of the same color and set them on edge with their tabs pointing in. Arrange them so that the sides of the tabs line up and you can see four faces of the cube.

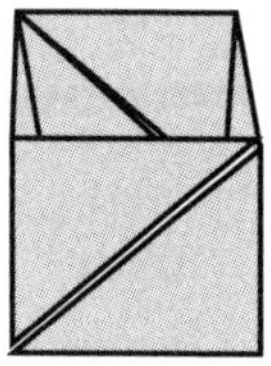

2. Take one unit of a different color and place it on top of the first two units as shown. Tuck the tabs into the pockets that are directly beneath them. Flip the cube over and repeat this process on the bottom with the second unit of that color.

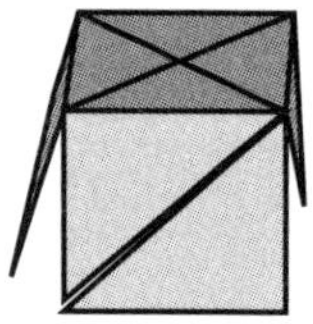

3. Turn the cube so that two of the remaining loose tabs are facing up. Place one unit of the third color across the top of the cube, making sure that the original tabs are on the **outside** of the unit. Tuck all four loose tabs into the pockets directly beneath them. Flip the cube over and repeat this process with the final remaining unit. If you have assembled your cube correctly, each face should have a "bow tie" pattern with two triangles each of two different colors.

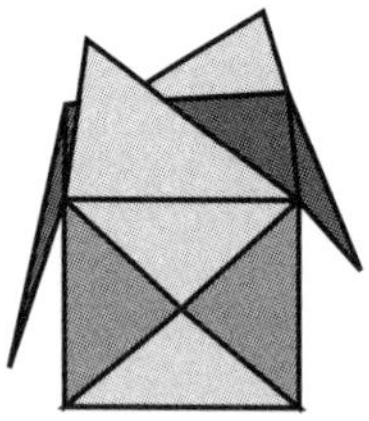

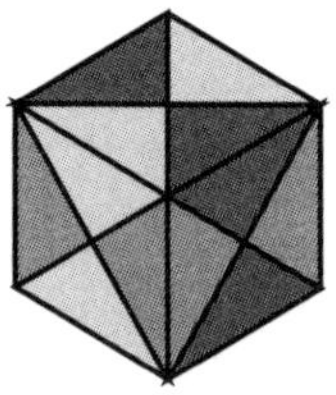

CUBE Exploration

Use your completed cube to respond to the following questions.

1. What shapes are the faces of the figure?

2. What can you say about their relationship to each other and how do you know?

3. How many faces, edges, and vertices does your figure have?

4. List some properties of the cube.

5. How would you find the surface area of one face? ...of the whole figure? Describe your plan.

6. If the length of one edge is equal to 2 units, what is the surface area of the whole figure according to the method you described in question five? Show your work.

7. What kinds of symmetry can you find in the cube? Identify and describe each kind that you can find.

OPEN-FACED CUBE Folding Instructions

1. Fold the square into thirds, using a valley and a mountain fold.

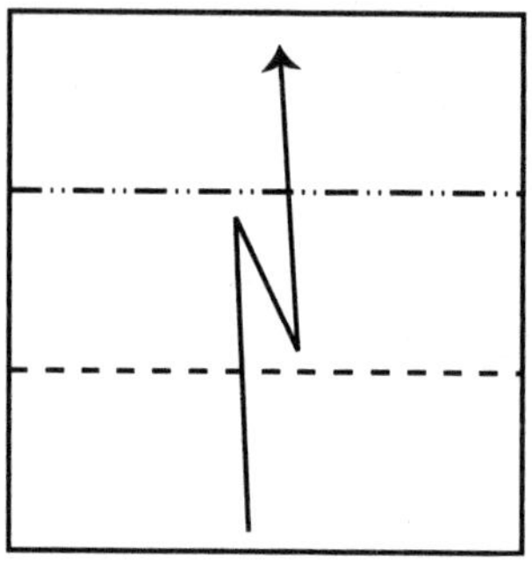

2. Fold the resulting rectangle in half horizontally and unfold.

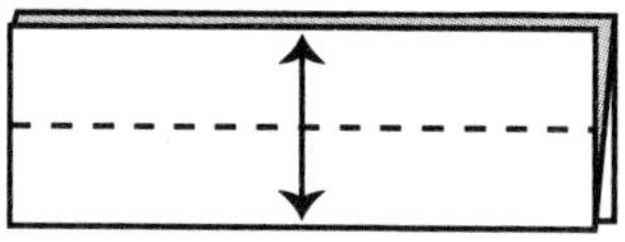

3. Fold the top right and bottom left corners in to meet the center crease, and unfold.

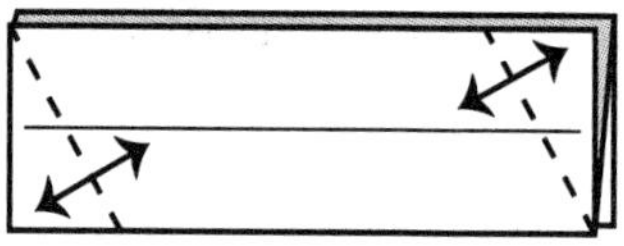

4. Crease the paper where indicated by the dashed line so that there is a diagonal connecting the two corner crease lines.

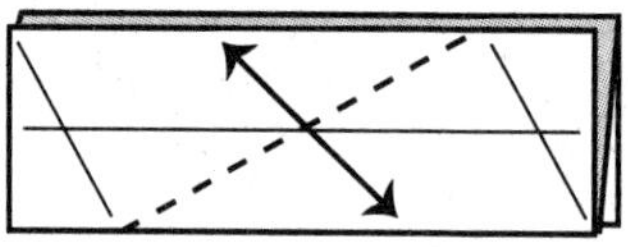

5. Repeat steps one through four 11 more times so that you have a total of 12 pieces like the one below.

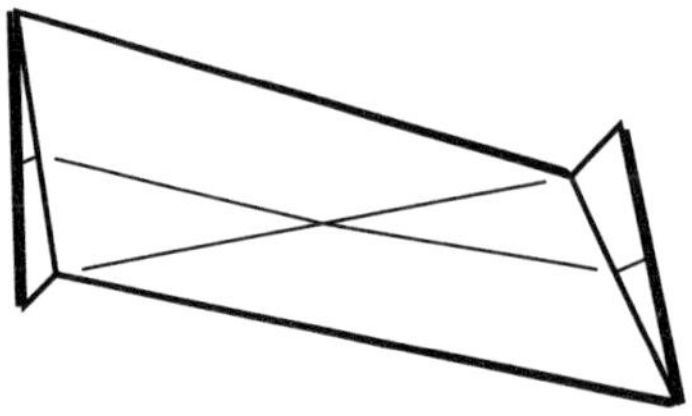

OPEN-FACED CUBE Folding Instructions

1. Connect four of the units by inserting one end of each unit between the flap on the side of another unit as shown. This should result in a square framework with a square hole in the middle. (The colored side of your units should be facing out.)

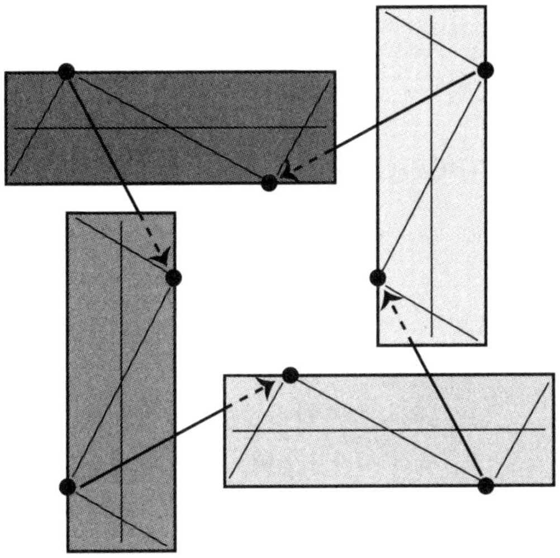

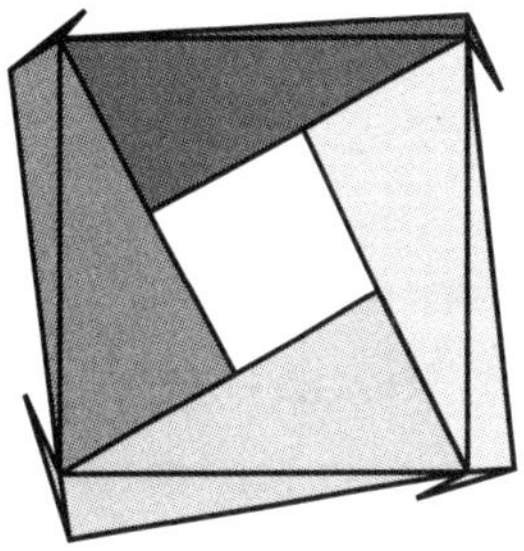

2. Connect an additional unit to each corner of the framework, then use the remaining four units to complete the sixth face of the cube.

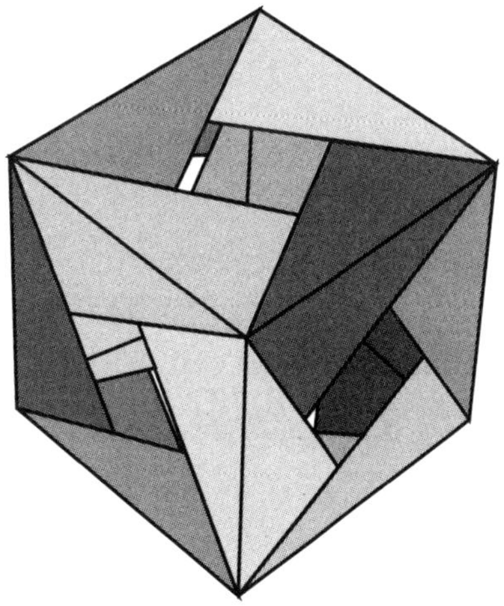

OPEN-FACED CUBE Exploration

You should have both the original cube, and your open-faced cube to answer these questions.

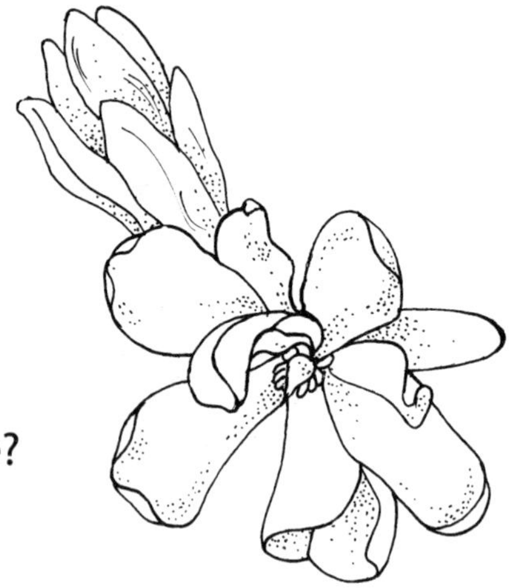

1. Which cube is bigger, the original cube or the open-faced cube? How can you explain this?

2. What shape are the openings on each face of the cube? How could you prove this?

3. If you round to the nearest half-centimeter, what is the ratio of one side of the original square of paper to one side of the open-faced cube? How does this ratio compare to the ratio for the regular cube?

4. Based on these ratios, how big would your original squares of paper need to be in order to have the original cube be about the same size as the open-faced cube?

5. How do the overall sizes of the open-faced cube and the regular cube compare? How does this relate to the ratios you discovered above?

6. Use the ratios you discovered to determine the approximate surface area of the open-faced cube if one edge of the regular cube is 2 units. Show your work.

OCTAHEDRON

FOCUS

Students will fold an octahedron and look at the geometric properties in the completed figure to see how these compare to the other figures they have folded.

KEY QUESTIONS

What are the geometric properties of a completed octahedron?

How do these properties compare to those of the models you have already folded?

MATH

Properties of polyhedra
- faces
- edges
- vertices
- similarity

Surface area

INTEGRATED PROCESSES

Observing
Comparing and contrasting
Generalizing

PAPER

Five squares per model in two colors

CREATOR

Tomoko Fusè

Procedure

1. Hand out the folding instructions (pages 50-56) and five paper squares to each student. The three loop units should all be made of one color, and the top and bottom pieces of another color.
2. Go over the folding instructions for the loop units as a class. Have students fold the remaining two units and guide them through the loop assembly step by step.
3. Repeat this process for the top/bottom units, guiding students through the assembly of their octahedron.
4. When all students have successfully assembled their models, hand out the remaining student sheet.
5. Have students work together in groups to answer the questions about their models and make comparisons with the previously folded models.
6. When all groups have finished, close with a time of class discussion where students share their discoveries and the things they learned about their octahedrons.

Discussion

1. How many faces does the octahedron have? [eight] How many vertices? [six] ...edges? [12]
2. How does this compare with the other figures you have folded so far? Be specific.
3. What shape are the faces? [equilateral triangles] What other figure(s) have this same shape for their faces? [The regular tetrahedron. (The icosahedron also has equilateral triangles for faces, but students should not have folded an icosahedron yet.)]
4. How many faces converge at each vertex? [four] How does this compare to other figures?
5. How are the pockets into which you put the top and bottom pieces related to the faces geometrically? [They are similar, smaller triangles.] Explain your reasoning.
6. If the base of one face is 3 units and the height is 2.5 units, what is the surface area of the octahedron? [30 units^2 $(\frac{1}{2} \times 3) \times 2.5 = 3.75$, $3.75 \times 8 = 30$]

Extensions

1. Have students fold another octahedron using the second method and compare the two versions. Which is easier to fold? Which one do you think looks better?
2. Have students fold the lid to make their octahedron into a decorative box. (If students will be using the octahedrons to hold anything, the paper used should be sturdier than regular origami paper.) Leaving the lid off can give students a decorative pencil box for their desks.

REGULAR OCTAHEDRON

Part One: Making and assembling the loop units

1. Fold the square in half vertically and unfold.

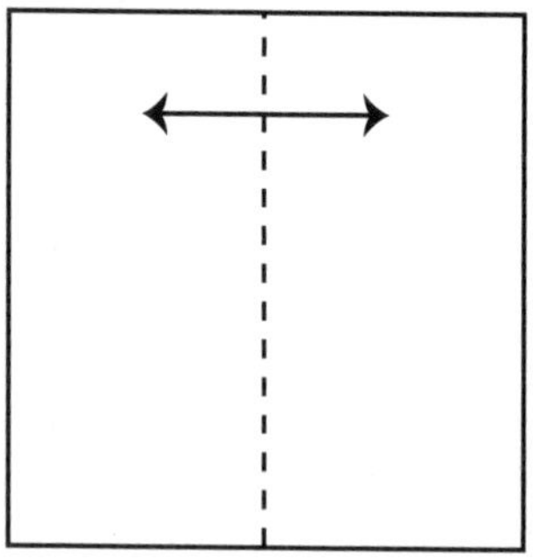

2. Fold from the bottom left corner as indicated by the dashed line so that the bottom right corner touches the midline.

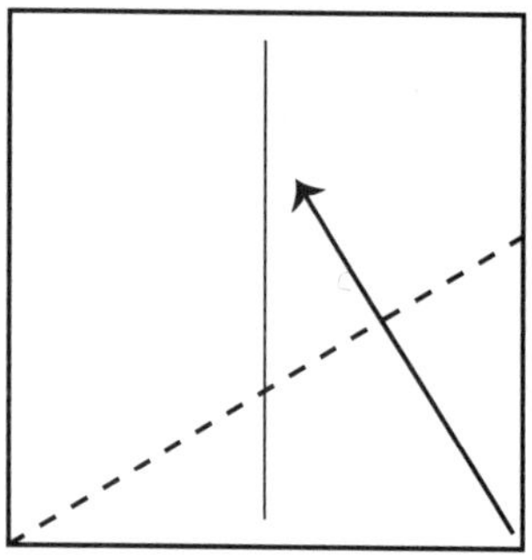

3. Fold the right side over so that the two points marked with dots meet as shown.

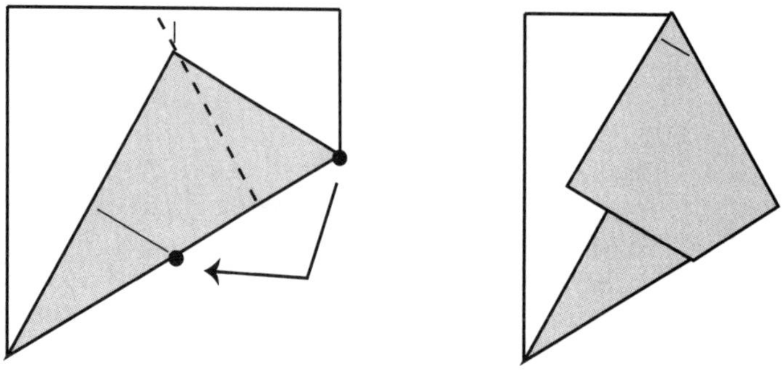

4. Unfold completely and fold the paper horizontally so that the two points marked by dots meet. The horizontal fold should go through the intersection of the two diagonals.

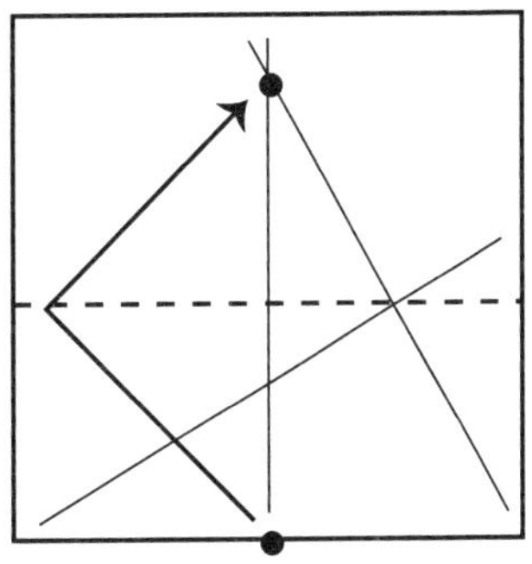

5. a. Fold the top part of the paper down at the point where the bottom edge meets the paper.
   b. Unfold the bottom half of the paper, leaving the top part folded down.

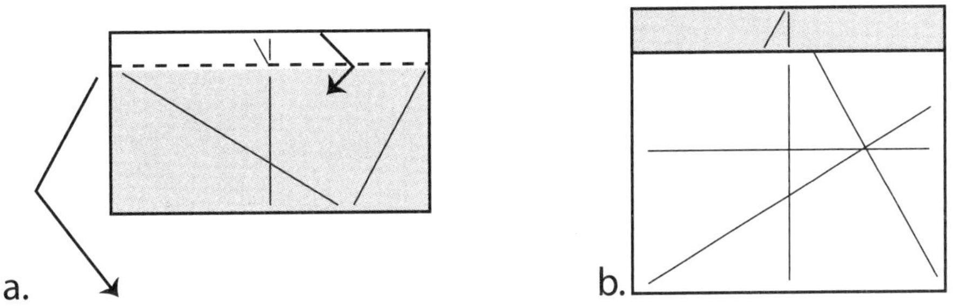

6. Crease as indicated by each of the dashed lines, bringing the corners in to meet the horizontal midline.

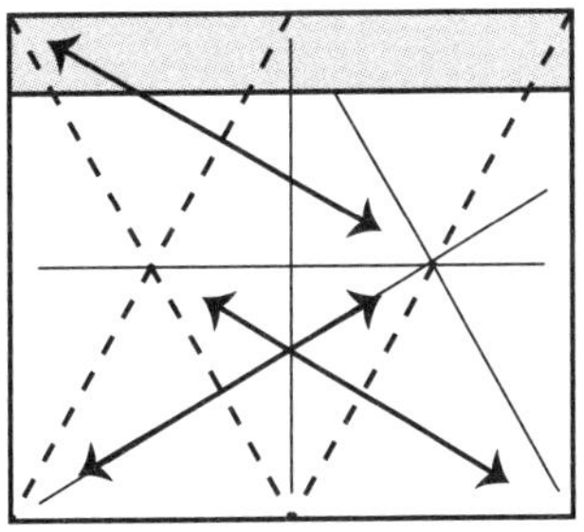

7. Fold the top left and bottom right corners where indicated by the dashed lines so that the corners touch the nearest diagonals. Notice that the two new sides formed are parallel to the nearest diagonals.

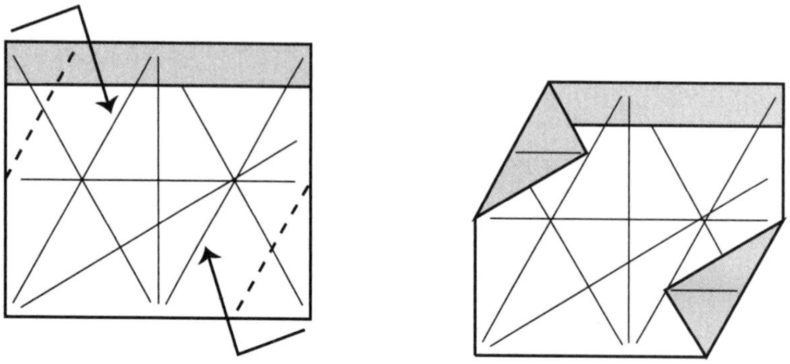

8. Fold again along the diagonals so that the two sides meet in the center.

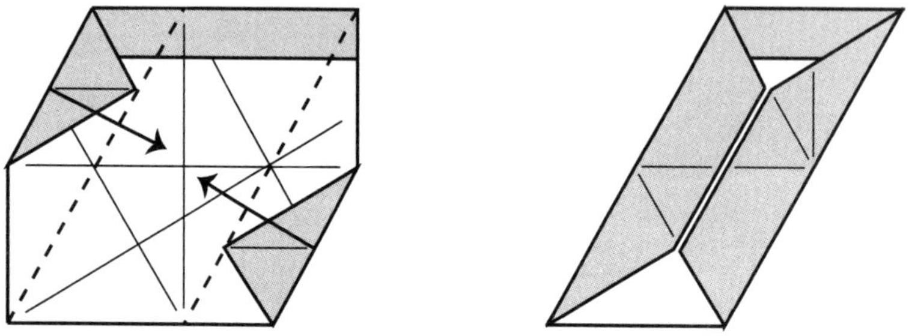

9. Flip the paper over and crease where indicated by the dashed lines. Repeat steps one through nine with the remaining two pieces of paper so that you have a total of three pieces like the one below.

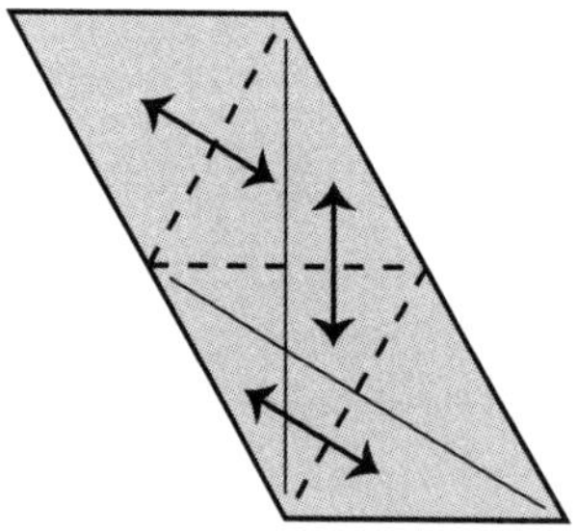

10. Slide the three pieces together as shown in the diagram below. One piece goes inside the next to the point indicated by the dots. The third piece and the first piece must be connected at the end, forming a complete loop. This loop should have six faces that are all equilateral triangles. It should be open at the top and at the bottom, and both openings should also be equilateral triangles. **Be sure to complete the loop so that the sides with the pockets are on the outside, not the inside.**

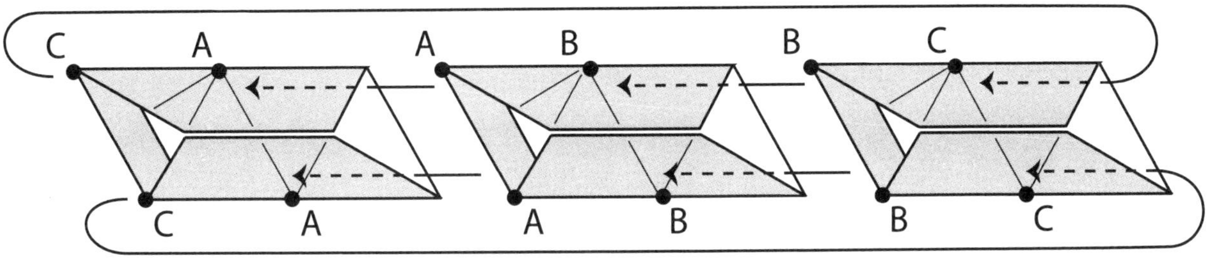

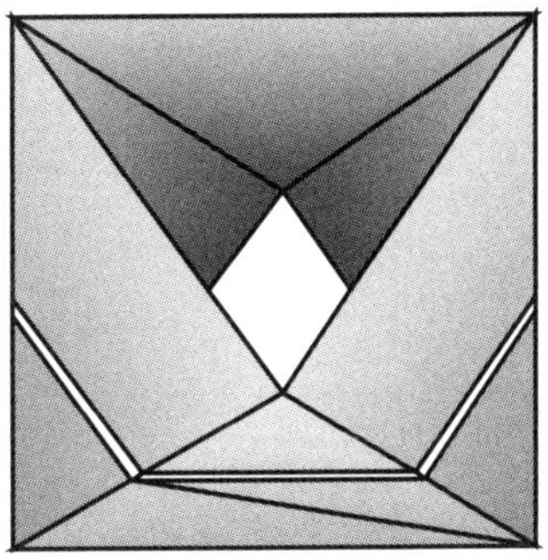

REGULAR OCTAHEDRON

Part Two: Making the top and bottom units and assembling the octahedron

1. Fold the square in half vertically and unfold.

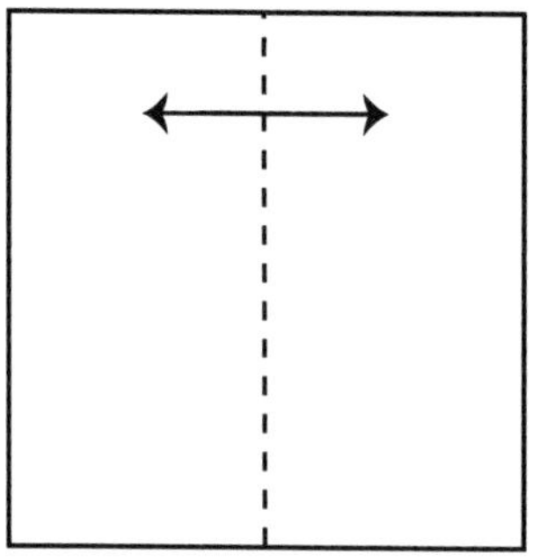

2. Fold the left side in to meet the midline.

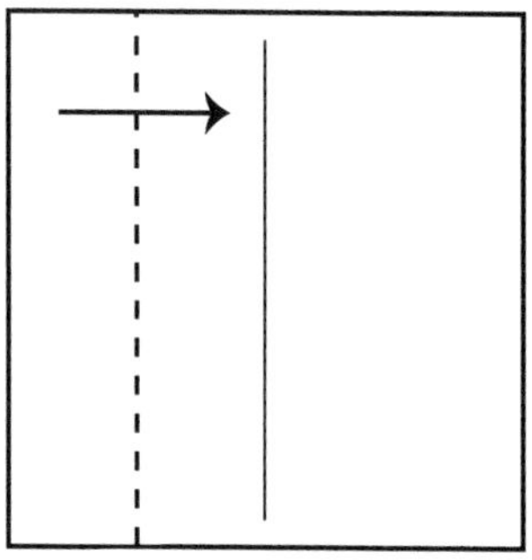

3. Fold as indicated by the dashed line so that the bottom right corner touches the left side of the paper.

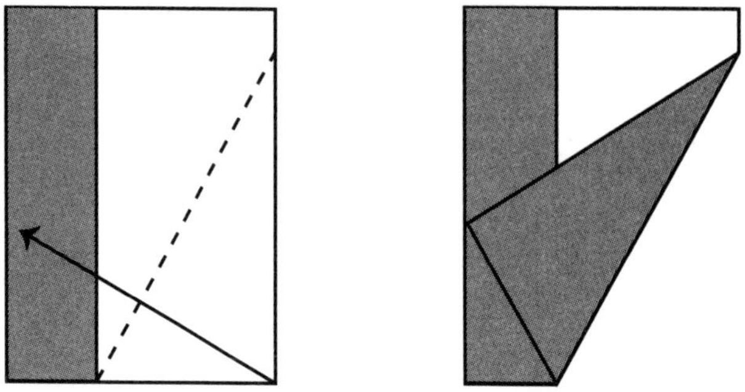

4. Unfold the entire paper and fold the bottom half up so that it meets the place where the diagonal intersects with the right side.

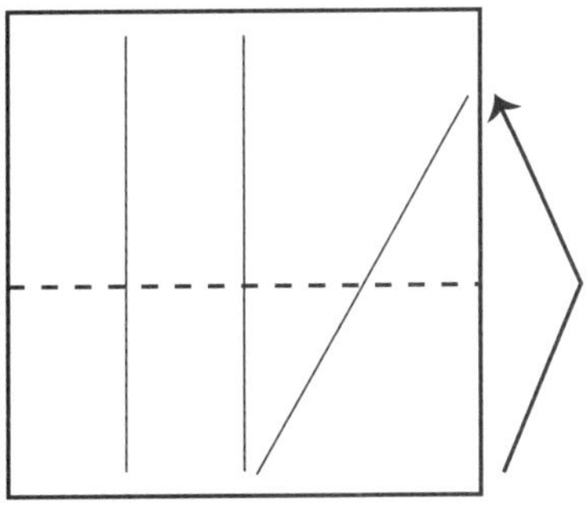

5. a. Fold the top part of the paper down at the point where the bottom edge meets the paper.
   b. Unfold the bottom half, but leave the top part folded down.

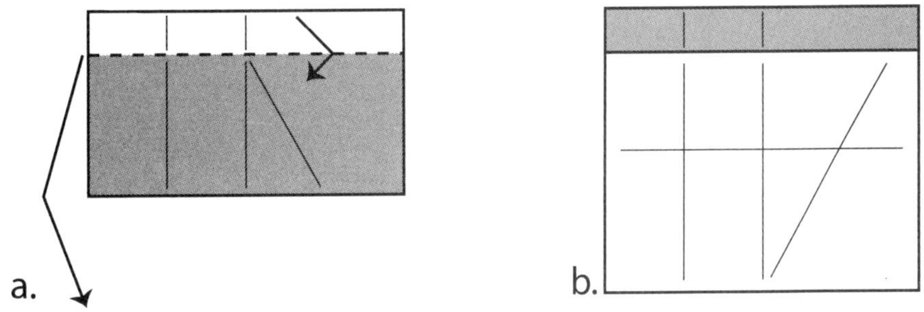

6. Fold the bottom left corner to the point where the right diagonal meets the horizontal midline. Repeat this process on the right side.

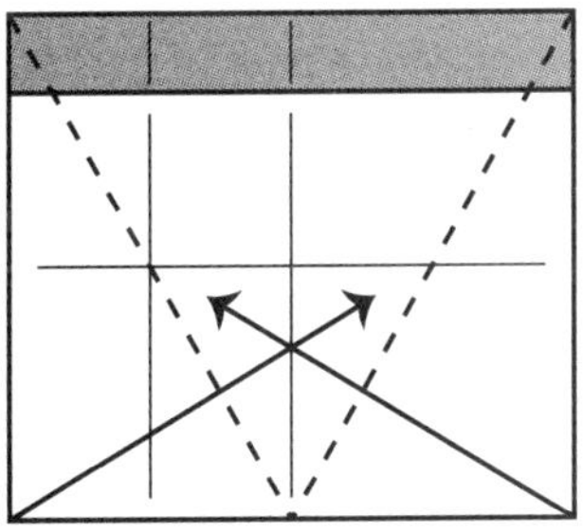

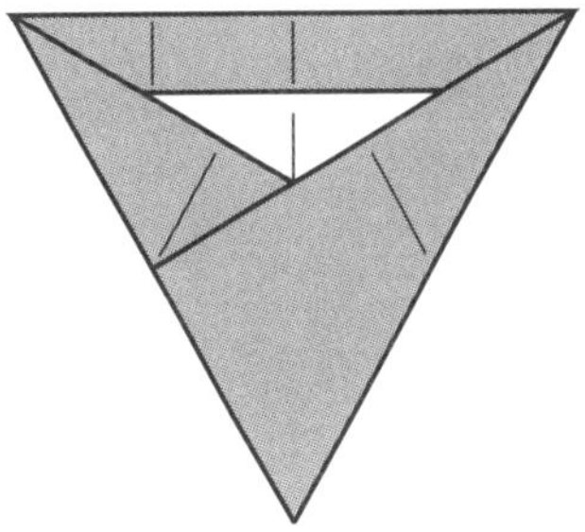

7. Fold each point of the triangle in to touch the opposite side as indicated, crease well and unfold. Repeat steps one through seven with your second piece of paper so that you have a total of two triangular pieces.

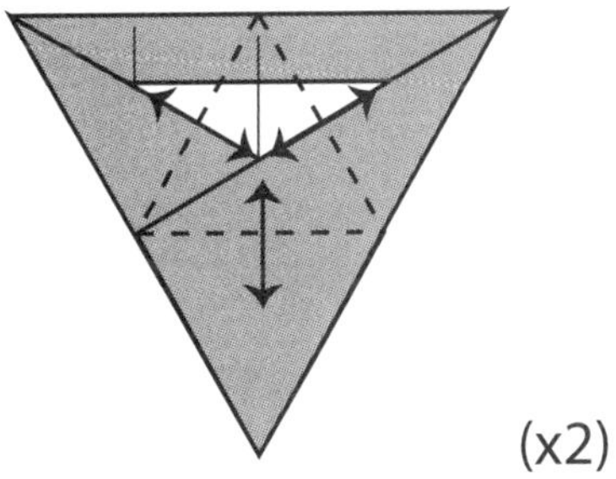

Octahedron Assembly: The two triangular pieces are the top and bottom pieces of your octahedron. Line up one triangle so that it fits over the hole in the top of the loop from *Part One*. Stick the points of the triangle into the slots on the sides of the loop. Turn the figure over so that the bottom hole is showing. Repeat this process with the second triangular piece. You should now have a completed octahedron with eight faces, each of which is an equilateral triangle.

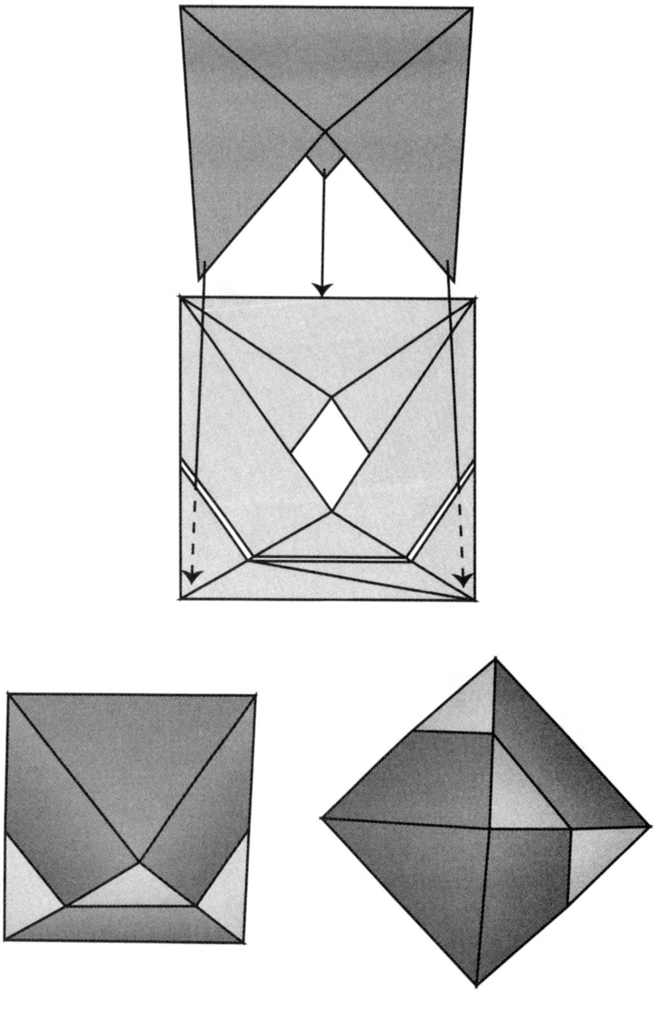

REGULAR OCTAHEDRON Exploration

Use your completed octahedron model to answer the following questions.

1. How many faces does the octahedron have? How many vertices? ...edges?

2. How does this compare with the other figures you have folded so far? Be specific.

3. What shape are the faces? What other figure(s) have this same shape for their faces?

4. How many faces converge at each vertex? How does this compare to other figures?

5. How are the pockets into which you put the top and bottom pieces related to the faces geometrically? Explain your reasoning.

6. If the base of one face is 3 units and the height is 2.5 units, what is the surface area of the octahedron?

OCTAHEDRON 2 Folding Instructions

1. Fold the square in half vertically and unfold.

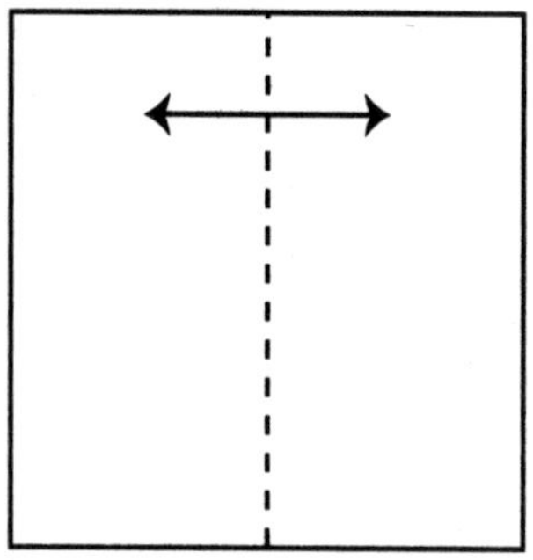

2. Fold from the bottom left corner as indicated by the dashed line so that the bottom right corner touches the midline.

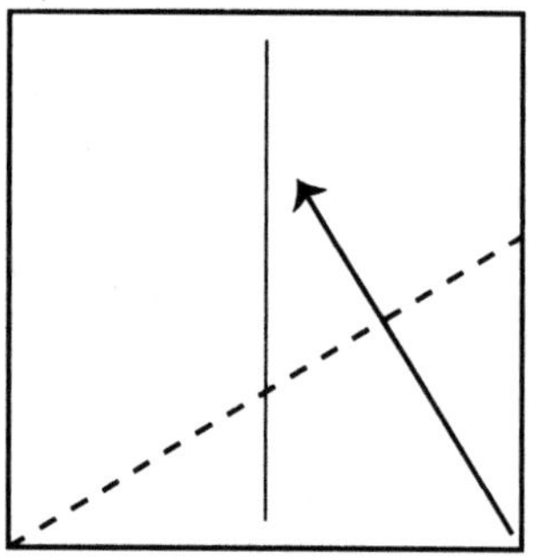

3. Fold the right side over so that the two points marked with dots meet as shown.

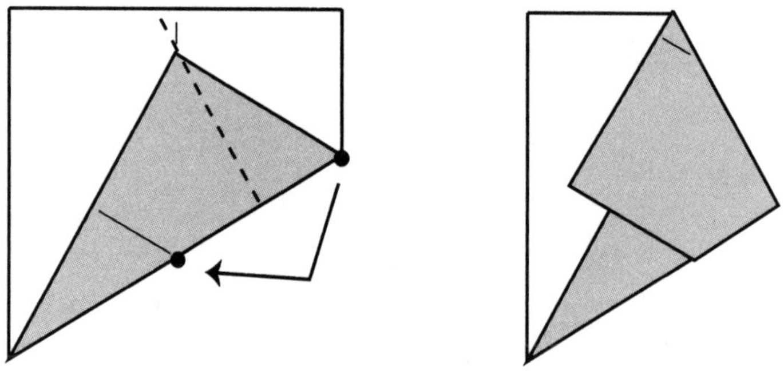

4. Unfold completely and fold the paper horizontally so that the two points marked by dots meet. The horizontal fold should go through the intersection of the two diagonals.

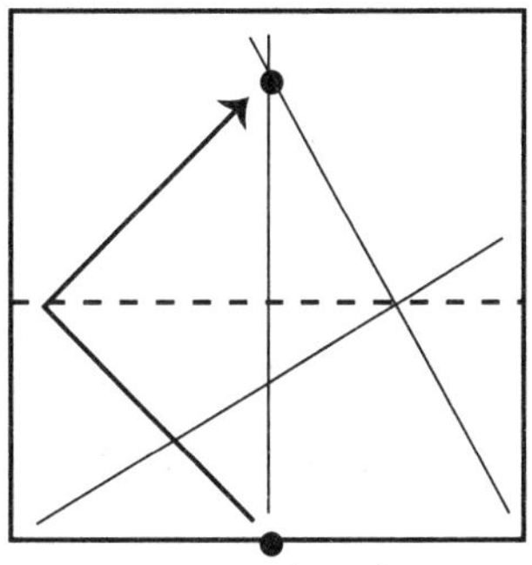

5. a. Fold the top part of the paper down at the point where the bottom edge meets the paper.
   b. Unfold the bottom half, but leave the top part folded down.

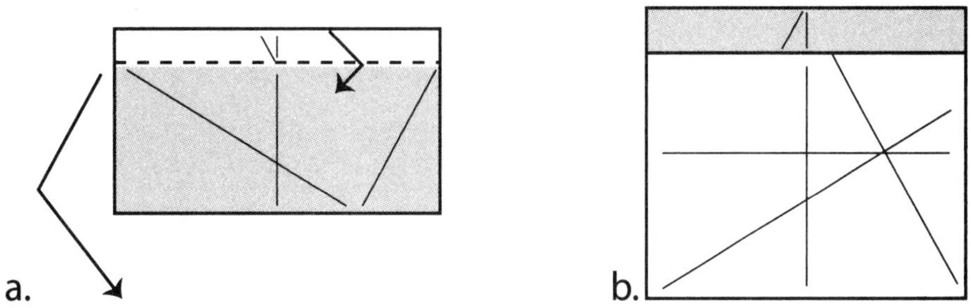

6. Crease as indicated by each of the dashed lines, bringing the corners in to meet the horizontal midline.

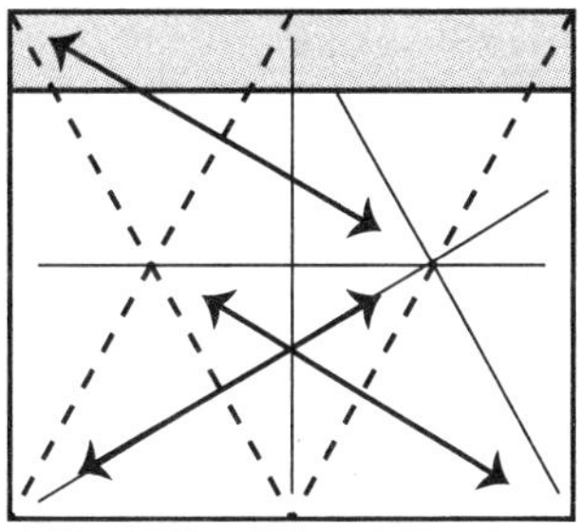

7. Fold the top left and bottom right corners where indicated by the dashed lines so that the corners touch the nearest diagonals. Notice that the two new sides formed are parallel to the nearest diagonals.

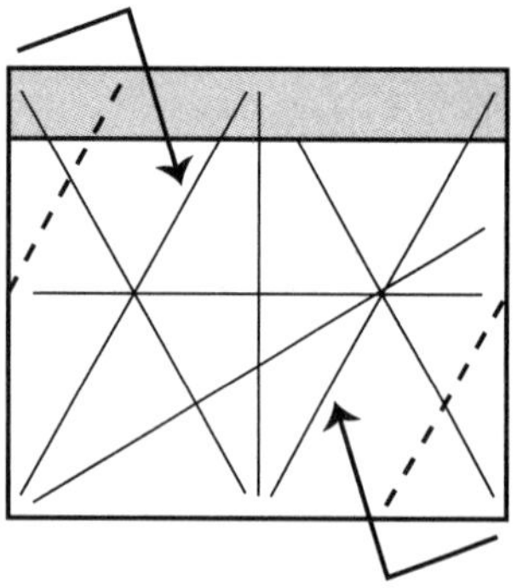

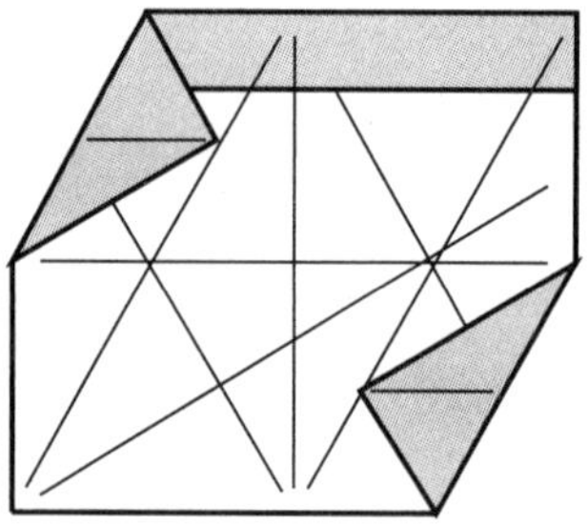

8. Fold again along the diagonals so that the two sides meet in the center.

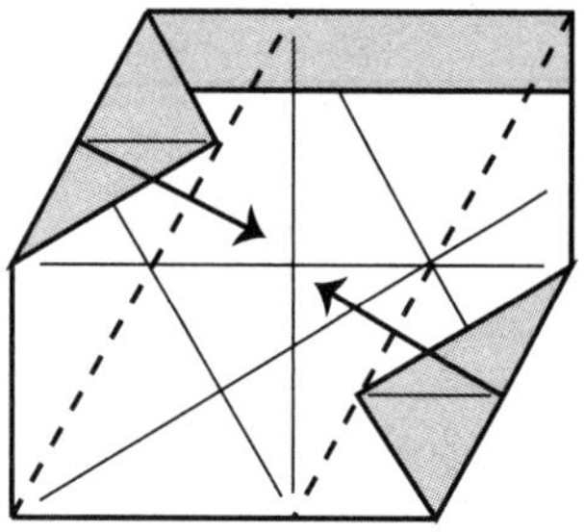

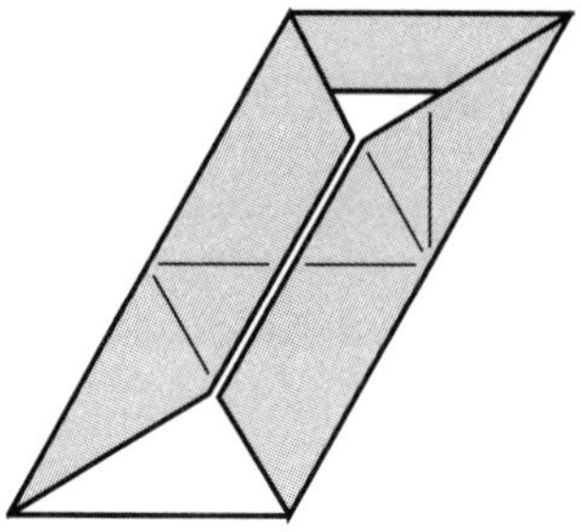

9. Flip the paper over and crease where indicated by the dashed lines. Repeat steps one through nine three more times so that you have a total of four pieces.

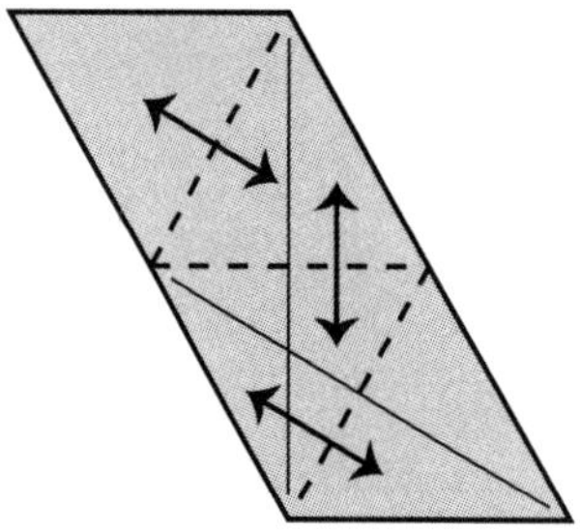

(x 4)

REGULAR OCTAHEDRON 2 Assembly

1. Take two pieces and fit them together as shown to form a square-based pyramid shape. Repeat this process with the other two pieces so that you have two square-based pyramid shapes.

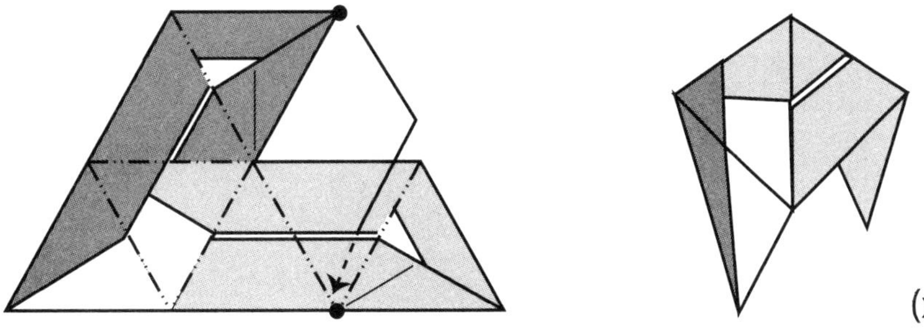

(x 2)

2. Fit the two pieces together as shown, inserting the tabs from one piece into the pockets on the other to form a regular octahedron.

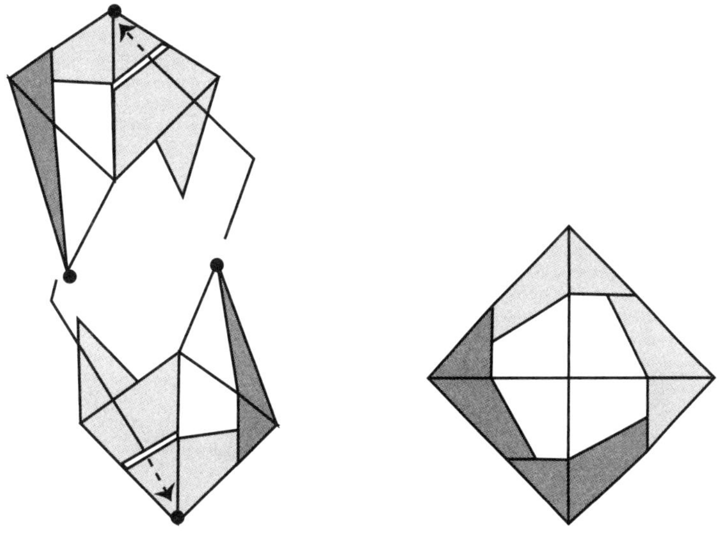

OCTAHEDRON BOX LID Folding Instructions

1. Fold the square in half vertically and unfold.

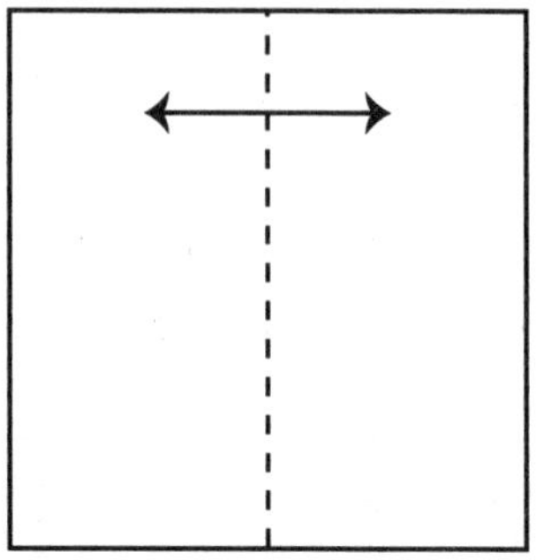

2. Fold the left side in to meet the midline.

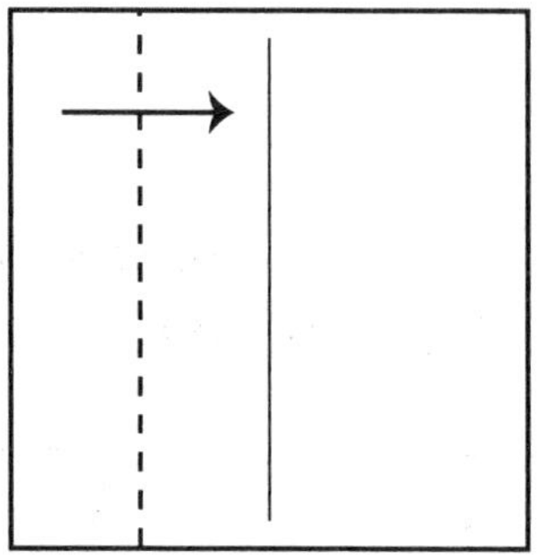

3. Fold as indicated by the dashed line so that the bottom right corner touches the left side of the paper.

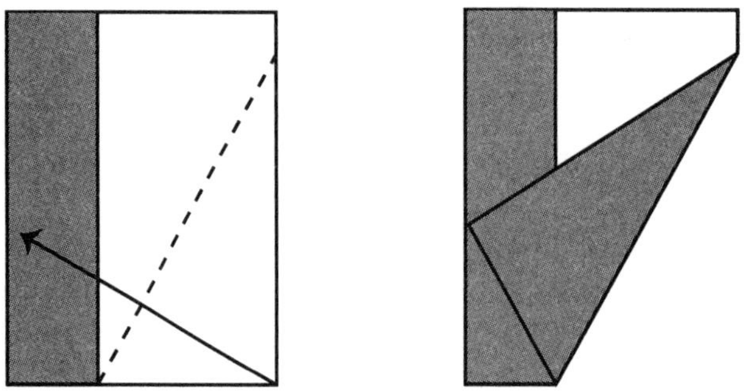

4. Unfold the entire paper and fold the bottom half up so that it meets the place where the diagonal intersects with the right side.

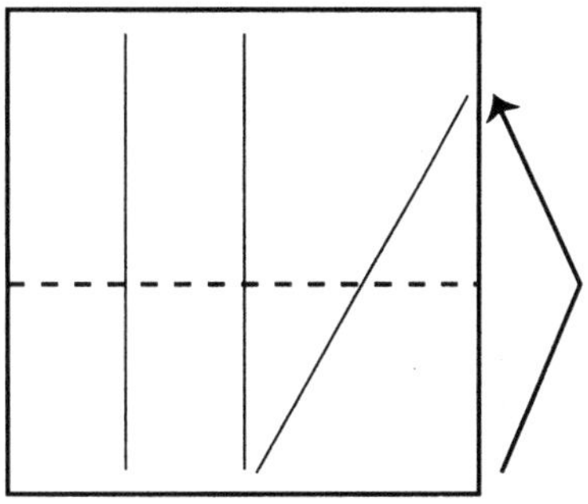

5. a. Fold the top part of the paper down at the point where the bottom edge meets the paper.
   b. Unfold the bottom half, but leave the top part folded down.

a.

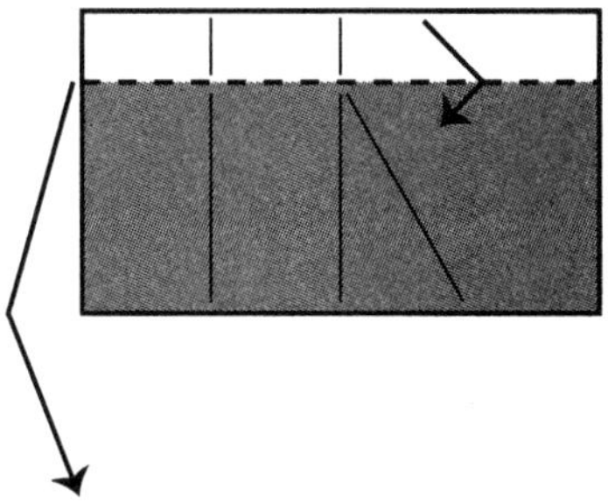

b.

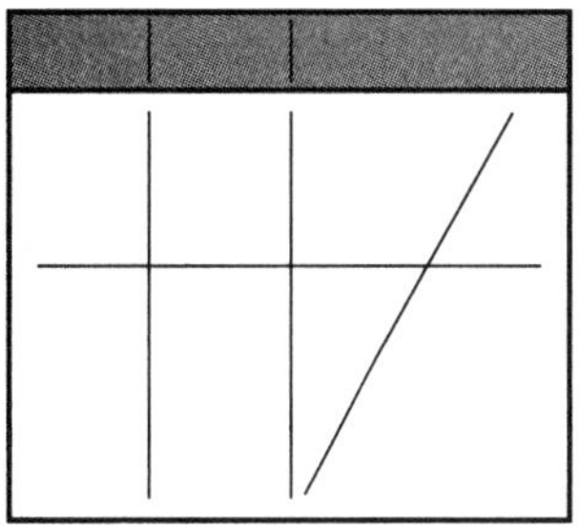

6. Fold the bottom left corner to the point where the right diagonal meets the horizontal midline. Repeat this process on the right side.

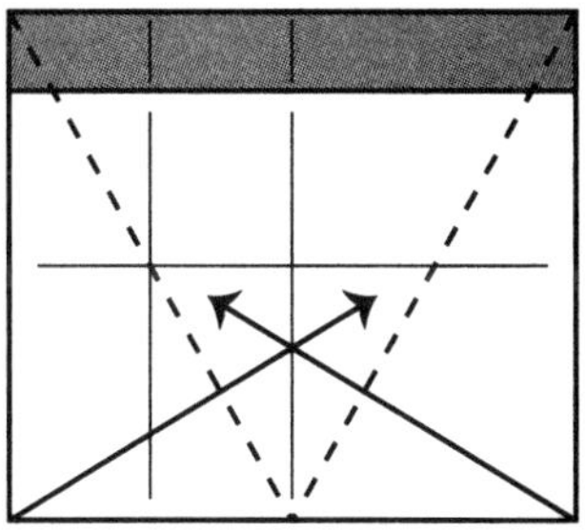

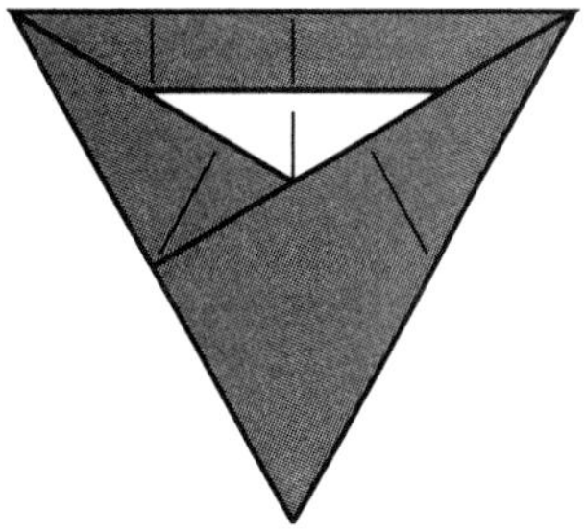

7. Fold the bottom point of the triangle up so that it touches the place where the top of the paper is folded over as indicated by the dots.

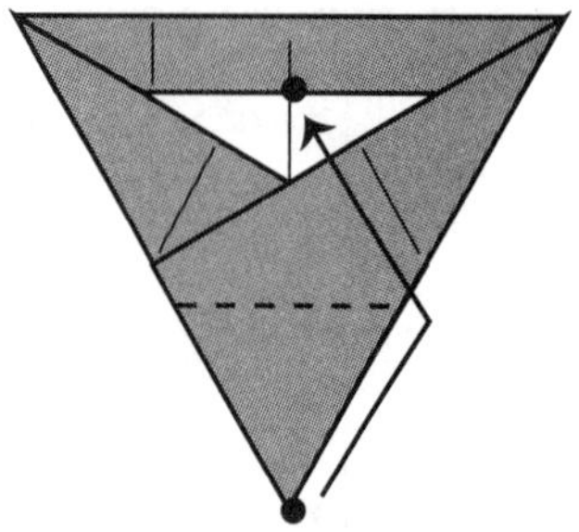

8. Fold the left and right points in so that they just touch the edges of the flap that you just folded. Glue or tape the flaps in place.

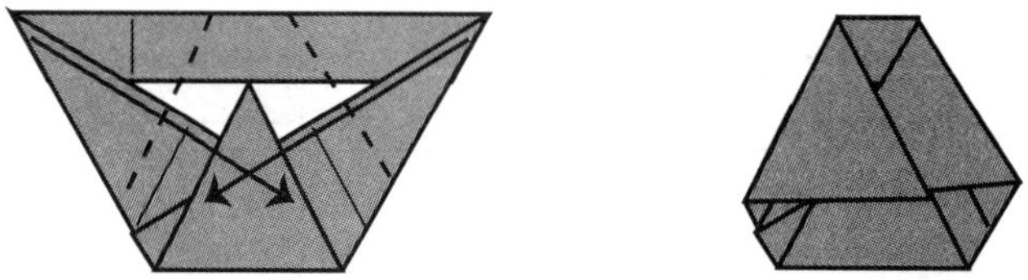

9. Crease the flaps so that the piece will just fit on the top of your octahedron.

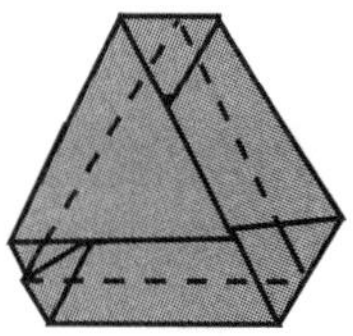

10. Make a handle from a piece of scratch paper and attach it to the top of your octahedron. You now have your completed octahedron box.

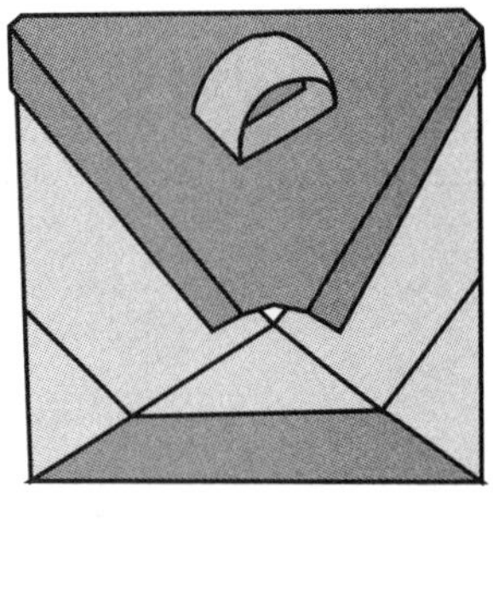

DODECAHEDRON

Key Questions

What are the geometric properties of a regular dodecahedron?

How do these properties compare to those of the other models you have constructed?

Math

Properties of polyhedra
- faces
- edges
- vertices

Integrated Processes

Observing
Collecting and recording data
Comparing and contrasting

Paper

12 squares per model in at least three different colors

Additional Materials

Previously folded models

Creator

Michelle Pauls

Focus

Students will construct a dodecahedron and identify some of its geometric properties. They will also compare these properties to those of the other models they have constructed.

Procedure

1. Hand out the folding instructions (pages 66-70) and 12 squares of paper to each student.
2. Go over the folding instructions for one unit of the dodecahedron step by step. Be aware that the folds in this model are somewhat more difficult than any encountered up to this point, so you may need to spend some extra time helping students.
3. Have students fold the remaining 11 units and guide them through the assembly of their dodecahedron model.
4. When all students have successfully assembled their models, have them get into small groups and distribute the remaining student sheet.
5. Have students work together to answer the questions about their models. Students will need to have the other models they have folded on hand to compare to their dodecahedron models.
6. When all groups have finished, close with a time of class discussion where students share the geometric properties they discovered and how these compare to other models.

Discussion

1. What shapes are the faces of the figure? [regular pentagons]
2. What is the measure of each of the interior angles on the faces of the dodecahedron? [108°] How do you know? [The sum of all the interior angles in a pentagon is always 540°. Since each face is a regular pentagon, each interior angle must be 108° (540 ÷ 5 = 108°).]
3. What lines/axes of symmetry exist in the folded unit used to make the dodecahedron? [There is only one line of bilateral symmetry that goes directly through the center of the unit vertically.]
4. How many faces, edges, and vertices does the dodecahedron have? [faces: 12; edges: 30; vertices: 20]
5. How many faces converge at one vertex? [three] How does this compare to the other models you have constructed? [bird tetrahedron: four; regular tetrahedron: three; cube: three; octahedron: four]
6. What are the similarities and differences between the dodecahedron and the other models you have constructed? [Various. Shape of faces, number of units needed to construct, number of faces, edges and vertices, etc.]

Extension

Have students make the *Open-Faced Dodecahedron* and compare it to the regular dodecahedron. (The *Open-Faced Dodecahedron* unit was created by Robert Neale.)

REGULAR DODECAHEDRON

Part One: Folding the units

1. Fold the paper in half vertically and unfold.

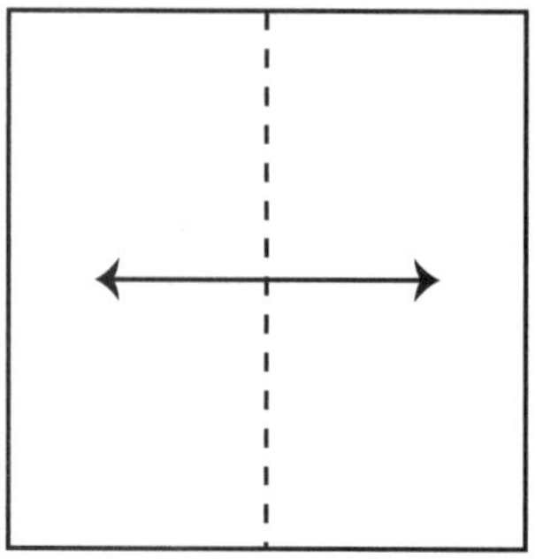

2. Fold each side in to meet the midline and unfold.

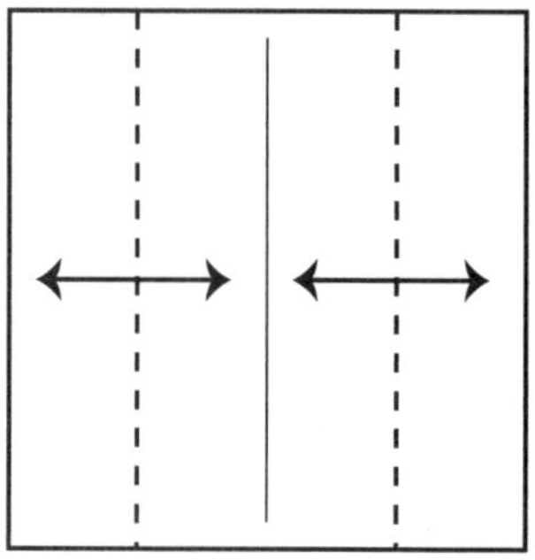

3. Fold the right edge over to meet the far left crease and unfold. Repeat this process in reverse with the left edge.

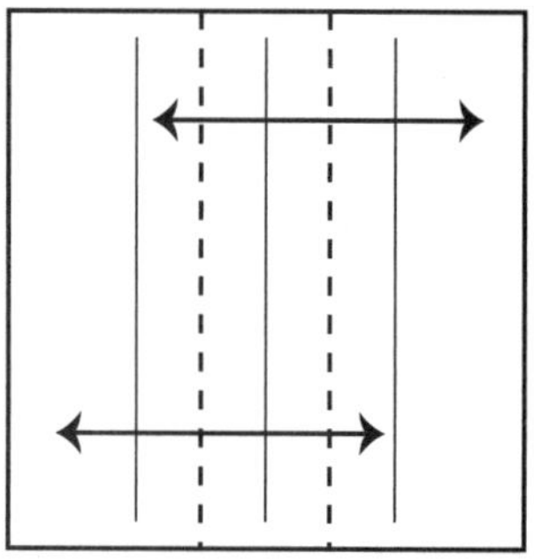

4. Fold the paper in half horizontally and unfold.

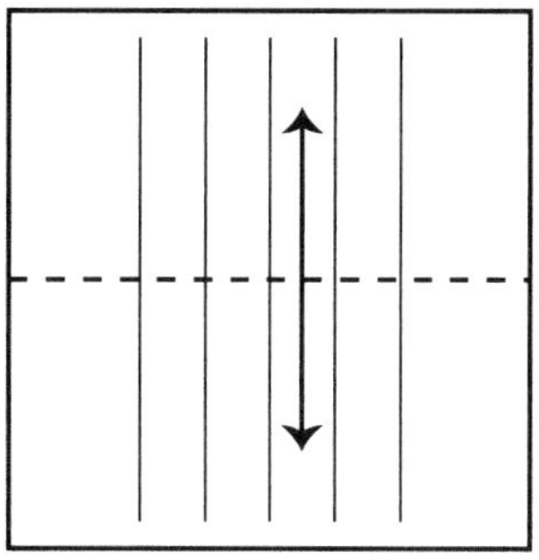

5. Fold the top left and bottom right corners into the center so that they meet as indicated by the diagrams. As you can see, each corner meets the opposite side at the first fold line.

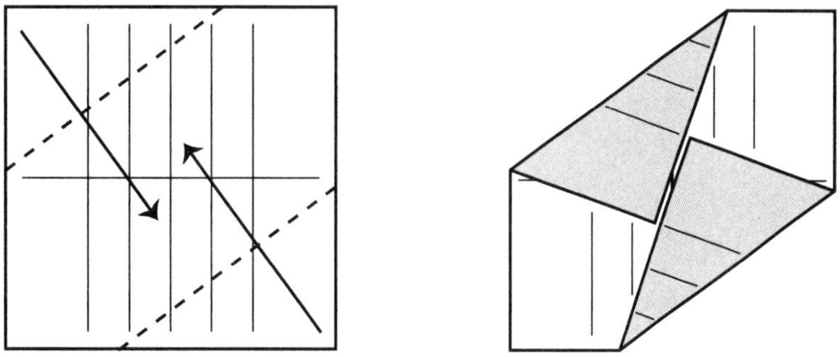

6. Unfold the paper, and repeat the previous step with the top right and bottom left corners. Again, each corner meets the opposite side at the first fold line.

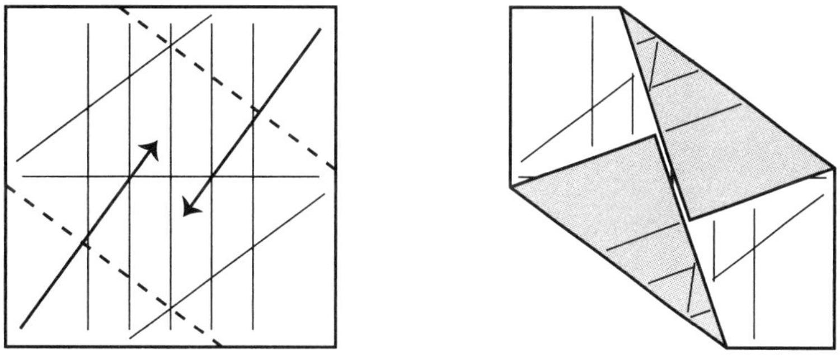

7. Unfold the paper and fold each corner down to meet the fold lines made in the previous two steps as shown.

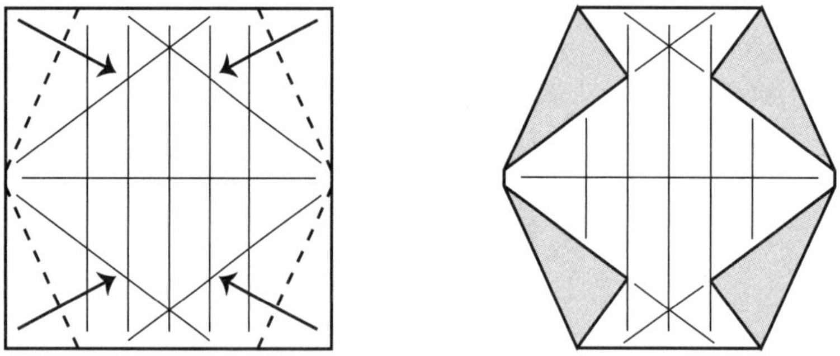

8. Fold the top right and bottom left corners in along the creases from step six.

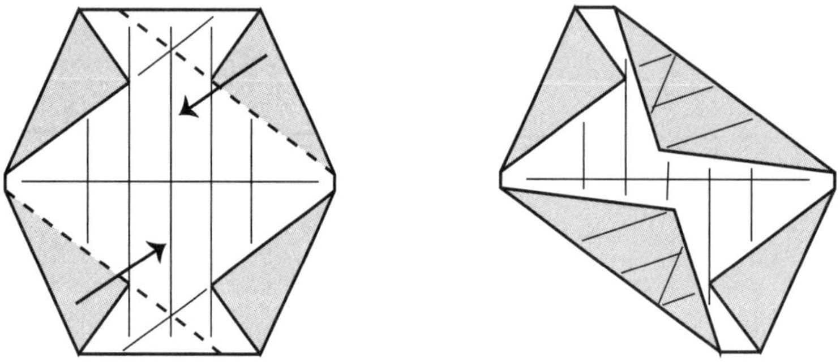

9. Fold the top left and bottom right corners in along the creases from step five.

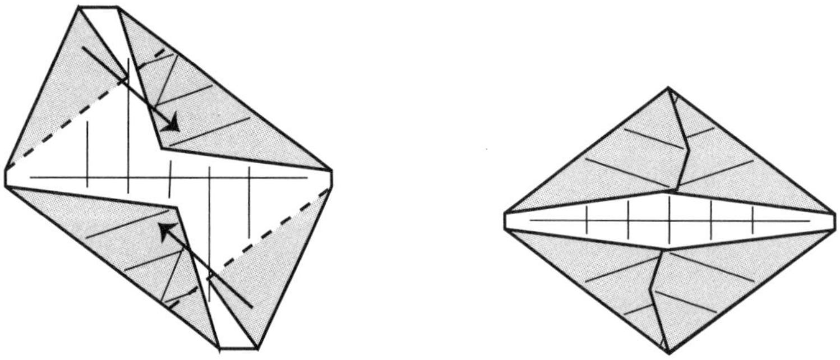

10. Fold the paper in half along the horizontal midline. As you fold, tuck the flap on the bottom into the flap on the top to lock the piece together.

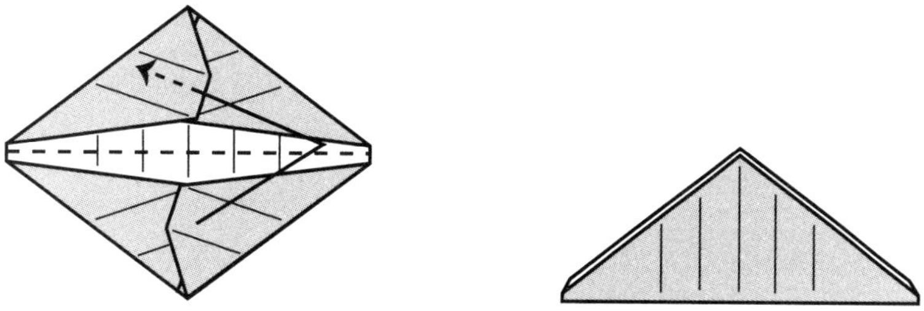

11. Fold the right and left sides of the figure in as shown. The folds should begin at the bottom of the paper where the middle set of creases meets the paper. The top edge of the folded section should be parallel to the bottom of the figure, as shown in the second diagram.

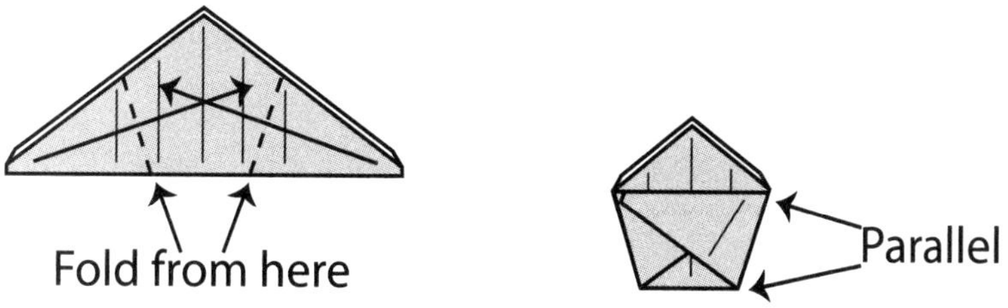

12. Repeat steps one through 11 until you have a total of 12 units like the one below.

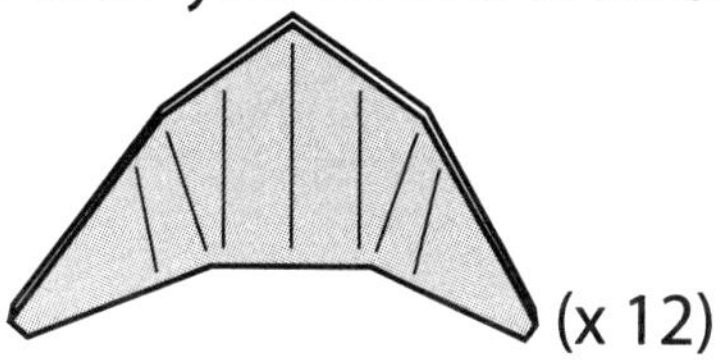

REGULAR DODECAHEDRON

Part Two: Assembling the dodecahedron

1. Take three units and connect them together as shown, inserting the points of one piece into the pockets of another.

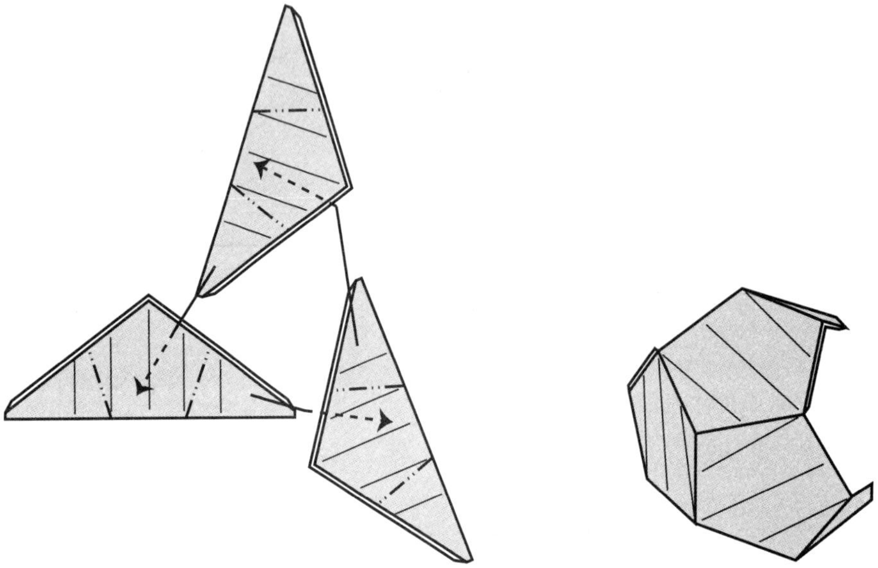

2. Continue to connect pieces in the same fashion to complete the dodecahedron. Always put the edges without pockets next to each other. This ensures that every tab will always be inserted into a pocket. The finished model should look something like the one below.

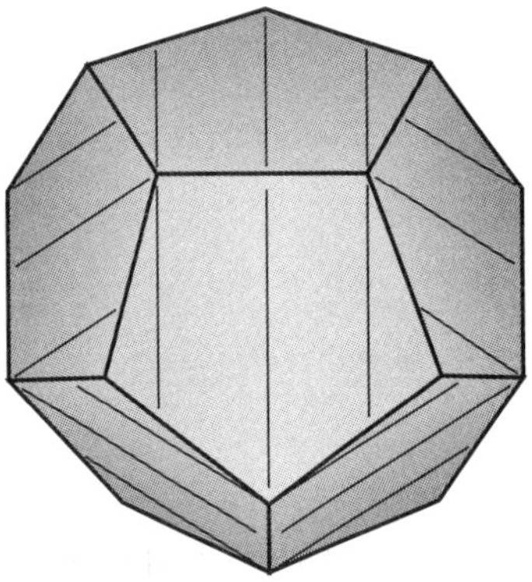

REGULAR DODECAHEDRON Exploration

Use your completed dodecahedron model to answer the following questions.

1. What shape are the faces of the dodecahedron?

2. What is the measure of each interior angle on the faces? How do you know?

3. What lines/axes of symmetry are there in the folded unit used to make the dodecahedron? Identify and label them on the diagram below.

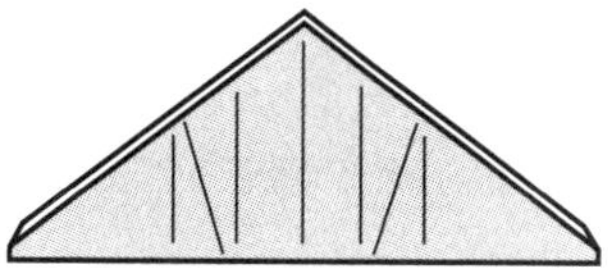

4. How many faces does the dodecahedron have? ...vertices? ...edges?

5. How many faces converge at each vertex? How does this compare to the other models you have constructed? Be specific.

6. What are some similarities and differences between the dodecahedron and the other models you have constructed?

OPEN-FACED DODECAHEDRON

1. Starting with the colored side of the paper facing up, fold the square in half using a valley fold.

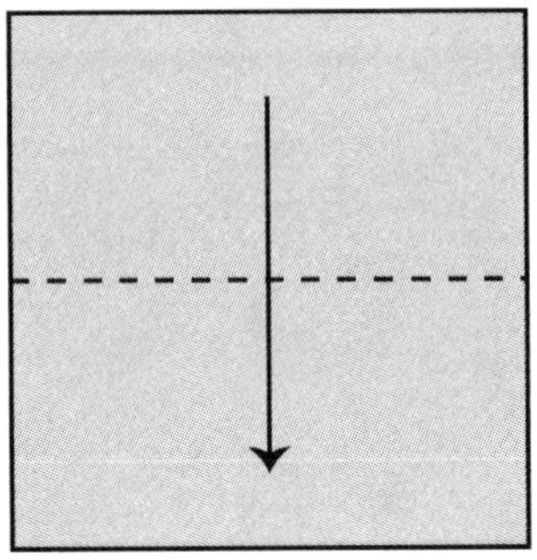

2. Fold the top layer up so that the bottom edge of the paper meets the top edge. Flip the paper over and do the same thing with the bottom layer so that the paper is folded into fourths with the colored side out.

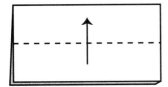

3. Fold the bottom left corner up to meet the top of the rectangle, and the top right corner down to meet the bottom of the rectangle. Unfold.

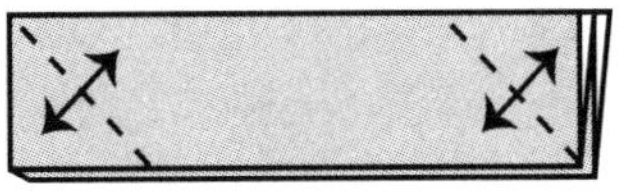

4. Make a valley crease connecting the two fold lines as shown.

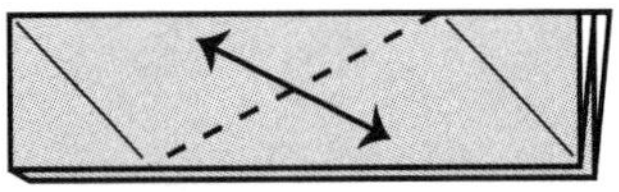

5. Repeat steps one to three so that you have a total of 30 units like the one below.

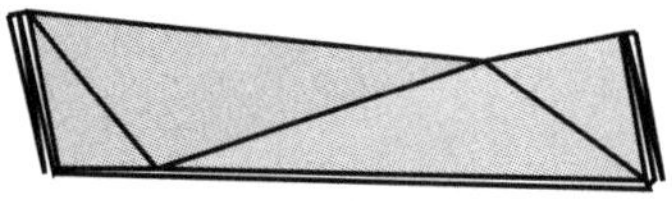
(x 30)

OPEN-FACED DODECAHEDRON Assembly

1. Connect two pieces as shown below, by inserting the corner of one piece between the flaps on the side of a second piece so that the creases are aligned.

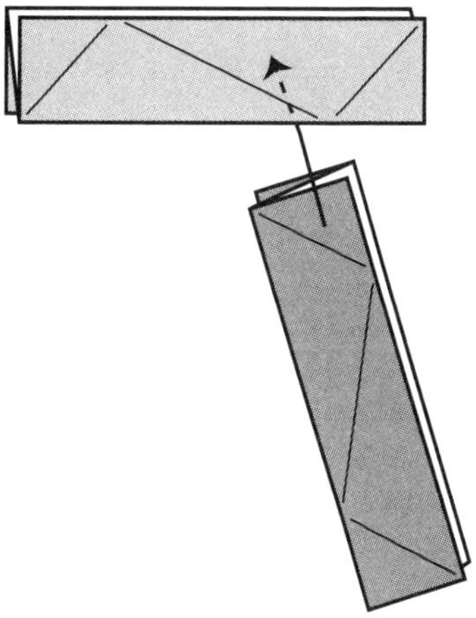

2. Connect three more pieces in the same fashion until you have formed a pentagon like the one below.

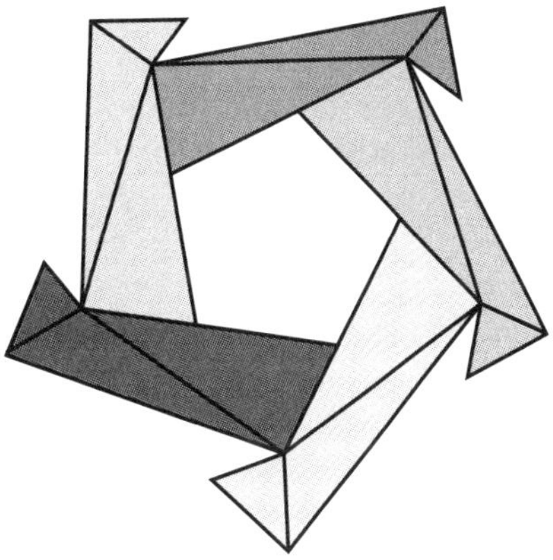

3. Add one more unit to each corner of the pentagon and continue to form faces like the one you just made until you have a completed dodecahedron.

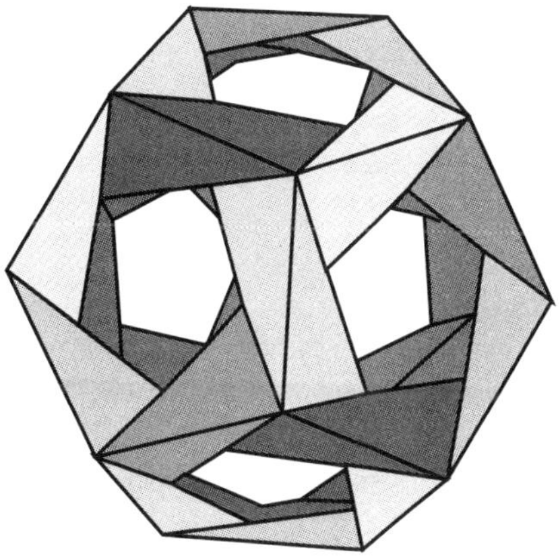

ICOSAHEDRON

Key Questions

What are the geometric properties of a completed icosahedron?

How do these properties compare to those of the other four Platonic solids?

Math

Properties of polyhedra
- faces
- edges
- vertices

Surface area
Platonic solids
Patterns

Integrated Processes

Observing
Collecting and recording data
Comparing and contrasting
Generalizing

Paper

15 squares per model in at least five different colors

Additional Materials

Completed models of the other four Platonic solids

Creator

Tomoko Fusè

Focus

Students will fold a model of an icosahedron. They will then identify the properties of their icosahedron and make comparisons between the icosahedron and the other four Platonic solids.

Management

1. In order for students to successfully complete the exploration sections they will need to have completed the symmetry worksheets found in the appendix or already be familiar with the topics those worksheets cover. They will also need to have made models of the other four Platonic solids (the tetrahedron, cube, octahedron, and dodecahedron) and have those available for comparisons.
2. Because of the large amount of folding required for each model, you may wish to have students work together in small groups to reduce the time it takes to construct each icosahedron.

Procedure

1. Hand out the folding instructions (pages 77-83) and 15 paper squares to each student or group.
2. Go over the folding instructions for the loop units step by step. Have students/groups fold the remaining four units and guide them through the loop assembly.
3. Repeat this process for the top/bottom units. It will be easier for students to follow the diagrams if they have five different colors of paper to use on their top/bottom units. Different colors also allow you to quickly see if the pieces have been correctly assembled. This is especially important with the icosahedron, since incorrect assembly can lead to unstable models.
4. When all students/groups have successfully assembled their models, hand out the exploration sheets and have students get out their models of the regular tetrahedron, the cube, the octahedron, and the dodecahedron.
5. Have students work together to answer the questions about their models and make comparisons between the five Platonic solids.
6. When all groups have finished, close with a time of class discussion where students share their discoveries and the things they learned about the Platonic solids.

Discussion

1. How many faces, edges, and vertices does the figure have? [faces: 20; edges: 30; vertices: 12]
2. How do these values compare to the other models you have built so far? (See *Solutions.*)
3. What shapes are the faces of the figure? [equilateral triangles]
4. What is the measure of each interior angle on any given face? [60°] How do you know? [Each face is an equilateral triangle, and the measure of each interior angle in an equilateral triangle is always 60°.]
5. How many faces converge at each vertex? [five] How does this compare to the other models you have built so far? (See *Solutions.*)

6. If the length of the base on one face is three units, and the height is 2.5 units, what is the surface area of the whole figure? [($\frac{1}{2}$ x 3) x 2.5 = 3.75, 3.75 x 20 = 75 units^2]
7. What patterns do you see in the Platonic solids table? (See *Solutions.*)
8. What relationship do you see between the number of faces, edges, and vertices in each figure? *(See Solutions.)*
9. What do you notice when you compare the cube and the octahedron? ...the dodecahedron and the icosahedron? (See *Solutions.*)
10. How many different kinds of rotational symmetry can you find in the Platonic solids? (See *Solutions.*)
11. Which models do you think have the most planes of bilateral symmetry? [The icosahedron and the dodecahedron have the most.] Why?
12. Which model do you think has the fewest planes of bilateral symmetry? [the tetrahedron] Why?

Extension

If students have not already done so, have them complete the *Equilateral Triangle Unit Exploration.*

Solutions

The completed table from the second student sheet along with some observations about the Platonic solids are given below.

The Platonic Solids

Polyhedron	Faces	Edges	Vertices	Shape of face	Faces per vertex
Tetrahedron	4	6	4	Triangle	3
Cube	6	12	8	Square	3
Octahedron	8	12	6	Triangle	4
Dodecahedron	12	30	20	Pentagon	3
Icosahedron	20	30	12	Triangle	5

Patterns/Observations about the Platonic solids:

- The number of faces, edges, and vertices is always even.
- The cube and the octahedron are said to be "dual." This means that they have the same number of edges, but the number of faces and vertices are opposite. The same is true of the dodecahedron and the icosahedron.
- When the faces of a polyhedron are triangular, there can be either three, four, or five faces converging at each vertex.
- The number of vertices plus the number of faces is equal to the number of edges plus two (V + F = E + 2). This is called *Euler's formula*, and is true for any polyhedron that is not a multiple structure and does not have holes, tunnels, or ring-shaped faces.

An in-depth discussion of all of the rotational and plane symmetries that exist in the Platonic solids moves quickly from the realm of geometry and into more advanced fields such as group theory, and is therefore avoided. The table below indicates which of the Platonic solids exhibit the different rotational symmetries, but does not attempt to identify how many of each axis exist, or how many different rotations there are around each of the axes.

Rotational Symmetry	Polyhedra with that symmetry
2-fold	Tetrahedron, Cube, Octahedron, Dodecahedron, Icosahedron
3-fold	Tetrahedron, Cube, Octahedron, Dodecahedron, Icosahedron
4-fold	Cube, Octahedron
5-fold	Dodecahedron, Icosahedron

Two planes of bilateral symmetry are shown below for each of the Platonic solids. There are many more planes of symmetry for each figure that are not indicated.

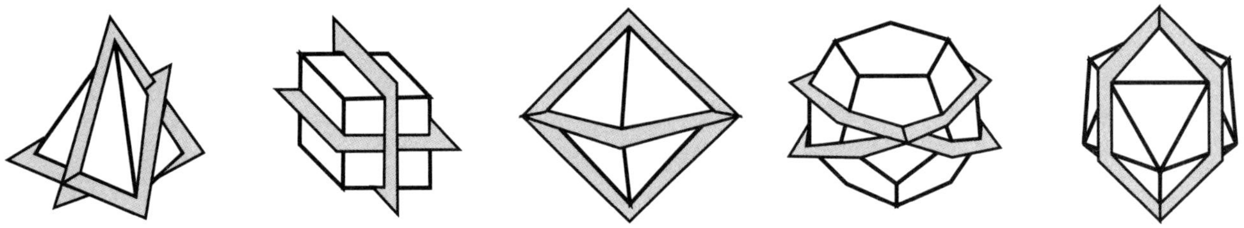

REGULAR ICOSAHEDRON

Part One: Making the units and assembling the loop

1. Fold the square in half vertically and unfold.

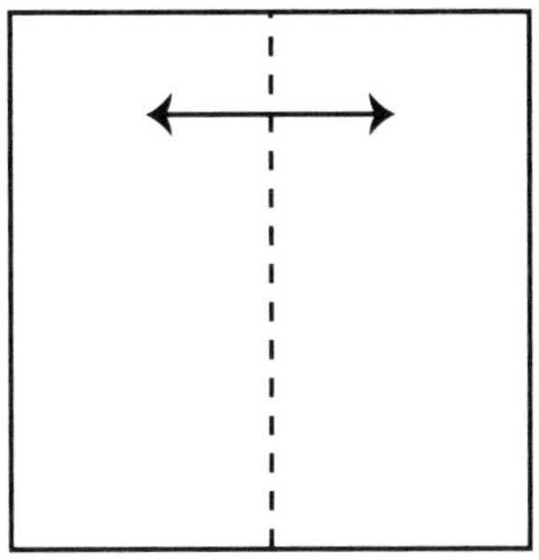

2. Fold from the bottom left corner as indicated by the dashed line so that the bottom right corner touches the midline.

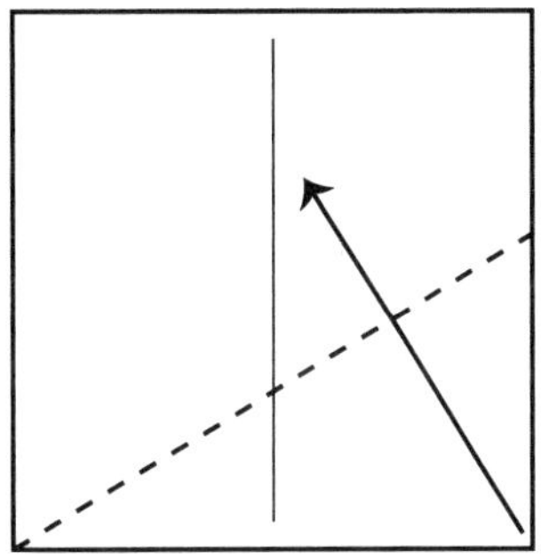

3. Fold the right side over so that the two points marked with dots meet as shown.

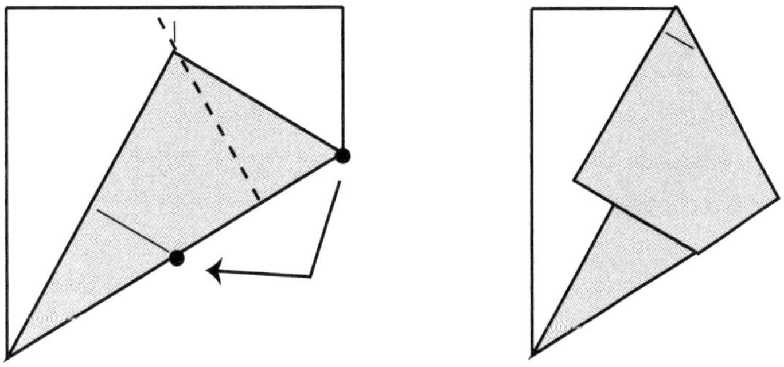

4. Unfold completely and fold the paper horizontally so that the two points marked by dots meet. The horizontal fold should go through the intersection of the two diagonals.

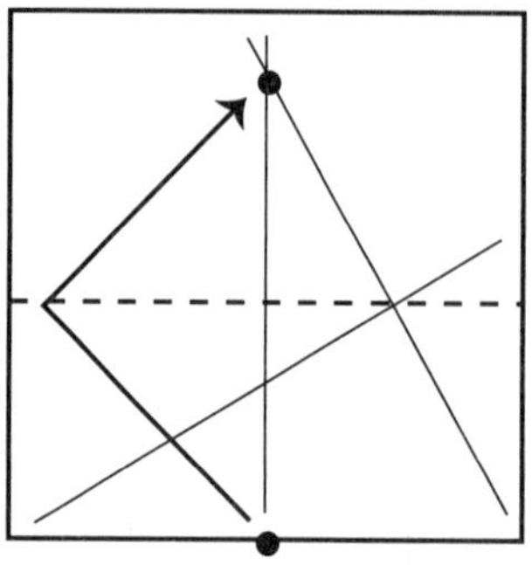

5. a. Fold the top part of the paper down at the point where the bottom edge meets the paper.
   b. Unfold the bottom half of the paper, leaving the top part folded down.

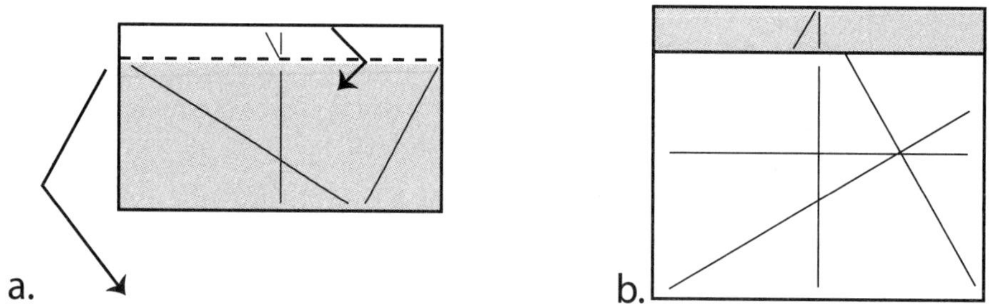

6. Crease as indicated by each of the dashed lines, bringing the corners in to meet the horizontal midline.

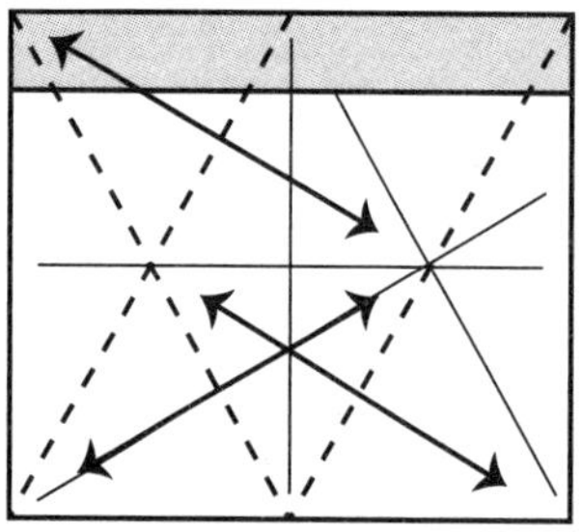

7. Fold the top left and bottom right corners where indicated by the dashed lines so that the corners touch the nearest diagonals. Notice that the two new sides formed are parallel to the nearest diagonals.

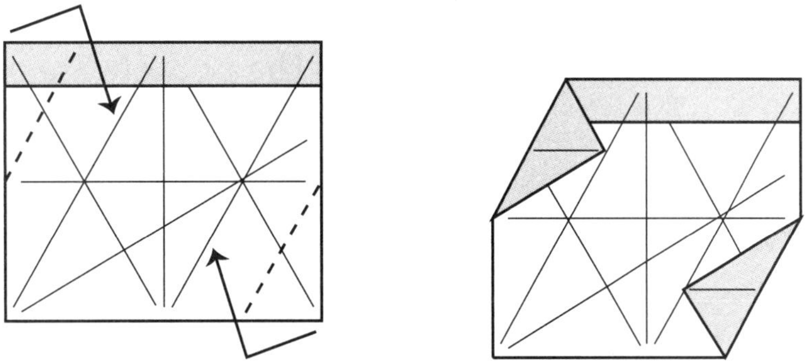

8. Fold again along the diagonals so that the two sides meet in the center.

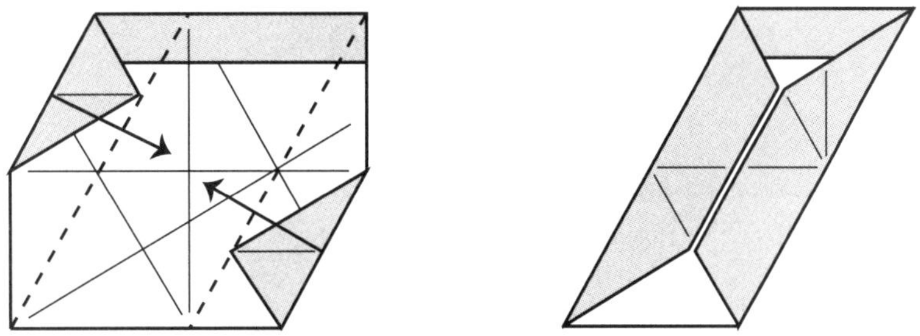

9. Flip the paper over and crease where indicated by the dashed lines. Repeat steps one through nine with your remaining pieces of paper so that you have a total of 15 pieces like the one below.

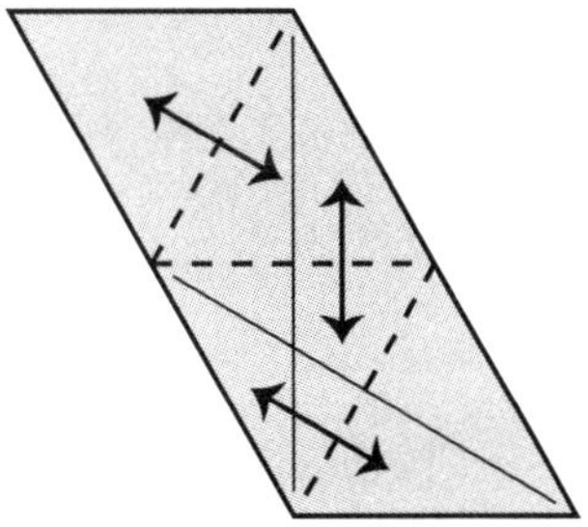

(x 15)

10. Connect five of the pieces using the same method that you used when you constructed the octahedron. One piece goes inside the next to the point indicated by the dots. The fifth piece and the first piece must be connected at the end, forming a complete loop. This loop should have 10 faces which are all equilateral triangles. It should be open at the top and at the bottom, and both openings should be regular pentagons. **Be sure to complete the loop so that the sides with the pockets are on the outside, not the inside.**

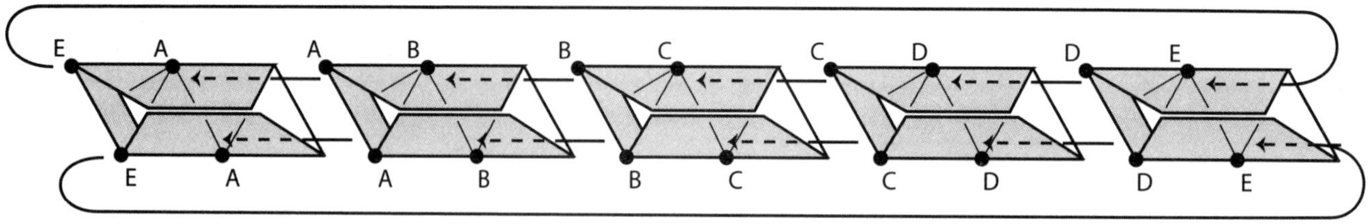

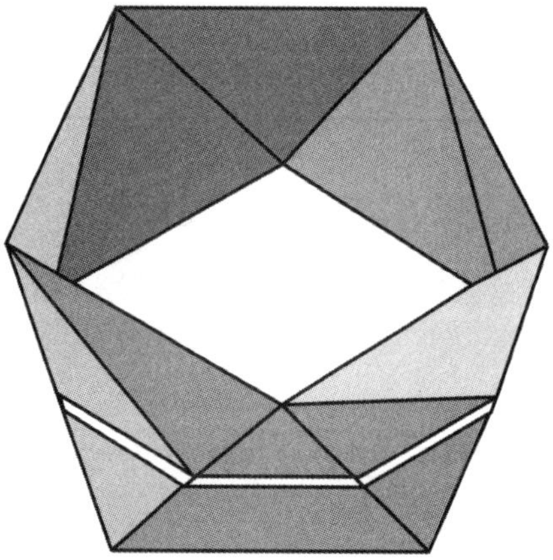

REGULAR ICOSAHEDRON

Part Two: Assembling the top and bottom and completing the icosahedron

1. Take one piece and insert it into a second piece as shown, so that the points marked with dots meet.

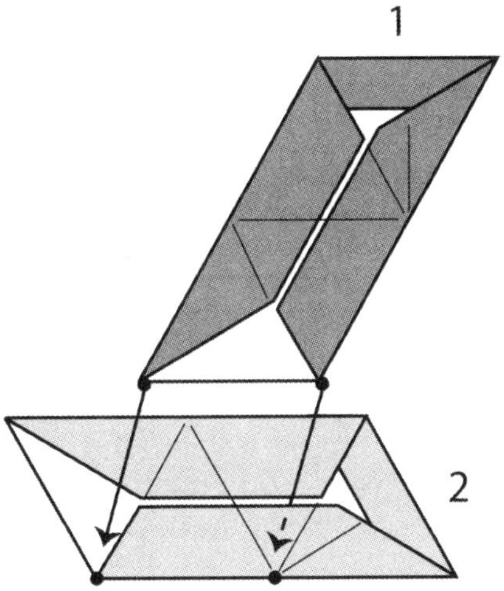

2. Take the third piece and fit it onto the side of the second piece in the same fashion as above.

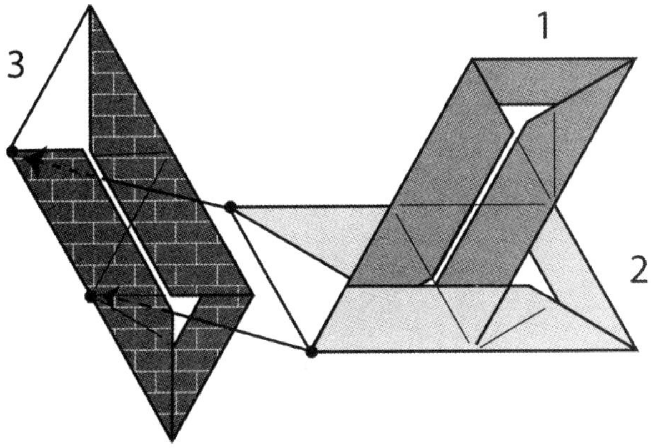

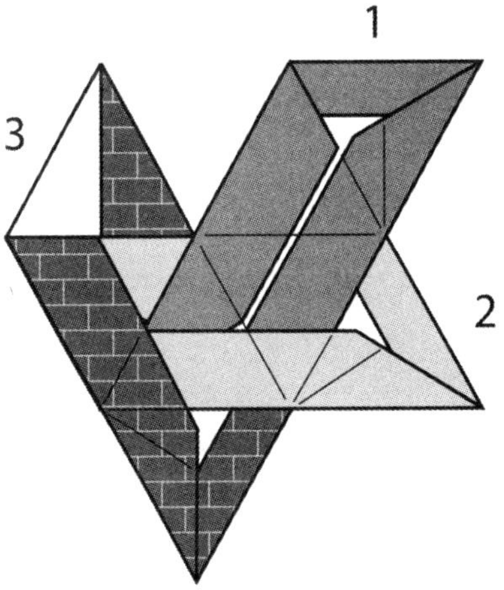

3. Take a fourth piece and slide it onto the third piece as shown.

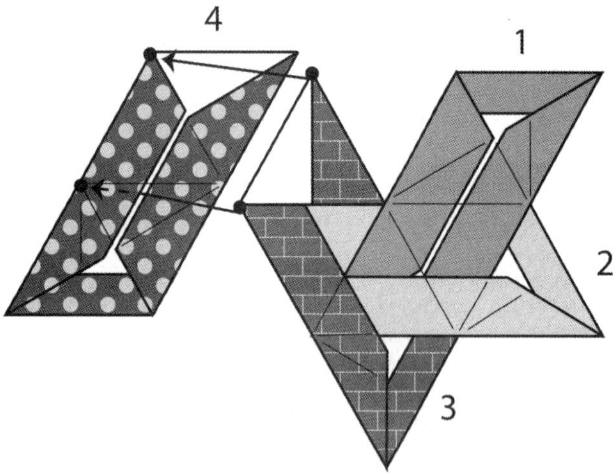

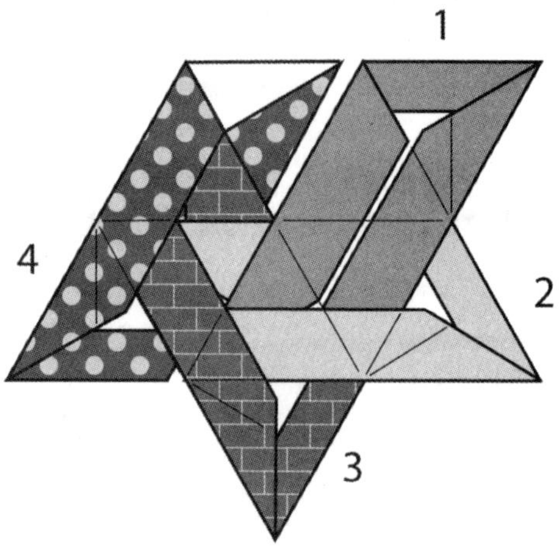

4. Before inserting the fifth piece, crease the figure (using mountain folds) where indicated by the dashed lines. Once you have carefully made the creases, begin by connecting pieces four and five as shown. Next, insert the end of piece five into the flap on piece one and push it all the way to the point marked by the dot. As you do this, the figure will not stay flat, but will take on the shape of a pentagonal "tent" with a peak and five tabs pointing down. Repeat this process with your other five pieces so that you have two identical "tents." These pieces will be attached to the loop from *Part One* to form the top and bottom of the icosahedron.

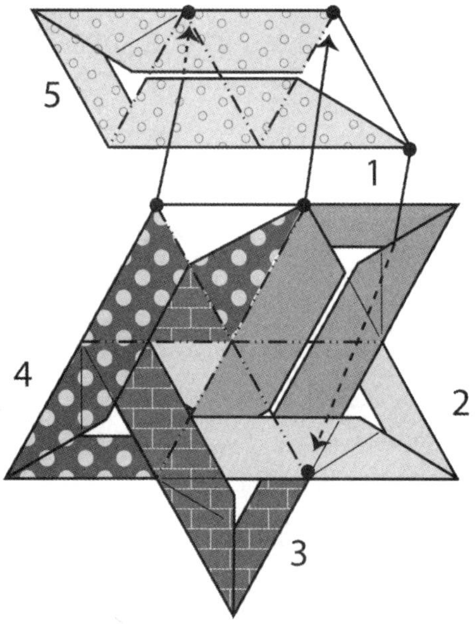

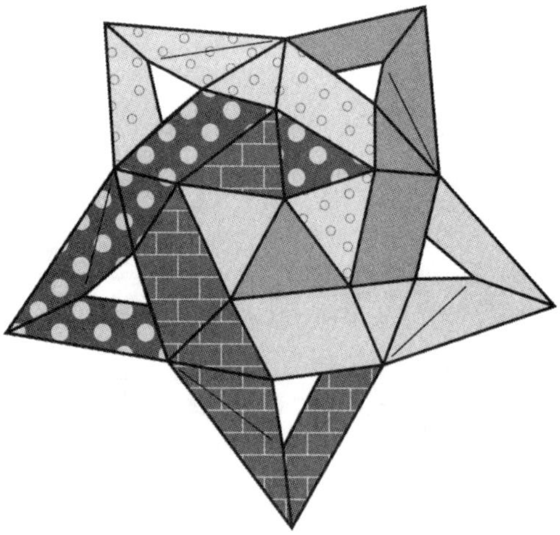

Icosahedron Assembly: Take one of the "tents" you just completed and line it up so that it covers the top of the loop from *Part One*. Place the tabs from the tent into the pockets on the side of the loop. Flip the shape over and repeat this process on the bottom.

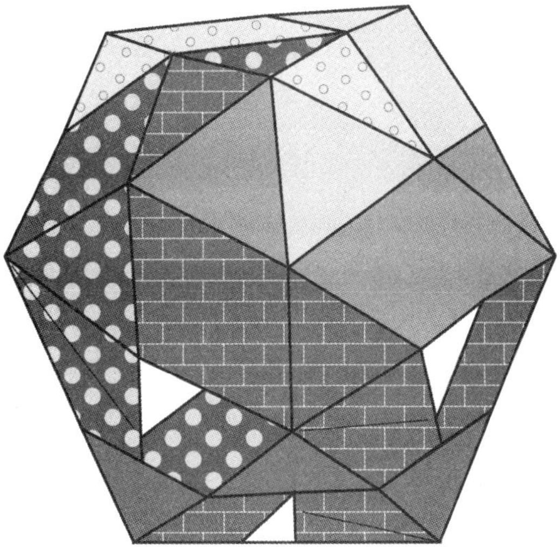

REGULAR ICOSAHEDRON Exploration

Use your completed icosahedron model to answer the following questions.

1. How many faces does the icosahedron have? How many vertices? ...edges?

2. How do these values compare to those for the other models you have built so far?

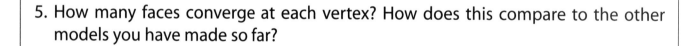

3. What shape are the faces?

4. What is the measure of each interior angle on any given face? How do you know?

5. How many faces converge at each vertex? How does this compare to the other models you have made so far?

6. What is the surface area of the icosahedron if one face has a base of 3 units and a height of 2.5 units? Show your work.

PLATONIC SOLIDS COMPARED

In geometry, there are five regular polyhedra known as the Platonic solids. They include the tetrahedron, the cube, the octahedron, the dodecahedron, and the icosahedron. By now you should have made a model of each of these Platonic solids. Using your models, fill in the table below, recording the number of faces, edges, and vertices, the shape of each face, and the number of faces that converge at each vertex for all five of the polyhedra.

The Platonic Solids

Polyhedron	Faces	Edges	Vertices	Shape of face	Faces per vertex
Tetrahedron					
Cube					
Octahedron					
Dodecahedron					
Icosahedron					

1. What patterns do you see in the table?

2. What relationship do you see between the number of faces, edges, and vertices in each figure?

3. What do you notice when you compare the cube and the octahedron?

4. What do you notice when you compare the dodecahedron and the icosahedron?

PLATONIC SOLIDS SYMMETRIES

Use your models of the Platonic solids to help you answer the questions below.

1. How many different kinds of rotational symmetry can you find in the Platonic solids? Use the table below to help you organize your findings. A few answers have been filled in to get you started.

Rotational Symmetry	**Polyhedra with that symmetry**
2-fold	Tetrahedron, Cube
3-fold	Tetrahedron,

2. Show at least two planes of bilateral symmetry that exist in each model.

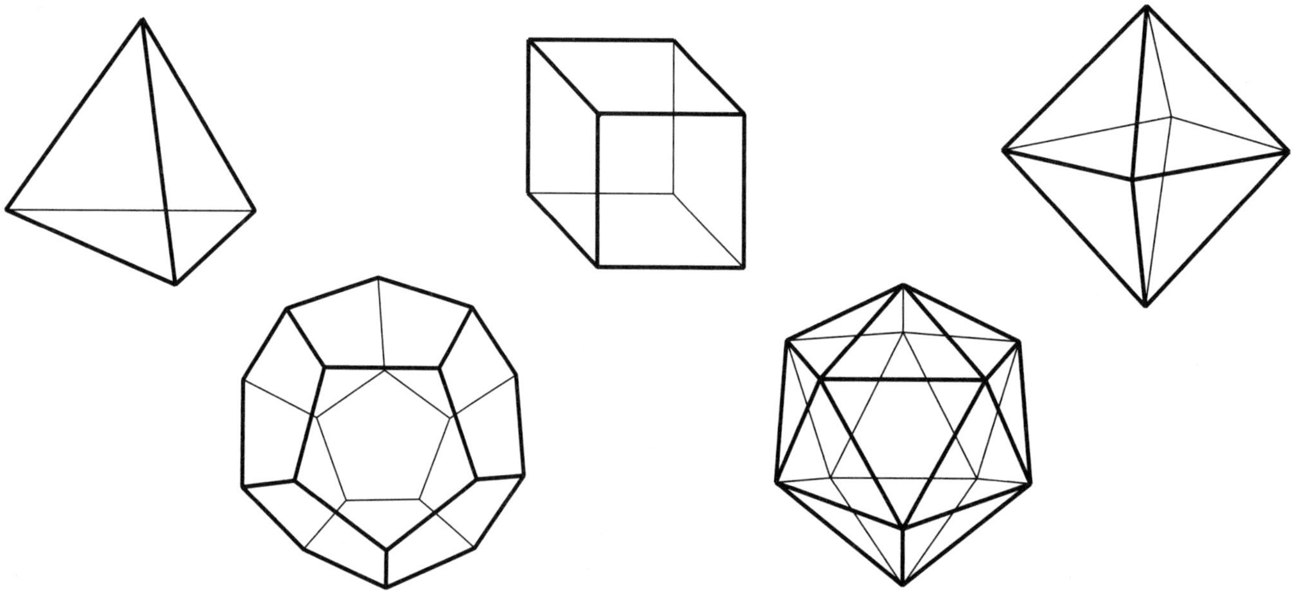

3. Which model(s) do you think has the most planes of bilateral symmetry? Why? Which model(s) do you think has the fewest planes? Why?

STELLATED OCTAHEDRON

FOCUS

Students will begin their exploration of stellations by constructing a stellated octahedron and examining its properties.

KEY QUESTIONS

What does it mean for a polyhedron to be stellated?

What are the properties of a stellated octahedron?

MATH

Stellation
Properties of polyhedra
- faces
- edges
- vertices

PAPER

12 squares per model in three different colors

ADDITIONAL MATERIALS

Stellated Polyhedra sheet
Octahedron models

CREATOR

Michelle Pauls

Management

1. When counting the faces, edges, and vertices of their models, students will likely encounter some confusion as to how many there are. As you can see in the diagram below, there are places where two edges fall on the same line. While it is tempting to count these as one edge, the fact that there is a vertex in the middle means that there are actually two edges. Be sure that students understand this distinction in this and subsequent stellation activities so that they will make accurate records of their models. They will also be asked to make a distinction between convex and concave edges, so be sure that this difference is clear in their minds.
2. Due to the amount of folding, you may wish to have students work together in small groups and make one model for every two or three students.

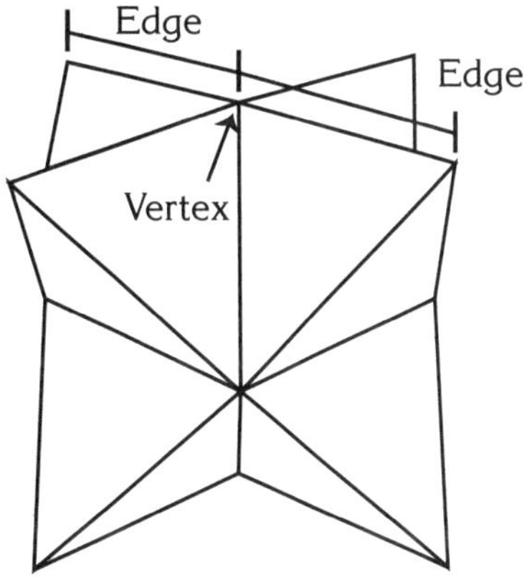

Procedure

1. Hand out the *Stellated Polyhedra* sheet and go over the information as a class. The concept of stellation is very complex, but students should be able to gain a basic understanding of what it means from the information sheet.
2. When students have had a chance to read through the explanation, hand out the folding instructions (pages 90-93) and 12 paper squares to each student/group.
3. Go over the folding instructions for one unit of the stellated octahedron. If this is the first time students have had to fold their paper into thirds, you may have to spend some time discussing possible techniques for doing this quickly and accurately.
4. Have students fold the remaining 11 units and guide them through the assembly of their stellated octahedron models.

5. When all students/groups have completed their models, hand out the exploration sheet and have students work together in groups to answer the questions. Be sure that they all understand how to count the number of faces, edges, and vertices accurately.
6. Close with a time of class discussion and sharing where students think about the geometric properties of their models and how these compare to other models.

Discussion

1. How many faces, edges, and vertices does the stellated octahedron have? [faces, 24; edges, 12; vertices, 14]]
2. How many of the edges are concave, and how many are convex? [12 concave, 24 convex]
3. What shape are the faces of the stellated octahedron? [equilateral triangles]
4. What other shapes that you have folded so far have these faces? [tetrahedron, octahedron, icosahedron]
5. What similarities exist between these other shapes and the stellated octahedron? [Stellated octahedron is actually a compound of two tetrahedra, similar angles, etc.] What differences exist? [Number of faces per vertex, concave edges in stellated model, etc.]
6. If the base of one face is 3 units and the height is 2.5 units, what is the surface area of the entire figure? [90 units^2 $(\frac{1}{2} \times 3) \times 2.5 = 3.75$, $3.75 \times 24 = 90$]

Extension

Older students can be challenged to do some research on stellation to develop a deeper understanding of the concept. There are many Internet sites that offer explanations and give diagrams of stellated figures.

STELLATED POLYHEDRA

An Introduction

What is a stellation?

When a polyhedron is stellated it means that the faces of that polyhedron have been extended until they intersect the extensions of the other faces. This must be done in such a way that the original symmetry of the polyhedron is preserved.

Which polyhedra can be stellated?

Of the five Platonic solids, only the octahedron, the dodecahedron, and the icosahedron have stellations. The tetrahedron and the cube do not have stellations because their faces, when extended, never intersect. The diagram below illustrates this fact.

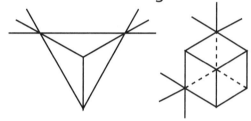

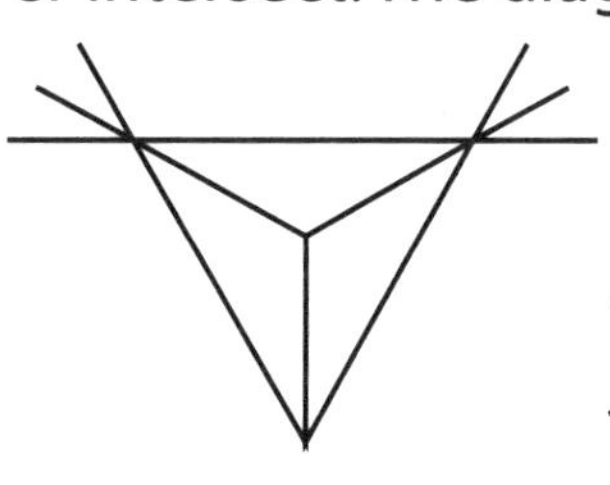

The Stellated Octahedron

To understand the stellation of the octahedron, look at the regular octahedron model that you constructed. Now imagine a tetrahedron being placed on each face of this octahedron. This is the stellated octahedron, or stella octangula. In the diagram below you can see the octahedron (indicated by the dashed lines), and the extensions of each face which form the stellated shape.

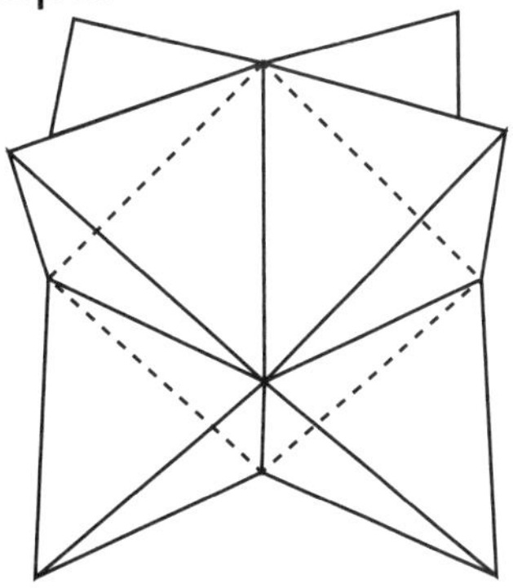

The Stellated Dodecahedron and Icosahedron

The stellations of the dodecahedron and the icosahedron are much more complex than that of the octahedron. There are three possible stellations for the dodecahedron, known as the small stellated dodecahedron, the great dodecahedron, and the great stellated dodecahedron. The icosahedron is the most complex of all with a total of 59 possible stellations!

STELLATED OCTAHEDRON Folding Instructions

1. Begin with the white side of your paper facing up. Fold the paper into thirds, using a combination mountain/valley fold. Be sure that the white side is still facing up and that the top flap opens on the right side.

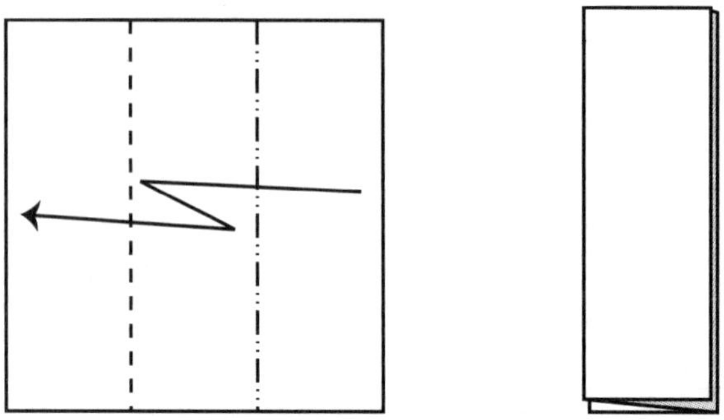

2. Unfold and fold the paper in half, making a short crease at the top of the paper.

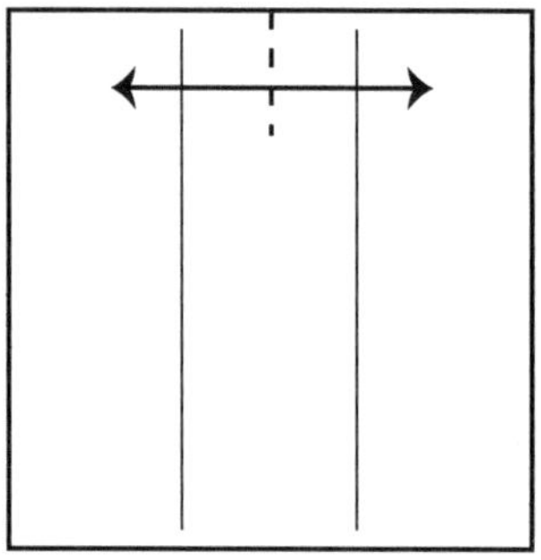

3. Starting the crease at the bottom left corner, fold the right corner up to meet the central fold line as indicated. Crease well and unfold.

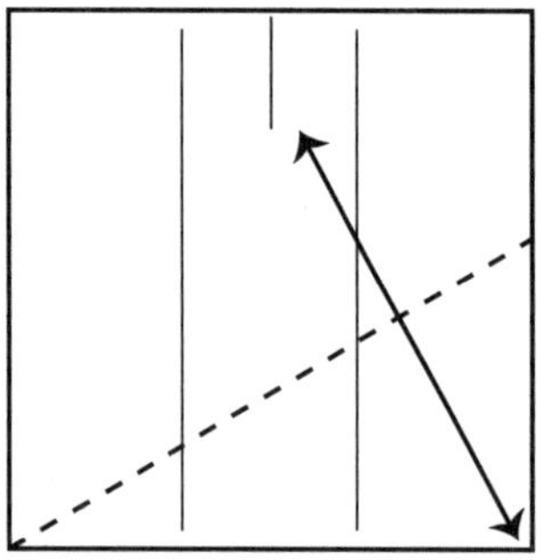

4. Refold the paper into thirds, being sure that it is oriented the same way as it was in step one.

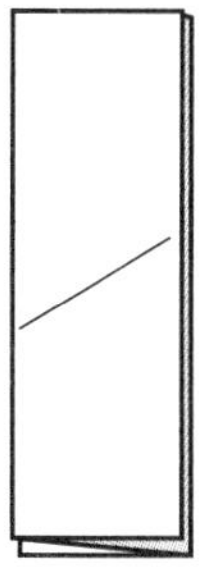

5. Fold the bottom half of the paper back along the existing fold line, using a mountain fold.

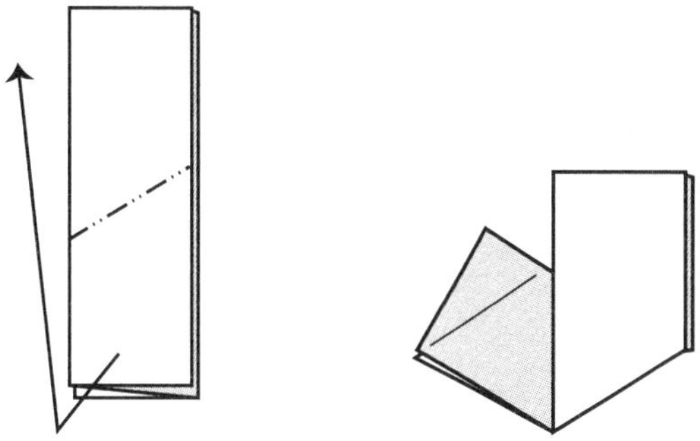

6. Fold the top of the paper down as indicated by the dashed line. The flap that you fold down should be flush on the one side with the bottom right edge of the paper and on the other side with the top right edge of the paper. The top right corner will hang over the edge a bit when it is folded down as you can see in the second diagram.

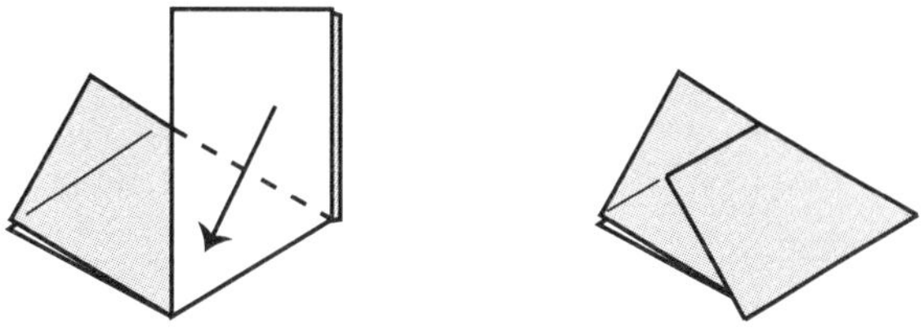

7. Flip the paper over and repeat this process on the back. Fold the right side over as indicated by the dashed line so that the flap is flush with both the fold beneath it and the bottom left edge of the paper. The resulting shape should be a rectangle, as shown.

8. Flip the paper back over to the front and fold the left side over as shown so that the corner folded is flush with the fold beneath it. Notice that the bottom left corner hangs over the edge slightly when it is folded over.

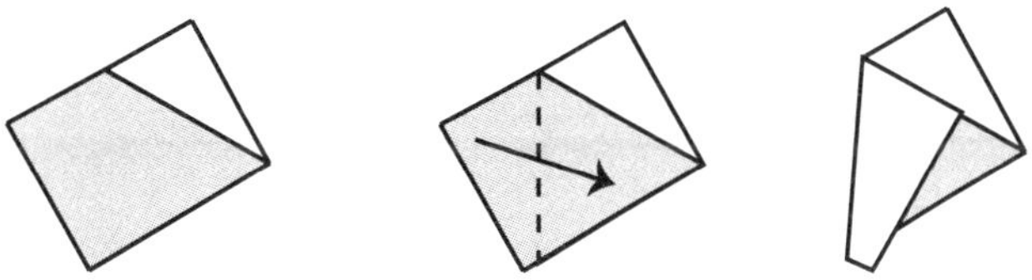

9. Flip the paper over and repeat this process on the back with the bottom flap. The resulting shape should look like the diagram on the right.

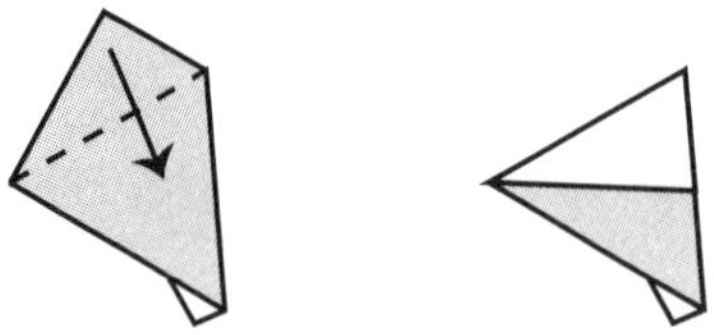

10. Unfold your paper to the tri-folded stage, making sure the white side is facing up again. The fold lines should look like those shown below.

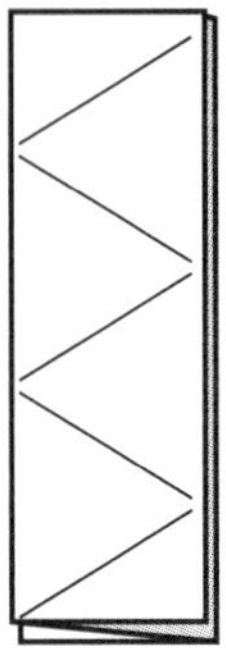

11. Using mountain folds, tuck the top triangular section in on itself so that it is completely inside the unit. You will need to open the unit in order to do this. Do the same with the bottom triangular section so that you are left with a unit that is divided into four equilateral triangles like the one shown below.

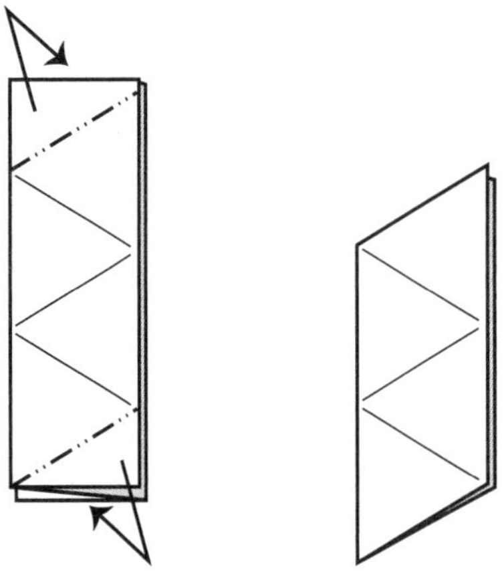

12. Turn the paper over so that the colored side is showing and reinforce the creases you made along each of the fold lines. The unit should look something like the one below. Repeat steps one to 12 so that you have a total of 12 units.

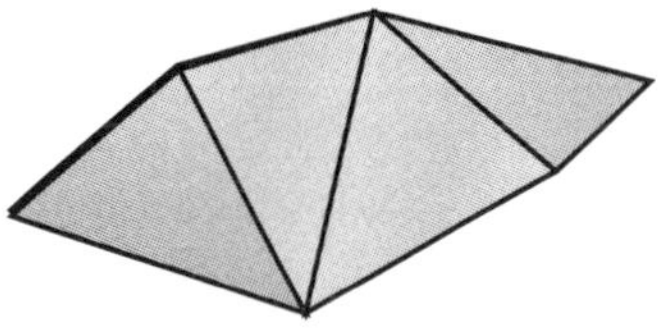

(x 12)

STELLATED OCTAHEDRON Assembly

1. Insert the end point of one piece into the pocket of the second triangle on another piece, as indicated.

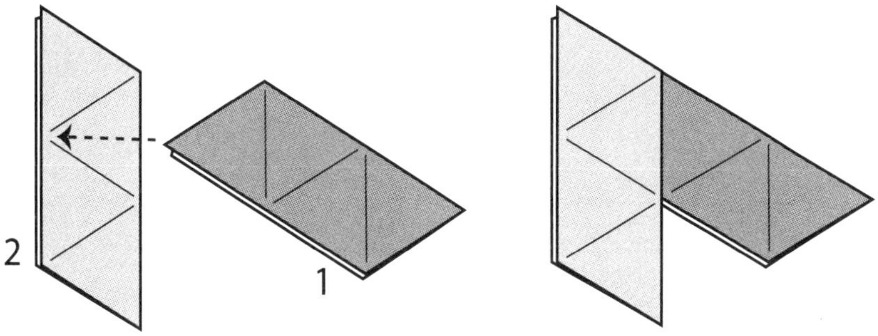

2. Insert a third piece into the first piece in the same fashion. Bring the second piece around and insert the point into the second pocket on the third piece. This should leave you with a triangular pyramid that has a tab coming from each side as shown.

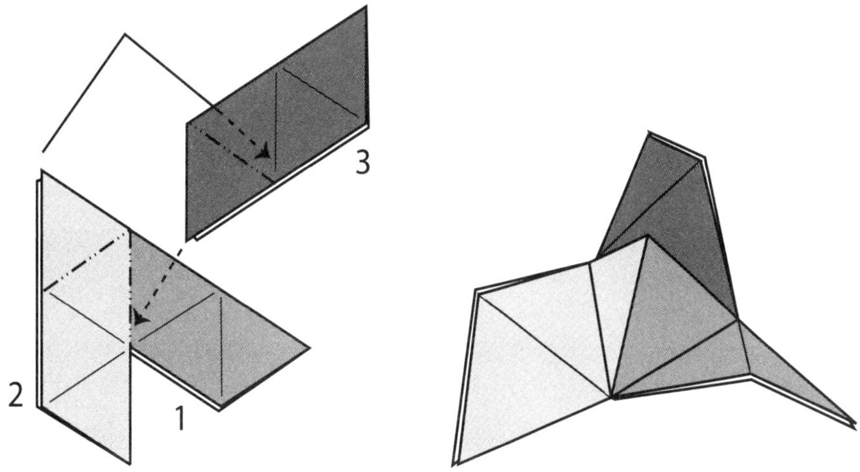

3. Continue attaching units one at a time so that each free tab is made into a triangular pyramid. Four triangular pyramids come together at each shared vertex. Your final result should look like the figure pictured below. This is your completed stellated octahedron.

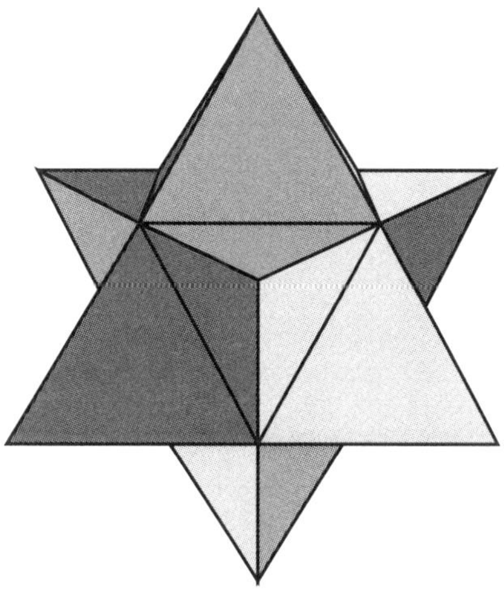

STELLATED OCTAHEDRON Exploration

Answer these questions once you have completed your model.

1. How many faces, edges, and vertices does the stellated octahedron have?

2. How many of the edges are concave, and how many are convex?

3. What shape are the faces of the stellated octahedron?

4. What other shapes that you have folded so far have these faces?

5. What similarities exist between these other shapes and the stellated octahedron? What differences exist?

6. If the base of one face is 3 units and the height is 2.5 units, what is the surface area of the entire figure? Show your work

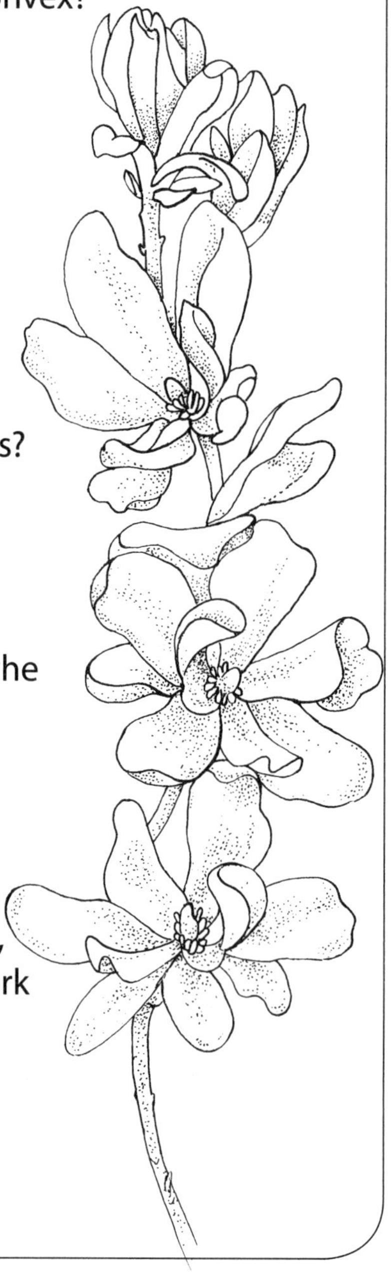

24-SIDED FIGURE

FOCUS

Students will fold a 24-sided figure and identify the geometric properties in the completed figures. They will then compare and contrast their 24-sided figures with their stellated octahedrons.

KEY QUESTIONS

What geometric properties are imbedded in the 24-sided figure?

How does the 24-sided figure compare to the stellated octahedron?

MATH

Properties of polyhedra
- faces
- edges
- vertices
- concave
- convex

Surface area

INTEGRATED PROCESSES

Observing
Comparing and contrasting

PAPER

12 squares per model in three or four different colors

ADDITIONAL MATERIALS

Stellated octahedron models

CREATOR

Mitsonobu Sonobè

Management
1. The 24-sided figure should be made with either three or four different colors of paper.
2. Due to the amount of folding, you may wish to have students work together in small groups and make one model for every two or three students.

Procedure
1. Hand out the folding instructions (pages 97-101) and 12 squares of paper to each student/group. Guide students through the construction of the basic unit for the 24-sided figure if necessary. (By this time they should be familiar with the folding process for the Sonobè unit.)
2. Have students work individually or in small groups to fold the remaining 11 pieces necessary for the figure.
3. When each student/group has completed all 12 units, go through the assembly procedure step by step, giving assistance to groups or individuals as needed.
4. When all students/groups have successfully completed their models, hand out the remaining student sheets.
5. Have students work together in small groups to answer the questions and explore the geometric properties of their 24-sided figures and how those compare to the stellated octahedron.
6. When all groups have finished the questions, close with a time of class discussion where students share their discoveries and experiences, including the properties of their figures and their methods for determining surface area.

Discussion
1. What shapes are the faces of the figure? [isosceles right triangles]
2. How many faces, edges, and vertices does your figure have? [faces, 24; edges, 36; vertices, 14]
3. How many of the edges are concave, and how many are convex? [12 concave, 24 convex]
4. How can you be sure that you have counted all of the faces, edges, and vertices correctly?
5. How would you find the surface area of one face? ...of the whole figure? Describe your plan. [Find the area of one face ($\frac{1}{2}$ base x height). Multiply this number by 24 for the total surface area.]
6. If the length of the base on one face is 3 units, and the height is 1 unit, what is the surface area of the whole figure according to the method you described in question five? [$(\frac{1}{2} \times 3) \times 1 = 1.5$, $1.5 \times 24 = 36$ units^2]
7. In what ways is the 24-sided figure the same as the stellated octahedron? [It has the same number of faces, edges, and vertices; it is made from the same number of units; each face is a triangle; the types of symmetry are the same; etc.]

8. In what ways is it different? [The faces are different types of triangles (right isosceles vs. equilateral), the angle at which the units meet is different, the unit used to construct it is different, etc.]
9. Based on what you know about stellation, why is the 24-sided figure not a true stellated octahedron? [The faces do not represent extensions of the sides of an octahedron, each of the faces in a stellated octahedron is an equilateral triangle, etc.]

Extensions

1. Have students make a 24-sided figure with the right triangle unit and make a comparison between the two units.
2. If they have not already done so, have students complete the *Sonobè Unit Exploration.*

24-SIDED FIGURE Folding Instructions

1. Fold the paper in half vertically and unfold.

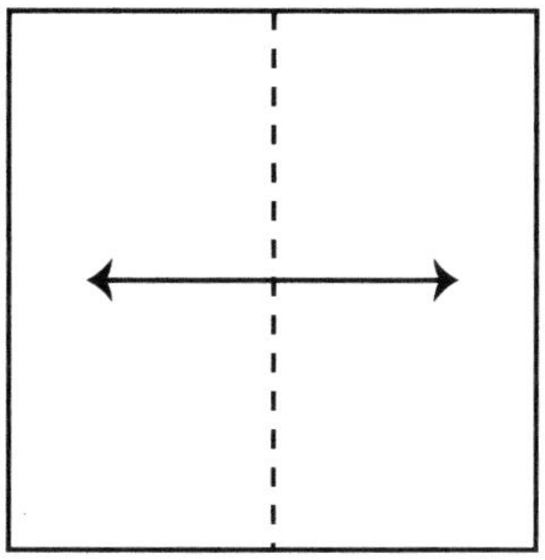

2. Fold the left edge and the right edge in to meet the center crease.

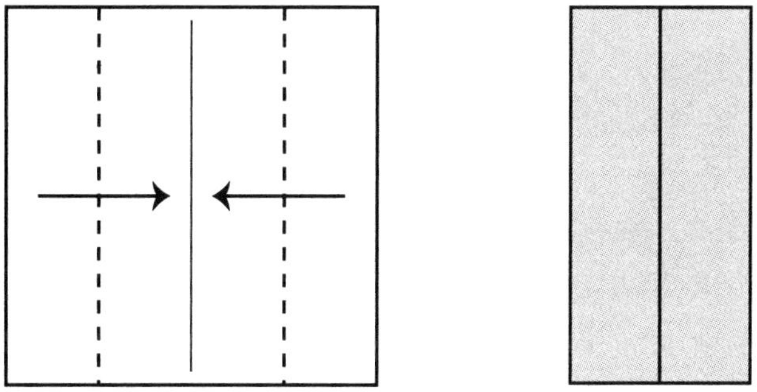

3. Fold as indicated by the dashed lines so that the top left corner meets the right side of the paper and the bottom right corner meets the left side of the paper.

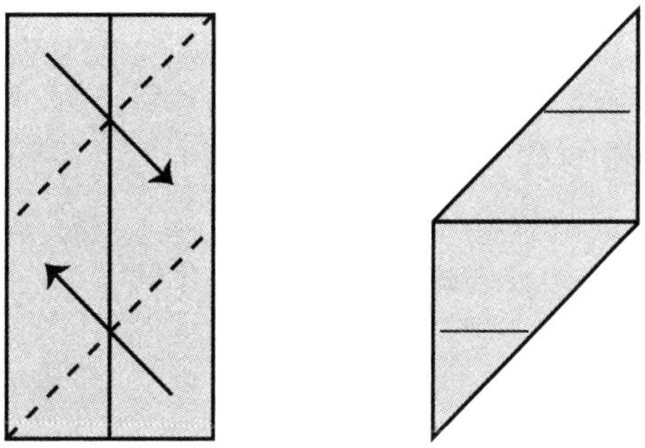

4. Unfold the paper completely. Fold the top right and bottom left corners in along the existing crease lines as shown.

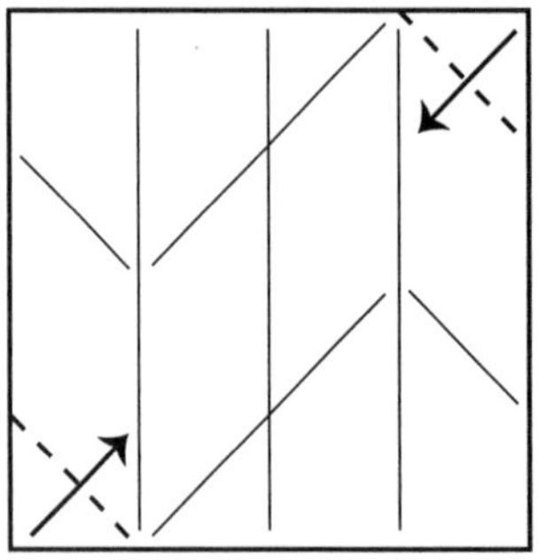

5. Fold the left and right sides of the paper in along the existing crease lines so that the edges meet in the middle.

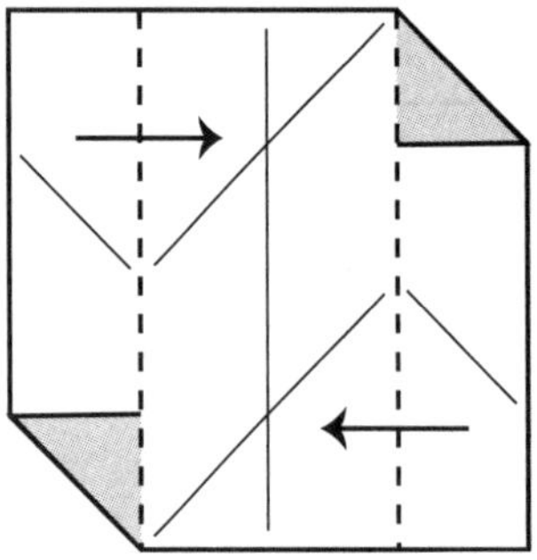

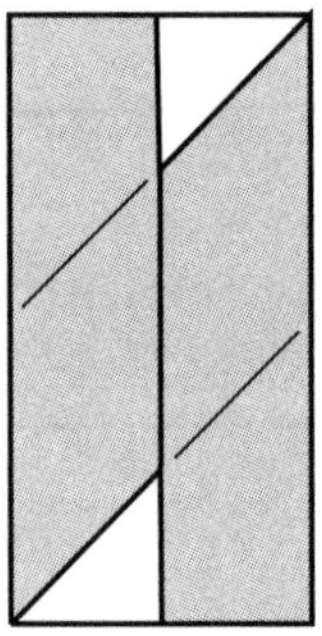

6. Fold the bottom right corner up along the existing crease line, tucking the corner underneath the flap as indicated.

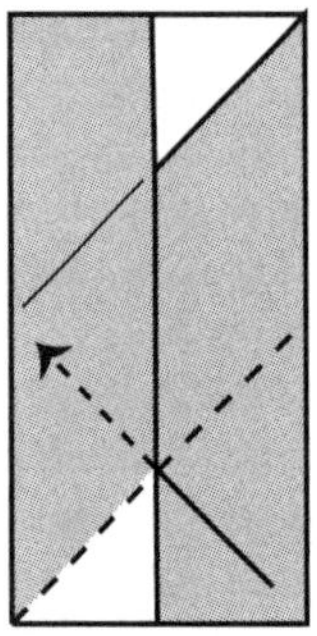

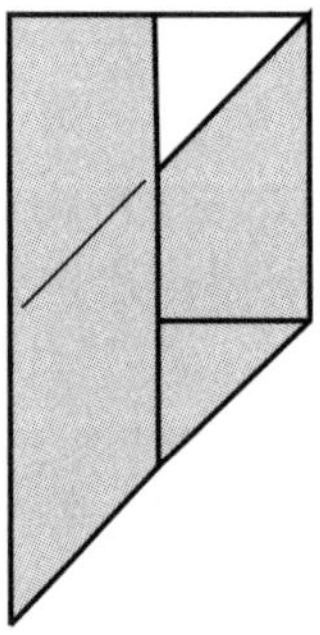

7. Repeat this process with the upper left corner, tucking it under the flap on the right side as indicated.

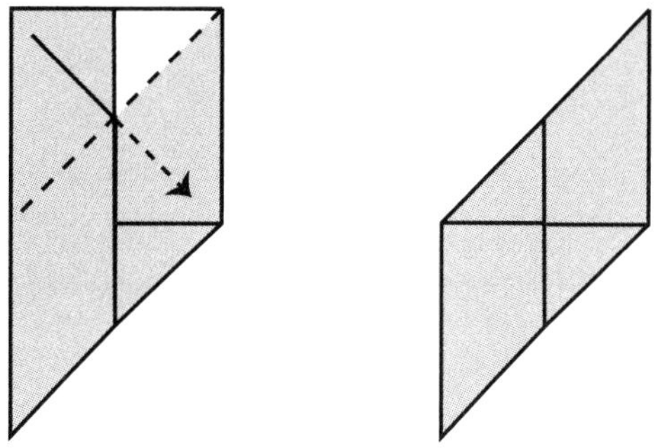

8. Flip the unit over and crease where indicated by the dashed lines.

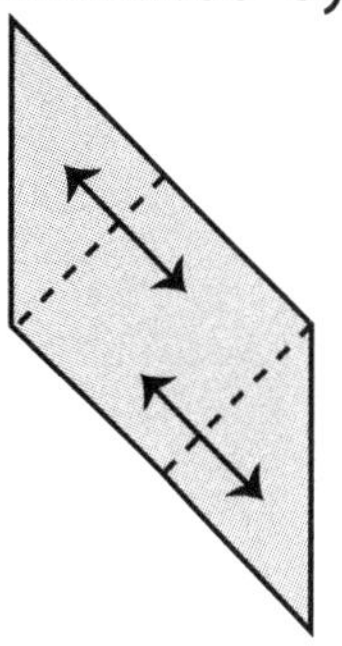

9. Flip the unit back to the front and crease well using a mountain fold along the line indicated. Repeat steps one through nine so that you have a total of 12 units like the one below.

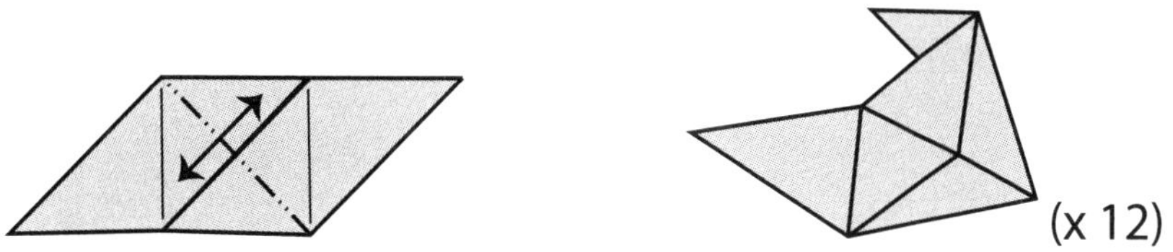

24-SIDED FIGURE Assembly

1. Take two pieces of different colors and join them together as shown.

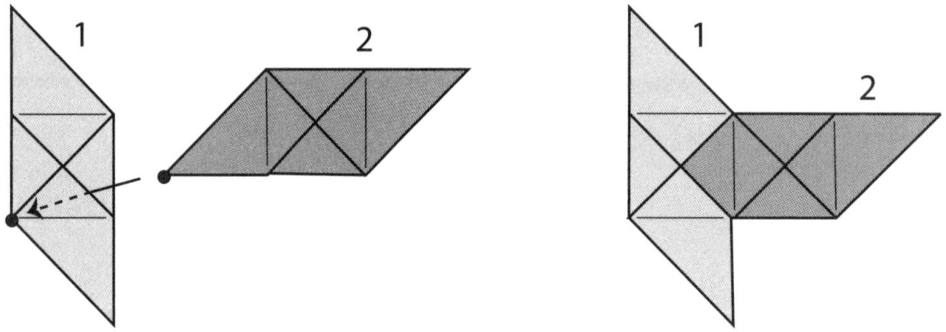

2. Take a third piece that is a different color and join it to the first two as shown. Note which of the creases are mountain, and which are valley. You should now have a triangular pyramid with three tabs sticking out.

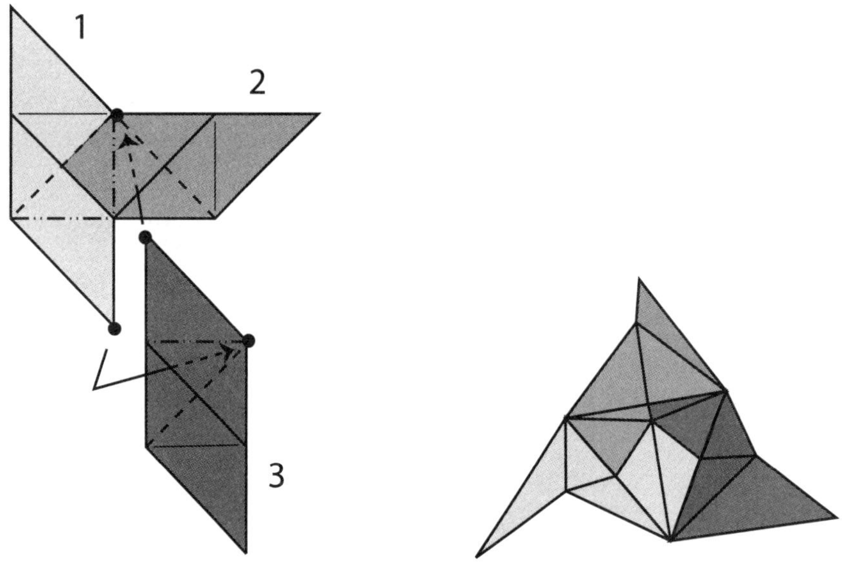

3. Make a second triangular pyramid in the same fashion by attaching two more units to one of the tabs as shown.

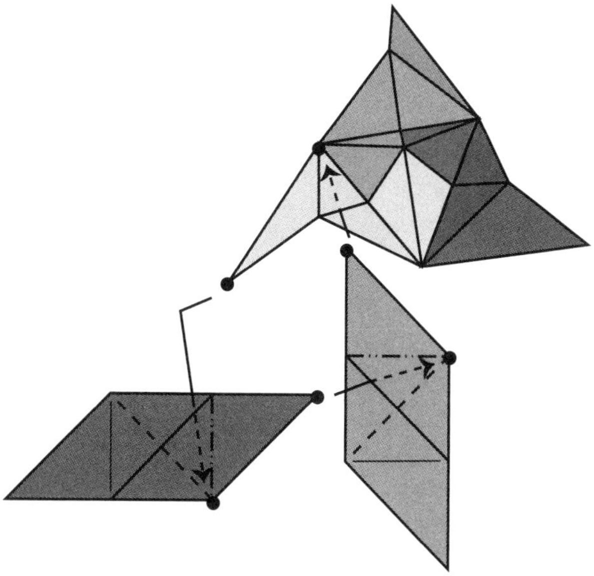

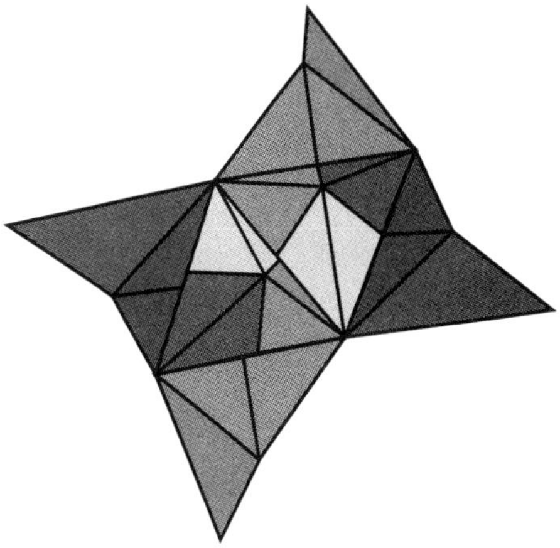

4. Repeat this process until all of the tabs have been made into pyramids and a closed figure has been formed. There should be four pyramids around each shared vertex. This is your completed 24-sided figure.

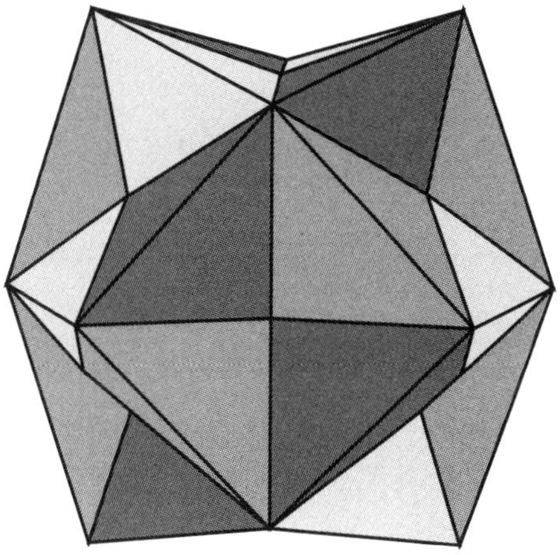

24-SIDED FIGURE Exploration

Use your completed 24-sided figure model to answer the following questions.

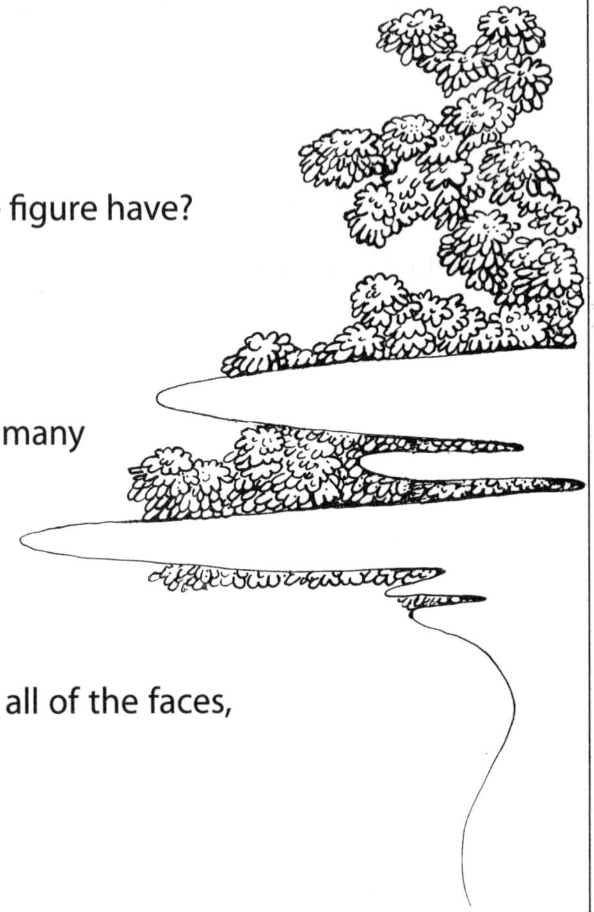

1. What shapes are the faces of the figure?

2. How many faces, edges, and vertices does the figure have?

3. How many of the edges are concave, and how many are convex?

4. How can you be sure that you have counted all of the faces, edges, and vertices?

5. How would you find the surface area of one face? …of the whole figure? Describe your plan.

6. If the length of the base on one face is 3 units, and the height is 1 unit, what is the surface area of the whole figure according to the method you described in question five? Show your work.

24-SIDED FIGURE Exploration

Use your stellated octahedron model to help you answer the remaining questions.

7. In what ways is the 24-sided figure the same as the stellated octahedron?

8. In what ways is it different?

9. If you were to cut off all of the triangular pyramids from the 24-sided figure, what shape would be left? Why?

10. How does this shape compare to the shape that would be left if you did the same thing to the stellated octahedron?

11. Based on your answers to the previous questions and what you know about stellation, why is the 24-sided figure not a true stellated octahedron?

STELLATED DODECAHEDRON

KEY QUESTIONS

What are the geometric properties of the small and the great stellated dodecahedron?

How do these two models compare?

MATH

Stellations
Properties of polyhedra
- faces
- edges
- vertices

Surface area
Volume

INTEGRATED PROCESSES

Observing
Collecting and recording data
Comparing and contrasting

PAPER

30 squares per model in at least five different colors

CREATOR

Jeannine Mosely

FOCUS

Students will fold a small and a great stellated dodecahedron, study their geometric properties, and make comparisons between the two.

Management

1. Because these models take 30 units each to make, you may want to have students work together in groups and make one model for every four or five students. You can also have students make the units at home for homework.
2. In order to complete the exploration section, students will need to have models of both the small and the great stellated dodecahedron. You may wish to have half of the groups make the small version and the other half make the great version. This will cut down on the time it takes to complete the activity.
3. The assembly of these models is fairly simple at first, but gets more difficult as you get down to the last few units. As you create your own models, pay attention to the techniques that you use to facilitate the assembly process so that you can share them with your students.
4. Both models should have five different colors of paper (or more). Because the "facets" are made up of either three- or five-sided pyramids, using five colors makes it possible for no two faces on one facet to be the same color. (A three-color assembly exists for the great stellated dodecahedron, but it is fairly difficult, and less aesthetic than a five-color assembly.) Arranging the units so that this occurs can be a puzzle more challenging than the actual assembly process, so have patience and be prepared to assist your students.

Procedure

1. Hand out 30 squares of paper and the appropriate folding instructions to each group.
2. Go over the procedure for folding one unit of the stellated dodecahedron step by step as a class. Be sure that students realize the importance of the paper being oriented exactly as it is in the diagrams. (This is less important if you are not using two-sided paper.)
3. Have students fold the remaining 29 units in their groups. When all groups have 30 units completed, go through the assembly procedure for each model with the class.
4. As groups assemble their models, move around the class giving assistance where needed. Try to help students assemble their models so that no facet has the same color in it twice.
5. Once groups have finished their models, hand out the exploration sheet. If each group does not have both models, combine groups so that students have both the small and the great stellated dodecahedron to look at when answering the questions.
6. Close with a time of class discussion and sharing.

Discussion

1. How many faces, edges, and vertices does the small stellated dodecahedron have? [faces, 60; edges, 90; vertices, 32]
2. How does this compare to the number of faces, edges, and vertices for the great stellated dodecahedron? [faces, 60; edges, 90; vertices, 32]
3. What method did you use to count the faces, edges and vertices? How do you know that you have counted them all?
4. What are some similarities between the two models? [The number of faces, edges, and vertices is the same; the shape of each face is the same; etc.]
5. What are some differences? [The number of faces on each "facet," the number of convex vertices, the number of facets that come together at each shared vertex, etc.]
6. Which of the two models has the greater surface area? [The surface area of each model is the same.] Justify your response. [Each model has the same number of faces. The area of each face is the same, therefore the surface area of the entire model is the same.]
7. Which of the models has the greater volume? [The small stellated dodecahedron has a greater volume.] Justify your response. [Although there are fewer facets on the small version, each facet has a volume four times that of the facets on the great version.]

Extension

Have students do some research to determine what the great dodecahedron looks like and see how it differs from the other two stellations.

* Some analyses of the stellated dodecahedron models indicate that they each have 12 star-shaped faces that intersect. However, the definition of face that we have given in this text does not allow for this interpretation of the models, and therefore we say that the stellations both have 60 faces that are triangular in shape, 90 edges, and 32 vertices.

STELLATED DODECAHEDRON

Part One: Folding the basic unit

1. Starting with the colored side up, fold the paper in thirds using a combination valley-mountain fold.

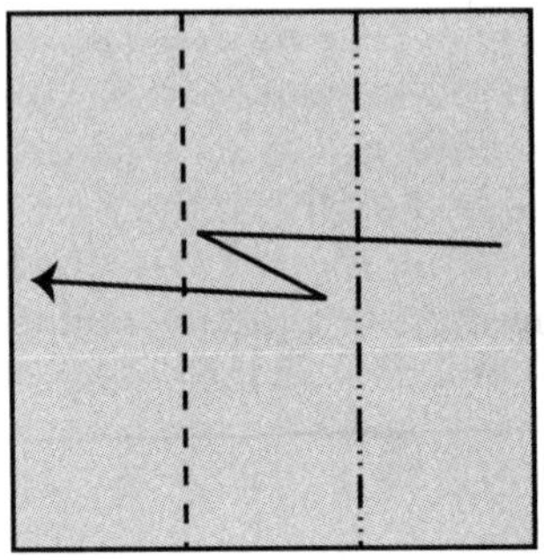

2. Fold the bottom left corner up to touch the upper right corner.

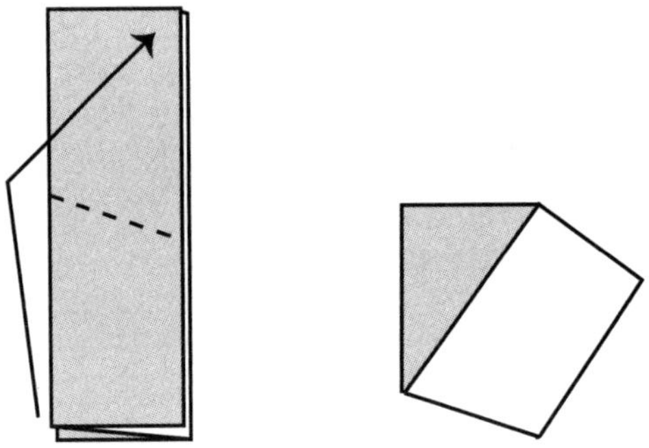

3. Unfold and fold where indicated by the diagonals, from the corners to the central fold line, using mountain folds.

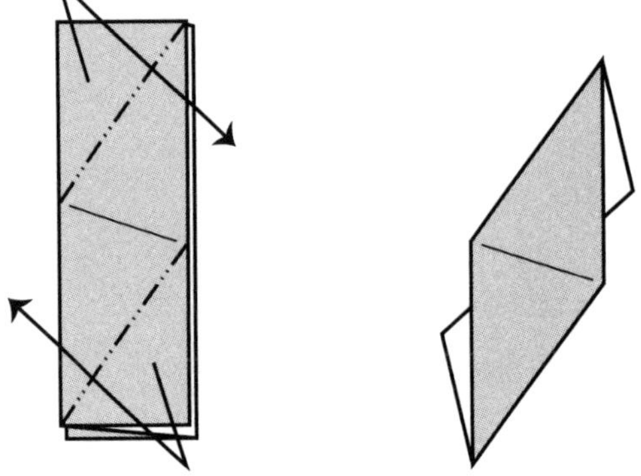

4. Crease the tabs that hang over the side of the paper as indicated.

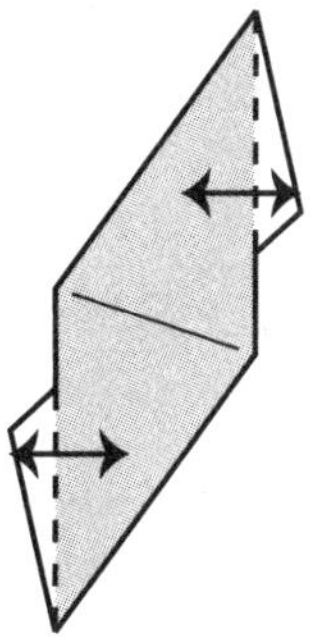

5. Unfold back to the rectangle. Repeat steps one to four so that you have a total of 30 units like the one below.

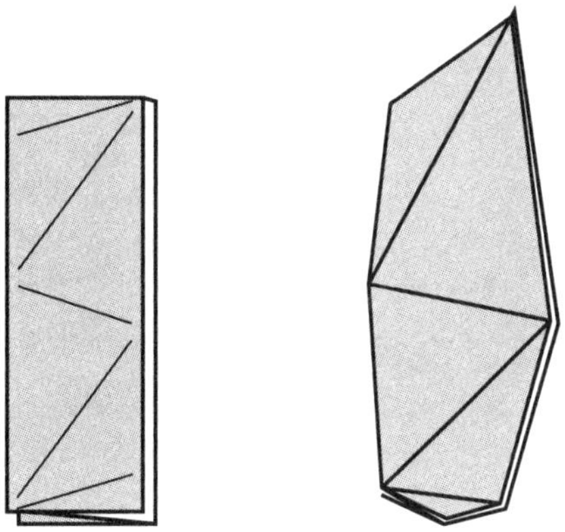

(x 30)

STELLATED DODECAHEDRON

Part Two A: Assembling the great stellated dodecahedron

1. Connect two units together as shown, inserting the top left corner of one into the side pocket of another so that the creases line up.

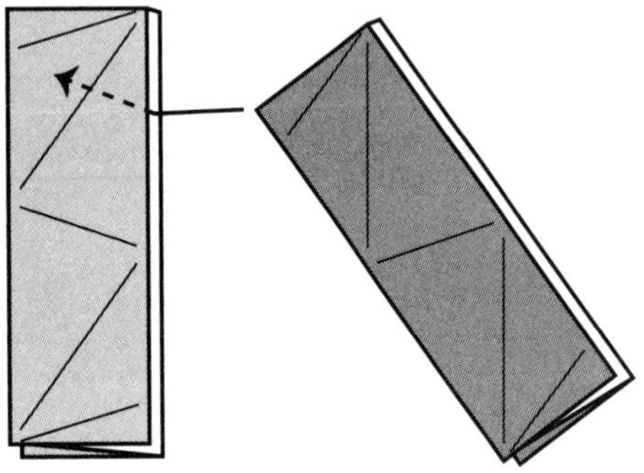

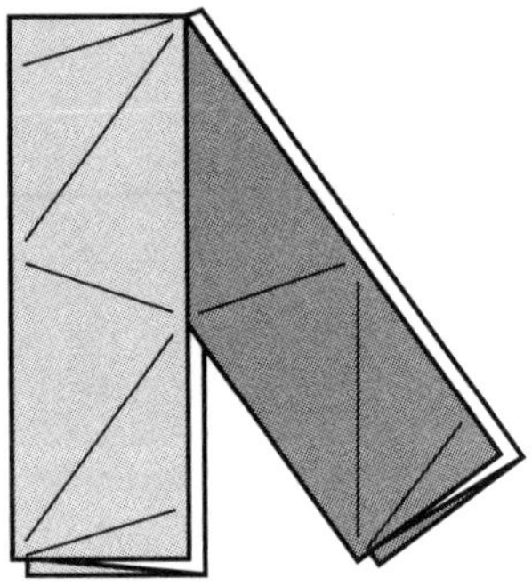

2. Insert a third piece into the first two in the same fashion and bring the first piece around to tuck into the third so that you are left with a triangular pyramid that has three tabs as shown.

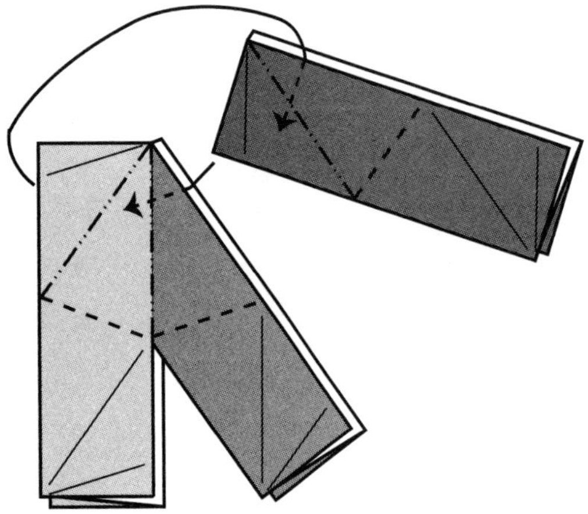

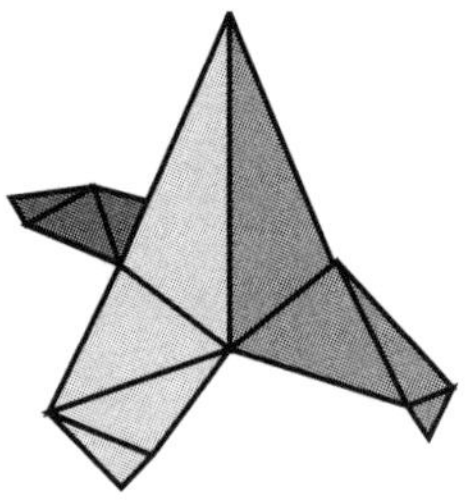

3. Continue to assemble pieces in this same fashion so that each tab becomes a part of a triangular pyramid, and five triangular pyramids come together at one vertex. Your completed great stellated dodecahedron should look something like the one below.

STELLATED DODECAHEDRON

Part Two B: Assembling the small stellated dodecahedron

1. Repeat steps one and two from *Part Two A*, but instead of connecting the first and third piece, add a fourth piece to the first three.

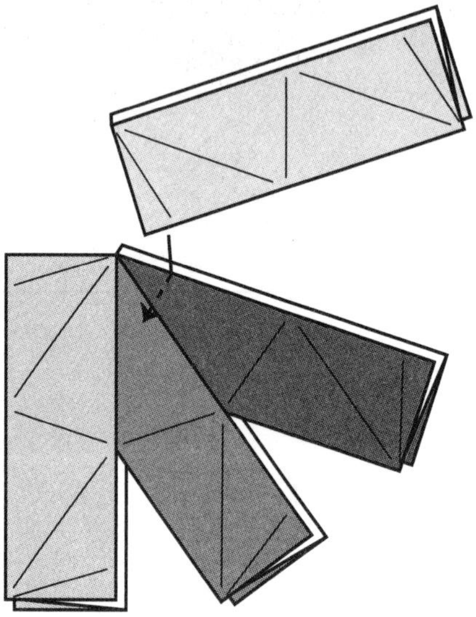

2. Insert a fifth piece into the first four, and connect the first and fifth pieces forming a pentagonal-based pyramid.

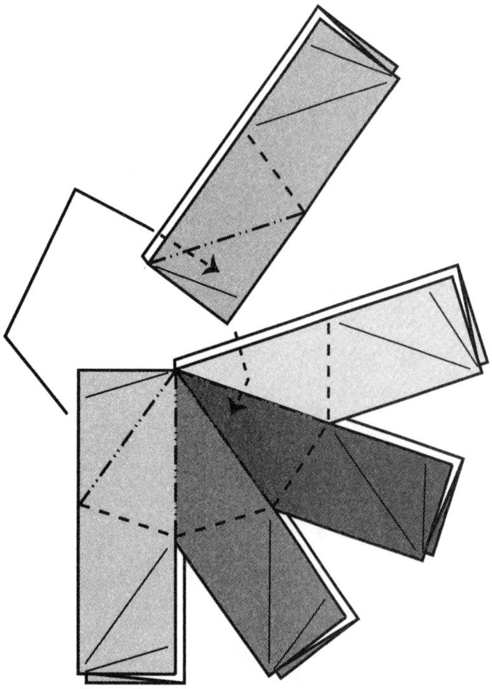

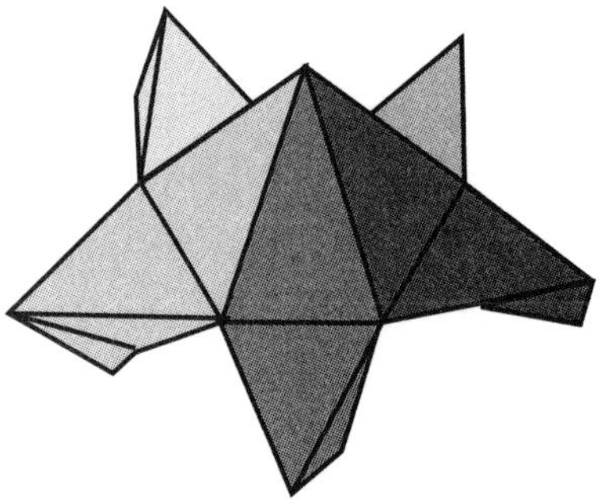

3. Continue to assemble pieces in this same fashion so that each tab becomes a part of a pentagonal pyramid, and three pentagonal pyramids come together at one vertex. Your completed small stellated dodecahedron should look something like the one below.

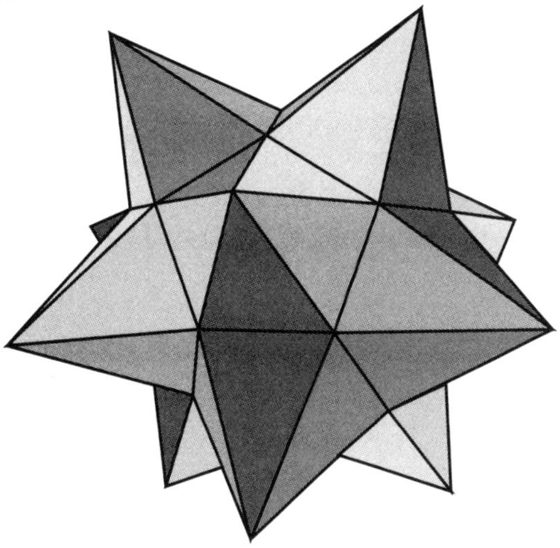

STELLATED DODECAHEDRON Exploration

You should have both the small and great stellated dodecahedron models on hand as you answer these questions.

1. How many faces, edges, and vertices does the small stellated dodecahedron have?

2. How does this compare to the number of faces, edges, and vertices for the great stellated dodecahedron?

3. What method did you use to count the faces, edges, and vertices? How do you know that you have counted them all?

4. What are some similarities between the two models?

5. What are some differences?

6. Which of the two models has the greater surface area? Justify your response.

7. Which of the models has the greater volume? Justify your response.

STELLATED ICOSAHEDRON

KEY QUESTIONS

What are the geometric properties of the stellated icosahedron?

What are the characteristics of the stellated solids, and how do these compare to the Platonic solids?

MATH

Stellations
Properties of polyhedra
- faces
- edges
- vertices

INTEGRATED PROCESSES

Observing
Collecting and recording data
Comparing and contrasting

PAPER

30 squares per model in at least four different colors

ADDITIONAL MATERIALS

Other stellated models for comparison
Platonic solid models for comparison
Platonic Solids Compared student sheet

CREATOR

Mitsonobu Sonobè

FOCUS

Students will fold a stellated icosahedron, study its geometric properties, and compare them to those of the other stellated solids they have folded.

Management
1. Because this model takes 30 units to make, you may want to have students work together in groups and make one model for every four or five students. You can also have students make the units at home for homework.
2. In order to complete the exploration section, students will need to have models of the previous stellated solids that they have folded, as well as their Platonic solid models so that they can compare and contrast the two groups.
3. The assembly of this model is fairly simple at first but gets more difficult as you get down to the last few units. As you create your own model, pay attention to the techniques that you use to facilitate the assembly process so that you can share them with your students.
4. Five colors of paper (or more) are recommended for the most aesthetic models. Although it is possible to have a three-color assembly such that no facet ever contains two of the same color, this is fairly difficult to do and less aesthetic than a five-color model.

Procedure
1. Hand out 30 squares of paper and the folding instructions to each group.
2. Go over the procedure for folding one unit of the stellated icosahedron as a class. (By this time students should be quite familiar with the unit, since it is the same one used to make the bird tetrahedron, the cube, and the 24-sided figure.)
3. Have students fold the remaining 29 units in their groups. When all groups have 30 units completed, go through the assembly procedure for the model with the class.
4. As groups assemble their models, move around the class giving assistance where needed. Try to help students assemble their models so that each facet uses three different colors.
5. Once groups have finished their models, hand out the exploration sheet. Students should have their previous models on hand as well as the *Platonic Solids Compared* student sheet to help them answer the questions.
6. When groups have completed the exploration, close with a time of class discussion and sharing.

Discussion
1. What patterns do you see in this table? [The number of faces, edges, and vertices are the same for both dodecahedrons and the icosahedron; each stellation has triangular faces; etc.]
2. Which figures are the most similar? [The two stellated dodecahedrons and the stellated icosahedron all have the same number of faces, edges, and vertices.] Why do you think that is?

3. Are there any characteristics that are true of each stellated solid? [Yes. Each stellation has some kind of triangular face] ...any that are different for each? [no] What are they?
4. What relationship exists between the number of faces, the total number of vertices and the total number of edges in each solid? [Faces + Vertices = Edges + 2 (this is Euler's formula)]
5. How does this relationship compare to the relationship that exists in the Platonic solids? [It is the same. Euler's formula works for all of the Platonic solids and all of the stellated solids in this book. The only cases where it does not hold true are when the polyhedra have holes, tunnels, ring-shaped faces, or are multiple structures.]
6. List some of the differences between the stellated solids and the Platonic solids. [Platonic solids do not have concave edges or vertices. The interior angles in stellated solids are not all the same, as they are in Platonic solids, etc.]
7. List some of the similarities between the stellated solids and the Platonic solids. [Each face of a given solid is the same. The relationship between the number of faces, edges, and vertices is the same, etc.]

Extensions

1. If students have not already done so, have them complete the *Sonobè Unit Exploration.*
2. Have students research some of the other 58 possible stellations of the icosahedron. Could any of the others be made with origami?

Solutions

The table from the student sheet is shown below with the correct answers filled in.

Stellations

Figure	Faces	Shape of face	Convex Edges	Concave Edges	Total Edges	Vertices
Stellated Octahedron	24	Equilateral triangle	24	12	36	14
24-Sided Figure	24	Isoceles right triangle	24	12	36	14
Small Stellated Dodecahedron	60	Isoceles triangle	60	30	90	32
Great Stellated Dodecahedron	60	Isoceles triangle	60	30	90	32
Stellated Icosahedron	60	Isoceles right triangle	60	30	90	32

STELLATED ICOSAHEDRON

Folding Instructions

1. Fold the paper in half vertically and unfold.

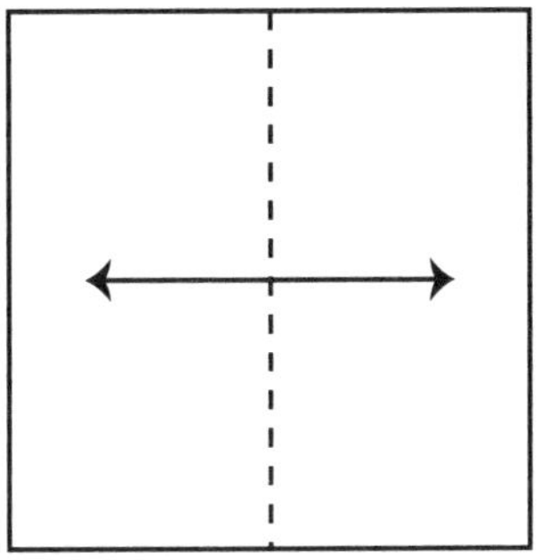

2. Fold the left edge and the right edge in to meet the center crease.

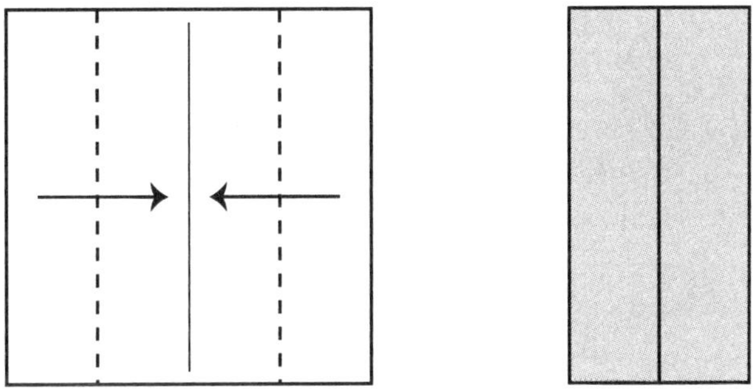

3. Fold as indicated by the dashed lines so that the top left corner meets the right side of the paper and the bottom right corner meets the left side of the paper.

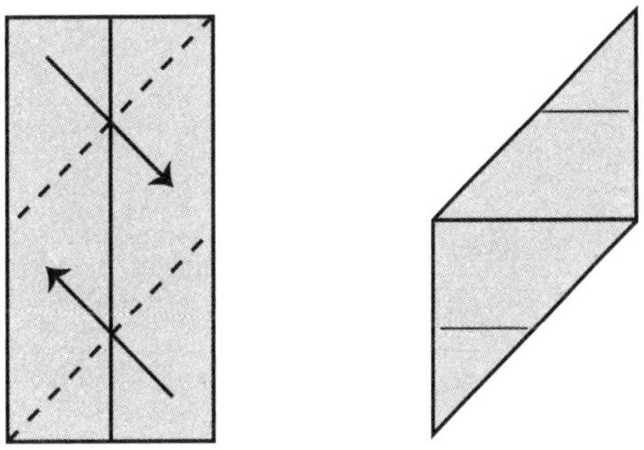

4. Unfold the paper completely. Fold the top right and bottom left corners in along the existing crease lines as shown.

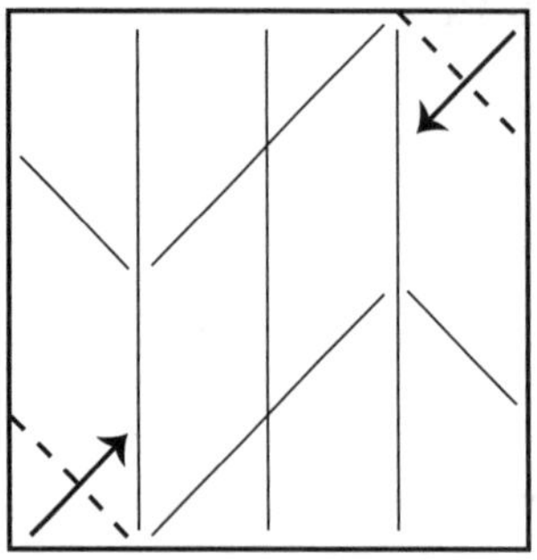

5. Fold the left and right sides of the paper in along the existing crease lines so that the edges meet in the middle.

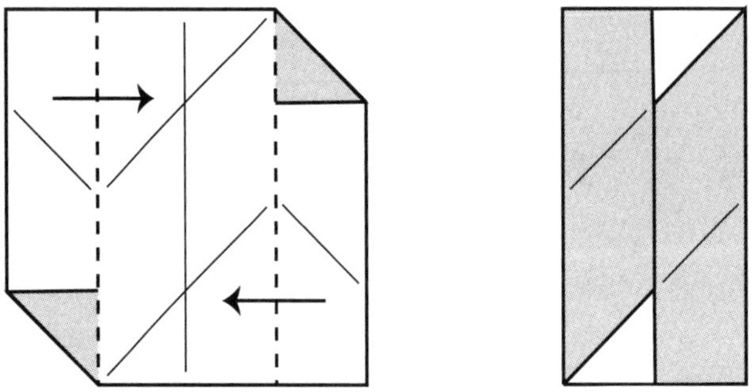

6. Fold the bottom right corner up along the existing crease line, tucking the corner underneath the flap as indicated.

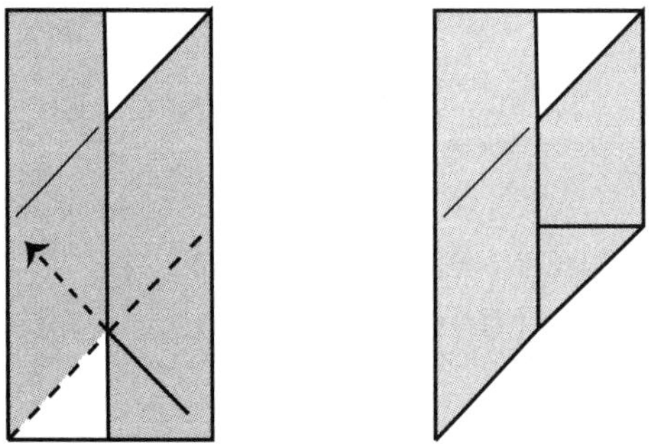

7. Repeat this process with the upper left corner, tucking it under the flap on the right side as indicated.

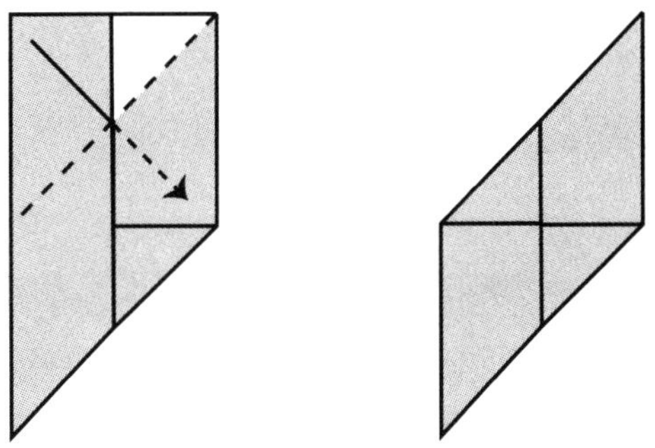

8. Flip the unit over and crease where indicated by the dashed lines.

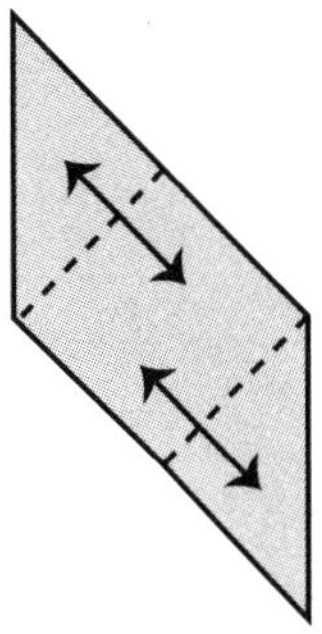

9. Flip the unit back to the front and crease well using a valley fold along the line indicated. Repeat steps one through nine so that you have a total of 30 units like the one below.

(x 30)

STELLATED ICOSAHEDRON

Assembly

1. Take two pieces of different colors and join them together as shown.

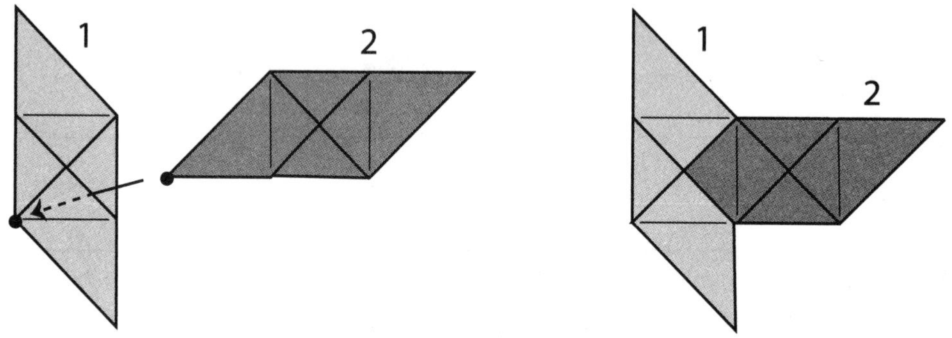

2. Take a third piece that is a different color and join it to the first two as shown, forming a triangular pyramid with three tabs sticking out.

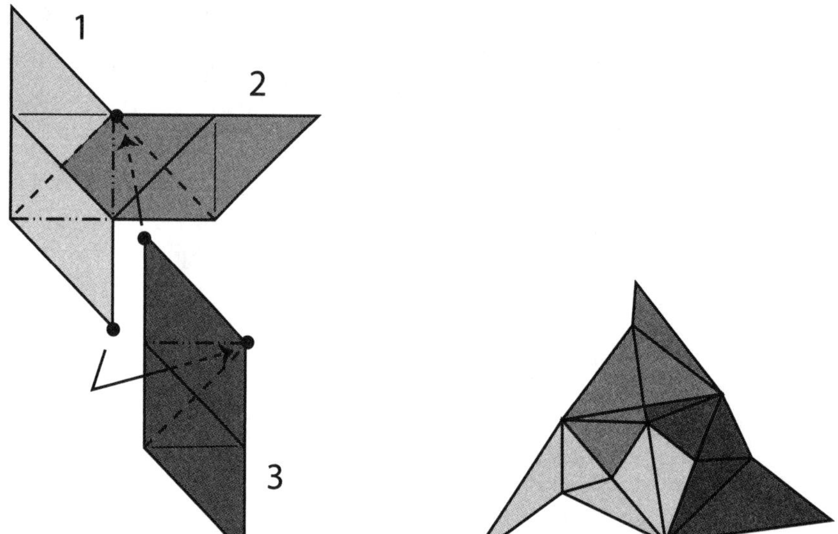

3. Each of the three tabs will be made into a triangular pyramid by adding two additional units. At each shared vertex, five triangular pyramids will come together as shown.

4. Continue inserting flaps and creating pyramids until you have used all 30 units and created a closed figure. This is your completed stellated icosahedron.

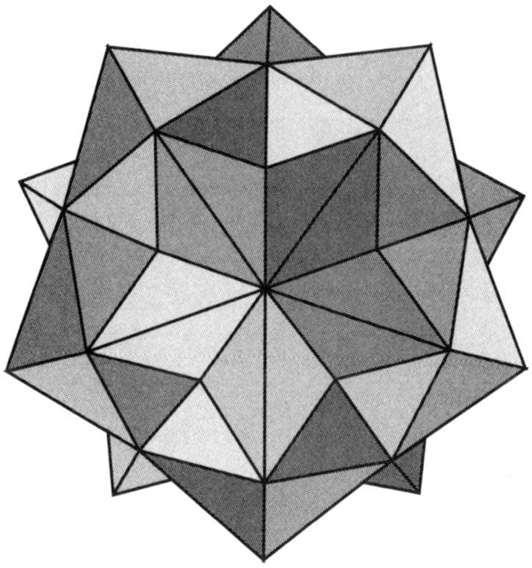

STELLATED SOLIDS COMPARED

Fill in the table below with the information for each of your stellations. Notice the distinction between convex and concave for the edges.

Stellations

Figure	Faces	Shape of face	Convex Edges	Concave Edges	Total Edges	Vertices
Stellated Octahedron						
24-Sided Figure						
Small Stellated Dodecahedron						
Great Stellated Dodecahedron						
Stellated Icosahedron						

Answer these questions after you have completed the table, using the back of your paper to record your answers.

1. What patterns do you see in this table?
2. Which figures are the most similar? Why do you think that is?
3. Are there any characteristics that are true of each stellated solid? ...any that are different for each? What are they?
4. What relationship exists between the number of faces, the total number of vertices and the total number of edges in each solid?
5. How does this relationship compare to the relationship that exists in the Platonic solids?
6. List some of the differences between the stellated solids and the Platonic solids.
7. List some of the similarities between the stellated solids and the Platonic solids.

FLEXASTAR

FOCUS

Students will build a flexastar and examine its geometric properties.

KEY QUESTION

What are the geometric properties of a flexastar and its unfolded unit?

MATH

Properties of geometric
- shapes
- congruence
- similarity
- angle

Transformations
Symmetry

PAPER

Eight squares per model in two different colors
One square for exploration

CREATOR

Unknown

COLLECTED BY

Florence Temko

Procedure

1. Hand out the folding instructions (pages 123-126) and eight paper squares to each student.
2. Go over the folding instructions for the flexastar unit step by step. Have students fold the remaining seven units and guide them through the assembly process.
3. When all students have successfully assembled their models, hand out the remaining two student sheets and an additional square of paper.
4. Have students work together in groups to fold an additional unit and answer the questions about their models.
5. When all groups have finished, close with a time of class discussion where students share their discoveries and the things they learned about their flexastar.

Discussion

1. What is the measure of each angle that originates at the center of the square? [22.5°] How do you know? [There are 16 lines radiating from the center in equal increments. When you divide 360° by 16, you get 22.5°.]
2. Are all of these central angles congruent? Why or why not? [All of the central angles are congruent. The diagonals bisect the four square regions created by the horizontal and vertical folds, and each of the eight triangles created by the diagonals is bisected again, leaving 16 congruent angles.]
3. What shape(s) do you see in each corner of the unfolded square? What can you say about these shapes and their relationship to each other? [There are two congruent isosceles right triangles in each corner. Seen together, they form a larger, similar isosceles right triangle.]
4. The paper has been divided into four smaller square sections by the center horizontal and vertical folds. How many triangles are there in one of these sections? [There are 12.]
5. Can you use this number to determine how many triangles there are in the entire square? [no] Why or why not? [When you are not limited to one corner, there are many larger and overlapping triangles that can be formed making the total much greater than 48 (12 x 4).]
6. What symmetries are there in the flexastar unit and model? (See *Solutions.*)

Extension

Try making flexastars of different sizes and using more and fewer units. What is the result?

Solutions

The symmetries that exist in the unfolded unit and in the flexastar model are discussed below.

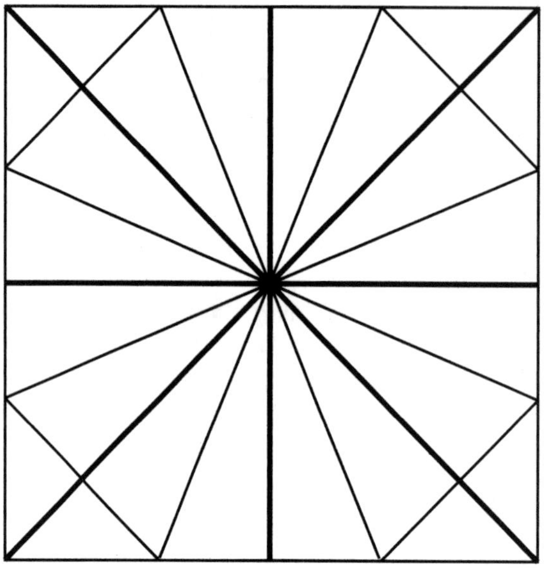

The dark lines in the diagram are the four lines of bilateral symmetry that exist in the unit. The unit also has 4-fold rotational symmetry around the center point.

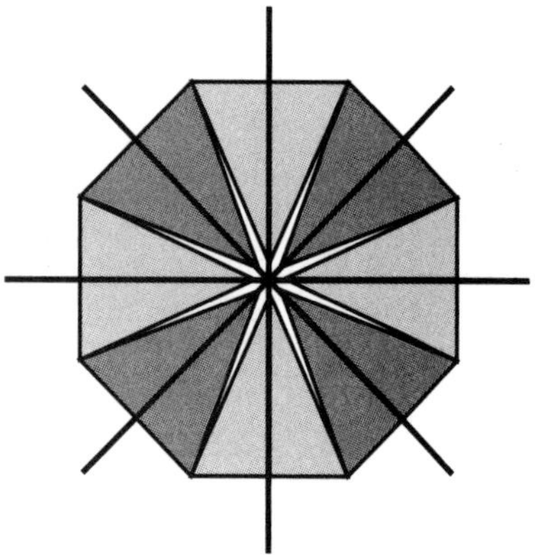

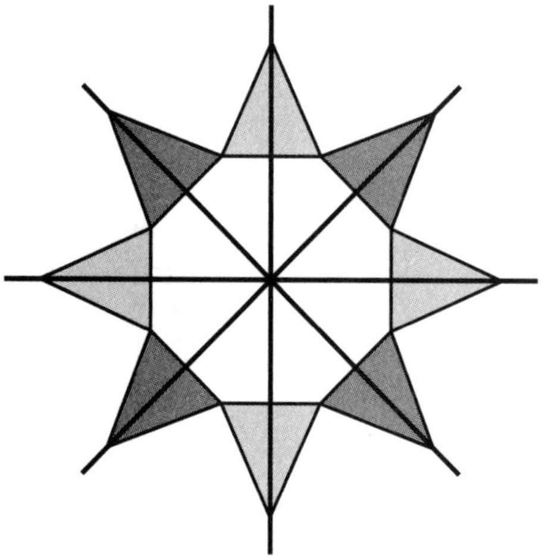

Both the closed and open forms of the flexastar have 8-fold rotational symmetry when rotated around their center points. They also both have eight lines of bilateral symmetry, indicated by the dark lines. (There is also a plane of bilateral symmetry that goes through both forms of the model cutting through its thickness, but this is not as relevant as the other symmetries.)

FLEXASTAR Folding Instructions

1. Start with the colored side of the paper facing up. Fold the square in half vertically and unfold and then horizontally and unfold.

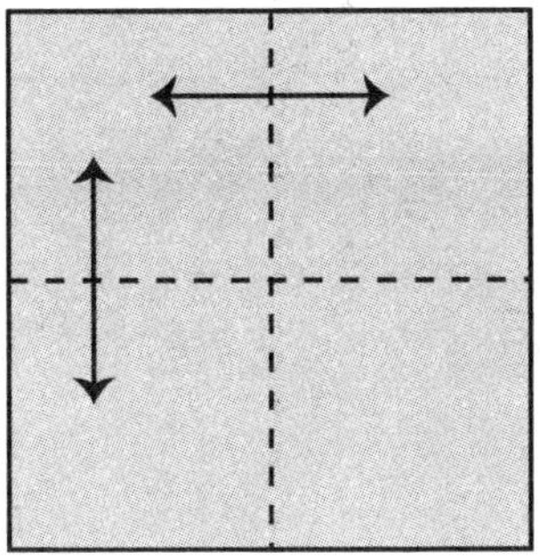

2. Flip your paper over and fold the top right corner down to meet the bottom left corner and unfold.

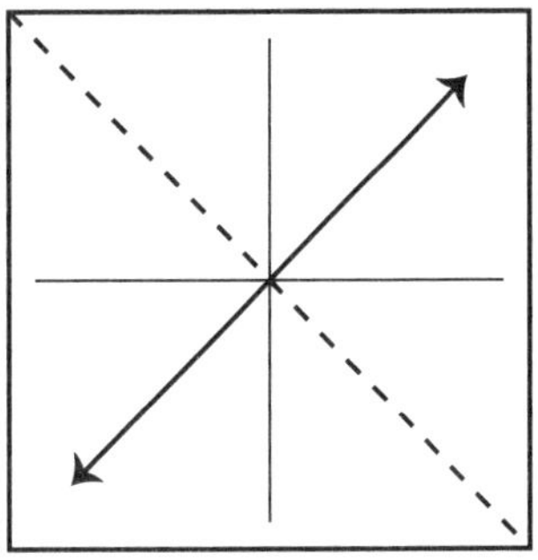

3. Fold the top left corner down to the bottom right corner.

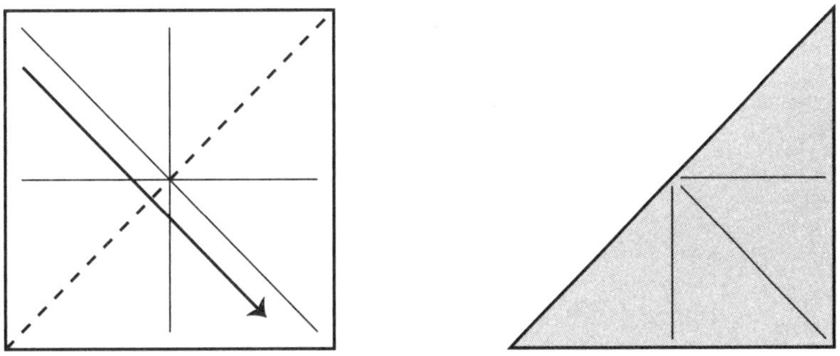

4. Bring the two corners down by making two valley folds and a mountain fold as indicated (this must be done on both sides at the same time). Press the paper flat to create a triangular shape like the one shown below.

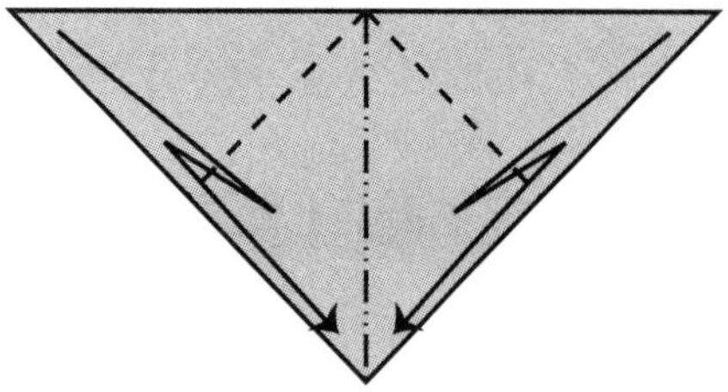

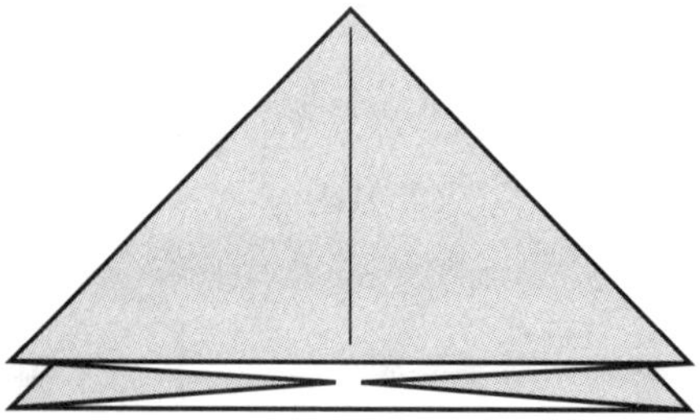

5. Fold the sides of the top flap in so that they are flush with the center line. Flip the paper over and repeat this process on the other side.

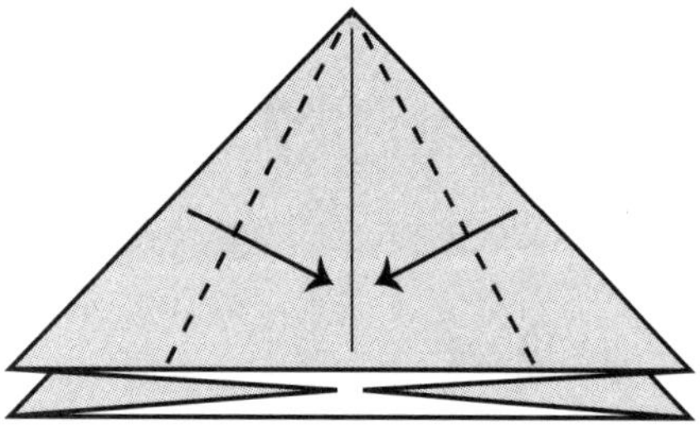

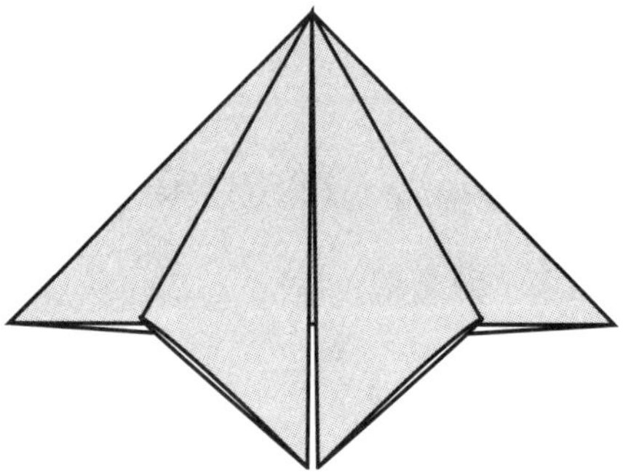

6. Repeat steps one through five with your remaining seven pieces of paper so that you have a total of eight units like the one below, four of one color, and four of another color.

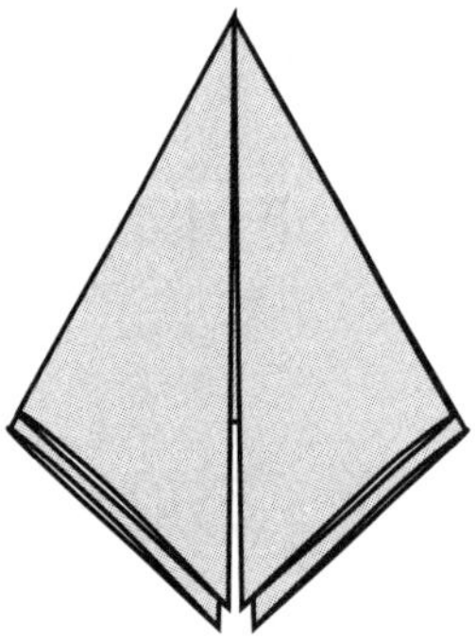

(x 8)

FLEXASTAR Assembly

1. Take two units of different colors and insert the tabs from the top flap of one into the pockets on the top flap of another. Be sure to **only insert the tabs from the top flap**.

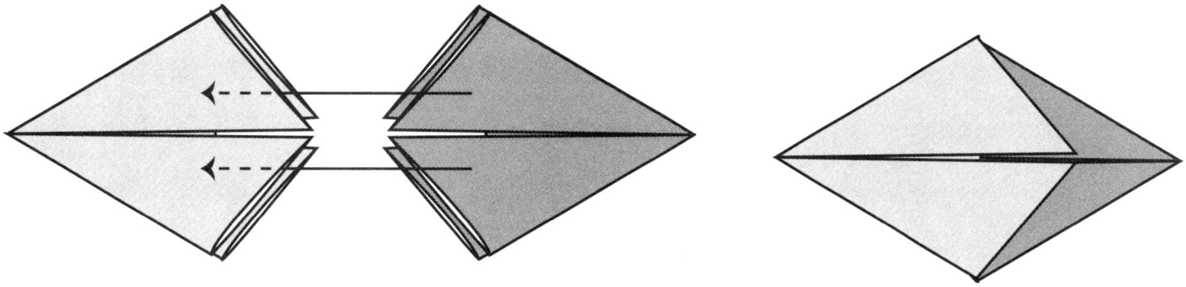

2. Fold the right piece over where indicated so that it aligns with the left piece.

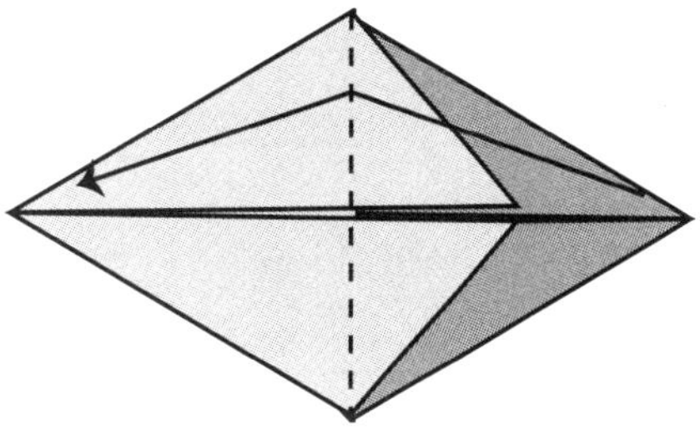

3. Insert the tabs from the top flap on a third piece into the remaining pockets on the second piece. Continue to attach pieces in this fashion—every other color and one unit at time, until all eight have been attached.

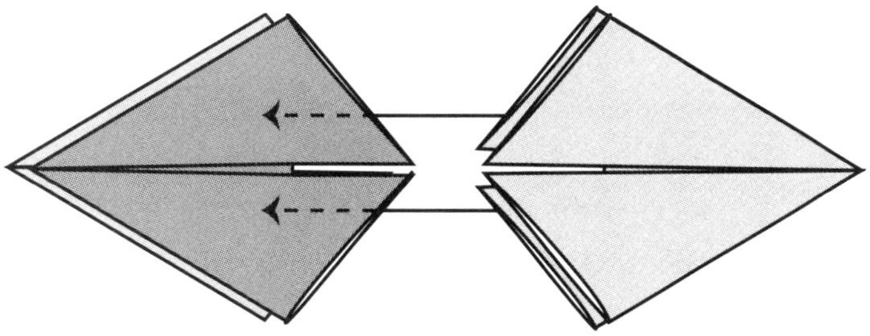

4. Connect the first and eighth piece, making a complete loop. This loop can be "flexed" by bringing all of the points into the center to create a closed wheel as shown. This is your completed flexastar.

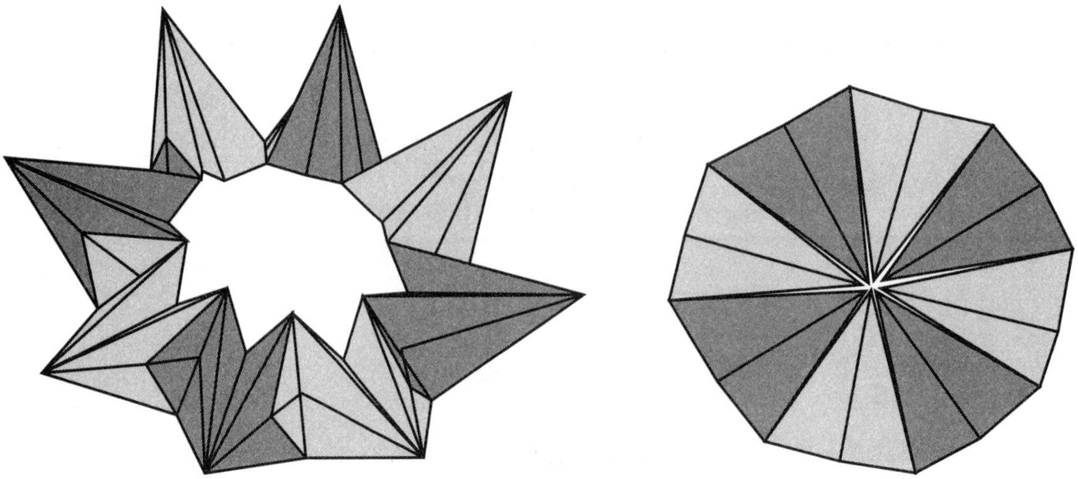

FLEXASTAR Exploration

Fold an additional flexastar unit, unfold it, and use it to answer the questions below.

1. Without using a protractor, determine the measure of each angle that originates at the center of the square. Justify your response.

2. Are all of these central angles congruent? Why or why not?

3. What shape(s) do you see in each corner of the unfolded square? What can you say about these shapes and their relationship to each other?

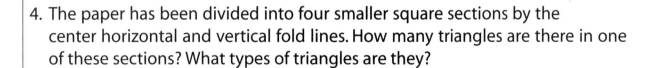

4. The paper has been divided into four smaller square sections by the center horizontal and vertical fold lines. How many triangles are there in one of these sections? What types of triangles are they?

5. Can you use this number to determine how many triangles there are in the entire square? Why or why not?

FLEXASTAR Exploration

Identify and label all of the symmetries that exist in the unfolded flexastar unit below.

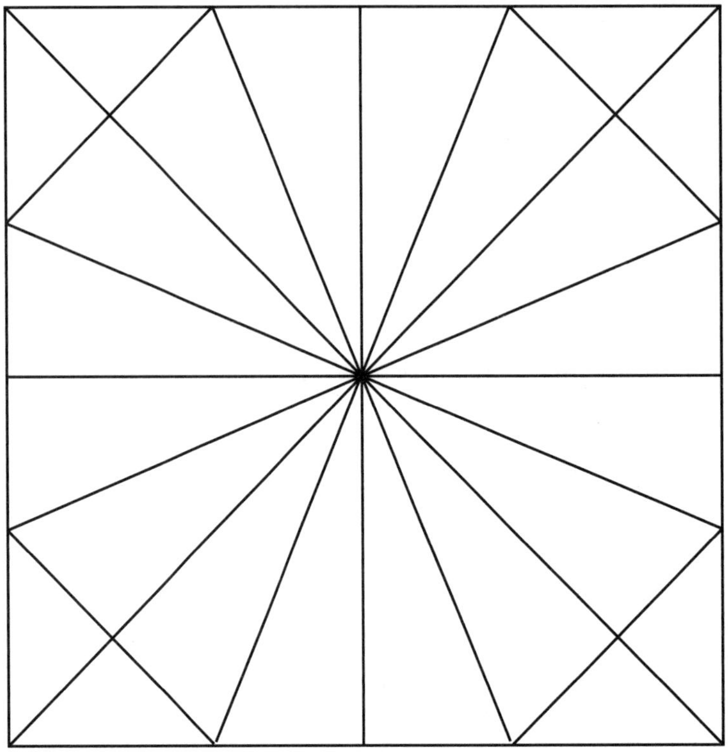

Identify and label all of the symmetries that exist in the open and closed form of the flexastar shown below.

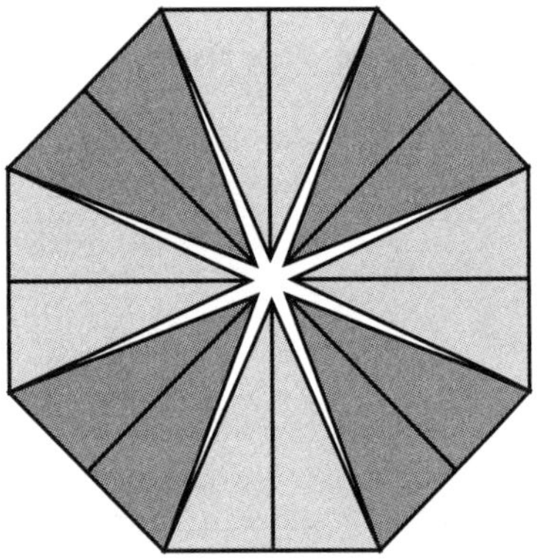

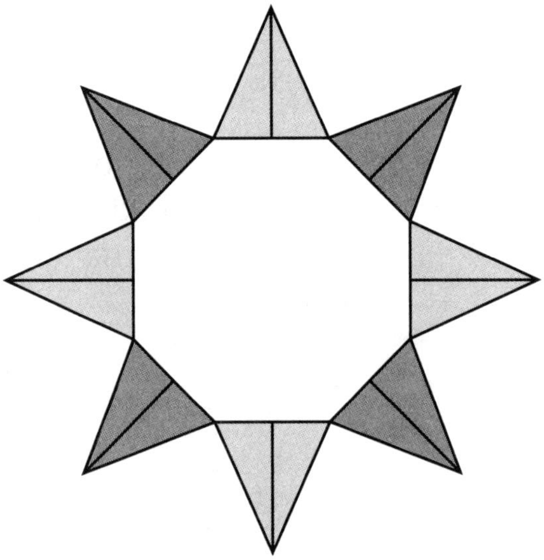

TRANSFORMING PINWHEEL

Key Question

What are the characteristics of the transforming pinwheel in both its ring and pinwheel forms?

Math

Properties of
- geometricshapes
- similarity
- congruence
- diameter

Symmetry

Integrated Processes

Observing
Comparing and contrasting
Predicting

Paper

Eight squares per model in two colors
One square for exploration

Additional Materials

Rulers

Creator

Robert Neale

Focus

Students will explore the characteristics and properties of the transforming pinwheel in both of its possible forms.

Management

1. The transforming pinwheels look the nicest when at least two colors of paper are used so that no two adjacent sections are the same color.

Procedure

1. Hand out the folding instructions (pages 131-134) and eight paper squares to each student.
2. Go over the folding instructions for the pinwheel unit as a class. Once you have completed a single unit, have students fold the remaining seven units.
3. When all students have completed their units, go through the assembly process step by step. Students may have a difficult time linking the first and last pieces together to form a closed ring, so be prepared to offer assistance as needed.
4. When students have completed their transforming pinwheel models, hand out the exploration pages, an additional square of paper, and rulers to each student.
5. Have students work together in groups to fold an additional unit, draw in the fold lines, and answer the exploration questions.
6. When all groups have completed the exploration section, close with a time of class discussion and sharing.

Discussion

1. How were you able to draw in the diagonal fold lines accurately?
2. What angles are the diagonal lines in the unfolded unit? [45°] How do you know? [They connect the midpoints on two adjacent sides of the square.]
3. Are there any lines of symmetry in this unit? [Yes, one.] Where is it? (See *Solutions.*)
4. What are all of the different shapes that are created by the fold lines? [There is a variety of triangles, quadrilaterals, and other polygons.]
5. What congruent shapes exist in the fold lines? [There are congruent parallelograms, triangles, and squares.] How do you know they are congruent?
6. What similar shapes exist in the fold lines? [There are isosceles right triangles that are similar.] How do you know they are similar?
7. What shape is the large section that forms the center of the pinwheel? [a regular octagon]
8. What shape is each of the smaller sections that make up this central section? [irregular quadrilateral] How are these shapes related to each other? [They are all congruent, or would be in a perfectly folded and assembled model.]
9. What shape are the "points" that come off of the center section of the pinwheel? [parallelograms] How are these shapes related to each other? [They are congruent.]

10. When the model is in the ring form, what shape is in the center? [a regular octagon] How does this shape relate to the shape in the center of the pinwheel? [It is similar, but smaller in diameter.]
11. What shape are the sections that make up the ring? [They are irregular pentagons (five sides each).] How do these shapes relate to the shapes that make up the center section of the pinwheel? [If you add a rectangle to each irregular quadrilateral that makes up the center of the pinwheel, you get the irregular pentagons that make up the ring.]
12. Which model did you predict has the greater diameter? Why?
13. Which form actually has the greater diameter? [the pinwheel] Is this what you predicted? Why or why not?
14. What types of symmetry exist in this model when it is in the pinwheel form? [The pinwheel has an 8-fold rotational symmetry. (See *Solutions* for lines of symmetry.)]
15. What types of symmetry exist in this model when it is in the ring form? [The ring has an 8-fold rotational symmetry. (See *Solutions* for lines of symmetry.)]

Solutions

The fold lines for the *Transforming Pinwheel* unit are shown below, with the one line of bilateral symmetry indicated.

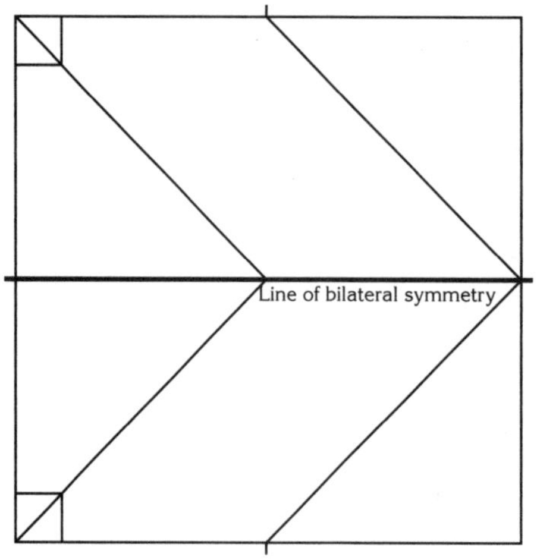

Both the pinwheel form and the ring form of the model exhibit 8-fold rotational symmetry, as indicated by the lines below.

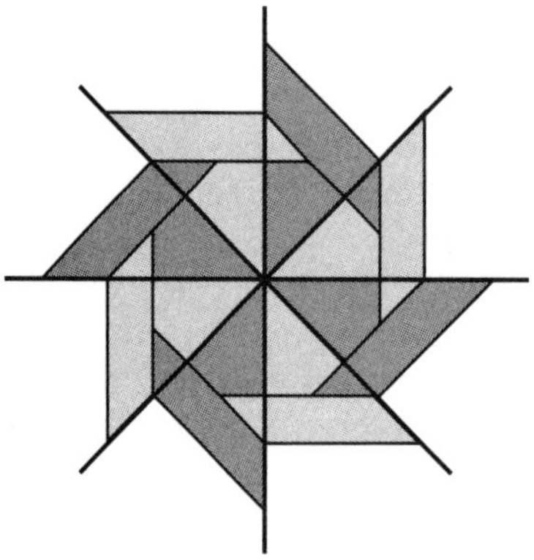

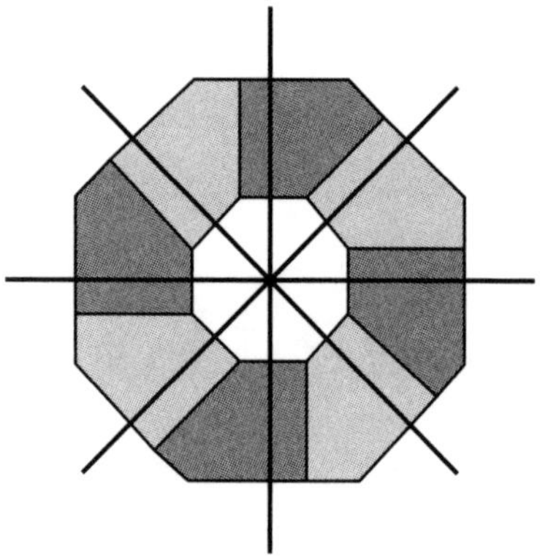

TRANSFORMING PINWHEEL

Folding Instructions

1. Starting with the white side up, fold the paper in half horizontally, and unfold.

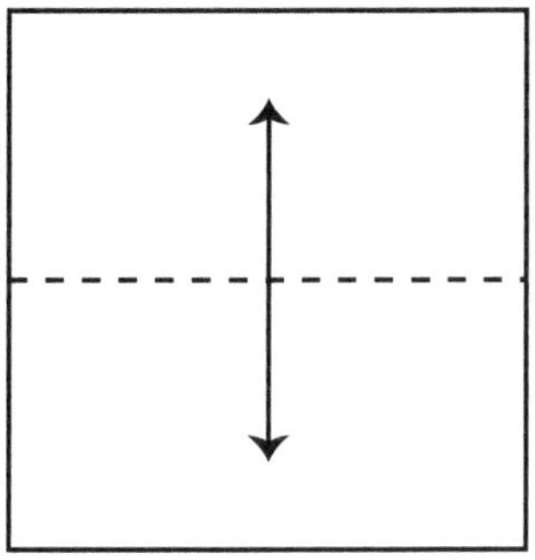

2. Fold the top right and bottom right corners in to meet the midline.

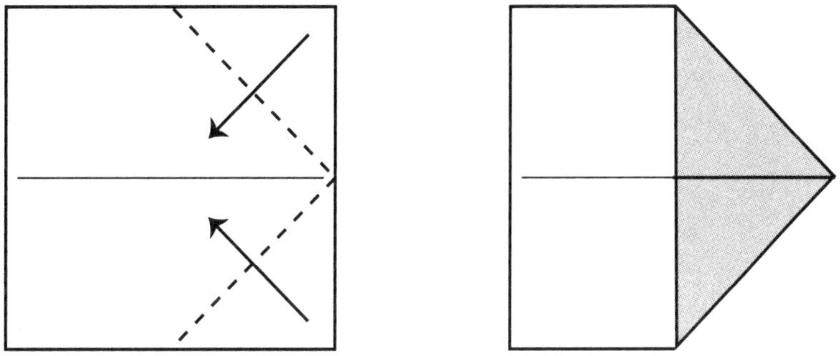

3. Fold the paper in half along the midline.

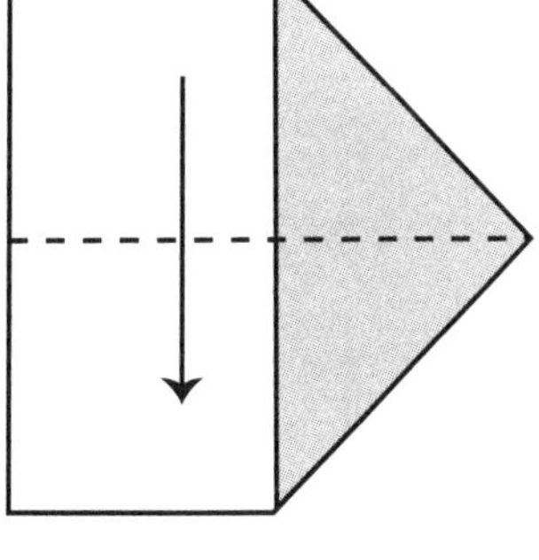

4. Fold the top left corner down as indicated by the dashed line and unfold.

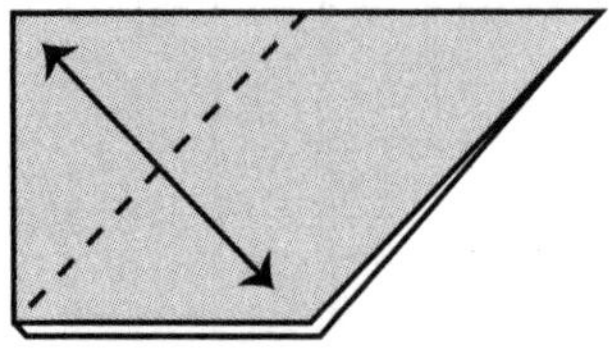

5. Tuck the top left corner into the shape by reversing the fold you made in the previous step.

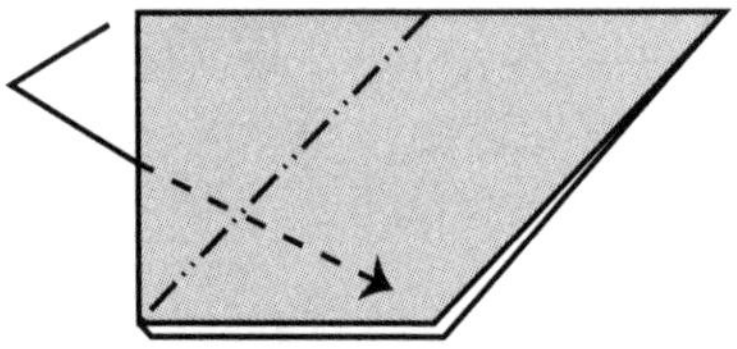

6. Your shape should look like the one below. Repeat steps one through five so that you have a total of eight units, four of one color, and four of another.

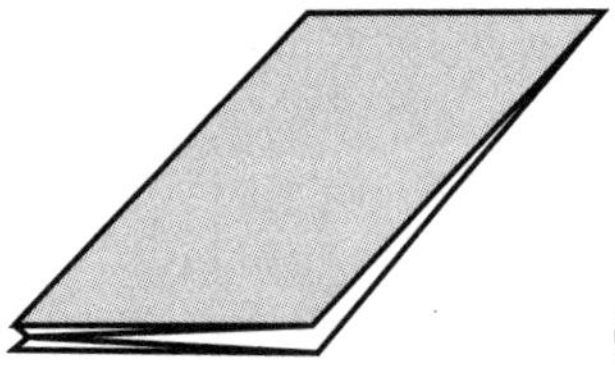

(x 8)

TRANSFORMING PINWHEEL Assembly

1. Take one piece of each color and place them together as shown. One piece should be between the flaps of the other piece.

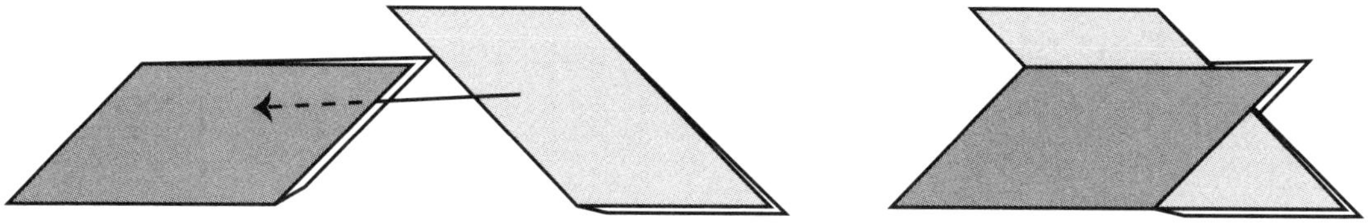

2. Fold both points from the first piece into the middle of the second as indicated so that they hold the pieces firmly together.

3. Connect a third piece onto the first two in the same fashion, again folding the points to lock the pieces in place.

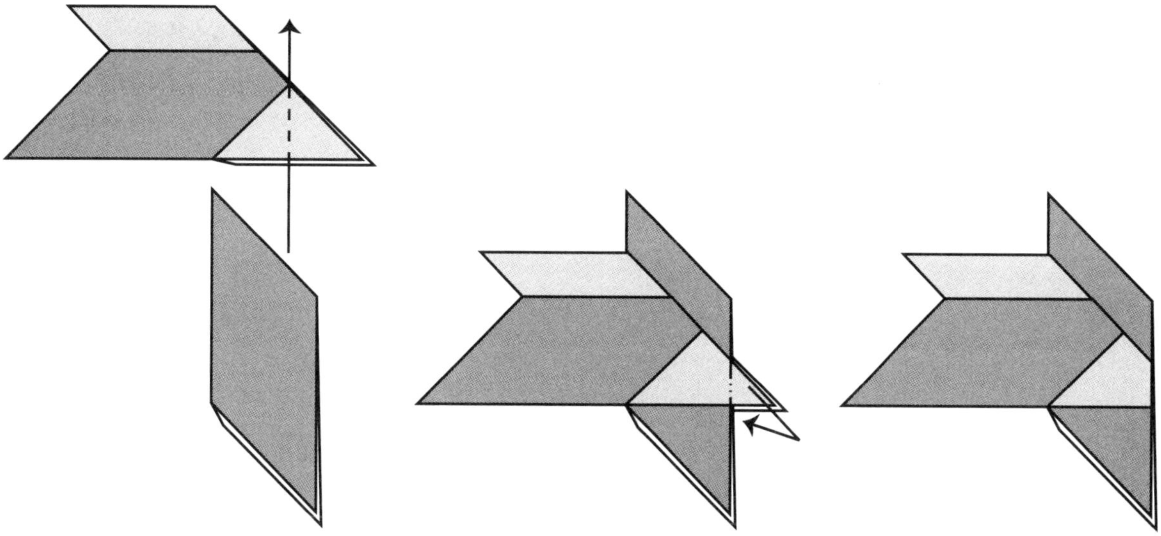

4. Continue to attach all of the remaining pieces to form a closed pinwheel like the one below.

5. Once you have secured your pinwheel, hold the pieces marked with arrows (two at a time) and pull gently outwards. Your pinwheel should stretch itself into the ring shape shown at the right. Pushing the pieces back together will return the ring to the pinwheel shape.

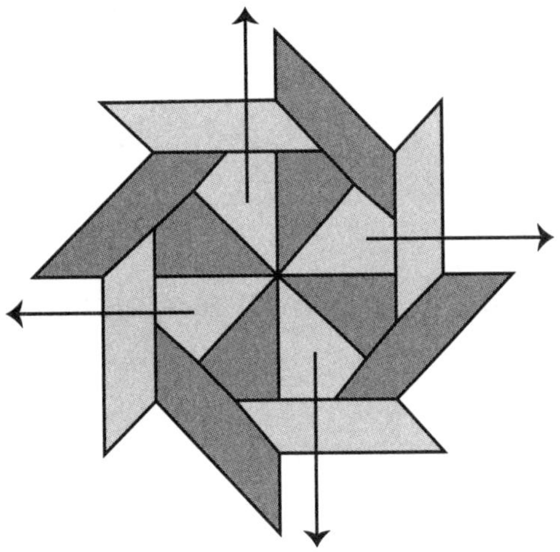

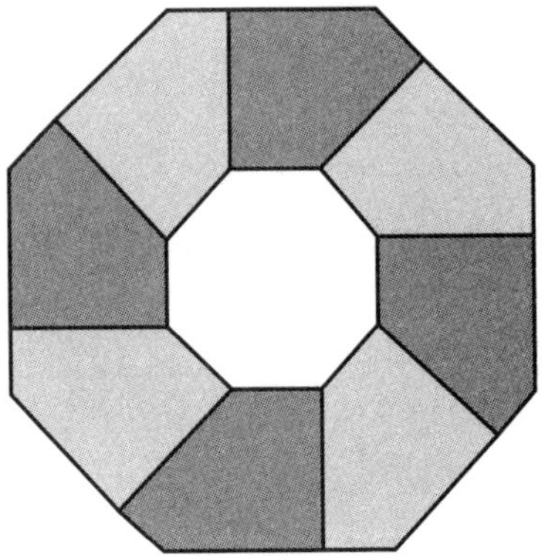

TRANSFORMING PINWHEEL Anatomy

Fold an additional pinwheel unit. Unfold it and use it to help you draw the fold lines in the square below. (You do not need to draw in the two small squares in the corners.) The center of each side of the square has been marked to help you draw in the lines accurately.

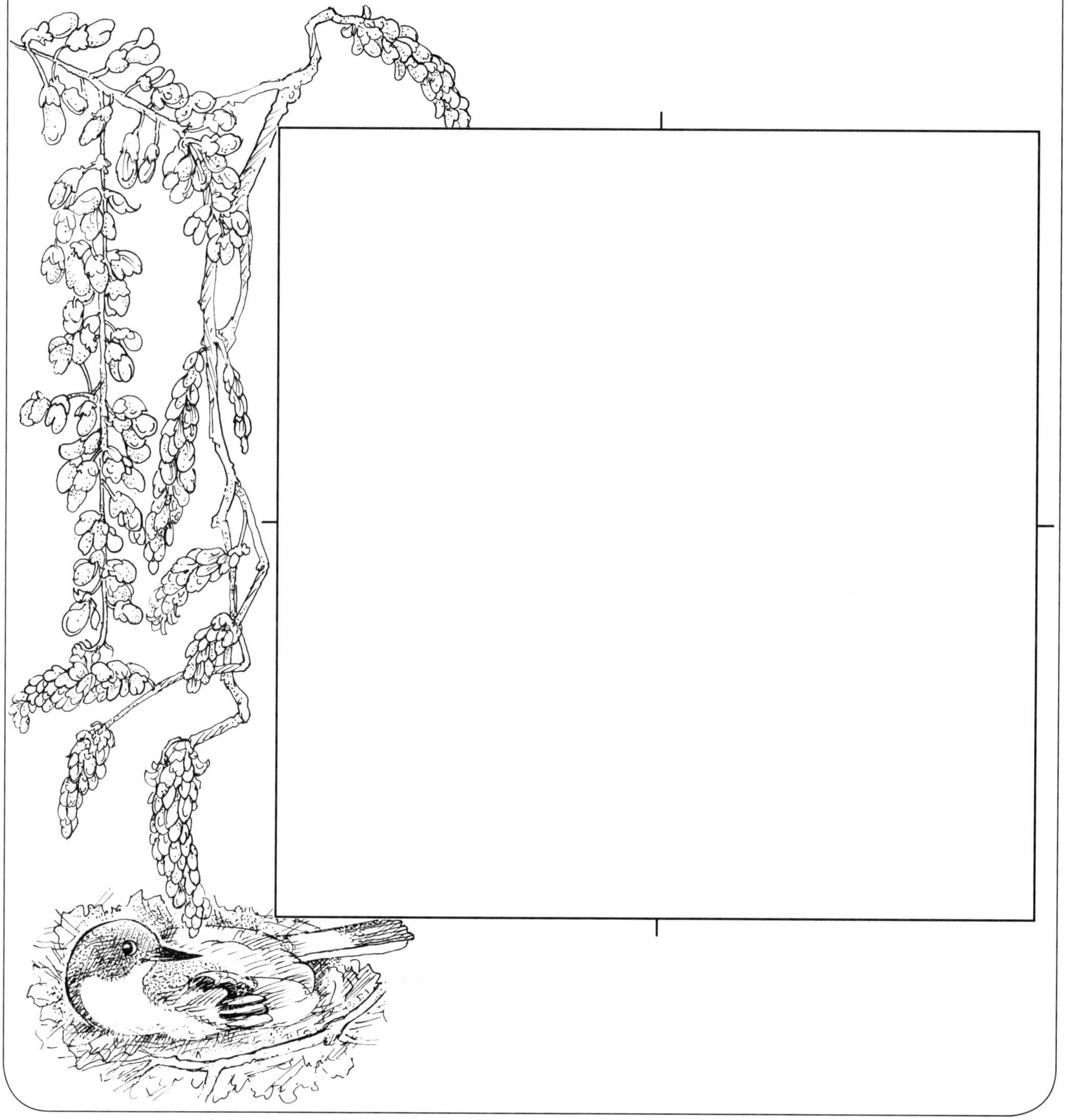

TRANSFORMING PINWHEEL

Exploration

1. How were you able to draw in the diagonal fold lines accurately?

2. What angles are the diagonal lines in the unfolded unit? How do you know?

3. Are there any lines of symmetry in this unit? If so, mark them on the diagram and list what kind they are below.

4. List each different kind of shape that is created by the fold lines. Organize your list by the number of sides each shape has.

5. What congruent shapes exist in the fold lines? How do you know they are congruent?

6. What similar shapes exist in the fold lines? How do you know they are similar?

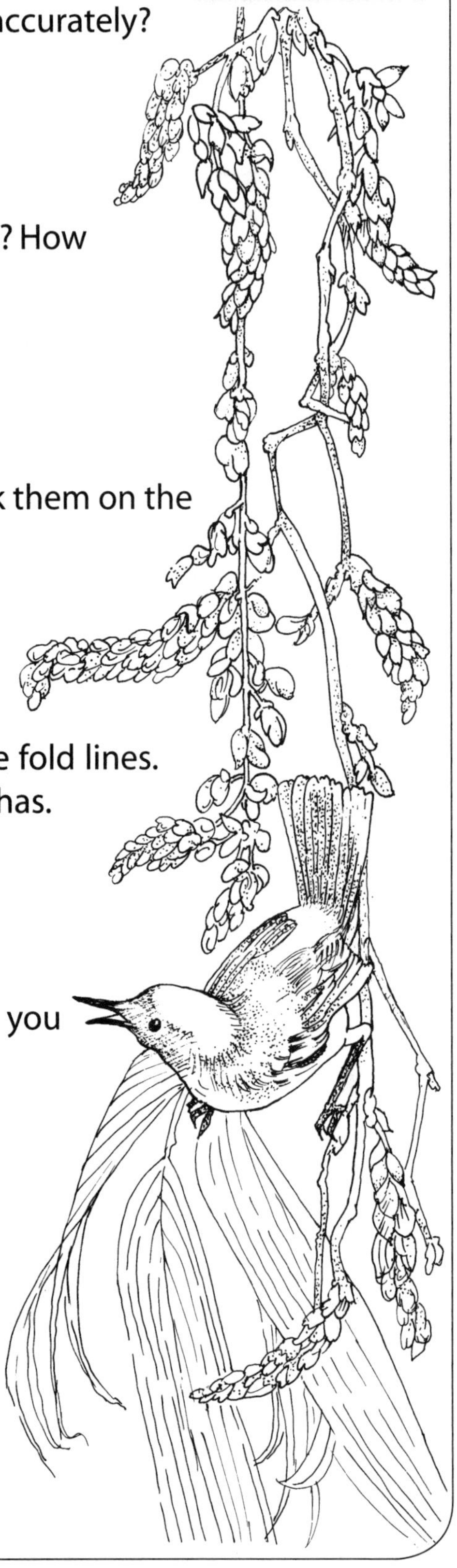

TRANSFORMING PINWHEEL Exploration

Use your completed model to help you answer the following questions.

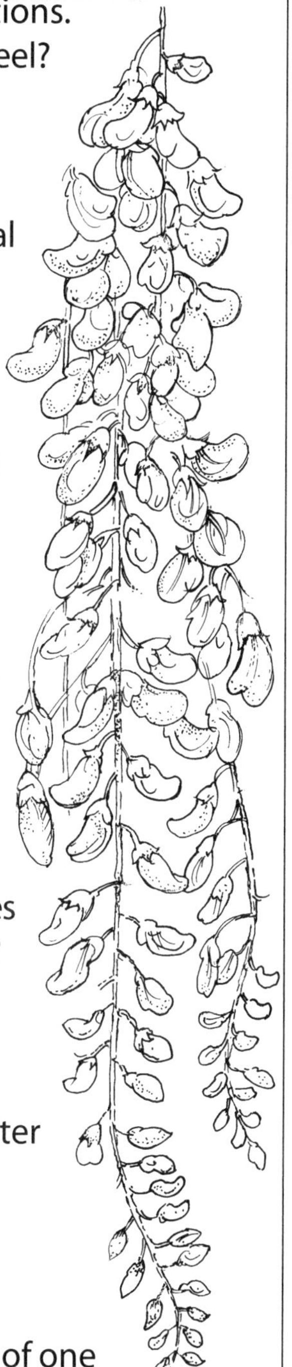

1. What shape is the large section that forms the center of the pinwheel?

2. What shape are each of the smaller sections that make up this central section? How are these shapes related to each other?

3. What shape are the "points" that come off the center section of the pinwheel? How are these shapes related to each other?

4. When the model is in the ring form, what shape is in the center? How does this shape relate to the shape in the center of the pinwheel?

5. What shape are the sections that make up the ring? How do these shapes relate to the shapes that make up the center section of the pinwheel?

6. Without measuring, predict which form of this model has the greater diameter, the ring or the pinwheel. Justify your prediction.

7. Measure the model in each form. (Be sure to measure from the tip of one point to the tip of the opposite point of the pinwheel.) Which form actually has the greater diameter? Is this what you predicted? Why or why not?

TRANSFORMING PINWHEEL

Symmetry

1. What types of symmetry exist in this model when it is in the pinwheel form?

2. Identify and label all lines/points of symmetry on the diagram below.

3. What types of symmetry exist in this model when it is in the ring form?

4. Identify and label all lines/points of symmetry on the diagram below.

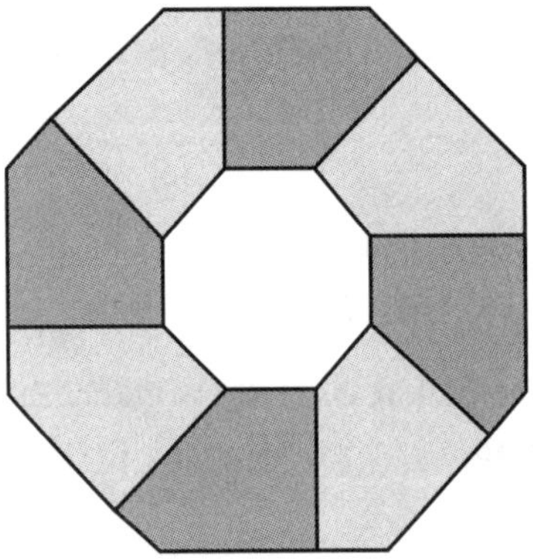

ROTATING TETRAHEDRON

KEY QUESTION

What are the properties of your rotating tetrahedron, and how do they compare to those of a regular tetrahedron?

MATH

Properties of geometric figures
- faces
- edges
- vertices

Surface area

INTEGRATED PROCESSES

Observing
Comparing and contrasting

PAPER

Three squares per model
One square for exploration

ADDITIONAL MATERIALS

Rulers
Colored pens or pencils

CREATOR

Tomoko Fusè

FOCUS

Students will fold and decorate a rotating tetrahedron model and explore its properties.

Management

1. The paper used for this model is critical to the success of the final product. The heavier weight paper that is suited for the unit origami models in this book can be too thick and cumbersome when it is folded into the rotating tetrahedron shape. A lighter weight paper is recommended, although if the paper is too lightweight, it tends to tear easily. White copy paper is a good choice.
2. This model looks the nicest when it is made from three pieces that are all the same color and has designs drawn on each of the faces.

Procedure

1. Hand out the folding instructions (pages 141-144) and three squares of paper to each student.
2. Go through the folding instructions for the unit as a class, and have students fold the remaining two units individually.
3. Distribute colored pens or pencils to the class and have students decorate the faces of their rotating tetrahedron. Be sure that students understand that each face marked with the same letter should have the same design drawn on it. Also be sure that they understand that the faces labeled "a" will meet in the final model to form the same equilateral triangle shape as the other faces.
4. Once students have decorated the faces of their rotating tetrahedrons, take the class through the assembly process step by step.
5. After students have assembled their rotating tetrahedrons, hand out the remaining student sheets, rulers, and an additional square of paper to each student.
6. Have students work together in groups to fold an additional rotating tetrahedron unit and answer the exploration questions.
7. When all groups have finished, close with a time of class discussion and sharing.

Discussion

1. What shapes are the faces of the rotating tetrahedron? [isosceles triangles]
2. How many faces does the model have? [24] How many of these are visible at any given time? [18]
3. How many vertices does the rotating tetrahedron have? [12] How many edges? [36]
4. How does the number of faces, edges and vertices compare to those for the regular tetrahedron? [A regular tetrahedron has four faces, six edges, and four vertices. The rotating tetrahedron has six times as many faces and edges and three times as many vertices.]
5. Why do you think this model is called a rotating tetrahedron? [The shapes of which it is composed are very close to being tetrahedrons.]
6. What similarities does this model have to the tetrahedron? What differences does it have?

Extension

Challenge advanced students to determine the volume of the rotating tetrahedron model based on the actual size of the original squares that they used to fold the units.

Solutions

Rotating Tetrahedron Anatomy

1. Draw in the horizontal and vertical fold lines on the unit. Into what shapes do they divide the original square? [16 congruent squares] How do you know? [The fold lines divide the square into fourths horizontally and vertically.]
2. Draw in the diagonal fold lines. Into what shapes do they divide the original square? Be as specific as possible. [The diagonal fold lines create a series of triangular shapes. Some of the triangles are equilateral, and some are 30°-60°-90° triangles. When two equilateral triangles are combined edge-to-edge, they form a rhombus, and when two 30°-60°-90° triangles are combined edge-to-edge, they form an obtuse isosceles triangle.]
3. Identify the sections of your unfolded unit that become the faces of your rotating tetrahedron. (See diagram below.) How do you know which sections those are?
4. Look at the sections of the unfolded unit that become faces. How could you use the way the fold lines divide the paper to determine the surface area of one face? [The bases and heights of the triangles that form the faces are all one-fourth the length of a side of the original square. To determine the surface area of one face, divide the length of the side of the original square by four, and plug that number in to the formula to determine the surface area of a triangle ($\frac{1}{2}$ base x height).
5. Assume that the length of one side of the original square is 12 cm. What is the surface area of one face? [$12 \div 4 = 3$, $\frac{1}{2}(3) \times 3 = 4.5$ units^2] ...of the whole figure? [$4.5 \times 24 = 108$ units^2]

The square section outlined by the dashed line represents the portion of each original square that becomes the faces of the rotating tetrahedron.

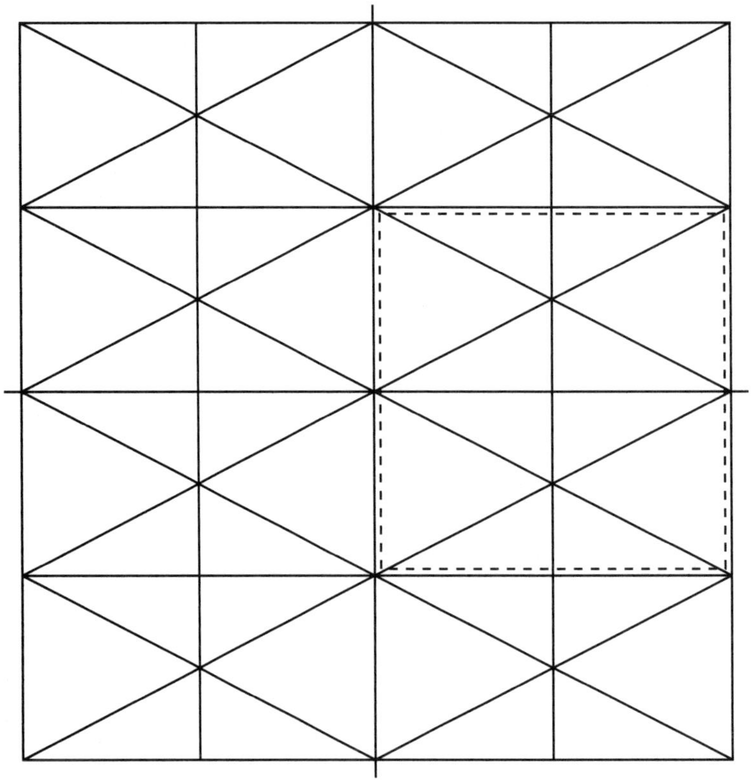

ROTATING TETRAHEDRON

Folding Instructions

1. Fold the paper in half horizontally and unfold.

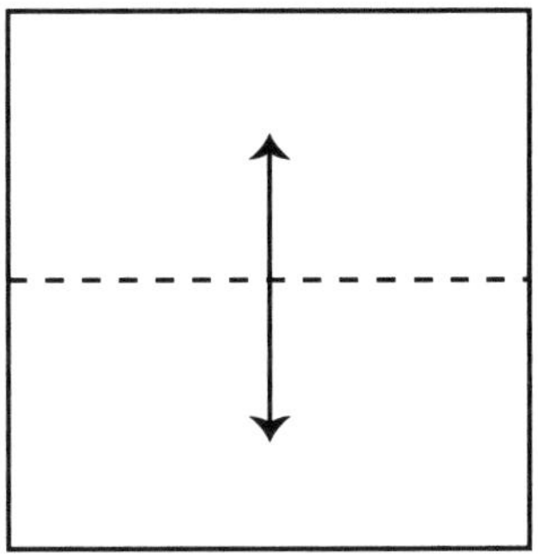

2. Fold the top and bottom edges in to meet the midline.

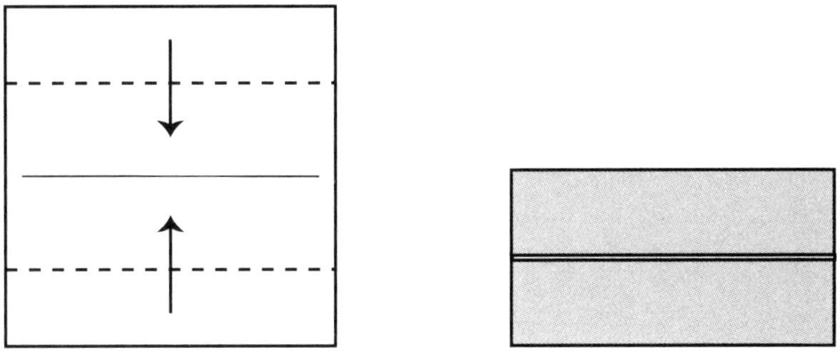

3. Fold the resulting rectangle diagonally, from corner to corner as shown, and unfold.

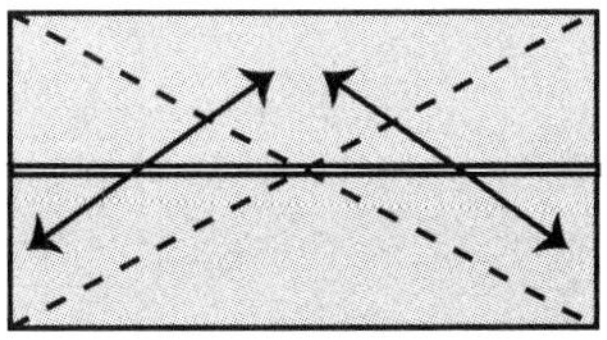

4. Filp the paper over, fold it in half vertically, and unfold.

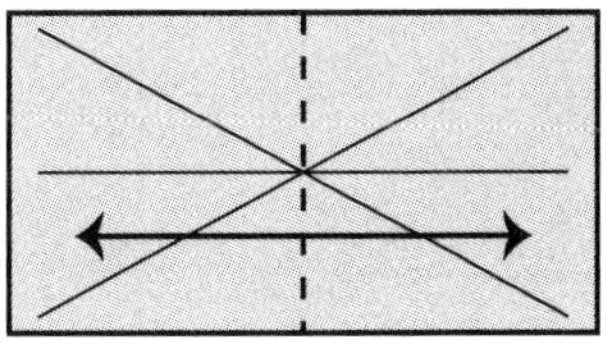

5. Fold the left and right edges in to the vertical midline and unfold.

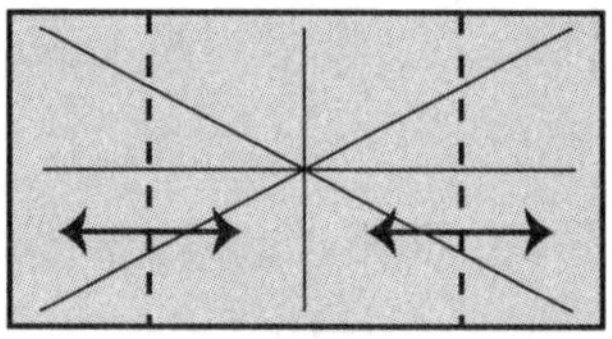

6. Flip the paper back to the front and fold diagonally as you did in step three, this time folding from the vertical midline to the horizontal midline on each side.

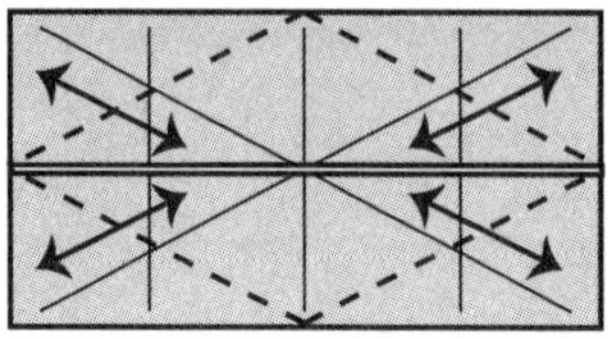

7. This is your completed piece. Repeat steps one through six so that you have a total of three pieces like the one below.

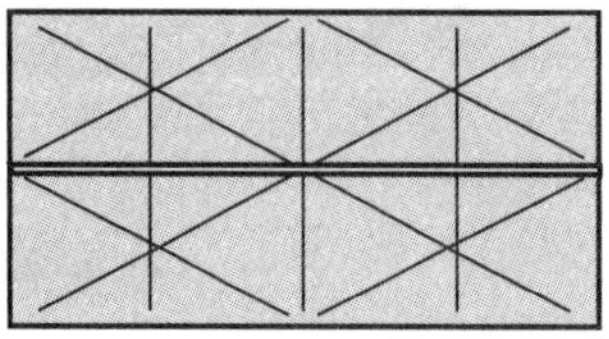
(x 3)

ROTATING TETRAHEDRON

Decoration

1. Take your three units and fit them together as shown below so that they make one long strip.

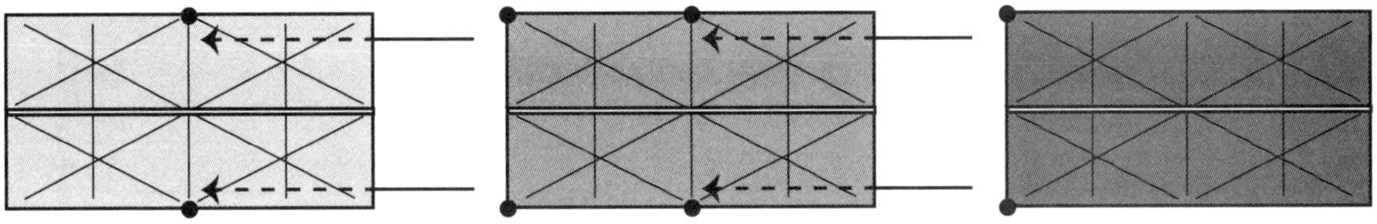

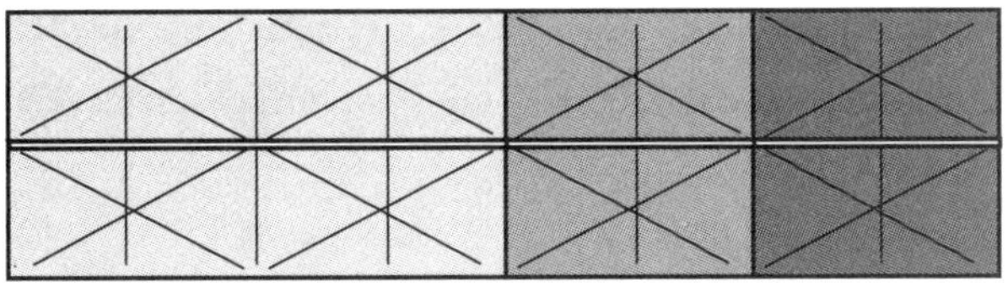

2. Turn the strip over and draw a pattern on each set of faces. The faces are marked by the letters a, b, c and d. Draw the same pattern on each face of the same letter.

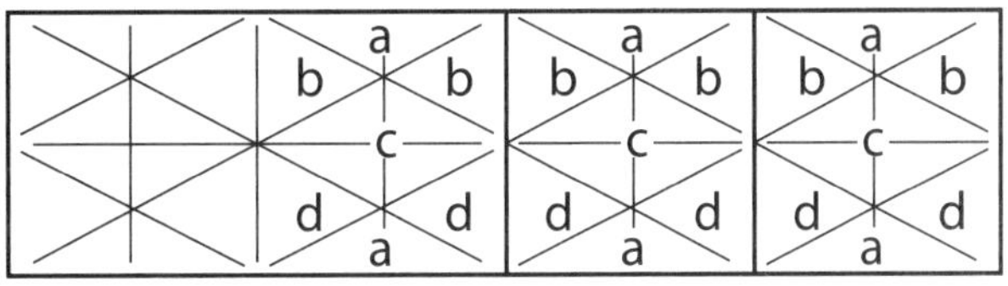

3. A sample decoration is shown below.

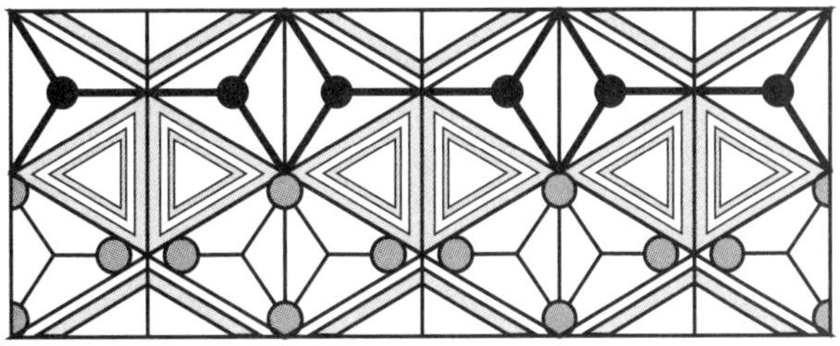

ROTATING TETRAHEDRON

Assembly

1. Make a loop out of the three units by connecting the first piece to the third piece as shown below. The faces that you colored should be on the outside of the loop.

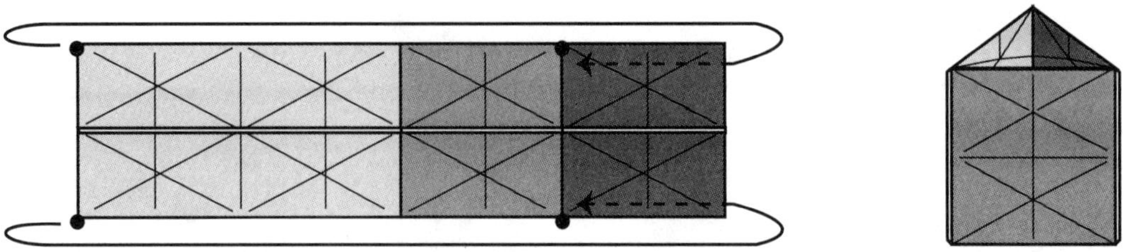

2. Using a combination of mountain and valley folds as shown, fold along the existing crease lines to tuck the top and bottom of the loop in towards the center.

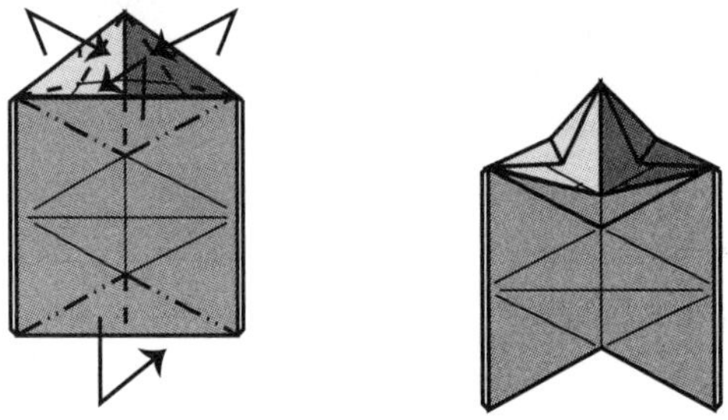

3. Bring each the resulting points in to the center by folding again along the existing crease lines. This is your completed rotating tetrahedron.

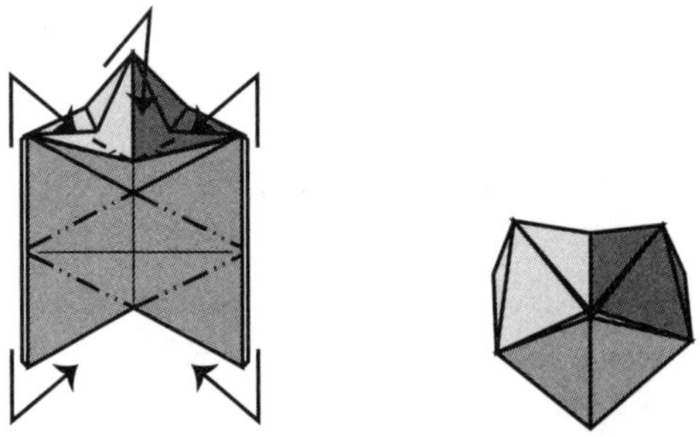

4. To rotate your shape, bring the three points on the top into the center. This should cause the ring to flip and reveal a different face. Carefully rotate the shape several times to enforce the creases. You should be able to rotate your ring in a continuous loop so that you can see each of the faces you colored in order.

ROTATING TETRAHEDRON

Exploration

Use your rotating tetrahedron model to answer the questions below.

1. What shapes are the faces of the rotating tetrahedron?

2. How many faces does the model have? How many of these are visible at any given time?

3. How many vertices does the rotating tetrahedron have? How many edges?

4. How do the number of faces, edges, and vertices compare to those for the regular tetrahedron?

5. Why do you think this model is called a rotating tetrahedron?

6. What similarities does this model have to the tetrahedron? What differences does it have?

ROTATING TETRAHEDRON

Anatomy

Fold an additional unit of the rotating tetrahedron, unfold it, and use it to help you answer the questions below. Use the square on the following page to draw in the fold lines as requested.

1. Draw in the horizontal and vertical fold lines on the unit. Into what shapes do they divide the original square? How do you know?

2. Draw in the diagonal fold lines. Into what shapes do they divide the original square? Be as specific as possible.

3. Identify the sections of your unfolded unit that become the faces of the rotating tetrahedron. How do you know which sections those are?

4. Look at the sections of the unfolded unit that become faces. How could you use the way the fold lines divide the paper to determine the surface area of one face? Describe your plan below.

5. Assume that the length of one side of the original square is 12 cm. What is the surface area of one face? ...of the whole figure? Show your work below.

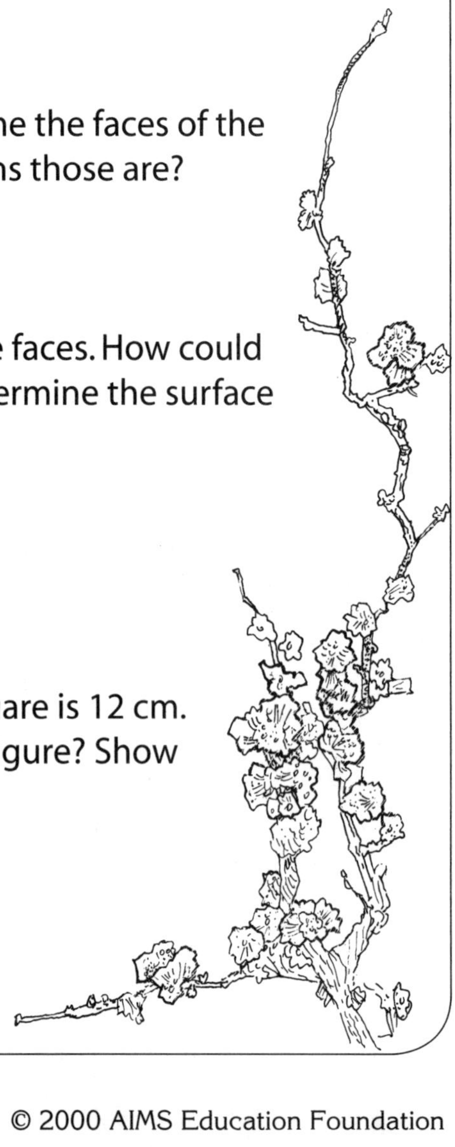

ROTATING TETRAHEDRON

Anatomy

Follow the instructions on the previous page to draw in the fold lines for the rotating tetrahedron.

HEXAFLEXAGON

FOCUS

Students will create a hexaflexagon and explore some of its properties and the patterns that are inherent in the process.

KEY QUESTIONS

What are the properties of your hexaflexagon?

What patterns can you discover in the way it works?

MATH

Properties of polygons
- faces
- angles

Math patterns

INTEGRATED PROCESSES

Observing
Collecting and recording data
Interpreting data

PAPER

One strip per model, 4 cm by 46 cm

ADDITIONAL MATERIALS

Colored pencils or pens
Rulers
Glue sticks
Scissors

CREATOR

Arthur Stone

Management

1. Each student will need a long thin strip of paper to construct the hexaflexagon. The models will be more durable and usable if they are made from paper about the weight of card stock. Sentence strips are the right weight and length, and can be cut in half or thirds to give a good width. The wider the strip, the longer it must be to complete the hexaflexagon. Although adding machine tape works well in terms of length and width, it is quite flimsy, and hexaflexagons made from it tend to deteriorate quickly.

Procedure

1. Hand out the folding instructions (sheets 151-154), paper strips, rulers, and glue sticks to each student. Go through the construction of the hexaflexagon step by step. Emphasize precision, because even slightly inaccurate folds can lead to a hexaflexagon that will get stuck or rip when flexed repeatedly.
2. Once students have successfully constructed their hexaflexagons, hand out the remaining student sheets and colored pencils. You may wish to give students multiple copies of the table on student sheet page 157 so that they can record more than one sequence of flexes.
3. Go through the instructions for flexing and coloring the hexaflexagon step by step, making sure that students are able to discover and color each of the six faces. Encourage creative and colorful designs that will look different when they are reoriented in another direction.
4. When students have colored each of the six faces and recorded the patterns they have used, have them practice flexing their hexaflexagon until they are comfortable with the procedure and can do it in a systematic and consistent way. Be sure that they record the method that they develop and use it consistently.
5. If students have not already been working in groups, have them get into groups of three or four. If the flexing techniques among group members differ, have them decide which technique is the best and use that one. Working together, have them record several different series of flexes. It is important for students to work in groups so that the person flexing the hexaflexagon does not have to write down the information and can concentrate on being consistent with the method being used.
6. When groups have data from each member's trial, have them work together to answer the questions on the final student sheet.
7. Close with a time of class discussion and sharing. Compare the various techniques used by the groups and help students search for patterns in the flexing process.

Discussion

1. What shape is the hexaflexagon? [hexagon] What is the measure of each interior angle? [120°] How do you know? [Each side is divided into six equilateral triangles. The measure of each interior angle of an equialteral triangle is 60°. Each interior angle of the hexagon is formed by two adjacent equilateral triangles, making the angle 120°.]
2. Why are there six different faces that can appear when you flex the hexaflexagon? [There were 18 triangles in the original strip of paper. Since you use both sides of the paper, that makes the total number of triangles 36. Each face of the hexaflexagon is made up of six triangles. Thirty-six triangles divided by six gives you six faces.] How many variations of these faces are there? [Each face appears in its original orientation and one alternate orientation, for a total of 12 variations.]
3. Do you think it would be possible to get more than six faces? [It is.] Less than six faces? [It is.] How would you do it? [To get differing numbers of faces, the original number of triangles must be different, and sometimes the shape of the original paper must also be different.]
4. Describe the technique your group used to flex the hexaflexagon.
5. Using this technique, what is the minimum number of flexes it takes to see each variation of all six faces? [The minimum possible is 12.] How do you know? (See *Solutions* for more detail.)
6. Based on your classmates' answers, does it appear that some techniques are better than others, or do they all let you see each face in the same number of moves? [This will depend largely on how the different groups decide to flex their hexaflexagons. If no groups were able to reach 12 as the minimum for the number of flexes to see each face, as a class you will want to discover how to reach that minimum. This will enable a discussion of the patterns that can only be found in a sequence that uses the minimum number of flexes to show each face.]
7. When you use the method to get all faces in the minimum number of moves, how many times does each face appear? (See *Solutions*.)
8. What other interesting things did you discover about the hexaflexagon?

Extensions

1. Explore the history of flexagons and the people who discovered them. Martin Gardner's *Hexaflexagons and Other Mathematical Diversions* is a good place to start.
2. Have students build flexagons with other numbers of faces. There are many internet sites that explore other possibilities and give diagrams.
3. Have students make a hexaflexagon puzzle where a hidden message or a series of clues appears on the different faces.

Solutions

There are only two possible sequences for flexing a hexaflexagon when you start with the same two faces on top and bottom and use a consistent technique. The two solutions shown both start with face A on the top and face B on the bottom. The method used is the one described on the student sheet where you begin by pinching two adjacent triangles together using a mountain fold, and continue with those same two triangles until you are no longer able to. Once you get stuck, you move one set of triangles counterclockwise and begin again. A star by the face indicates that the face was not in its original orientation.

Flex	Top Face	Bottom Face	Same Triangles?
0	A	B	Yes
1	C*	A*	Yes
2	F*	C*	No
3	A*	F	No
4	C*	A*	Yes
5	B*	C	Yes
6	D	B*	No
7	C*	D*	No
8	B*	C	Yes
9	A	B	Yes
10	E	A*	No
11	B*	E*	No
12	A	B	Yes

Flex	Top Face	Bottom Face	Same Triangles?
0	A	B	Yes
1	E	A*	No
2	B*	E*	No
3	A	B	Yes
4	C*	A*	Yes
5	F*	C*	No
6	A*	F	No
7	C*	A*	Yee
8	B*	C	Yes
9	D	B*	No
10	C*	D*	No
11	B*	C	Yes
12	A	B	Yes

The frequency of each face in the tables below is counted for the flexes from one to 12, not counting flex 0.

Face	Frequency	Face	Frequency	Total
A	2	A*	4	6
B	2	B*	4	6
C	2	C*	4	6
D	1	D*	1	2
E	1	E*	1	2
F	1	F*	1	2

Face	Frequency	Face	Frequency	Total
A	2	A*	4	6
B	2	B*	4	6
C	2	C*	4	6
D	1	D*	1	2
E	1	E*	1	2
F	1	F*	1	2

Patterns

All of these patterns assume the method described above, or one which produces identical results, was used.

- It takes a minimum of 12 flexes to see every variation of every face.
- The face on the top will always be on the bottom after the next flex. Sometimes it will be in the same orientation, sometimes in a different orientation.
- You can do two flexes using the same set of triangles, then you will be forced to rotate for the next two flexes. This pattern of twos continues indefinitely.
- Faces A, B, and C occur three times as often as faces D, E, and F.
- The variations of faces A, B and C occur twice as often as the original orientations.

HEXAFLEXAGON

Folding Instructions

1. Begin with a strip of paper about four centimeters (1.5 inches) wide and 46 centimeters (18 inches) long. Using a ruler, find the horizontal midline and draw a light line in pencil from the left edge of the paper as shown.

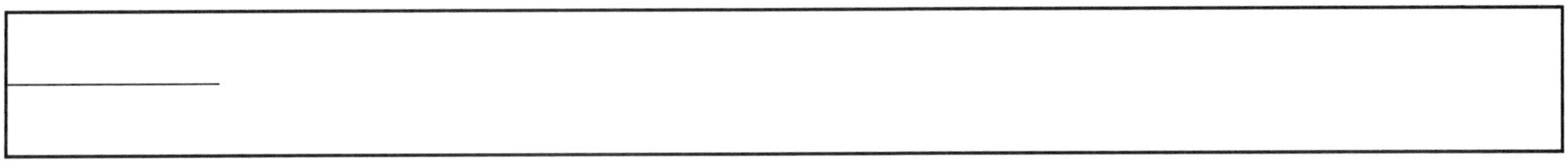

2. Crease the top left corner as indicated by the dashed line so that the corner touches the horizontal midline.

3. Cut the along the crease you just folded and discard the small triangle.

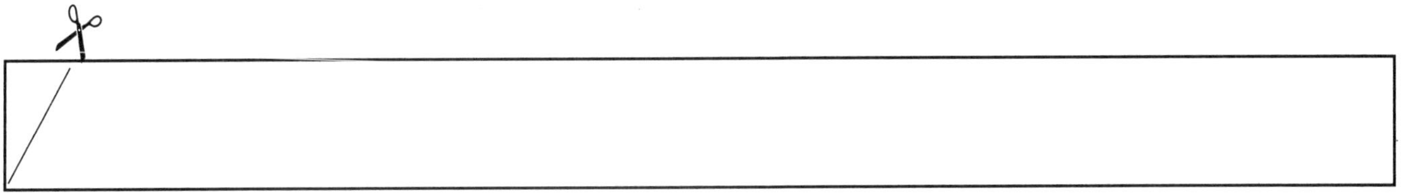

4. Valley fold the bottom left corner up so that the left side of the paper lies flush with the top of the paper. Mountain fold the paper back down so that the new left edge is flush with the bottom of the paper. Repeat this process of alternating valley and mountain folds to create equilateral triangles until you have reached the end of the paper.

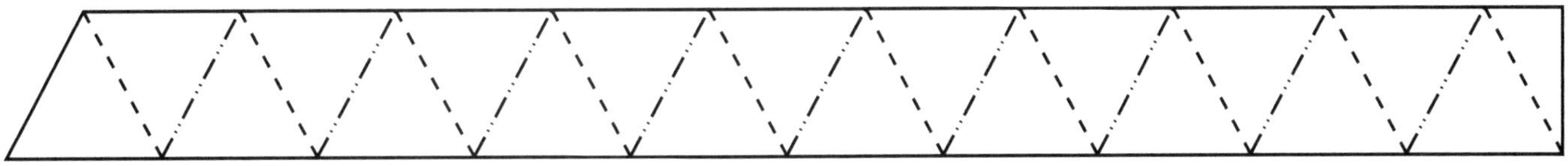

The paper should now look something like an accordion, with each face folded back on itself.

5. Unfold the paper and lay it flat. Count 19 triangles starting from the left side and cut off any extra.

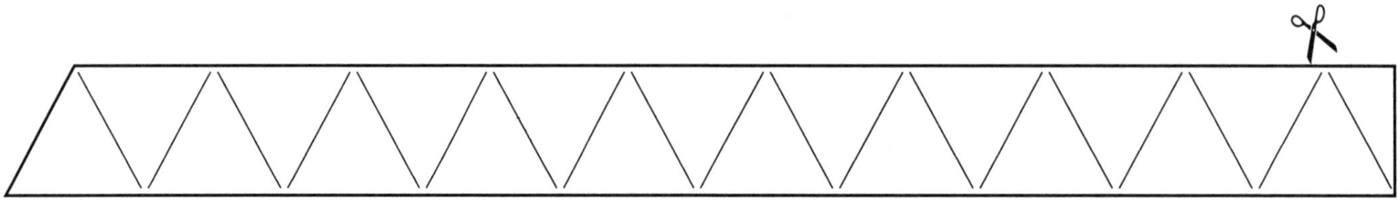

6. Lightly label both sides of the paper as shown below using pencil. Notice that the blank triangle is at opposite ends on the front and the back.

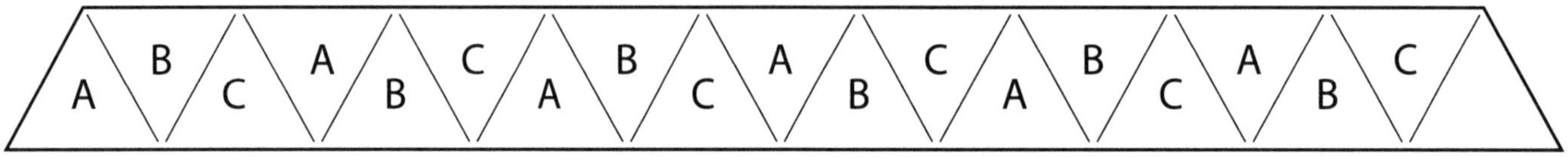

Front

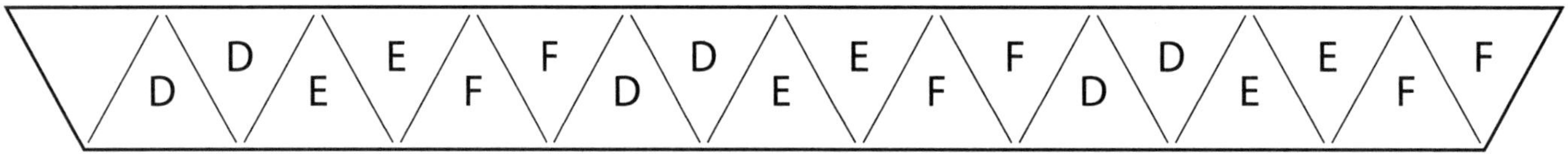

Back

7. Using mountain folds where indicated, fold the paper so that the letters on the back come together D with D, E with E, and F with F.

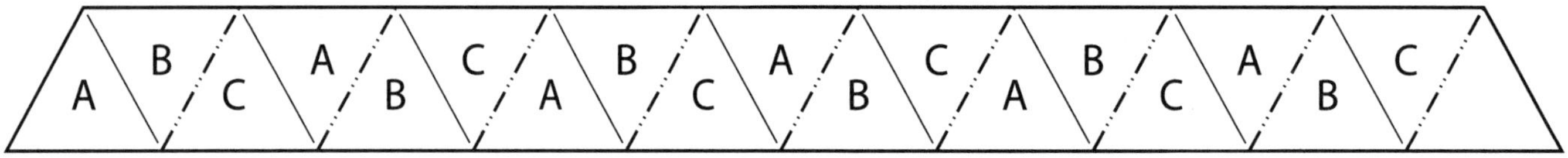

This should leave a paper that is folded around itself and looks like the diagram below.

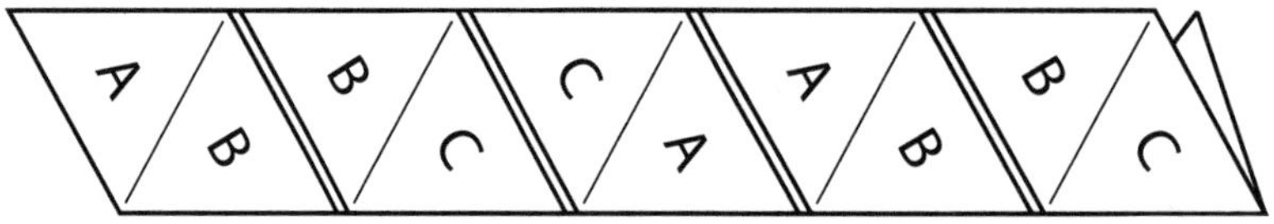

8. Using a mountain fold where indicated, bring the left side of the paper down as shown.

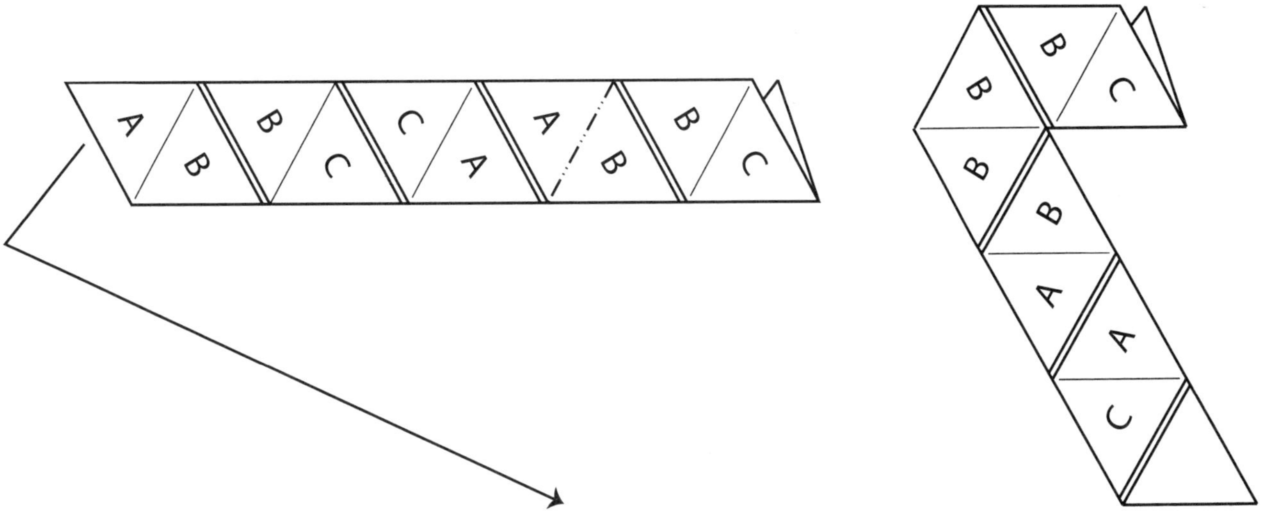

9. Using a mountain fold where indicated, bring the bottom edge back up to the top. The flap that you fold up should go in front of the flap labeled C so that each triangle on the front is labeled B.

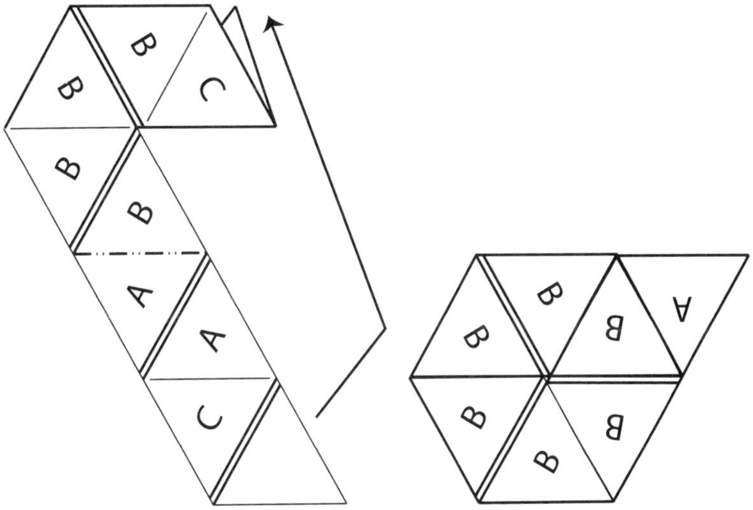

10. Fold the flap labeled A back and paste it to the blank flap directly behind it.

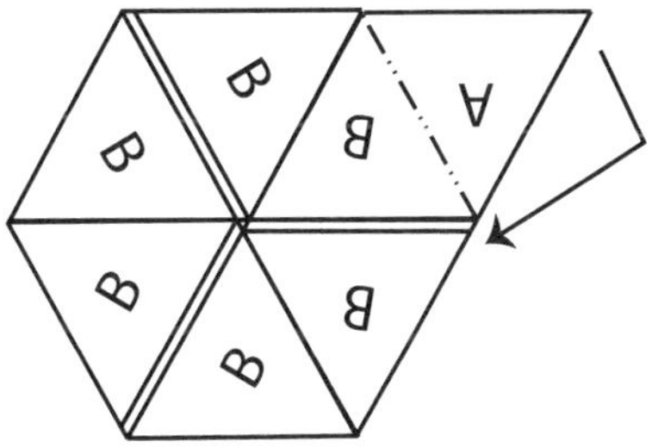

11. If you have done everything correctly, each triangle on the front will be labeled with B, and each triangle on the back with A.

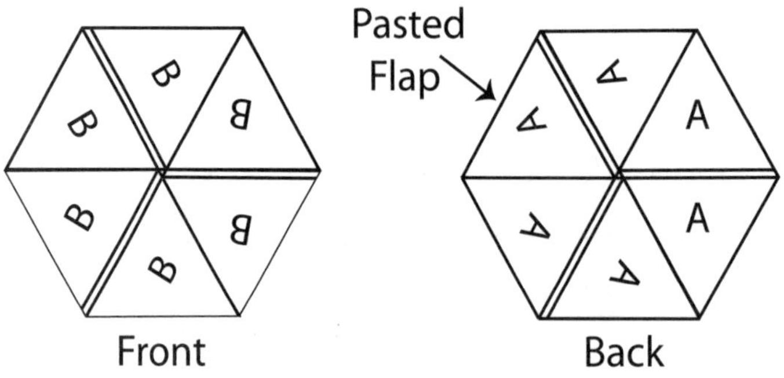

This is the completed hexaflexagon. The actual technical name for this shape is a hexa-hexaflexagon because it has six sides and six faces. This distinguishes it from the many hexaflexagon variations that all have six sides, but differing numbers of faces (tri-hexaflexagon, tetra-hexaflexagon, etc.). However, for simplicity, this shape will be referred to as a hexaflexagon.

HEXAFLEXAGON

Exploration

Coloring the Hexaflexagon

In order to use the hexaflexagon, color each set of faces. Begin by erasing the letters from both sides of the hexaflexagon that are currently visible (A and B). Color each individual triangle on one face the same way. The more creative the colors and patterns, the more impressive the hexaflexagon will be when it is used. Try to create patterns that use different colors and cover different sections of each triangle. A few sample patterns are shown below.

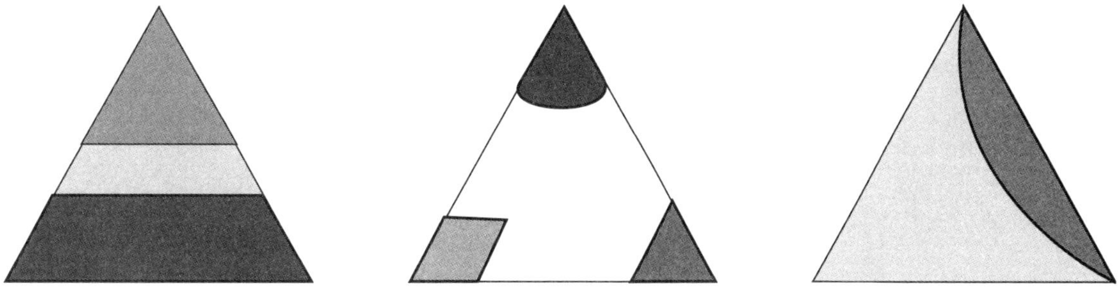

Flexing the Hexaflexagon

There are various methods and techniques which can be used to change the faces of the hexaflexagon. Use the technique described below or develop your own method.

1. Pinch two adjacent triangles on one face of the hexaflexagon together using a mountain fold. Hold these two triangles between your thumb and first finger, leaving the rest of the hexaflexagon loose.
2. While holding the triangles together, push the corner farthest from your fingers down as far as it will go.
3. This should cause the hexaflexagon to pop open, showing four triangles of a different face. Release the two triangles that you were holding together to reveal this new face.
4. Repeat steps one to three starting with the same two triangles pinched together until you are no longer able to continue. Then move over to an adjacent pair of triangles and begin again.

Continue to flex the hexaflexagon until you have discovered all of the six faces and colored each one with a unique pattern.

HEXAFLEXAGON

Exploration

Record the pattern you colored on each triangle of the faces in the appropriate space below.

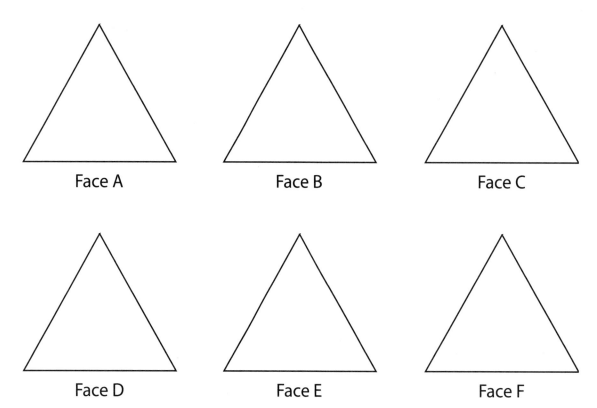

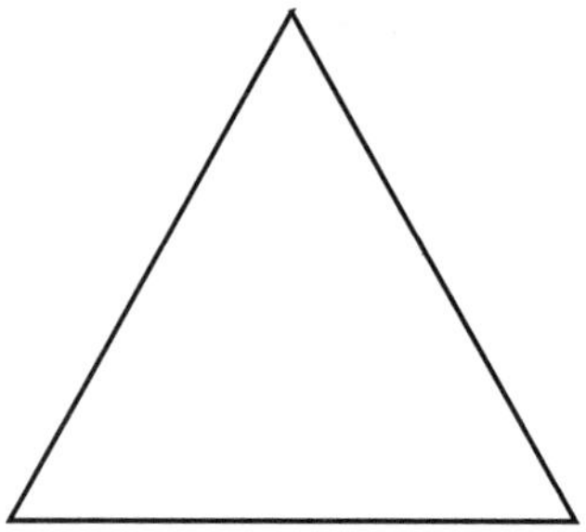

Face A

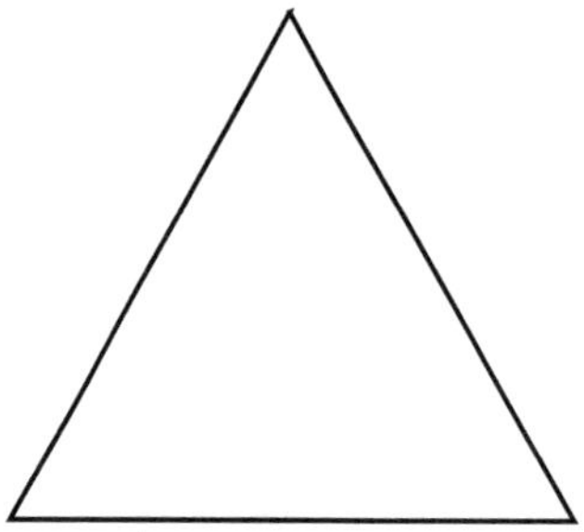

Face B

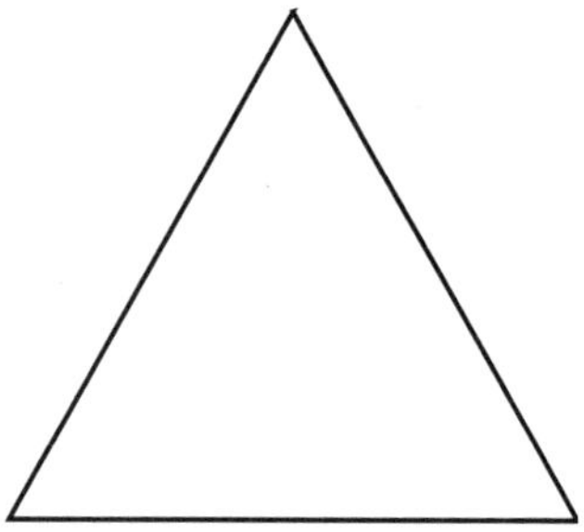

Face C

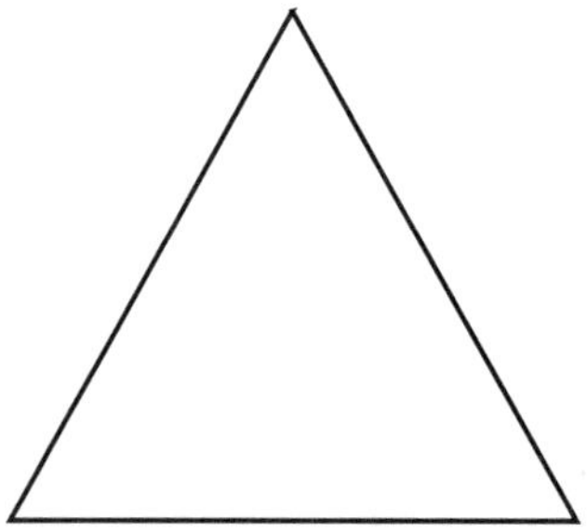

Face D

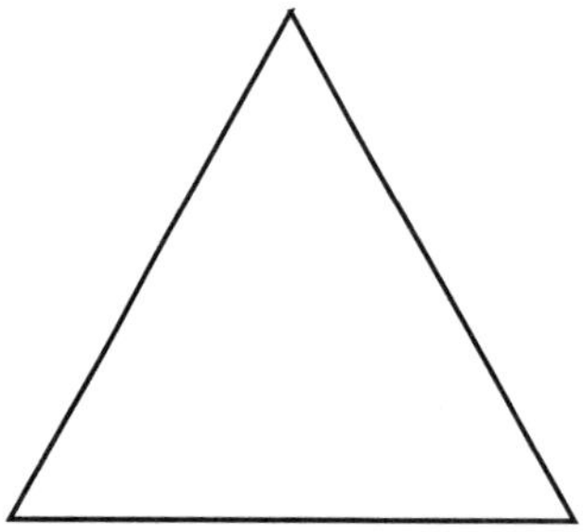

Face E

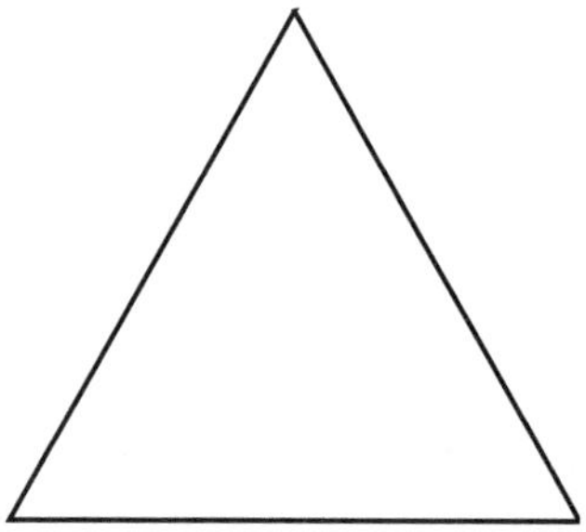

Face F

Now that all six faces of the hexaflexagon have been colored, practice flexing it so that you can see all six faces in the fewest number of flexes. Record the technique you develop below.

HEXAFLEXAGON Exploration

Using the method you developed, record each flex it takes for you to see all six faces of the hexaflexagon. The *Flex* column tells how many times you have flexed your shape. In the *Top Face* and *Bottom Face* columns, record which faces are on the top and bottom after each flex. Put a star by the letter of the face if it has a different orientation than it did when you originally colored it. In the *Same Triangles?* column indicate whether you pinched the same two triangles together for the next flex (Yes) or if you used two different triangles to continue (No).

Flex	Top Face	Bottom Face	Same Triangles?
0	A	B	Yes
1			
2			
3			
4			
5			
6			
7			
8			
9			
10			
11			
12			
13			
14			

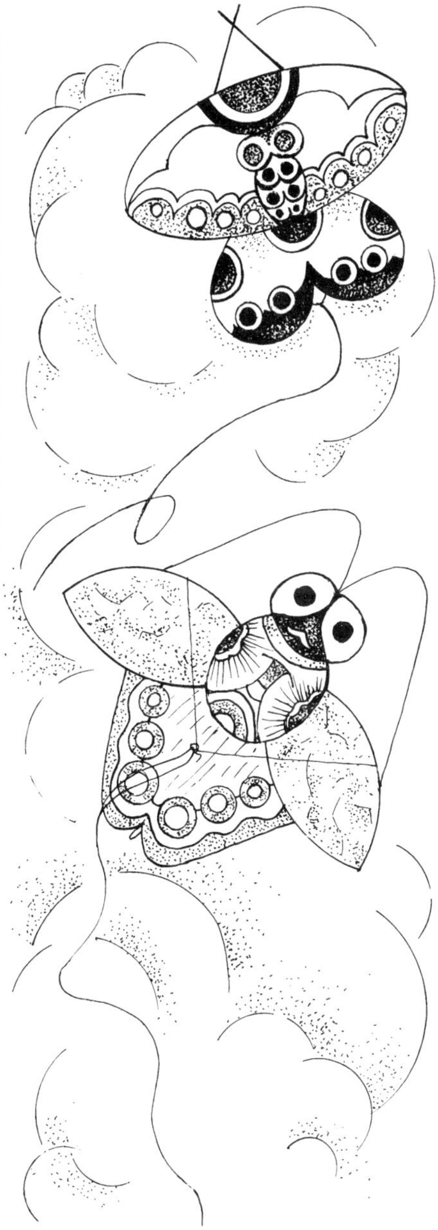

HEXAFLEXAGON Exploration

Answer these questions after you have finished your exploration.

1. What shape is the hexaflexagon? What is the measure of each interior angle? How do you know?

2. Why are there six different faces that can appear when you flex the hexaflexagon? How many variations of these faces are there?

3. Do you think it would be possible to make a flexagon with more than six faces? ...less than six faces? How would you do it?

4. What is the minimum number of flexes it takes to see each variation of all six faces? How do you know?

5. When you use the method to get all faces in the minimum number of moves, how many times does each face appear?

6. What other interesting things did you discover about the hexaflexagon?

ORIGAMI SQUARED

Focus

Students will fold the five pieces of a classic geometric puzzle and put them together to form a square.

Key Question

How can you arrange your five folded shapes to form a square?

Math

Geometric properties
- perimeter
- area

Puzzles

Integrated Processes

Observing
Comparing and contrasting
Generalizing

Paper

Five squares per puzzle

Creator

Marc Kirschenbaum

Management

1. Unlike a majority of the activities in this book, these puzzle pieces are best made with traditional origami paper because of its light weight. Using the heavier weight paper that is well-suited for unit origami models results in bulky and less precise pieces in this puzzle.
2. This activity will probably need to be spread over several days to give students a chance to solve the puzzle. The folding can be done in one period, but it will take most students much longer than that to figure out how to make a square with their puzzle pieces. Only after students have solved the puzzle will they be able to go on to the explorations.
3. There are two parts to the exploration section. In the first part students are challenged to develop a plan that would allow them to determine the area of each individual puzzle piece if they were given the area of only one piece. In the second section, students will compare the perimeters and areas of the three possible squares that can be made with one or more of the puzzle pieces. Depending on the needs and abilities of your students, only one, or neither of these explorations may be appropriate.
4. In order to complete the second part of the exploration successfully, students must be able to work with square roots.

Procedure

1. Hand out the folding instructions (pages 163-171) and five squares of paper to each student.
2. Go over the instructions for folding each piece step by step. Note that the first three to seven steps are the same for each puzzle piece.
3. Once students have folded all five pieces correctly, hand out the next student sheet and go over the objective of the puzzle with the class.
4. When students have had a chance to solve the puzzle and discover all of the possible squares, they will be ready to move on to the exploration section.
5. If students will be doing the first part of the exploration, you will need to give them an area value (actual or arbitrary) for the puzzle piece that they choose once they have developed their plan. Using this value, they will then determine the areas of the other puzzle pieces.
6. Once students have solved the puzzle and completed the appropriate explorations, close with a time of class discussion and sharing.

Discussion

Main Puzzle

1. How do the five puzzle pieces fit together to make a square? (See *Solutions*.)
2. Is it possible to make squares using different numbers of puzzle pieces? [Yes, see *Solutions* for details.]
3. What other squares are possible? [A four-piece square and a one-piece square.]

Exploration Part One

1. Which puzzle piece did you choose to know the area of? Why?
2. Describe your plan for finding the area of each piece based on that information.
3. Are there other pieces that would also have worked with your plan? Why or why not?
4. What does this tell you about the way that the puzzle pieces are related to each other?

Exploration Part Two

1. If the perimeter of the five-piece square is 24 units, what is the area of that square? [36 units^2] How do you know? [If the perimeter is 24 units, each side is 6 units ($24 \div 4 = 6$), and 6 squared is 36.]
2. What is the area of the four-piece square? [32 units^2] ...the perimeter? [$16\sqrt{2}$] How do you know? (See *Solutions*.)
3. What is the area of the small square piece? [4 units^2] ...the perimeter? [8 units] How do you know? (See *Solutions*.)
4. What is the difference in area between the five-piece square and the four-piece square? [4 units^2] Why? [The four-piece square does not use the small square puzzle piece, which has an area of 4 units^2.]

Extension

Based on what students learned about how the puzzle pieces are related to each other, challenge them to make a new square dissection puzzle that uses different shapes, but the same principles. They can even be challenged to make origami models of their puzzles.

Solutions

There is only one possible way to make a square using all five puzzle pieces. By using only four of the five puzzle pieces, a second, slightly smaller square is possible. If you also count the square puzzle piece itself, there are three possible squares that can be made by using different numbers of puzzle pieces. All three possibilities are shown below.

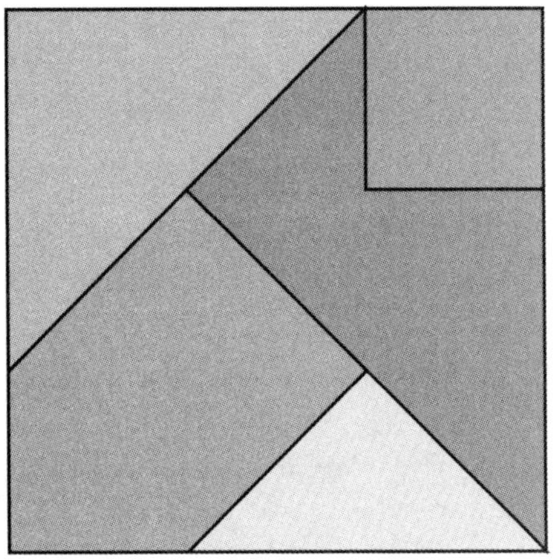

Square using all five pieces

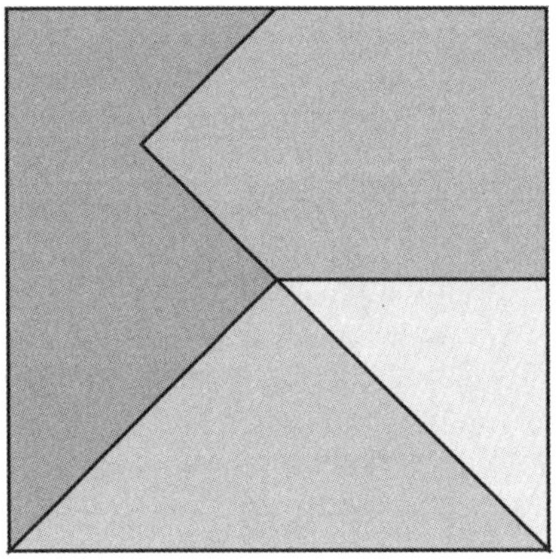

Square using only four pieces

Square puzzle piece

Exploration Part One

In the first part of the exploration, students are asked to choose one puzzle piece and develop a plan that would let them determine the area of each piece, given the area of the one piece they chose. One of many possible methods for doing this is described below. Your students may develop other, equally valid, stategies.

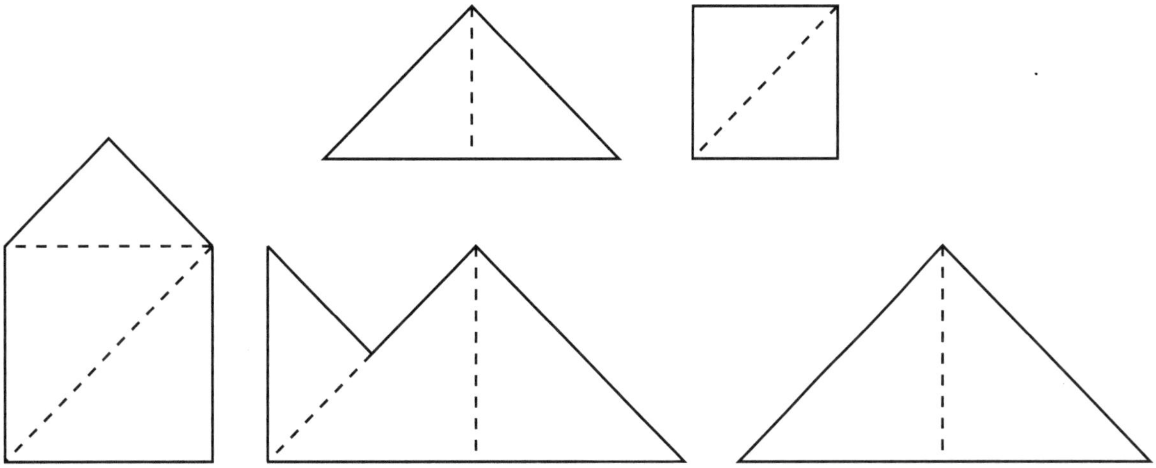

As you can see, each puzzle piece can be divided into either two or three triangles. These triangles are two different sizes: congruent with the small triangular puzzle piece, or congruent with half of the small triangular puzzle piece. Notice also that the square puzzle piece and the small triangular puzzle piece can both be divided into two congruent triangles, indicating that they have the same area.

When the pieces are divided in this way, it is easy to see that knowing the area of either the small triangular puzzle piece or the square puzzle piece would quickly allow you to determine the area of every other puzzle piece.

Let us assume that we know the area of the square puzzle piece to be six units^2. This means that the area of the small triangular puzzle piece is also six units^2, and one-half of the square puzzle piece (or the small triangular puzzle piece) is three units^2. The large triangular puzzle piece would threfore have an area of 12 units^2 because it is made up of two small triangular puzzle pieces. The remaining two pieces would both have areas of 15 units^2 because they are each made up of two small triangular puzzle pieces and one-half of the square puzzle piece.

Exploration Part Two

In the second part of the exploration, students are asked to determine the area and perimeter of the three possible squares based on the knowledge that the perimeter of the largest square is 24 units.* If the perimeter is 24 units, this means that each side of the square is six units (24 ÷ 4 = 6), making the area 36 units^2.

Knowing this information allows us to determine the dimensions of the small square puzzle piece because, as you can see in the diagram, the small square piece has sides that are one third the length of the sides in the large square. Once it is determined that the square puzzle piece has sides that are two units each (6 ÷ 3 = 2), it quickly follows that it has a perimeter of 8 units and an area of 4 units^2.

With this knowledge, it can be determined that the square that uses only four pieces has an area of 32 units^2 because it does not use the small square puzzle piece (36 units^2 - 4 units^2 = 32 units^2). If the area of the four-piece square is 32 units^2, then the length of each side is $\sqrt{32}$ units, which can be reduced to $4\sqrt{2}$ units. This makes the perimeter of the smaller square $16\sqrt{2}$ units.

* Note: If you are using six-inch squares of paper, the units are the actual dimensions of the pieces in inches.

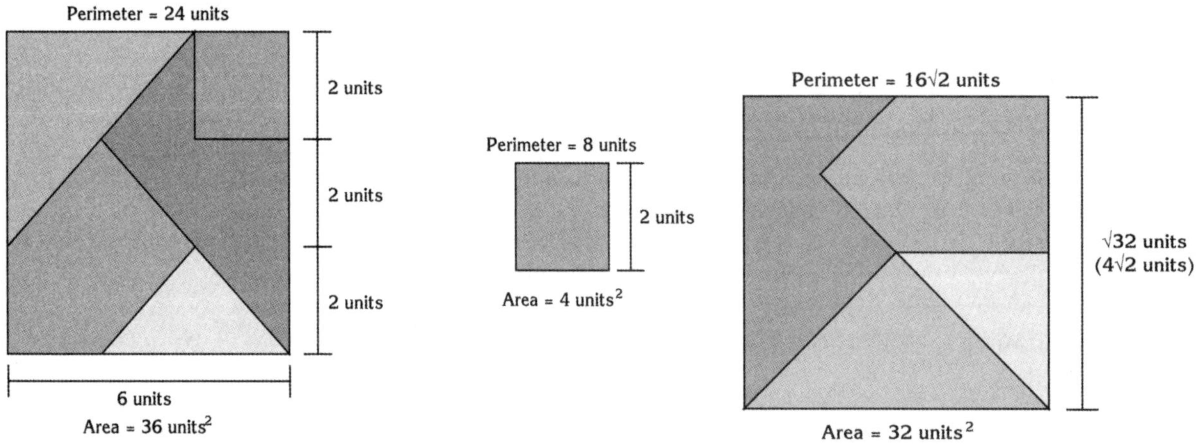

The information described above is summarized in this table from the student sheet.

# of pieces in square	Perimeter in units	Length of each side	Area in units^2
5	24	6	36
4	$16\sqrt{2}$	$\sqrt{32}$ ($4\sqrt{2}$)	32
1	8	2	4

ORIGAMI SQUARED

Puzzle Piece One

1. Start with the square of paper colored side up. Fold it in half vertically, making only a short crease at the top of the paper.

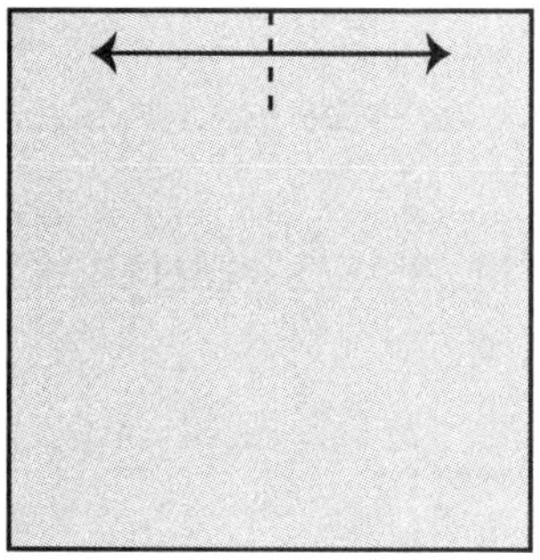

2. Fold the bottom left corner up so that it touches the top of the crease.

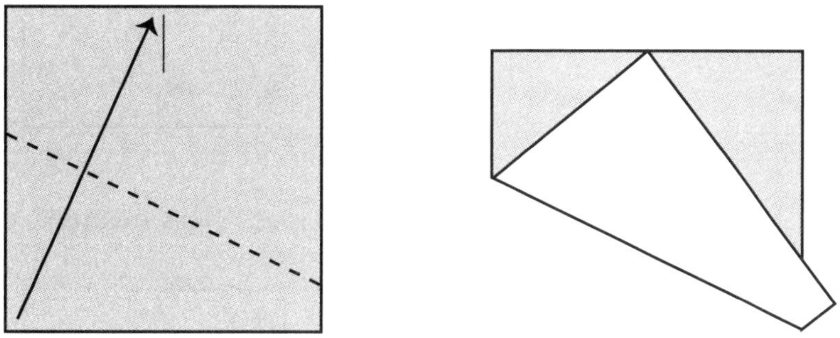

3. Flip the paper over and make a horizontal fold across the paper so that the top left corner meets the point where the front of the paper crosses the left edge.

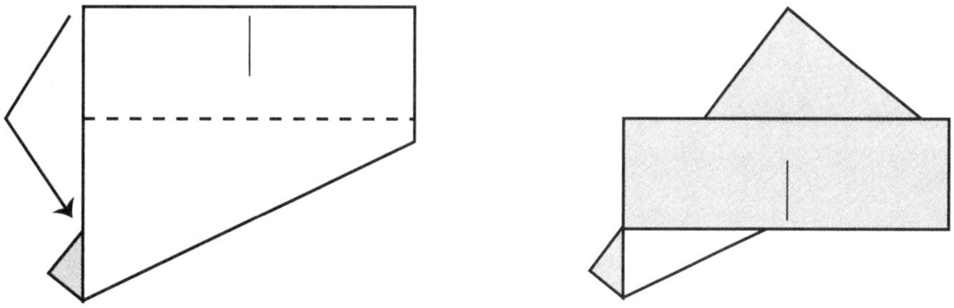

4. Unfold the paper so that the white side is face up, being sure to orient it as shown in the diagram. Fold the right edge in to meet the vertical fold line, crease, and unfold.

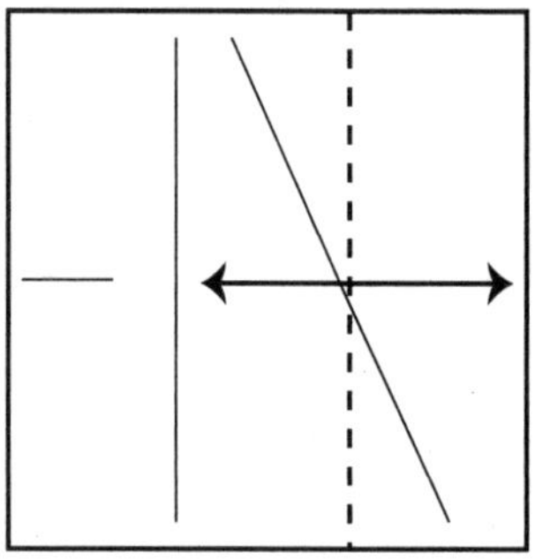

5. Fold the top right and bottom left corners in so that the top and bottom edges are flush with the nearest vertical fold lines.

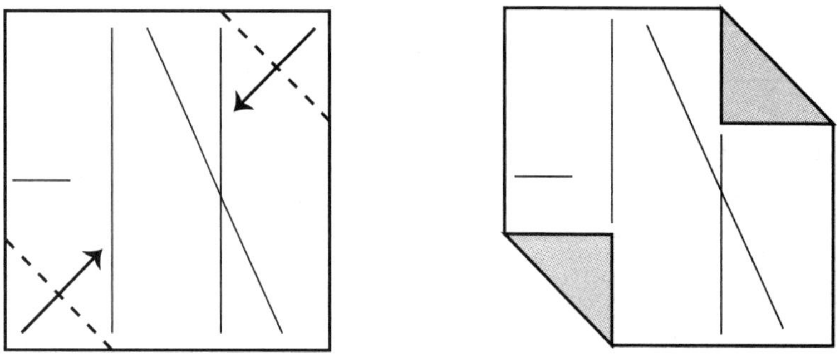

6. Fold both sides in so that the edges of the paper meet the nearest vertical fold lines.

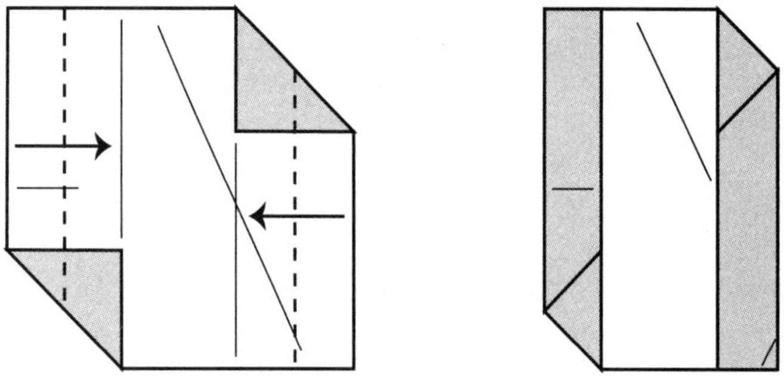

7. Crease the top of the paper horizontally as shown. Fold the bottom of the paper up in the same fashion.

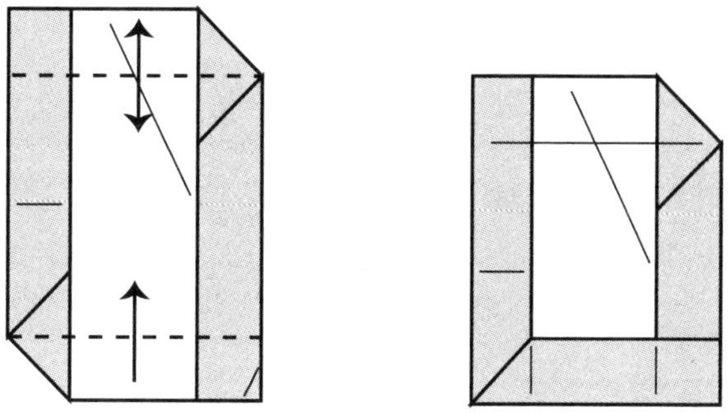

8. Fold the bottom right corner up to the point where the top horizontal crease meets the left side of the paper.

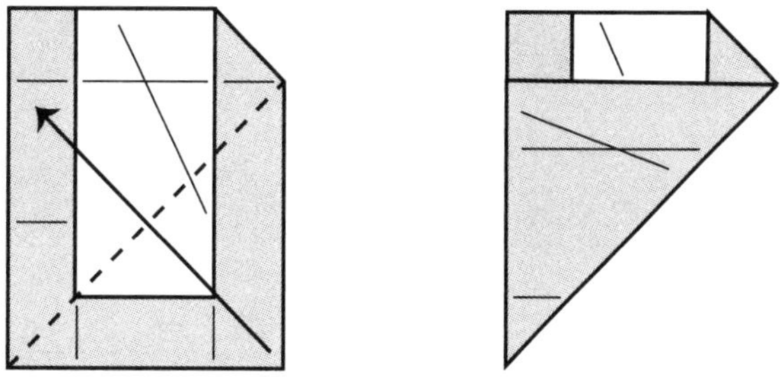

9. Tuck the top flap into the pocket created by your last fold. This is the first puzzle piece.

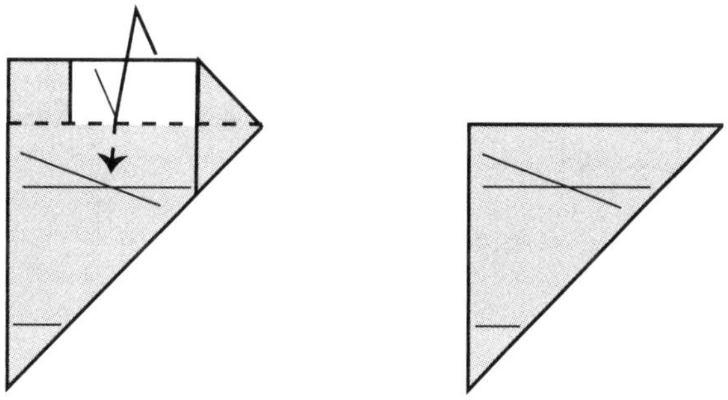

Puzzle Piece Two

1. Repeat the first four steps from *Puzzle Piece One* with the second square of paper. Fold the paper in half along the diagonal, as shown.

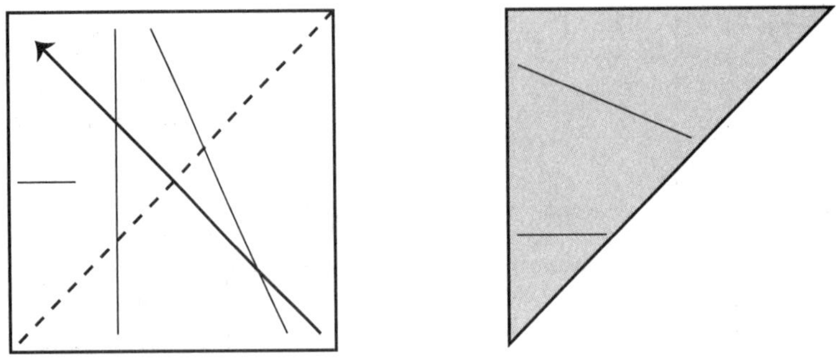

2. Fold the top right corner down as indicated so that the two points marked with dots meet.

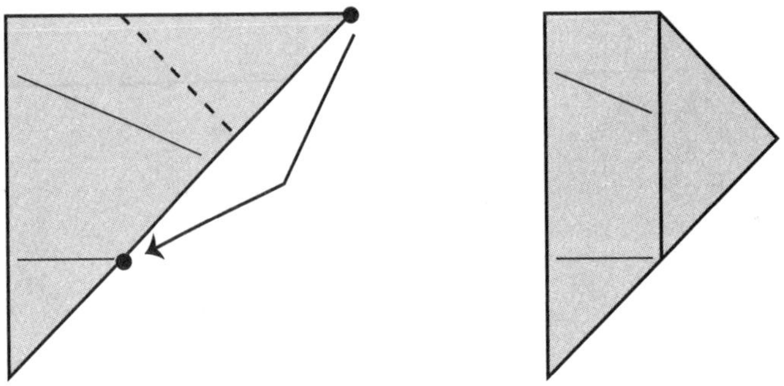

3. Fold the bottom left point up to meet the right point as shown. As you make the fold, tuck the point into the pocket. This is the second puzzle piece.

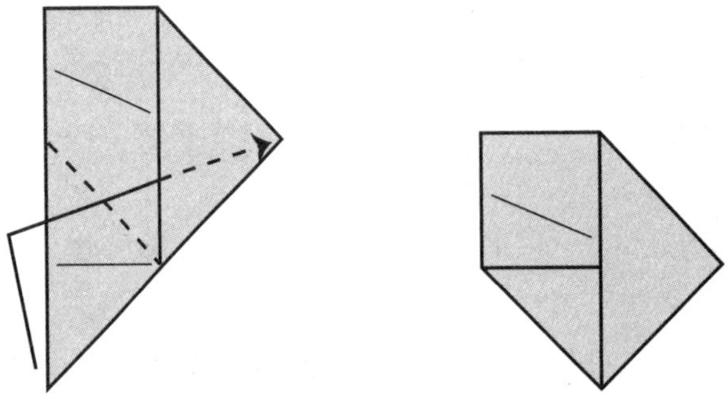

Puzzle Piece Three

1. Repeat the first five steps from *Puzzle Piece One* with the third square of paper. Fold the top left corner in along the diagonal indicated.

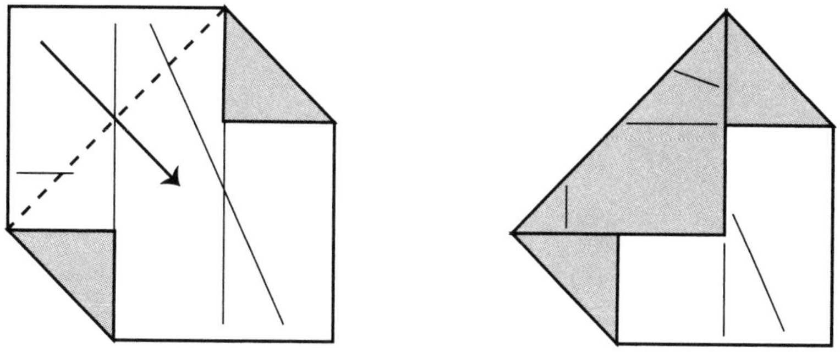

2. Fold the top of the paper down so that the point meets the corner that was folded down in the previous step.

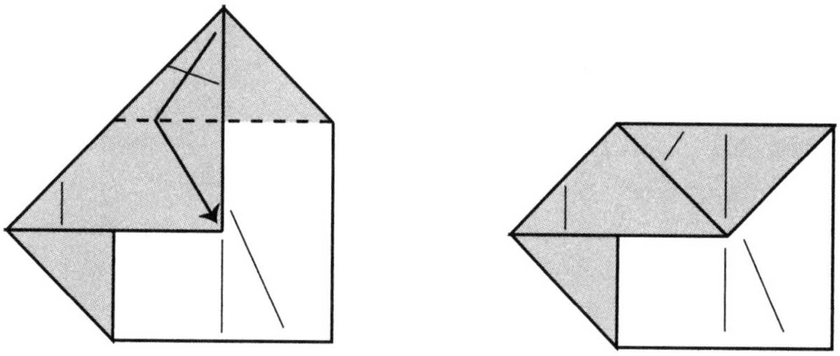

3. Fold the bottom right corner of the paper up as indicated.

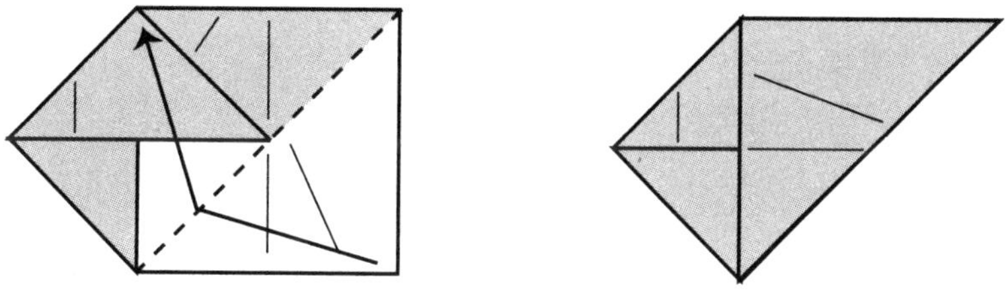

4. Fold the top right corner down to meet the bottom point of the shape.

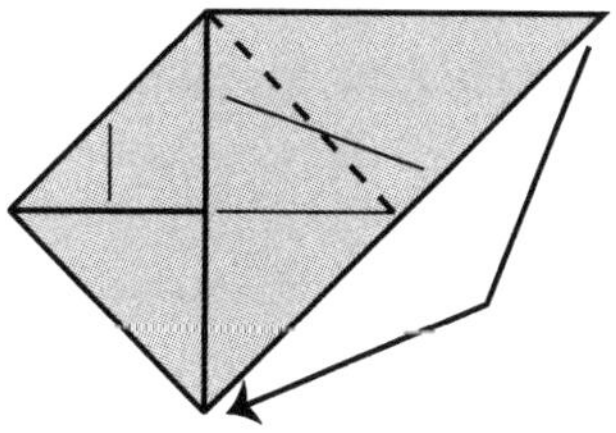

5. Fold the shape in half vertically, tucking the left side into the right pocket as you do. This is the third puzzle piece.

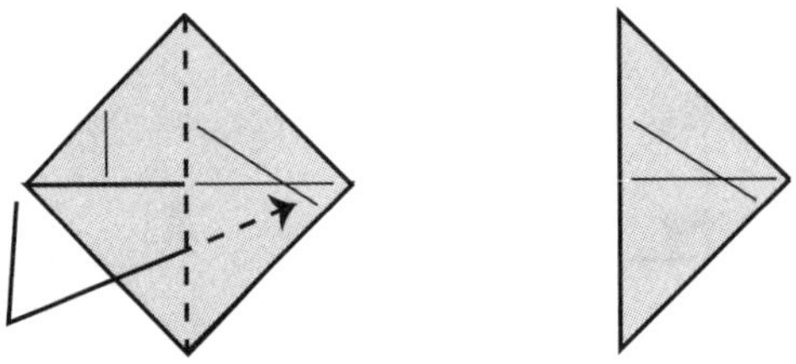

Puzzle Piece Four

1. Repeat the first three steps from *Puzzle Piece One* with the fourth piece of paper. Unfold the paper so that the white side is face up, bring sure to orient it as shown in the diagram. Fold the bottom left corner up so that the bottom edge is flush with the vertical fold line.

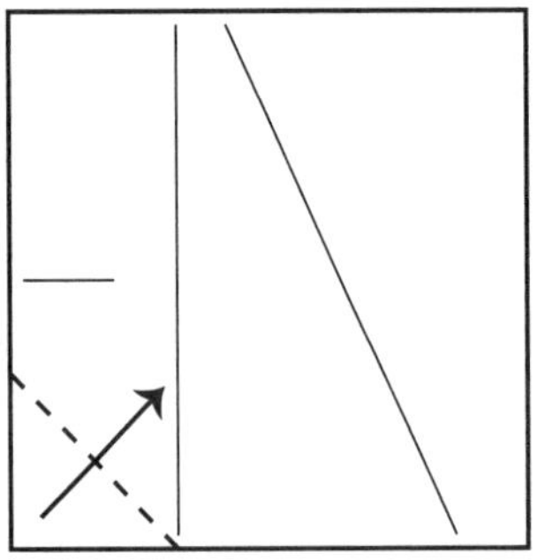

2. Fold the top of the paper down to meet the edge of the fold you just created, crease, and unfold.

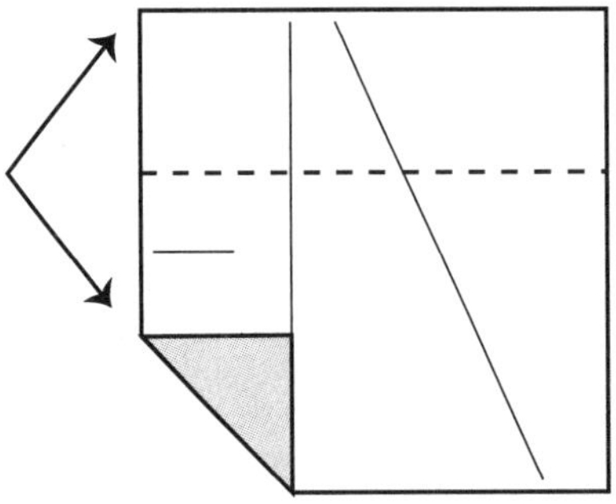

3. Make two creases on the left side of the paper as indicated. The upper of the two creases should be a valley crease, and the lower a mountain crease.

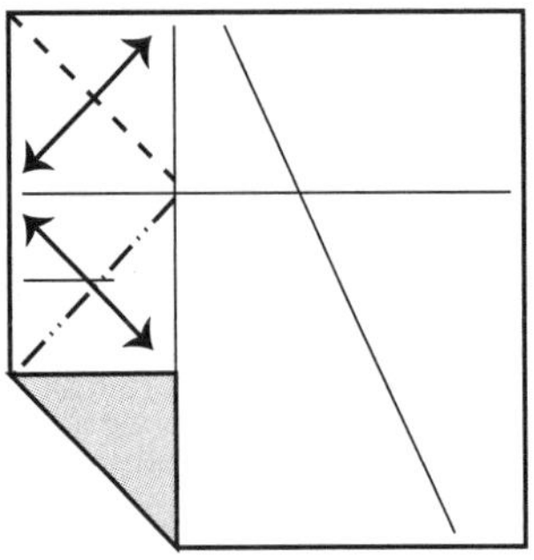

4. Using a series of simultaneous folds, bring the top of the paper down, while bringing the right side in. This should result in the shape shown at the right.

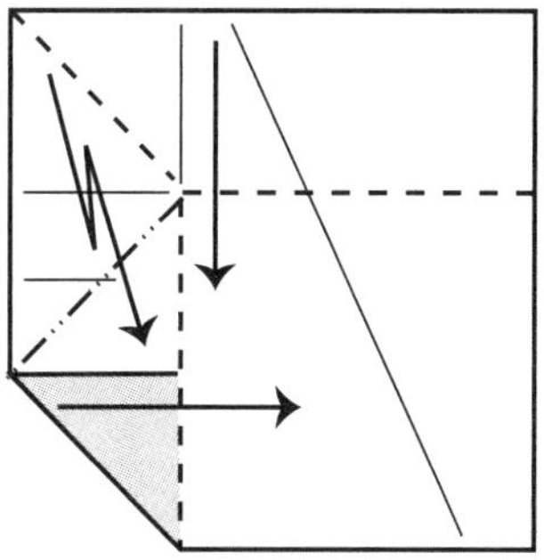

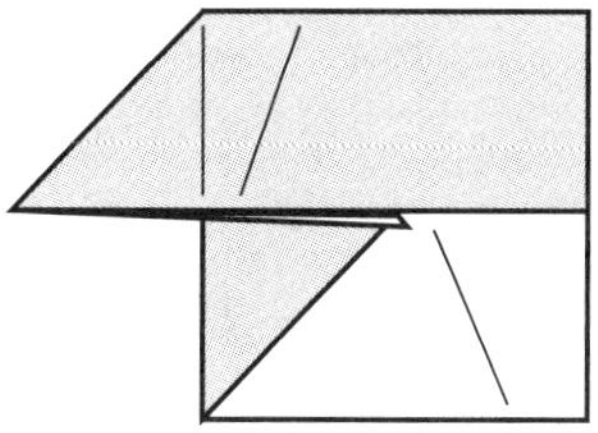

5. Crease the top layer of the paper as indicated.

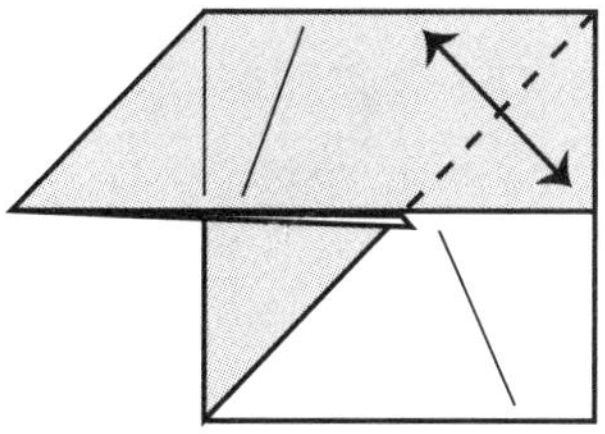

6. Fold the paper in half diagonally as indicated by the dashed line. As you fold, tuck the flap that was creased in the previous step into the triangular pocket as shown. This is the fourth puzzle piece.

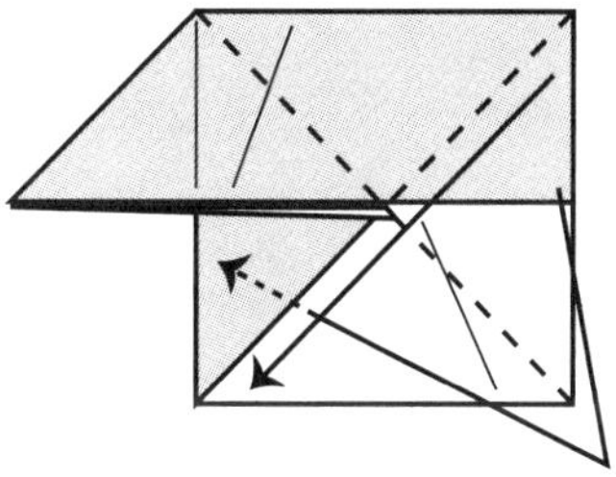

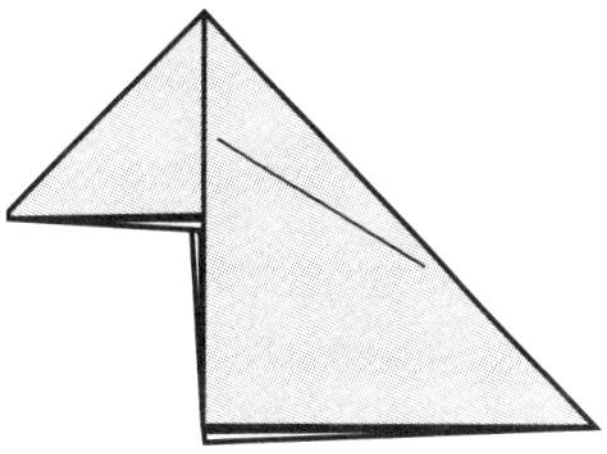

Puzzle Piece Five

1. Fold the paper into thirds using two valley folds.

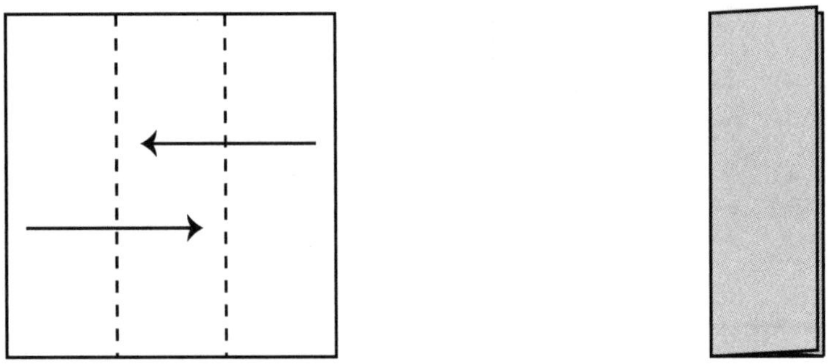

2. Crease the paper as indicated so that the top of the paper is flush with the left side.

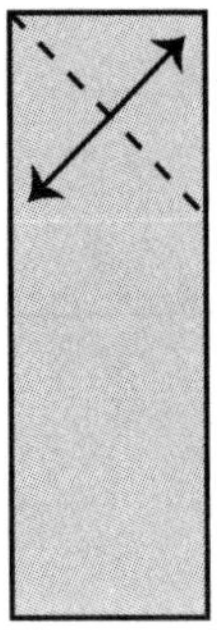

3. Fold the top of the paper down at the point where the diagonal fold line meets the right side.

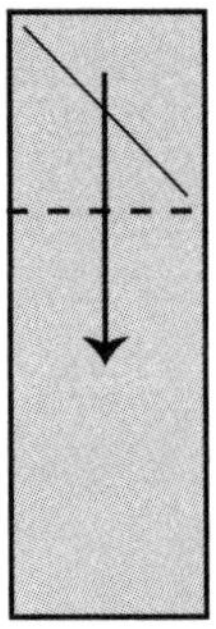

4. Fold the bottom left corner up along the diagonal to make a triangular tab as shown.

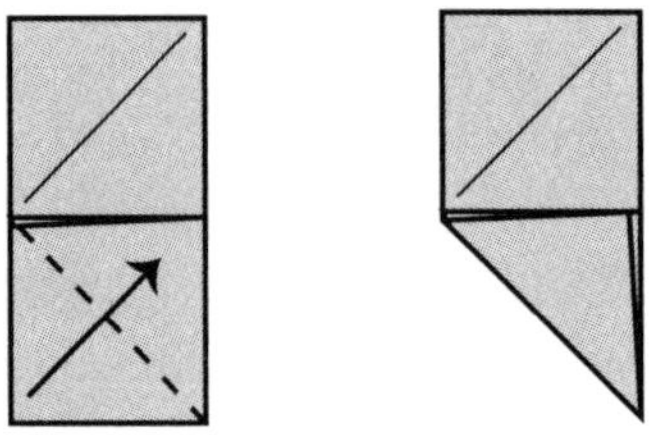

5. Tuck this triangular tab into the pocket formed by the previous folds. This is the fifth puzzle piece.

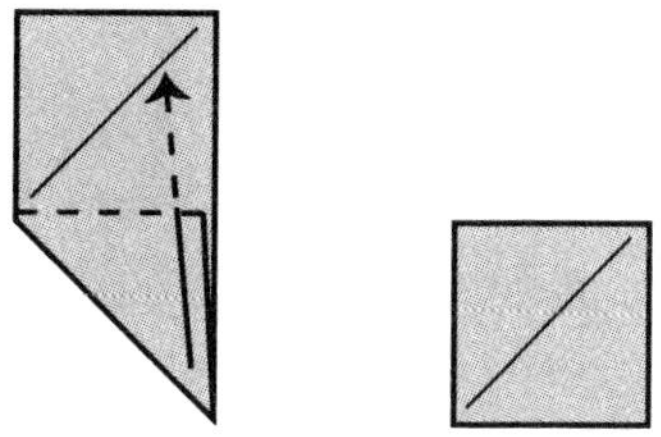

Your five completed puzzle pieces should look like the ones below.

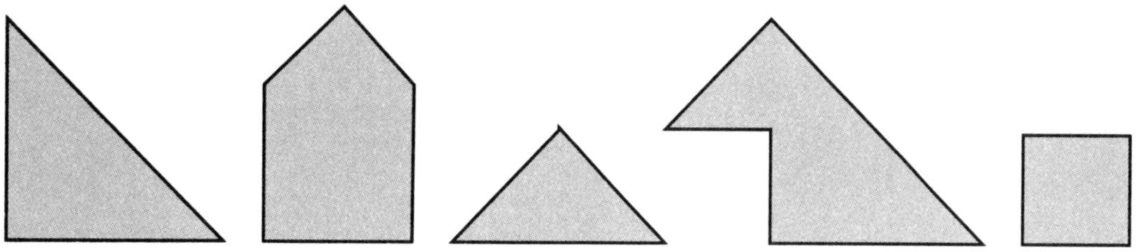

ORIGAMI SQUARED

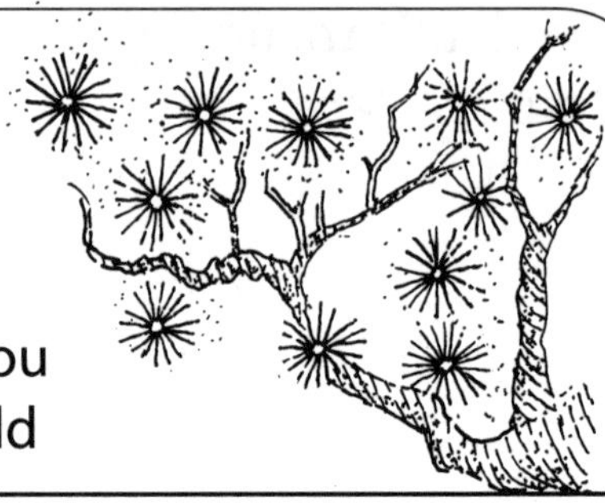

The object of this puzzle is to take the five pieces that you folded and arrange them to form a square. This square should be the same size as the paper from which each piece was folded. Once you discover a solution, draw it in the space provided.

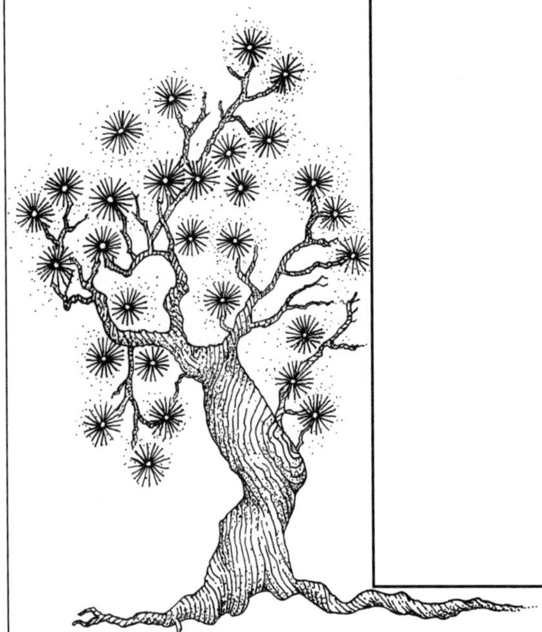

Is it possible to make a square using fewer than five puzzle pieces? How? How many different squares are possible using one or more of the puzzle pieces? Draw a picture of each additional solution you discover in the spaces below.

ORIGAMI SQUARED
Exploration

Part One

If you could be told the area of any one puzzle piece and had to use that information to determine the areas of the other four puzzle pieces, which piece would you choose? Explain your reasoning using words and/or pictures. Show how you would use this piece to determine the area of each other piece.

Use the area value that your teacher gives you for the puzzle piece you have chosen to determine the area of each other puzzle piece. Show your work below.

ORIGAMI SQUARED Exploration

Part Two

Once you have solved the puzzle, fill in the table below with the required information for each possible square that can be made using one or more of the puzzle pieces. The perimeter for the five-piece solution has been given to get you started. Show your work in the space below the table using words and/or diagrams.

# of pieces in square	Perimeter in units	Length of each side	Area in units^2
5	24		

ORIGAMI SQUARED

Exploration

Part Two

Once you have completed the table on the previous page, answer the questions below.

1. If the perimeter of the square that is made with all five pieces is 24 units, what is the length of each side? What is the area of that square? How were you able to determine this?

2. How does this information let you determine the area and perimeter of the small square puzzle piece?

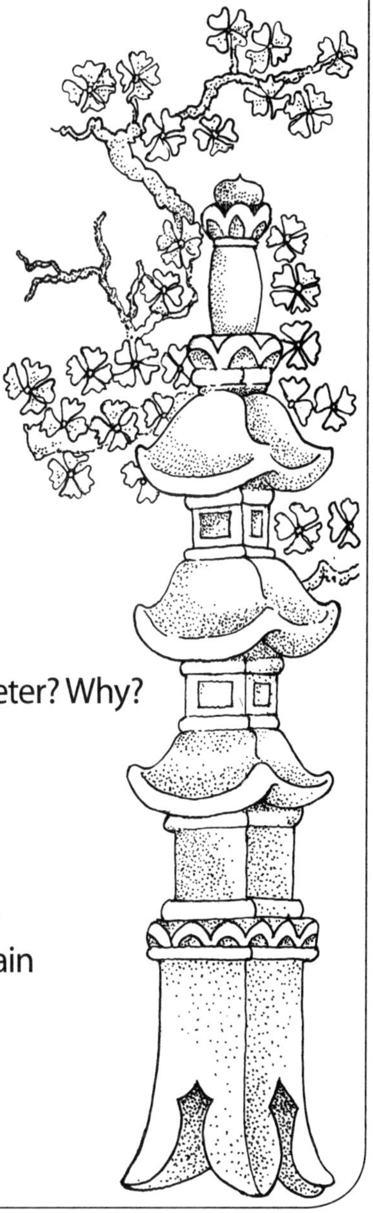

3. What is the area of the square that can be made with four of the five puzzle pieces? How do you know?

4. What is the length of one side of this square? ...the total perimeter? Why?

5. What is the difference in area between the square that uses five puzzle pieces and the square that uses four puzzle pieces? Explain your reasoning.

TANGRAM

FOCUS

Students will create the seven pieces of the classic tangram puzzle and use them to construct the 13 convex polygons that can be made with these pieces. They will also look at the areas of the individual pieces and of similar shapes which can be made using fewer than seven tangram pieces.

KEY QUESTIONS

How can you use your tangram pieces to make the 13 possible convex polygons?

What is the area of each tangram piece?

What are the areas of the squares, triangles and parallelograms you can make using fewer than seven pieces?

MATH

Convex polygons
Similar shapes
Area
Problem solving

INTEGRATED PROCESSES

Observing
Comparing and contrasting
Collecting and recording data
Generalizing

PAPER

Seven squares per puzzle

CREATOR

Michelle Pauls*

Management

1. Unlike a majority of the activities in this book, the tangram pieces are best made with traditional origami paper because of its light weight. Using the heavier weight paper that is well-suited for unit origami models results in bulky and less precise pieces in this puzzle.
2. There are three separate challenges presented on the student sheets. Depending on the needs and abilities of your students, you may choose to use only one or two of these challenges rather than all three.
3. The nature of this activity lends itself to being spread over several days to a week so that students have time to discover solutions to the various shapes presented in *Challenge One*.

Procedure

1. Hand out the folding instructions (pages 181-190) and seven squares of paper to each student.
2. Go over the folding instructions for each piece step by step. Be sure that students make two each of the second and fifth puzzle pieces.
3. Choose the challenges which are best suited for your students and distribute the corresponding student pages. You may want to provide scratch paper for students to record their solutions to *Challenge One*.
4. At the end of the time you have allotted for this activity, close with a time of class discussion and sharing.

Discussion

Challenge One

1. Were you able to come up with solutions to all 13 of the convex polygons?
2. Did you find more than one solution for any of the shapes? Which ones? (All of the shapes except for the square have more than one solution.)

Challenge Two

1. What are the areas of each of the tangram pieces? (See *Solutions*.)
2. How were you able to determine these values?
3. What would the area of each piece be if the small triangle had an area of two units? ...three units? ...0.5 units? How do you know?

Challenge Three

1. Did thinking about how the various tangram pieces are related help you to determine all of the possible piece combinations for different areas? How?
2. What are all of the possible areas for similar squares? [16, 8, 4, 2]

3. What do you notice about the possible areas for similar squares? [They are all even, with each smaller area being half of the one before it.]
4. What are all the possible areas for similar parallelograms? [16, 12, 8, 4, 2]
5. How do these areas compare to those for the square? [There are five possible areas, they are all even, etc.]
6. What are all of the possible areas for similar triangles? [16, 9, 8, 4, 2, 1]
7. How do the possible areas for the triangle compare to those for the square and the parallelogram? [There are more possible areas for triangles than for squares and parallelograms, two of the areas are odd, one piece can be used for three different areas, etc.]
8. Which shape has the most possible areas using different shape combinations? [the triangle] What do you think are some reasons for this? [Three of the tangram pieces are triangles, any two isosceles right triangles can be put together to form a larger similar triangle, etc.]

Extensions

1. As a class, try to find every possible unique solution for each of the 13 convex polygons. Which have more than one solution? ...more than two solutions?
2. Repeat *Challenge Three* with some of the other convex polygons that can be made using the tangram pieces. Which shapes can be made with fewer than seven pieces? Are there any that cannot be made unless all seven pieces are used?
3. Advanced students can be challenged to use the area values they calculated to determine the perimeters of the pieces. Students must be familiar with the Pythagorean Theorem and be able to work with square roots in order to do this extension.

* Special thanks to Marc Kirshenbaum who designed the large triangle piece.

Solutions

Challenge One

One possible solution for each of the 13 convex polygons is shown below. Every shape except the square has more than one unique solution. (A unique solution is different from the others even when rotated and flipped.)

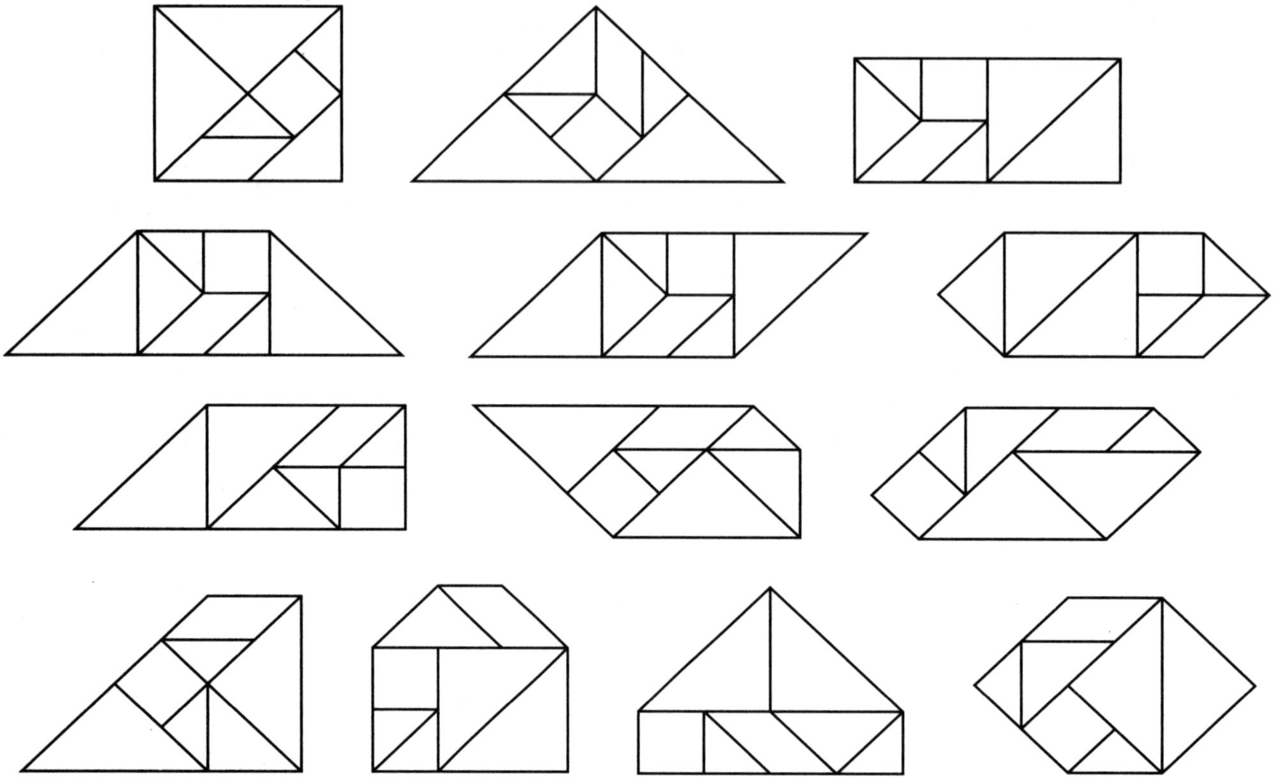

Challenge Two

Piece	Area
Small triangle	1 $unit^2$
Medium triangle	2 $units^2$
Large triangle	4 $units^2$
Square	2 $units^2$
Parallelogram	2 $units^2$

The total area for all seven tangram pieces is 16 $units^2$.

Challenge Three

Squares

# of pieces	Area	Piece combinations
7	16	All
5	8	Medium triangle, small triangles, square, parallelogram
4	8	One large triangle, medium triangle, small triangles
4	8	One large triangle, parallelogram, small triangles
4	8	One large triangle, square, small triangles
3	4	Medium triangle, small triangles
2	2	Small triangles
1	2	Square

Parallelograms

# of pieces	Area	Piece combinations
7	16	All
6	12	One large triangle, medium triangle, small triangles, square, parallelogram
4	8	One large triangle, medium triangle, small triangles
4	8	One large triangle, parallelogram, small triangles
4	8	One large triangle, square, small triangles
3	4	Medium triangle, small triangles
3	4	Parallelogram, small triangles
3	4	Square, small triangles
2	8	Large triangles
2	2	Small triangles
1	2	Parallelogram

Triangles

# of pieces	Area	Piece combinations
7	16	All
5	8	Medium triangle, small triangles, square, parallelogram
4	9	One large triangle, medium triangle, parallelogram, one small triangle
4	9	One large triangle, medium triangle, square, one small triangle
4	9	One large triangle, parallelogram, square, one small triangle
4	8	One large triangle, medium triangle, small triangles
4	8	One large triangle, parallelogram, small triangles
4	8	One large triangle, square, small triangles
3	4	Medium triangle, small triangles
3	4	Parallelogram, small triangles
3	4	Square, small triangles
2	2	Small triangles
1	4	Large triangle
1	2	Medium triangle
1	1	Small triangle

Extension #3

The perimeter values in the table below assume that the area of the small triangle is one square unit.

Piece	Perimeter
Small triangle	$2 + 2\sqrt{2}$
Medium triangle	$4 + 2\sqrt{2}$
Large triangle	$4 + 4\sqrt{2}$
Square	$4\sqrt{2}$
Parallelogram	$4 + 2\sqrt{2}$

TANGRAM Folding Instructions

Piece One:

1. Fold the square in half diagonally, from corner to corner.

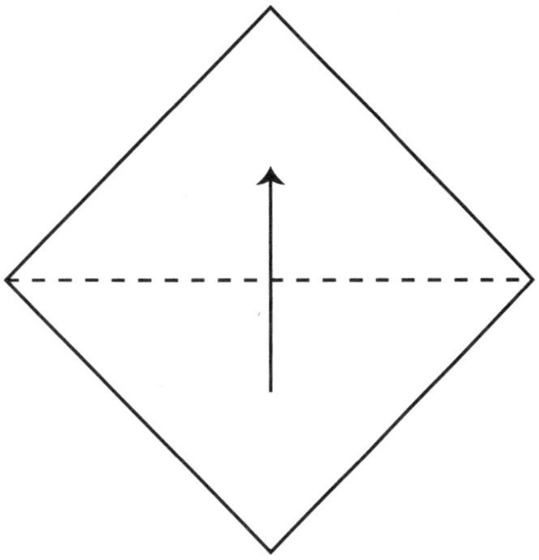

2. Fold the bottom two corners of the triangle up so that they meet the top corner, and unfold.

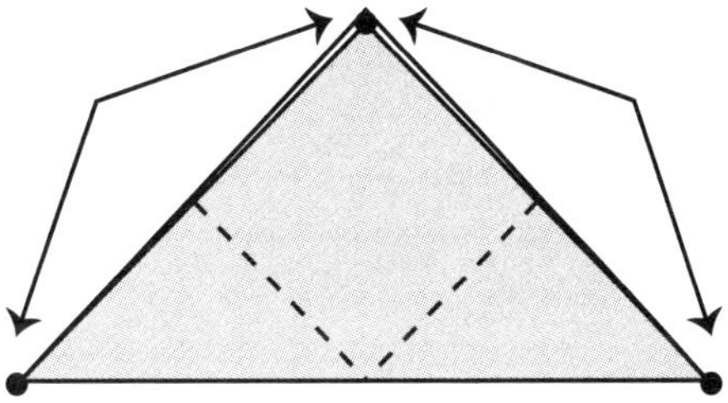

3. Unfold the paper completely and fold the top and bottom points in so that they meet at the center of the square.

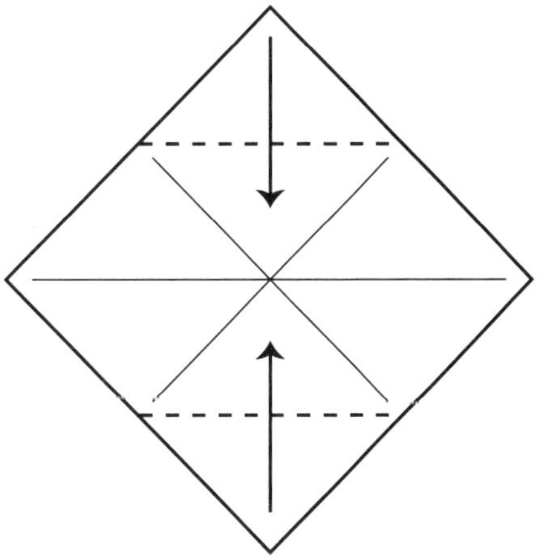

4. Fold the paper in half along the existing crease line.

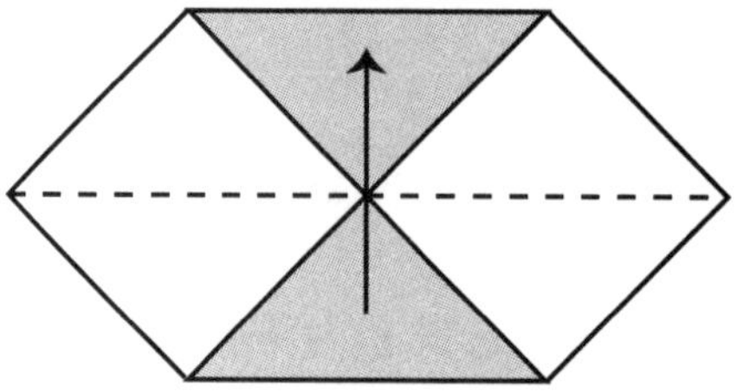

5. Fold both corners up as you did in step 2.

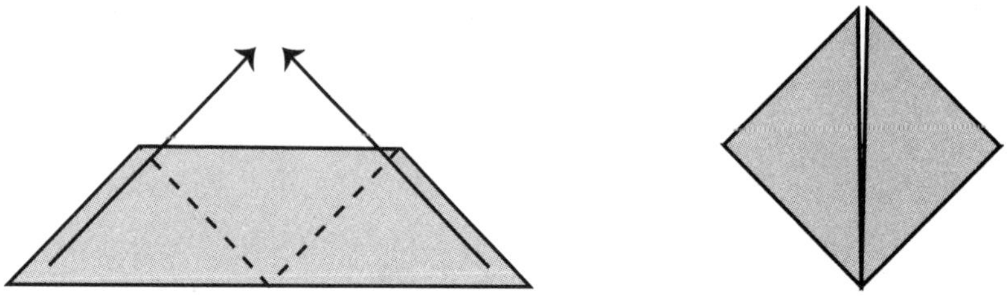

6. Using mountain folds as indicated, crease the top flaps and tuck them into the pocket directly behind them. This is the first tangram piece.

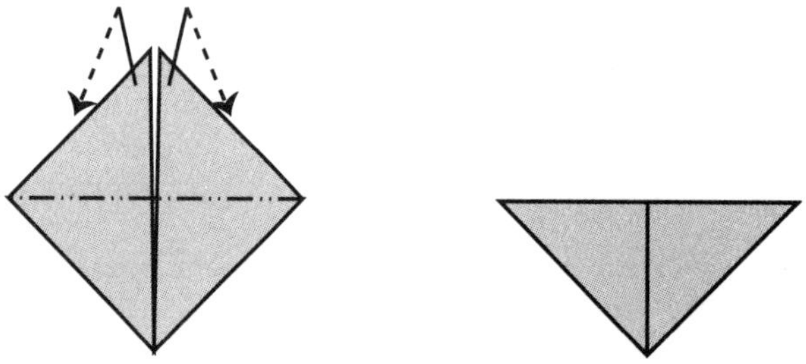

Piece Two:

1. Repeat steps 1-2 from *Piece One* on the second sheet of paper. Crease the bottom left corner of the triangle along the vertical fold line indicated.

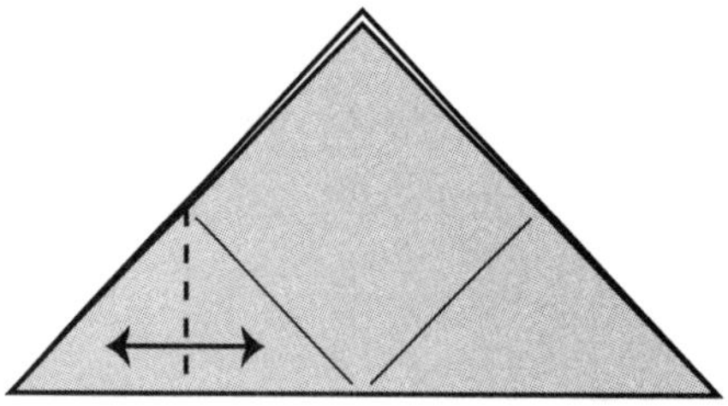

2. Reverse the fold that was just made and tuck the left point of the triangle into the inside of the unit.

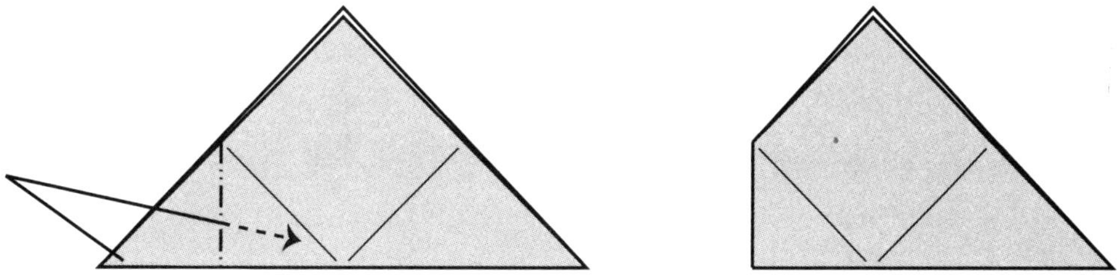

3. Fold the top point of the paper down to meet the bottom edge as indicated.

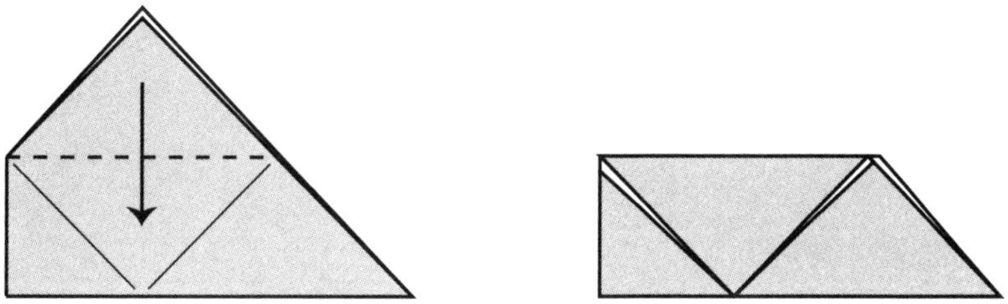

4. Fold the bottom left corner up along the existing fold line.

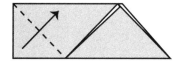

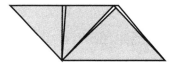

5. Fold the left side of the paper over so that the top left corner meets the top right corner.

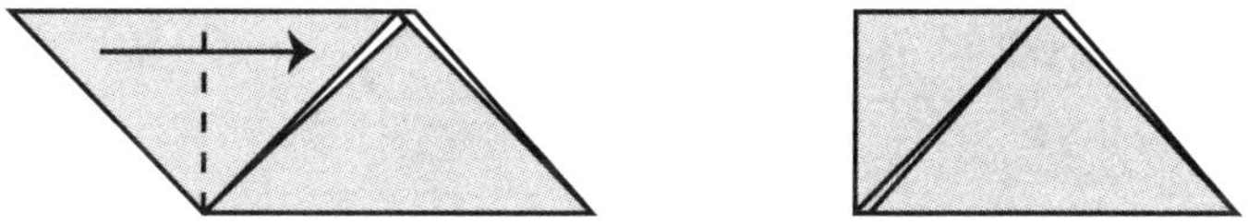

6. Fold the top left corner down along the existing fold line.

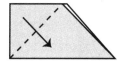

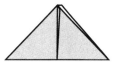

7. Fold the triangle in half, tucking the right side into the pocket on the left as you do so. This completes the second tangram piece. Repeat these steps so that you have two pieces like this one.

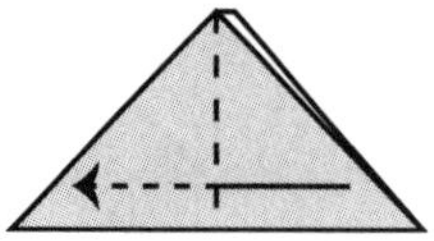

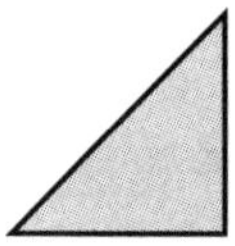

(x 2)

Piece Three:

1. Fold the square in half diagonally, from corner to corner.

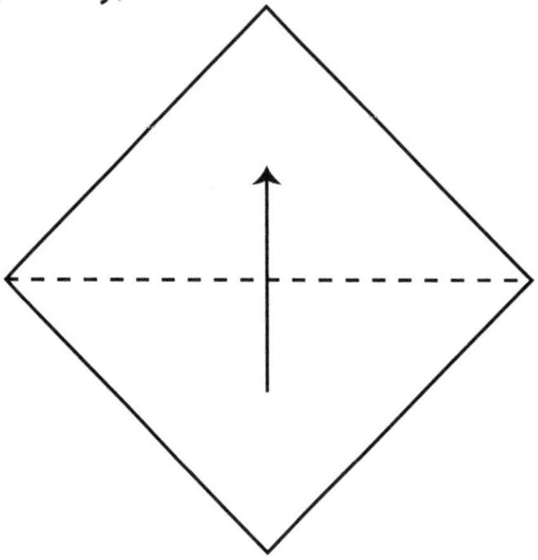

2. Fold the resulting triangle in half vertically and unfold.

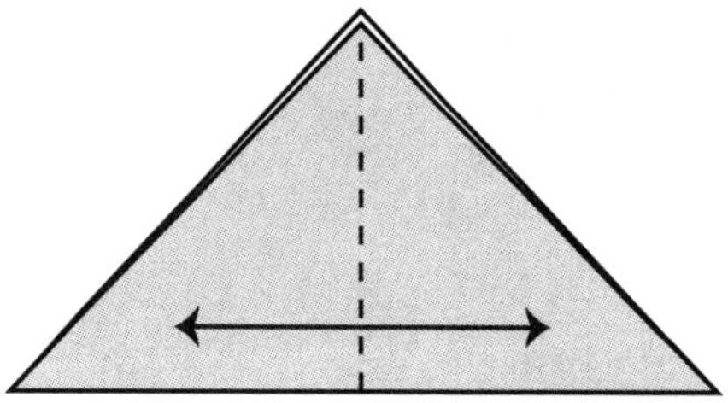

3. Fold the bottom left corner of the triangle in to meet the center crease and unfold.

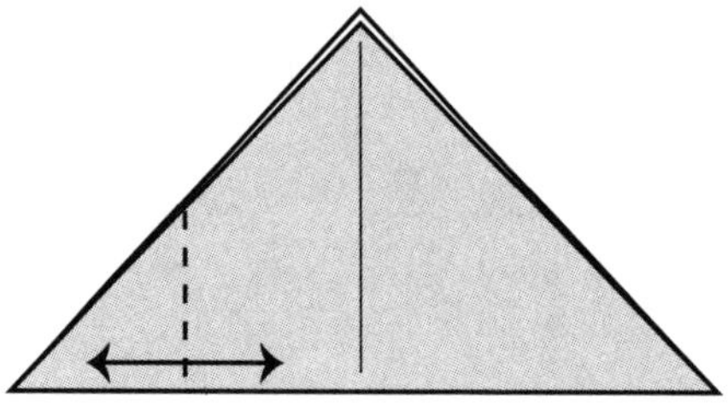

4. Reverse the fold that was just made and tuck the left point inside the triangle.

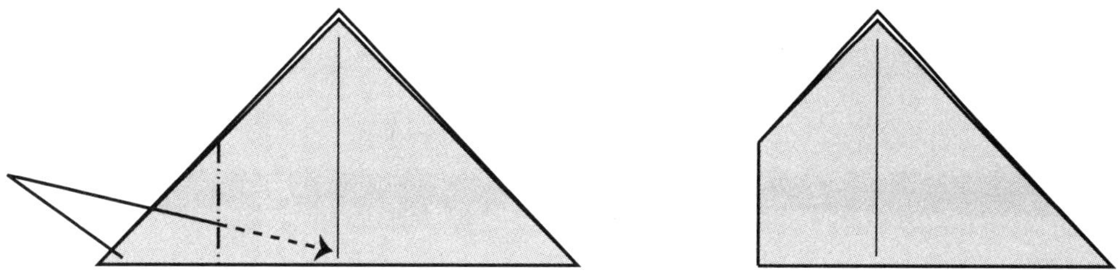

5. Fold the piece in along the existing crease.

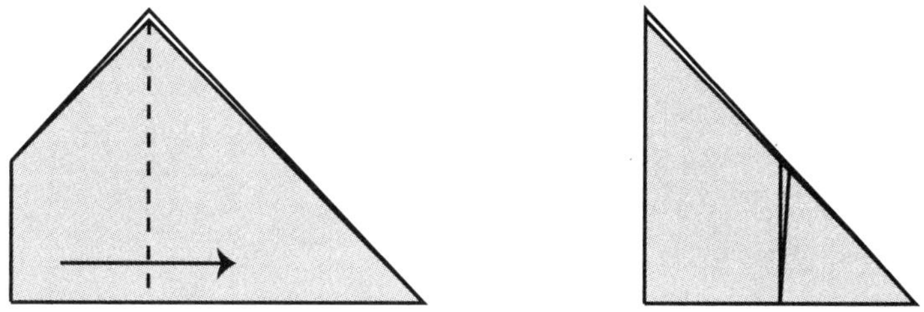

6. Fold the bottom left corner up to meet the center of the opposite side.

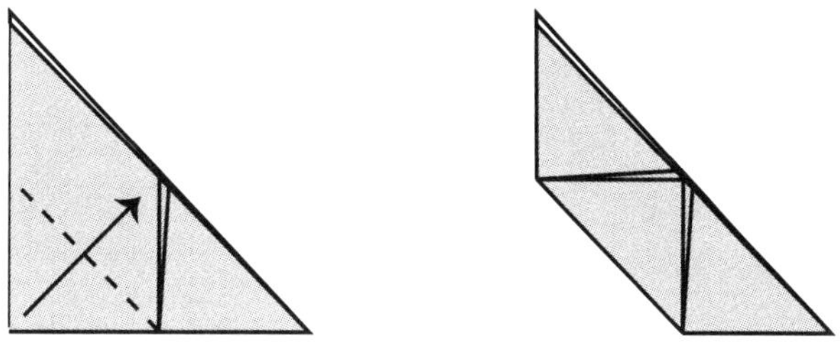

7. Fold the bottom triangular flap in half as indicated.

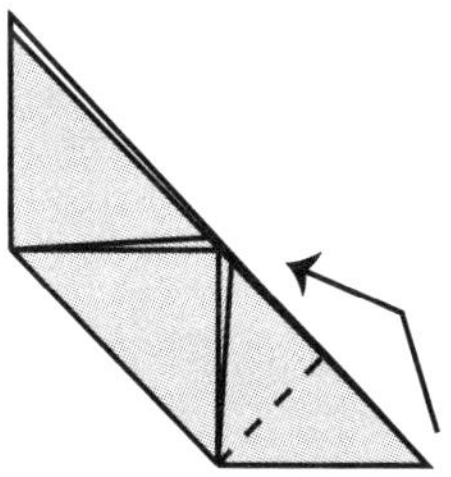

8. Tuck the triangular flap you just created into the pocket to its left as shown. This is the completed third piece.

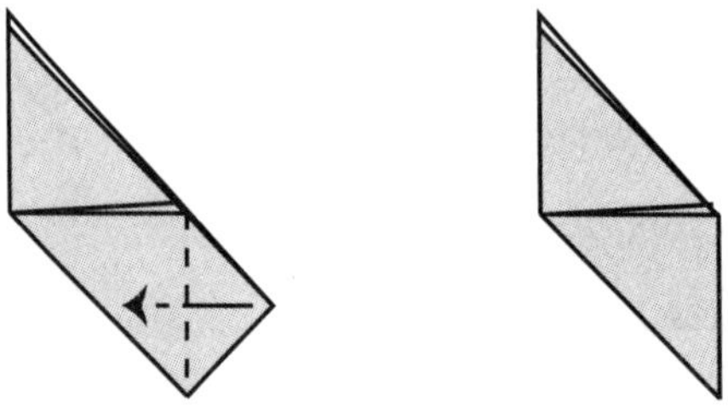

Piece Four:

1. Fold the paper in half vertically and unfold and then horizontally and unfold.

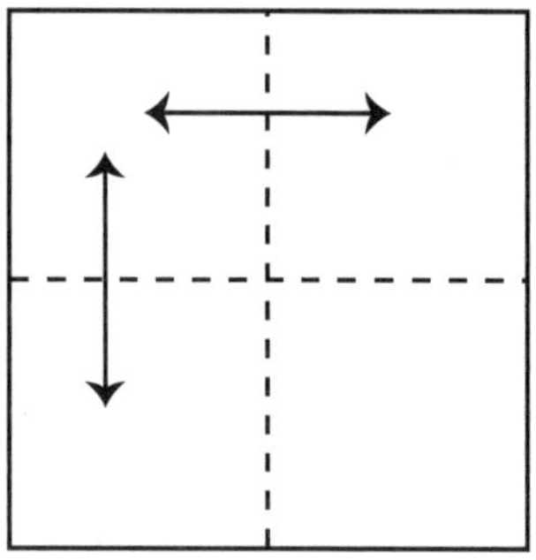

2. Fold all four corners in so that they meet in the center of the square. Unfold two of the corners and rotate the paper so that it is oriented as shown below.

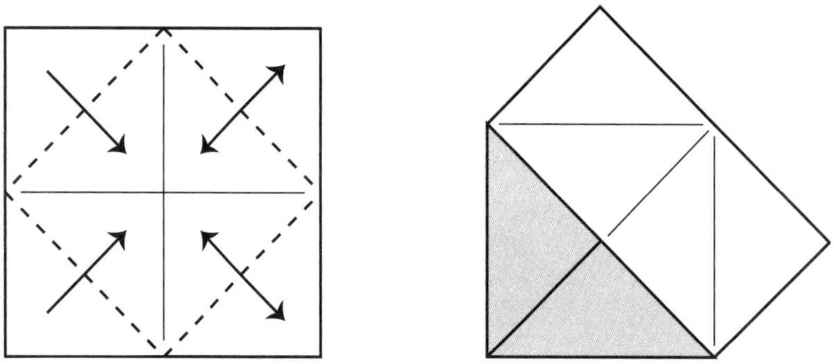

3. Fold the bottom edge of the paper to meet the top horizontal fold line.

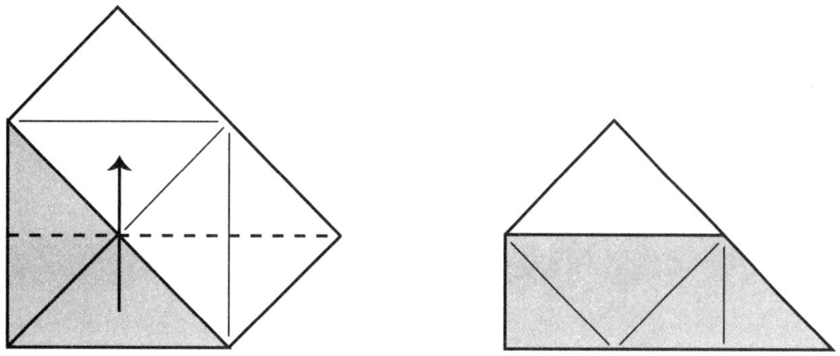

4. Fold the top triangular flap down as indicated.

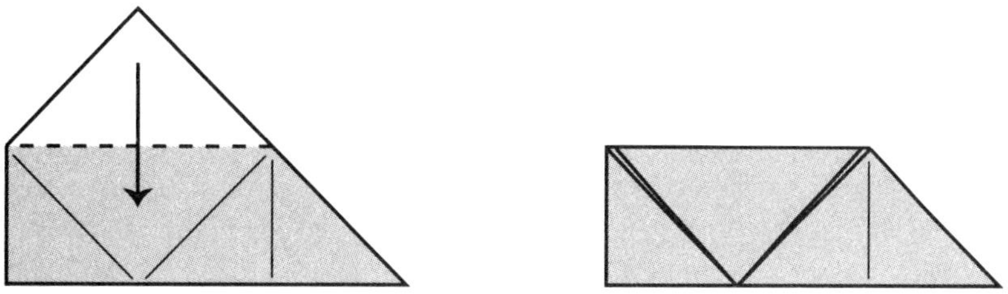

5. Fold the rectangular portion of the paper in half vertically.

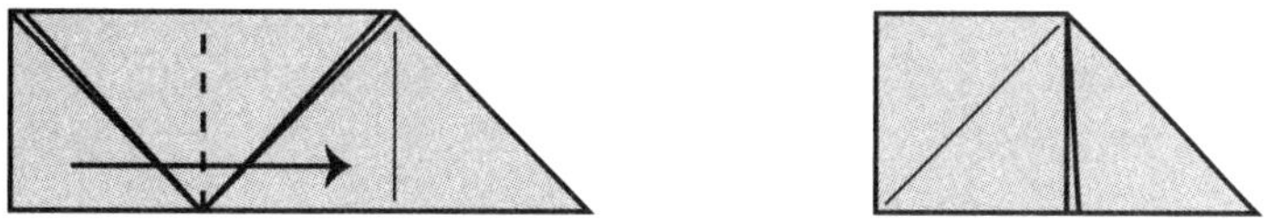

6. Using a valley fold, tuck the triangular tab on the right into the pocket of the flap that was just folded over. This is the completed fourth piece.

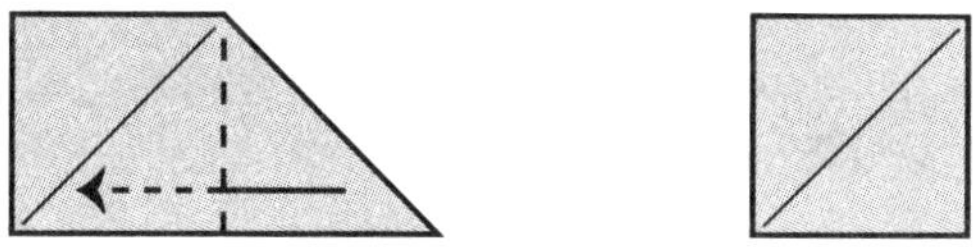

Piece Five:

1. Fold the square in half diagonally, from corner to corner.

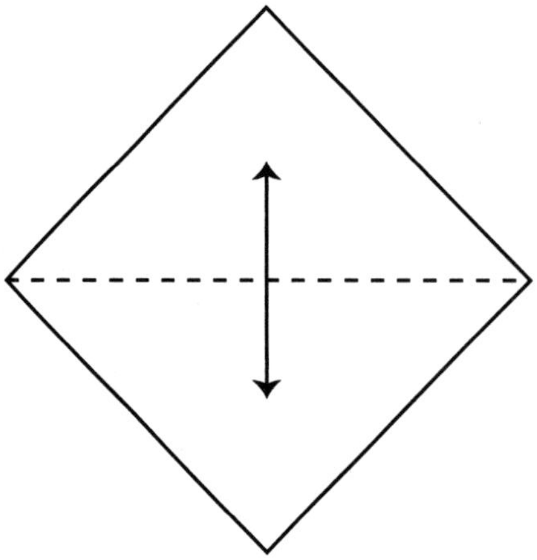

2. Fold the top left edge of the paper down to meet the diagonal fold line.

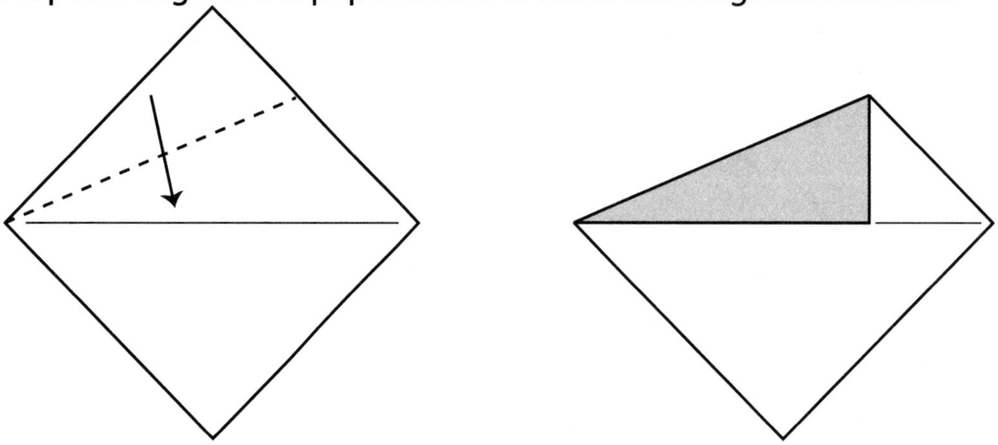

3. Fold the right corner in to meet the point where the top corner touches the midline, then unfold the top flap.

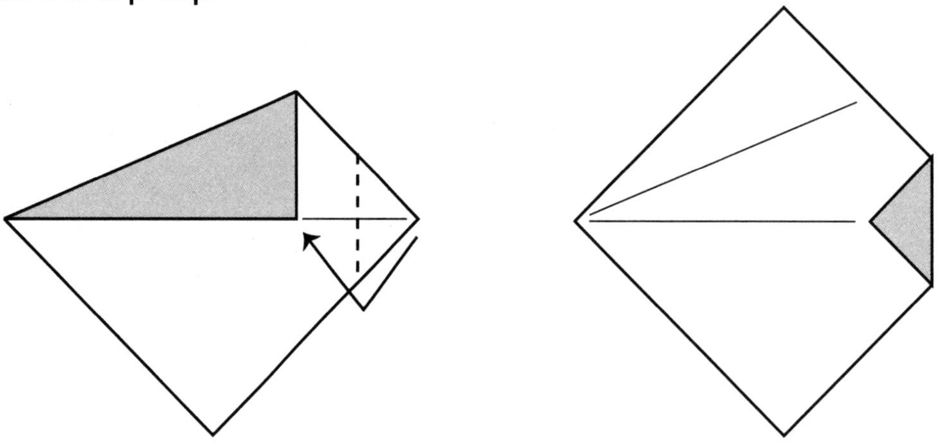

4. Fold the top left edge down to meet the diagonal fold line.

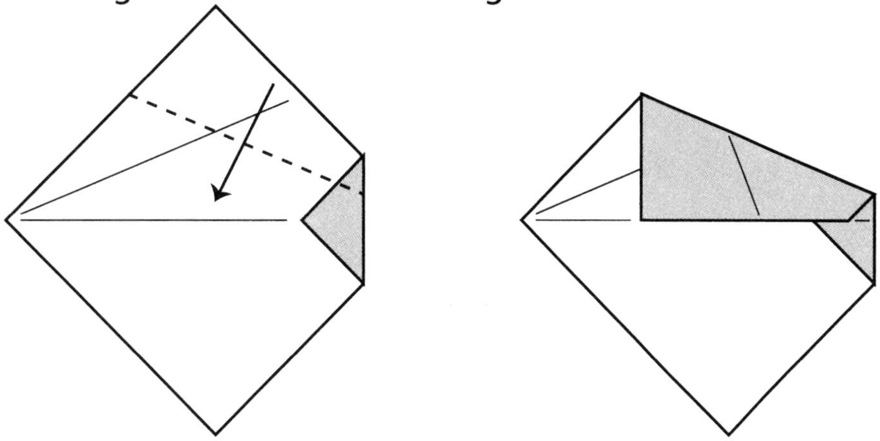

5. Fold the left corner in to meet the point where the top corner touches the midline, then unfold the top flap.

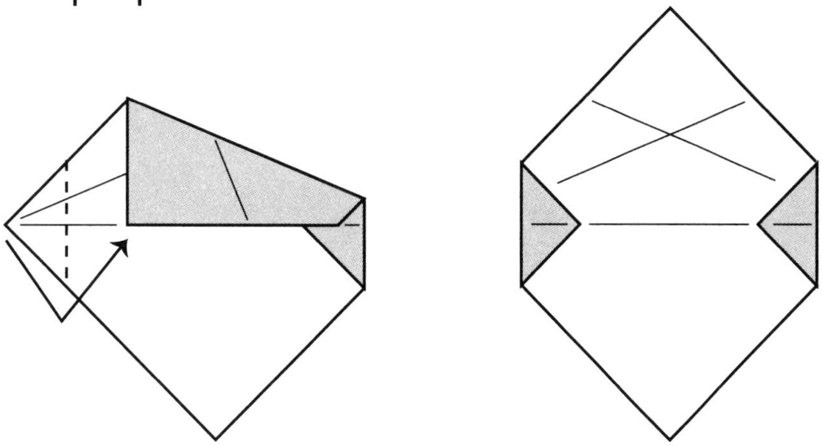

6. Fold the top left and bottom right edges in as indicated so that the points marked with dots meet.

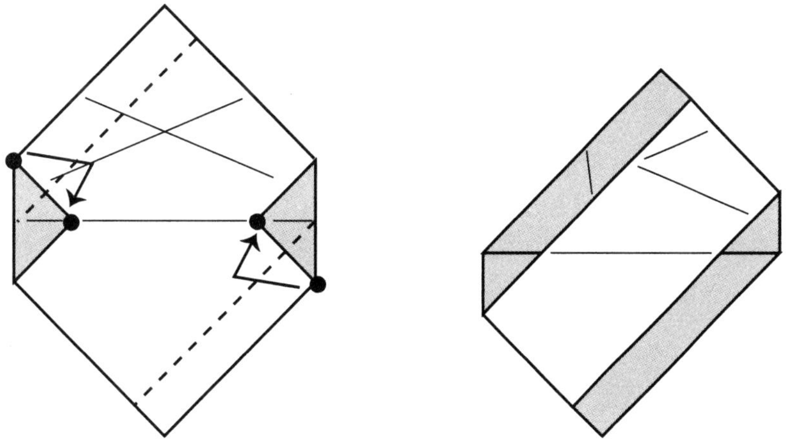

7. Fold the top and bottom edges of the paper in as indicated, and unfold the top edge.

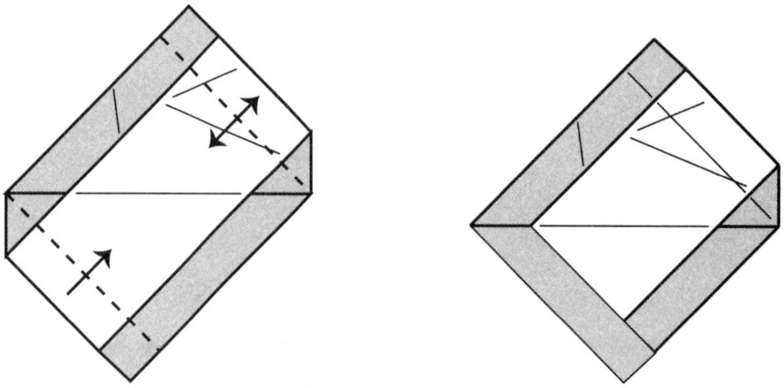

8. Using the existing crease, fold the paper in half.

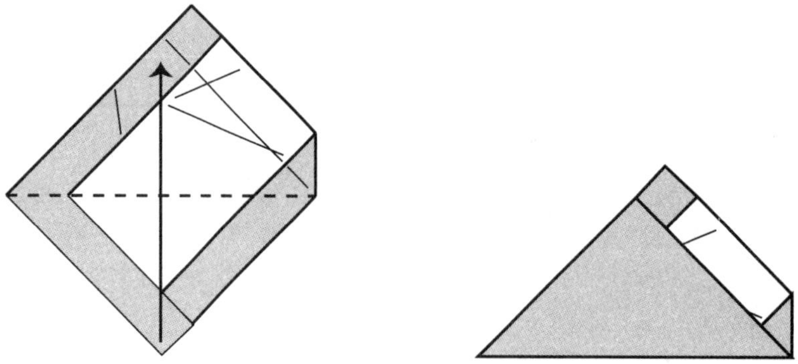

9. Using a valley fold, tuck the flap into the inside of the triangle. This is the completed fifth piece. Repeat steps one to nine so that you have two of these pieces.

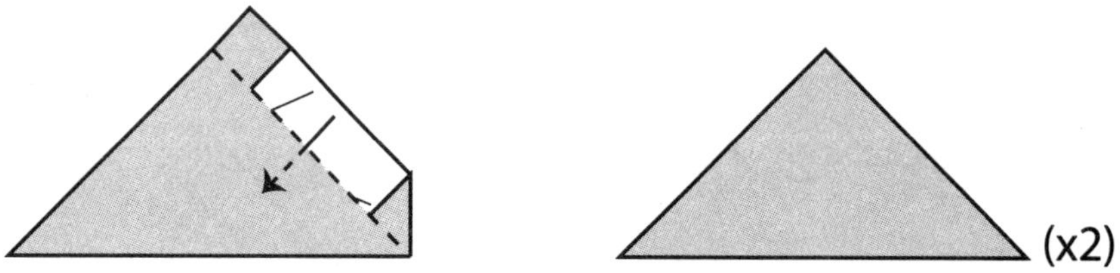

You should now have seven tangram pieces that look like the ones below.

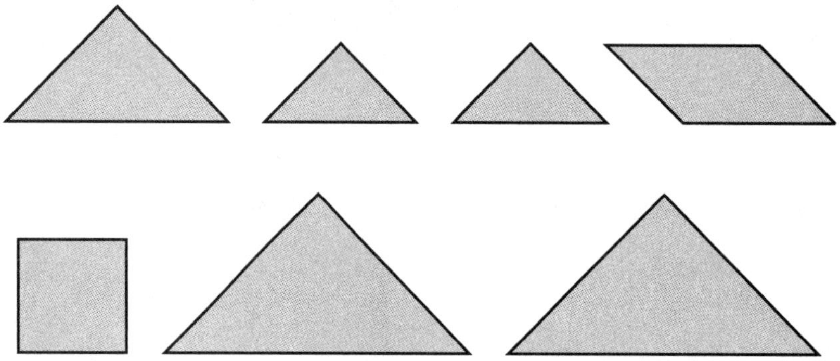

TANGRAM

The tangram is an ancient puzzle that has been traced to China, although no one knows how long ago it was actually created. Popular tradition says that the tangram shapes were first discovered when a man dropped a square tile and it broke into seven pieces. He spent a long time trying to return the pieces to their original square shape. Since then, the tangram has become popular all over the world. Some historical figures who were fascinated with the tangram include Lewis Carroll, Sam Loyd (the noted American puzzle creator), and Theodore Roosevelt.

Although the tangram can be used to create an infinite number of shapes, both regular and irregular, there are only 13 convex polygons that can be created using all seven pieces. (A convex polygon is defined as one that has no interior angles greater than 180°. In other words, it is never "dented in" on any of its faces.)

Challenge One: See how many of the 13 convex polygons shown below you can make using your tangram pieces. Record the solutions you find on the back of your paper. Many of the shapes have multiple solutions. See how many you can find for each one.

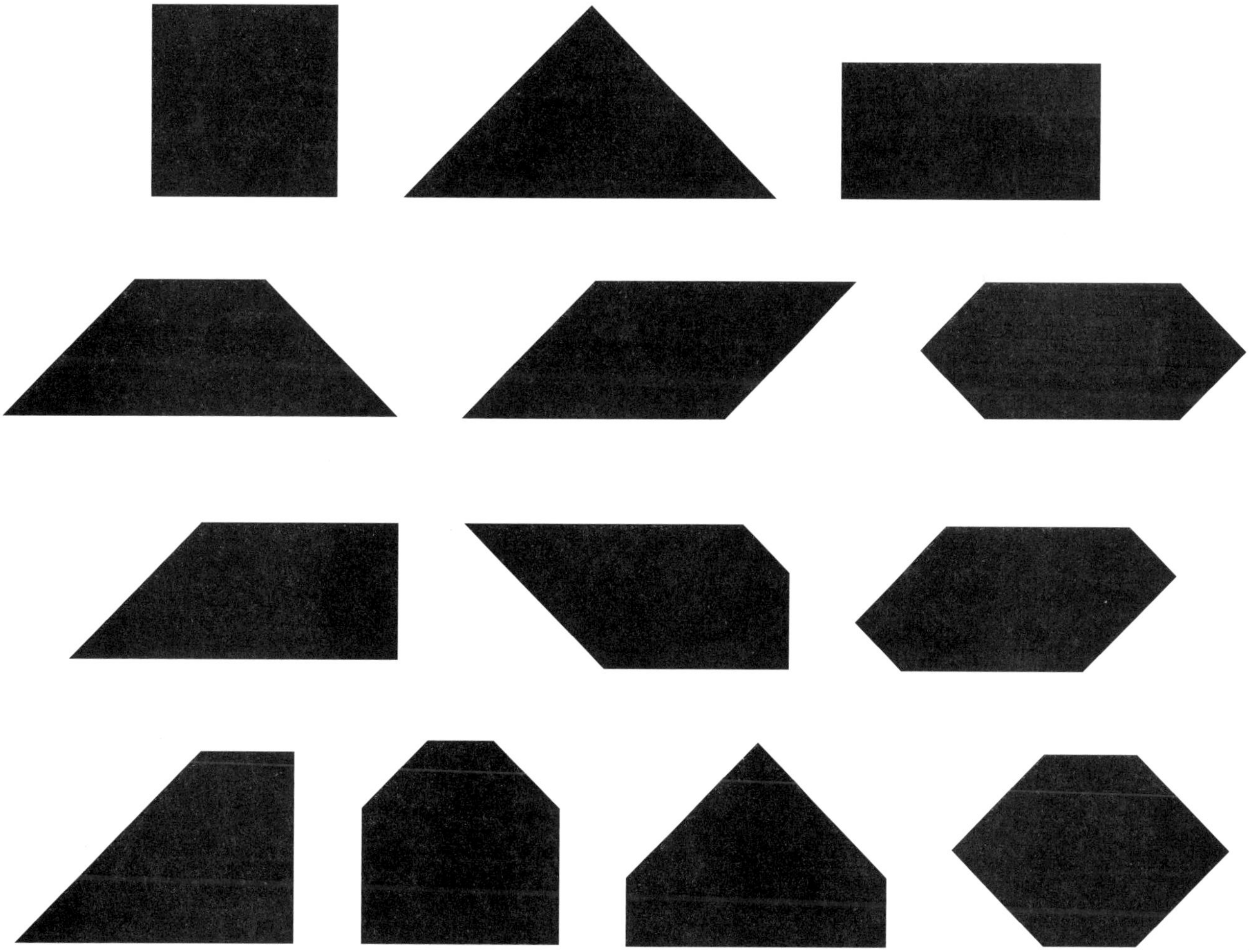

TANGRAM Exploration

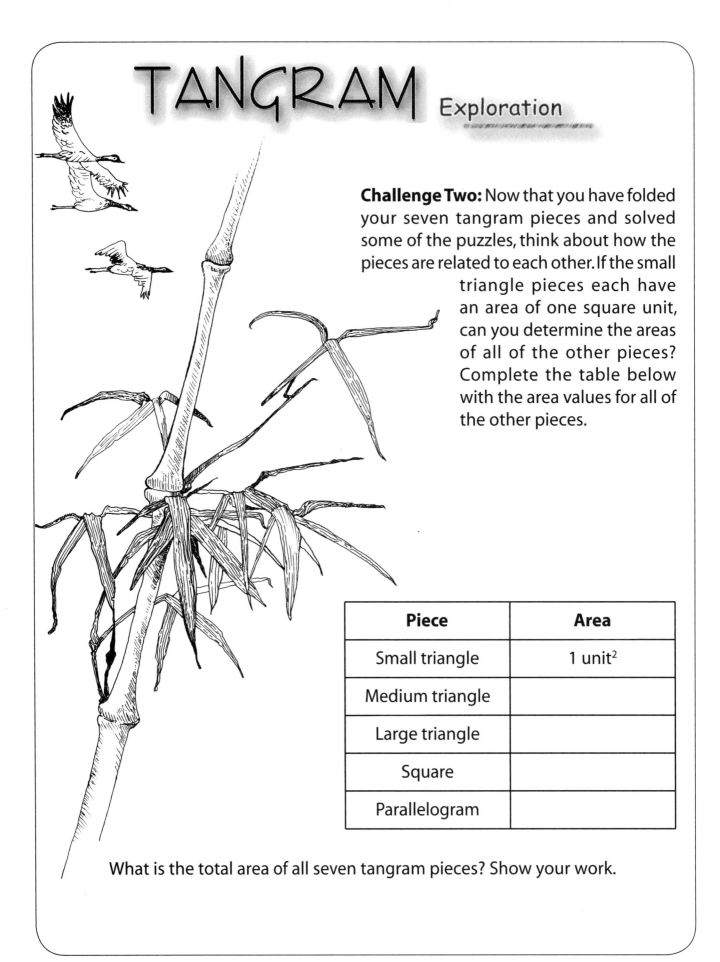

Challenge Two: Now that you have folded your seven tangram pieces and solved some of the puzzles, think about how the pieces are related to each other. If the small triangle pieces each have an area of one square unit, can you determine the areas of all of the other pieces? Complete the table below with the area values for all of the other pieces.

Piece	Area
Small triangle	1 $unit^2$
Medium triangle	
Large triangle	
Square	
Parallelogram	

What is the total area of all seven tangram pieces? Show your work.

TANGRAM Exploration

Challenge Three: Your tangram pieces consist of a square, a parallelogram, and three similar right triangles. You have already made these shapes using all seven tangram pieces. Now see how many of those shapes you can make using fewer than seven pieces. Record the number of pieces used to make each new square, triangle, and parallelogram in the tables on this page and the next two. Use the area values from *Challenge Two* to determine the areas of these new polygons. Write which pieces you used for each different area in the "Piece combinations" column. Record each possible piece combination for the same area and the same number of pieces. Two examples have been done for you.

Squares

# of pieces	Area	Piece combinations
7	16	All
5	8	Medium triangle, small triangles, square, parallelogram

TANGRAM Exploration

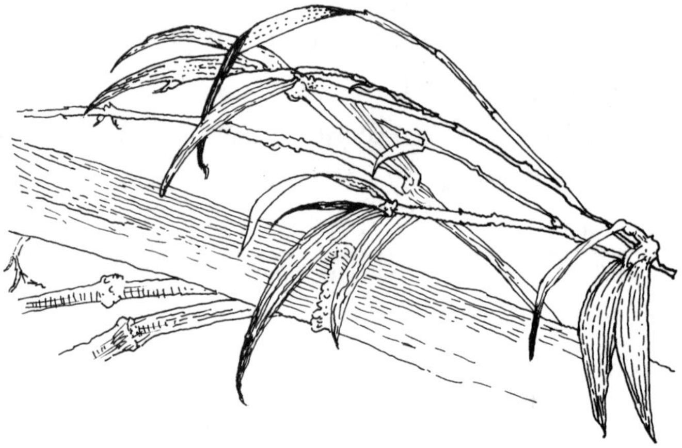

When you make your parallelograms from fewer than seven pieces, be sure that they are similar to the parallelogram puzzle piece. For example, while the shape pictured below to the left is a parallelogram, it is not similar to the original puzzle piece, and would therefore not be recorded in the table. The piece to the right, however, is similar, and would be recorded.

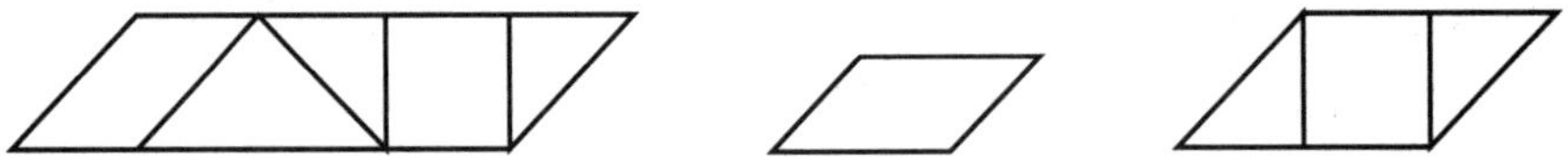

Not similar　　Tangram piece　　Similar

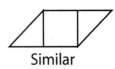

Parallelograms

# of pieces	Area	Piece combinations
7	16	All
6	12	One large triangle, medium triangle, small triangles, square, parallelogram

TANGRAM Exploration

Triangles

# of pieces	Area	Piece combinations
7	16	All
5	8	Medium triangle, small triangles, square, parallelogram

TETRAHEDRON PUZZLE

FOCUS

Students will fold and assemble the two pieces of a classic three-dimensional geometric puzzle. Once they have created the pieces they will attempt to solve the puzzle.

KEY QUESTION

How do the two puzzle pieces you have created fit together to form a tetrahedron?

MATH

Geometric solids
Congruence
Problem solving

PAPER

10 squares per puzzle in three different colors

CREATOR

Michelle Pauls*

Management

1. This activity will probably need to be spread over several days to give students a chance to solve the puzzle. The folding can be done in one period, but it will take most students much longer than that to figure out how to combine their two pieces to form a tetrahedron. This is made even more challengeing by the fact that the origami pieces are not as stable as wood or plastic would be, and can be difficult to keep in the correct orientation. Only after students have solved the puzzle will they be able to move on to the exploration.

Procedure

1. Hand out the folding instructions (pages 198-206) and 10 paper squares to each student. To make it easiest for students to follow the folding instructions, they should have four squares of one color, four of another color, and two of a third color.
2. Go over the folding instructions for the side units step by step. Have students fold the remaining seven side units.
3. Repeat this process for the square base units. Take students through the procedure for assembling one half of the puzzle. Have them assemble the second half on their own, giving assistance as needed.
4. When all students have successfully assembled their two puzzle pieces, hand out the next student sheet, which outlines the object of the puzzle.
5. When students have solved the puzzle, give them the exploration sheet and have them answer the questions. After all sudents have had time to complete the exploration, close with a time of class discussion and sharing.

Discussion

1. If you were to break each puzzle piece into three smaller pieces, two of which were congruent tetrahedrons, what shape would the third piece be? [a square-based pyramid]
2. How are these square-based pyramids oriented to each other in the solution? [They are placed base to base.]
3. If two square-based pyramids were joined base to base, what shape would be formed? [a regular octahedron] How do you know?
4. Based on this information, into what Platonic solids can a regular tetrahedron be broken? [four regular tetrahedrons and one regular octahedron]
5. If you had thought about how a tetrahedron can be broken down before you attempted to solve the puzzle, do you think it would have been easier for you? Why or why not?
6. Do you think any of the other Platonic solids can be broken down in similar ways? Why or why not?

* Michelle Pauls created the square base and designed the assembly of the tetrahedron puzzle using the equilateral triangle unit by Tomoko Fusè.

Solution

To make a tetrahedron from the two puzzle pieces, the square bases on both pieces must go together as shown.

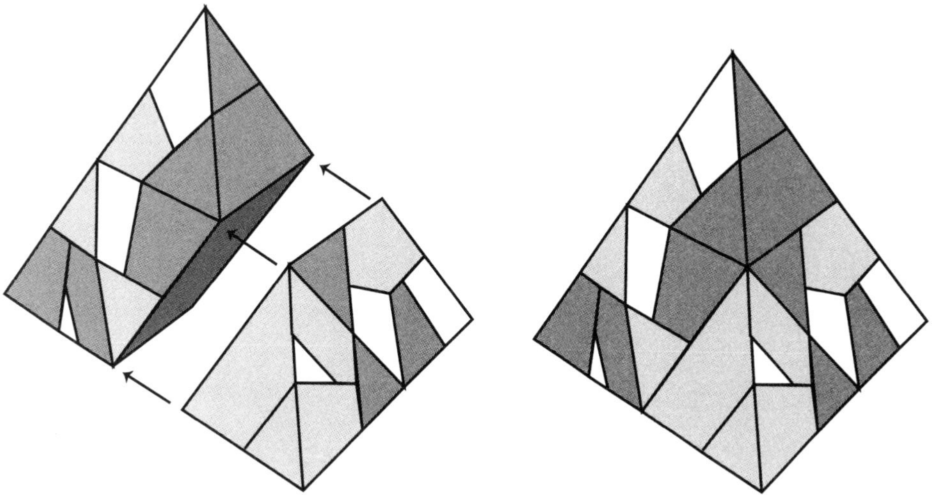

TETRAHEDRON PUZZLE

Part One: Folding the side units

1. Fold the square in half vertically and unfold.

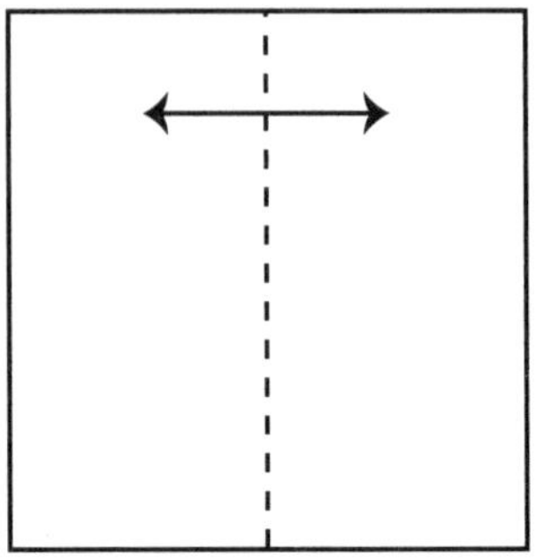

2. Fold from the bottom left corner as indicated by the dashed line so that the bottom right corner touches the midline.

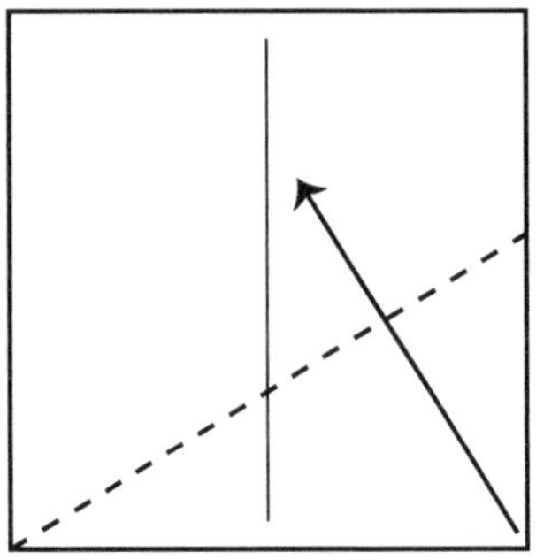

3. Fold the right side over so that the two points marked with dots meet as shown.

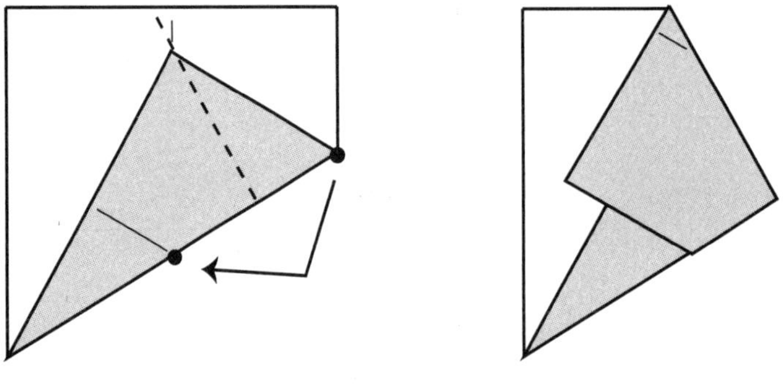

4. Unfold completely and fold the paper horizontally so that the two points marked by dots meet. The horizontal fold should go through the intersection of the two diagonals.

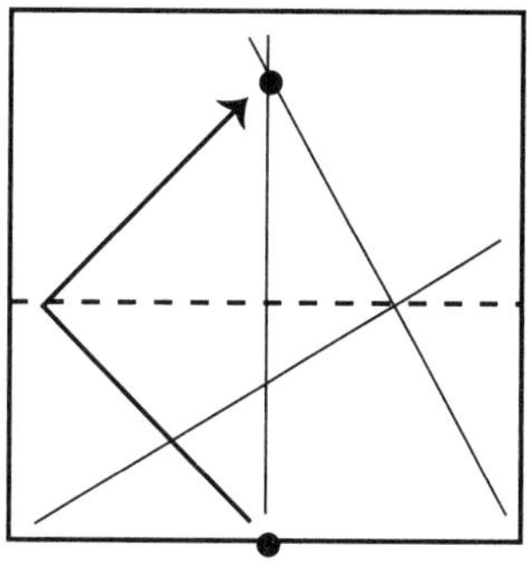

5. a. Fold the top part of the paper down at the point where the bottom edge meets the paper.
   b. Unfold the bottom half, but leave the top part folded down.

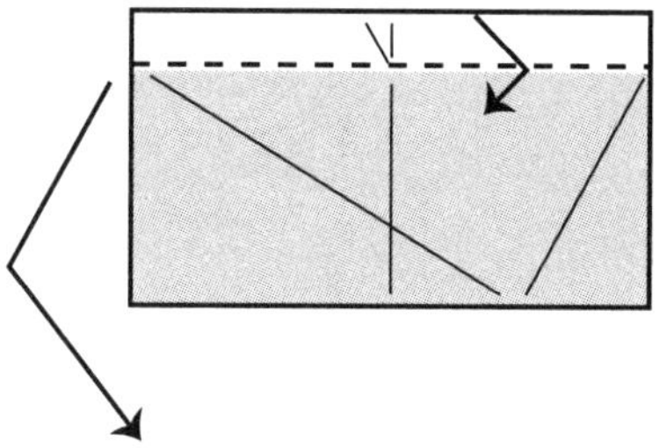

a.

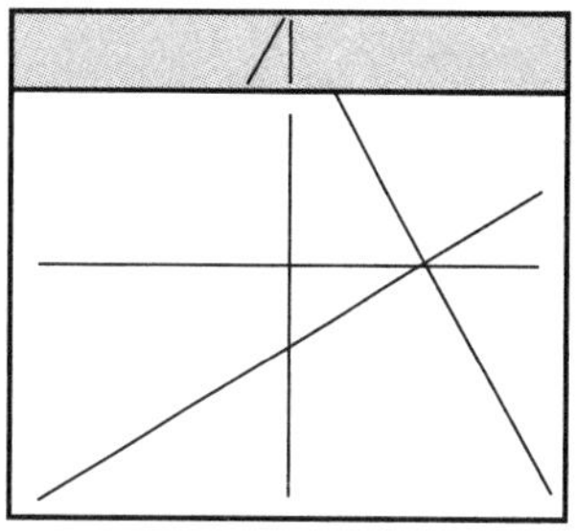

b.

6. Crease as indicated by each of the dashed lines, bringing the corners in to meet the horizontal midline.

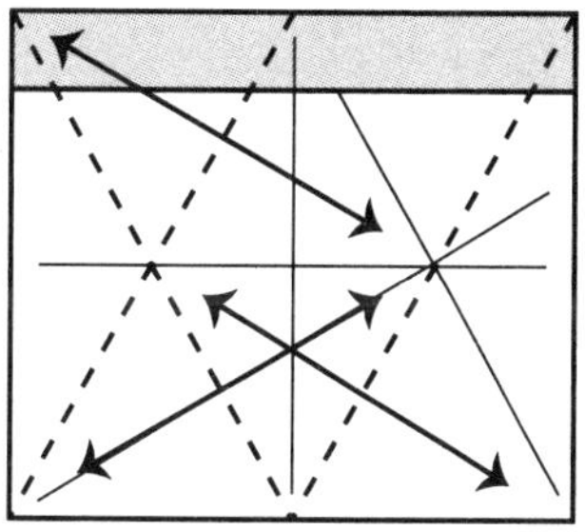

7. Fold the top left and bottom right corners where indicated by the dashed lines so that the corners touch the nearest diagonals. Notice that the two new sides formed are parallel to the nearest diagonals.

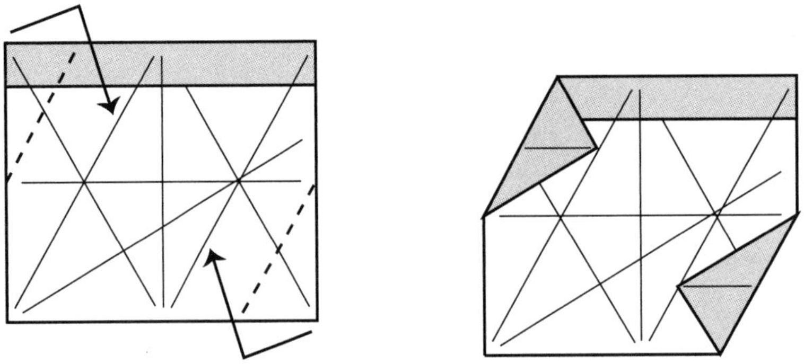

8. Fold again along the diagonals so that the two sides meet in the center.

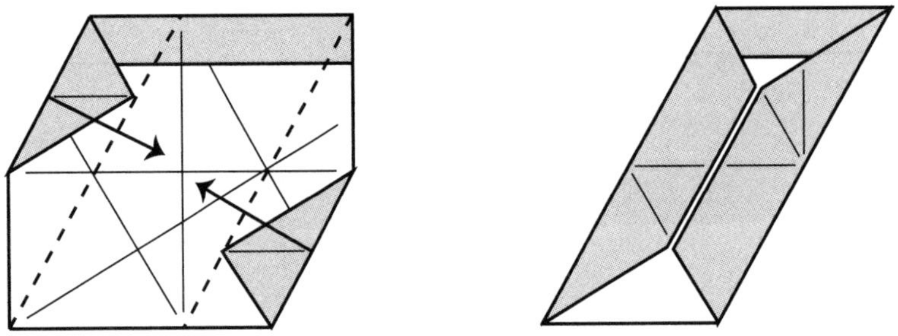

9. Flip the paper over and crease where indicated by the dashed lines. Repeat steps one through nine three more times so that you have a total of four pieces like the one shown below.

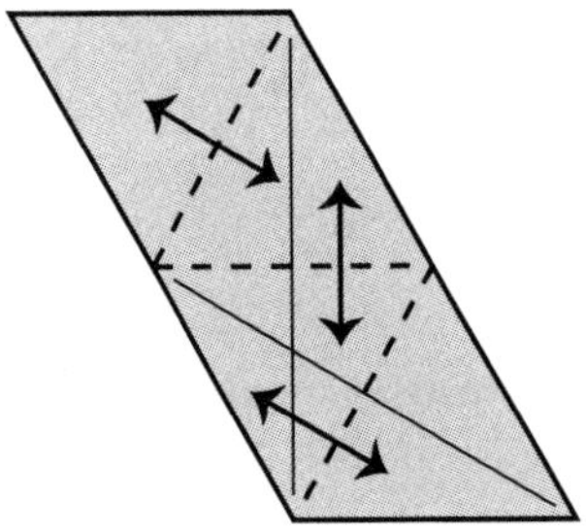
(x 4)

10. Repeat steps one through six with the remaining four squares. Steps seven through nine will be done as mirror images.
Fold the top right and bottom left corners where indicated by the dashed lines so that the corners touch the nearest diagonals. Notice that the two new sides formed are parallel to the nearest diagonals.

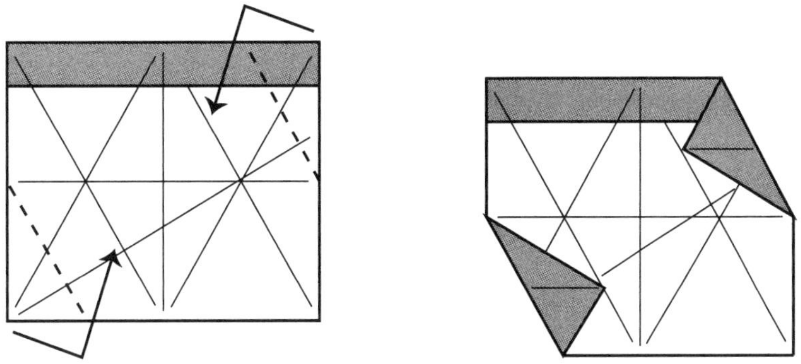

11. Fold again along the diagonals so that the two sides meet in the center.

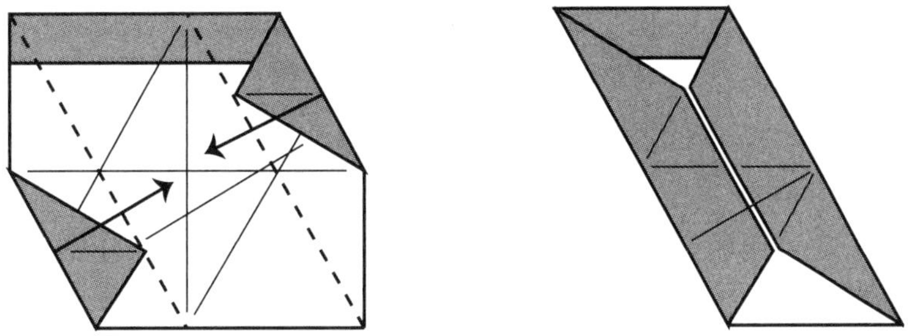

12. Flip the paper over and crease where indicated by the dashed lines. You should have four pieces like the one below that are mirror images of the first four you folded.

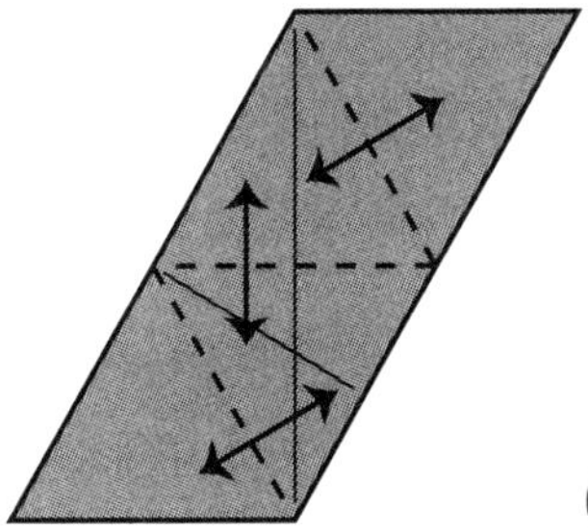

(x 4)

TETRAHEDRON PUZZLE

Part Two: Making the flat square base

1. Fold the square in half vertically and unfold and then horizontally and unfold.

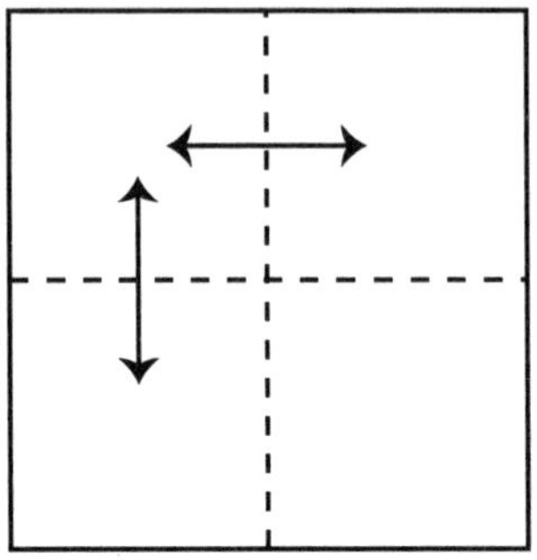

2. Fold the left and right edges in to meet the vertical midline and unfold.

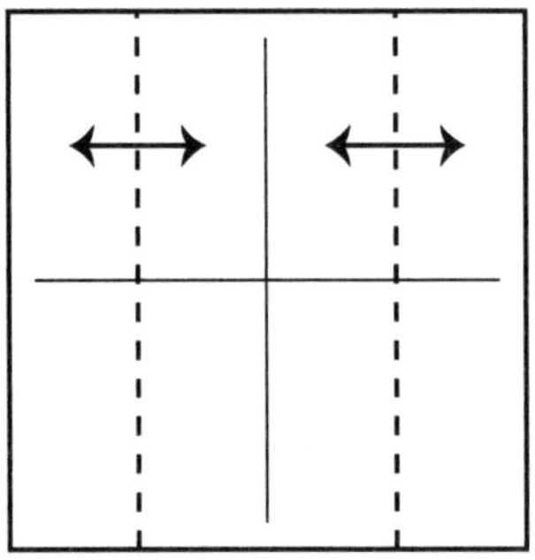

3. Fold the top and bottom edges in to meet the horizontal center fold line. Unfold only the bottom edge.

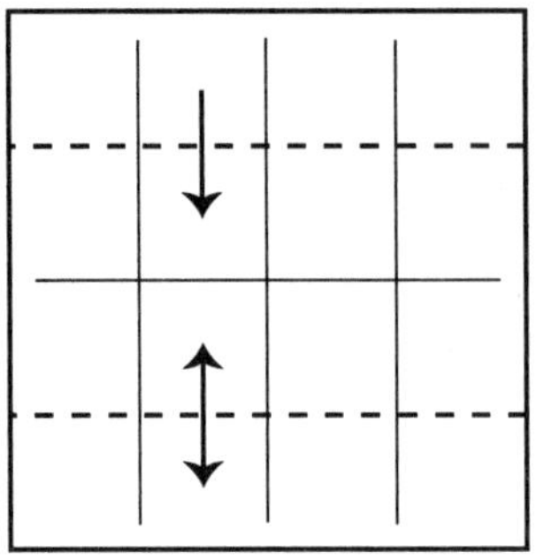

4. Take the corner of the flap that was just folded down and align it with the top edge of the paper. Do this by folding along the far right crease that was created in step 2. (Make sure you reinforce this crease well.) When you align the corner with the edge, flatten the paper, forming a small triangular flap that extends over the top edge as illustrated.

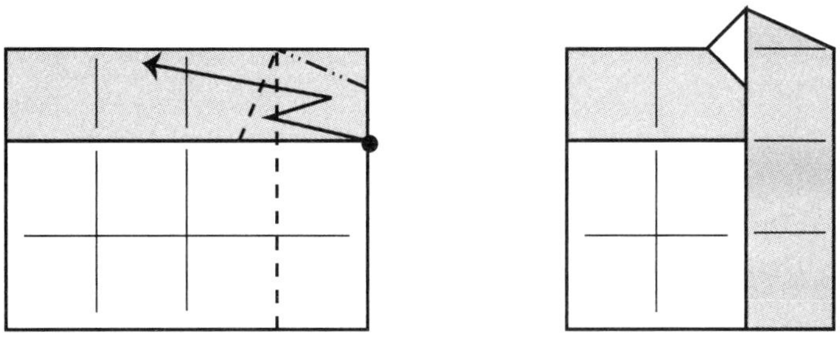

5. Repeat this process using the left side of the paper.

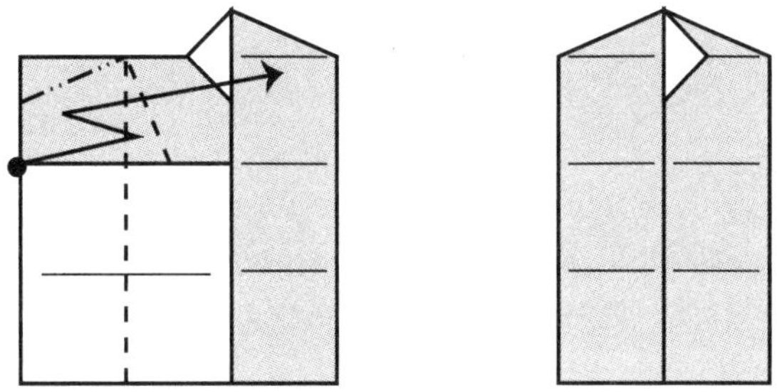

6. Unfold the paper, fold the bottom edge to meet the center horizontal fold line, and repeat the process from step 4.

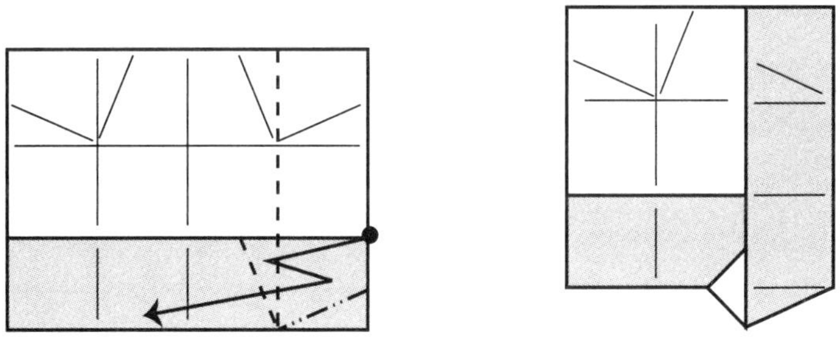

7. Do the same with the left side of the paper.

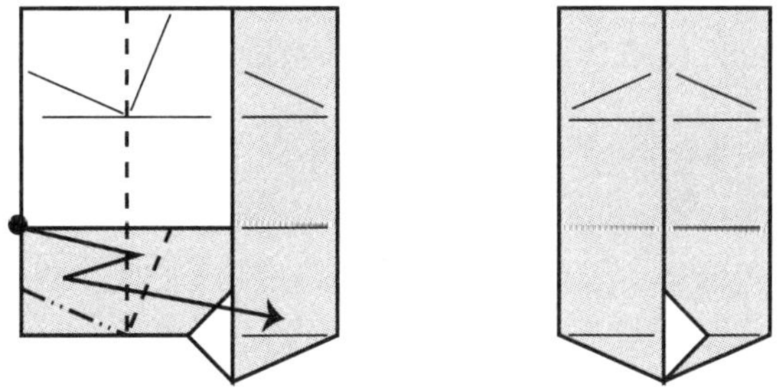

8. Refold the top section of the paper so that both the top and the bottom have identical triangular flaps.

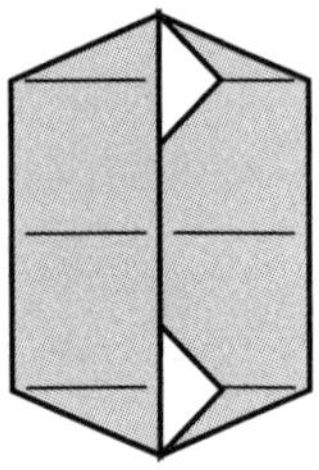

9. Tuck the small triangular pieces into the pockets directly beneath them.

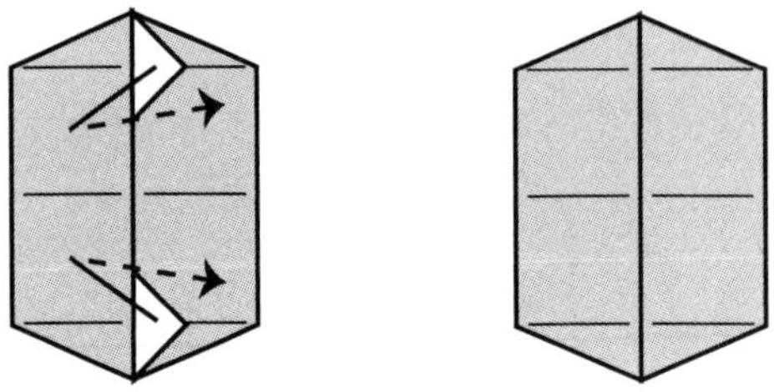

10. Using mountain folds, crease the triangular flaps as indicated and tuck them into the inside of the unit. This forms the completed square base.

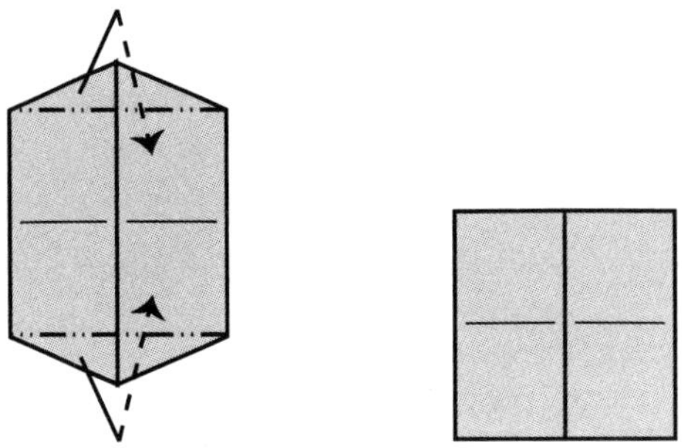

TETRAHEDRON PUZZLE

Part Three: Assembling the tetrahedron puzzle pieces

1. Insert two of the original units into the flat square piece as shown below so that the sides with pockets are facing the table.

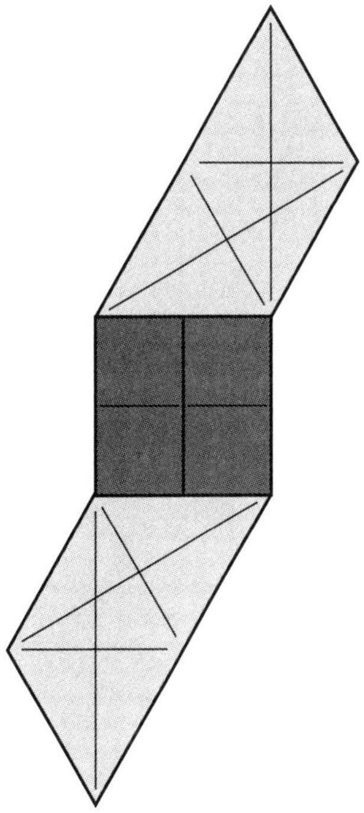

2. Lift the flaps and insert two of the mirror image pieces into the front flap as indicated.

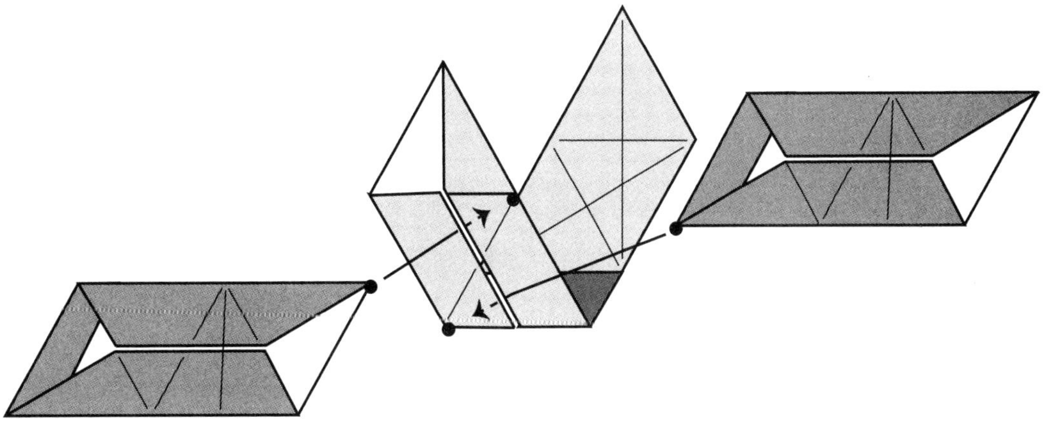

3. Insert the point from the back flap into the pocket on the indicated piece. This will create a sort of triangular tunnel over the square base.

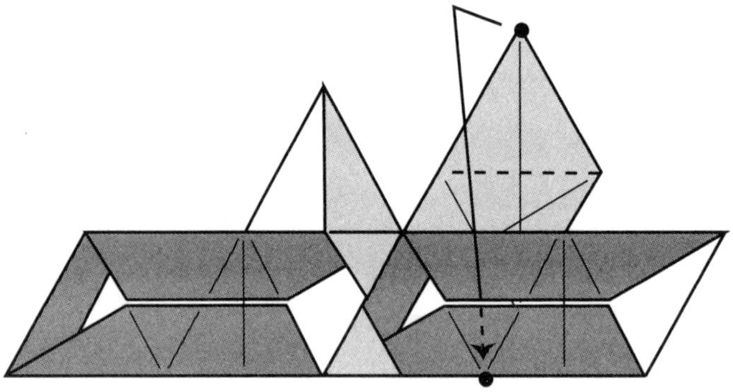

4. First, wrap the right and left flaps around to the back by mountain folding where indicated by the dashed lines. Once the flaps have been wrapped around, tuck the point marked with a dot into the pocket on the flap as shown. This pocket will now be on the back of the unit, and directly beneath the piece you are folding down. Finally, tuck the two loose tabs into the pockets lying directly beneath them.

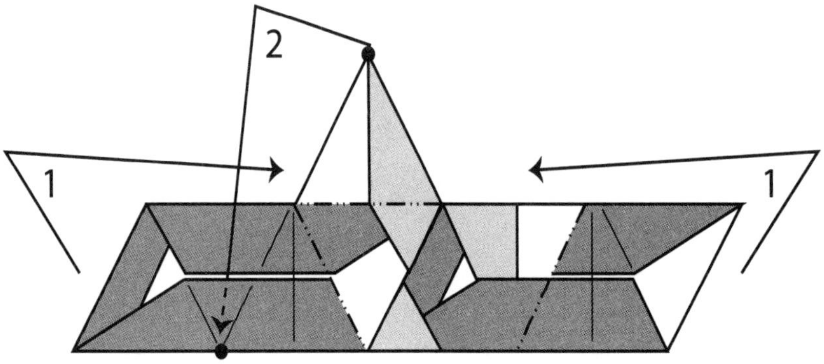

5. The final product should be a five-sided shape with one square face, two faces that are trapezoids, and two faces that are equilateral triangles. Repeat steps one through three with the remaining units so that you have a total of two identical puzzle pieces.

Top view

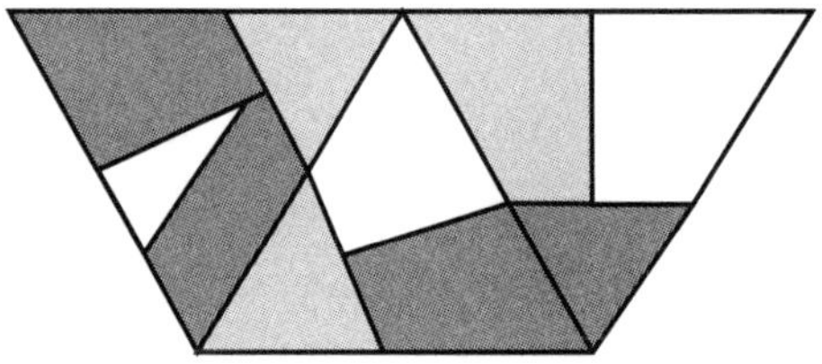

Side view

TETRAHEDRON PUZZLE

The object of this puzzle is to take the two identical pieces that you have created and put them together to form a regular tetrahedron.

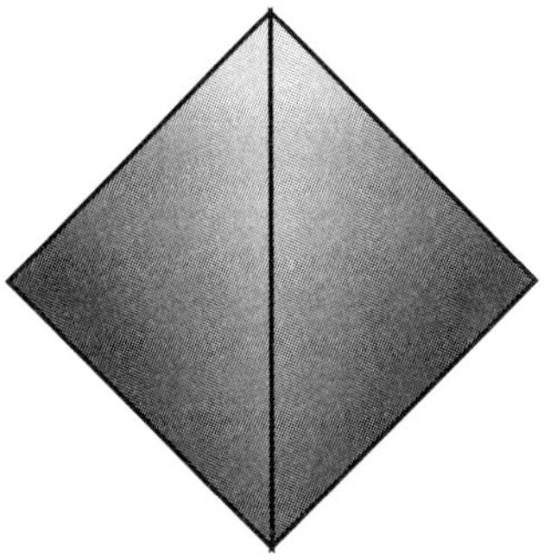

Side view

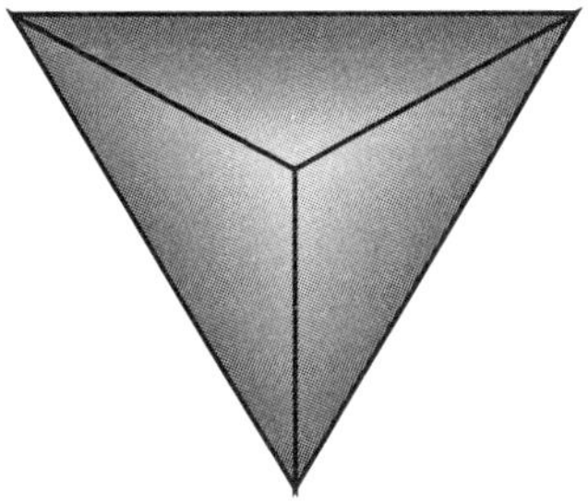

Top view

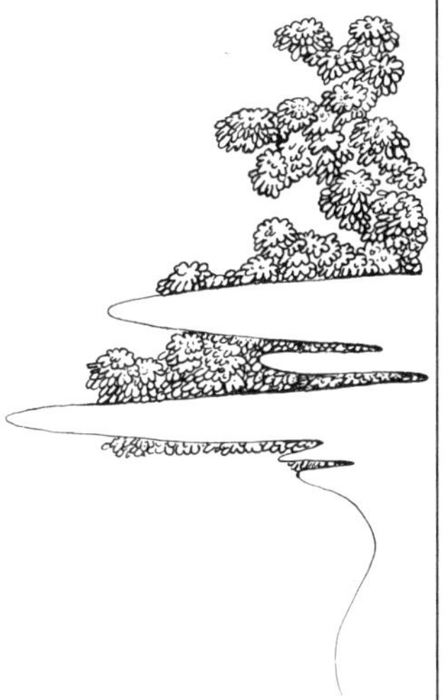

Draw a picture of your solution in the space below.

TETRAHEDRON PUZZLE

Exploration

Answer these questions after you have solved the puzzle.

1. If you were to break each puzzle piece into three smaller pieces, two of which were congruent tetrahedrons, what shape would the third piece be?

2. How are these "third pieces" oriented to each other in the solution?

3. If the two of the shapes mentioned above were joined base to base, what shape would be formed? How do you know?

4. Based on this information, into what Platonic solids can a regular tetrahedron be broken?

5. If you had thought about how a tetrahedron can be broken down before you attempted to solve the puzzle do you think it would have been easier for you? Why or why not?

6. Do you think any of the other Platonic solids can be broken down in similar ways? Why or why not?

SONOBÈ UNIT Folding Instructions

1. Fold the paper in half vertically and unfold.

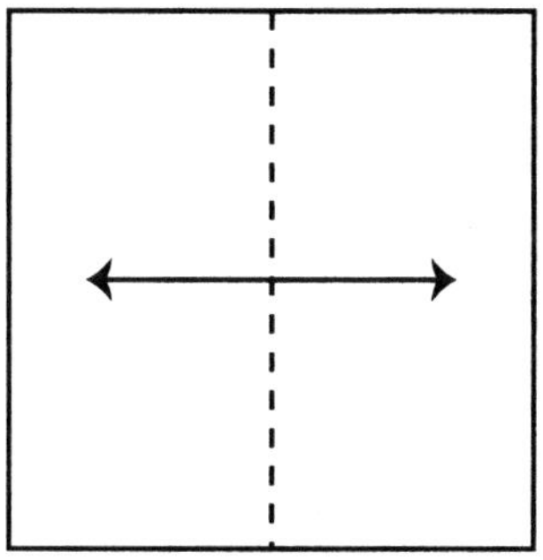

2. Fold the left edge and the right edge in to meet the center crease.

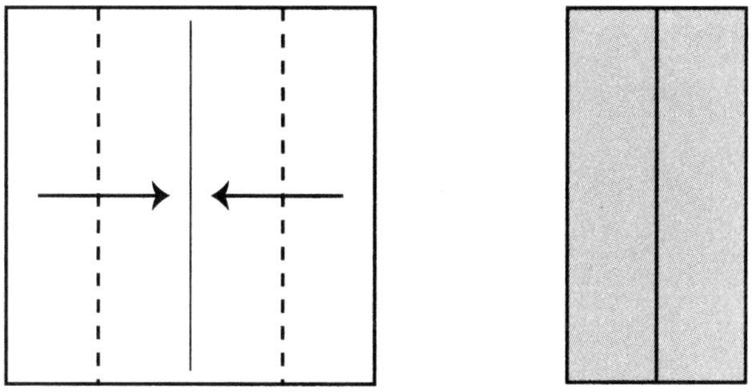

3. Fold as indicated by the dashed lines so that the top left corner meets the right side of the paper and the bottom right corner meets the left side of the paper.

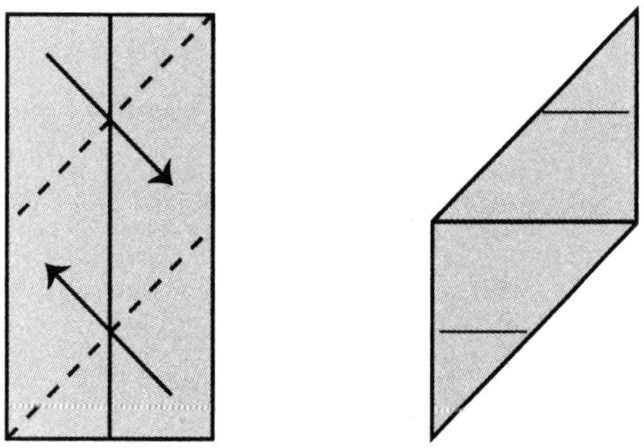

4. Unfold the paper completely. Fold the top right and bottom left corners in along the existing crease lines as shown.

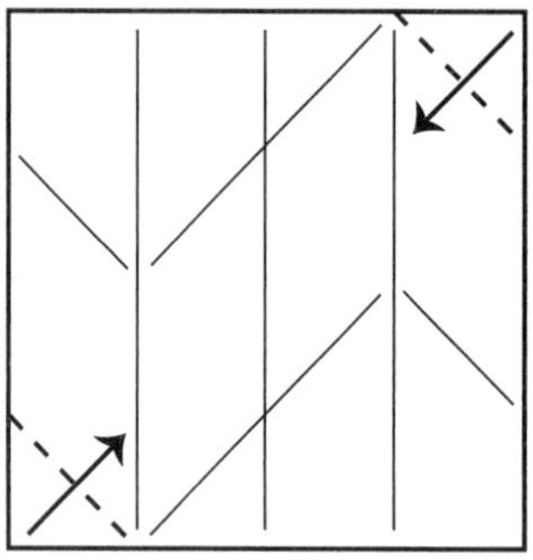

5. Fold the left and right sides of the paper in along the existing crease lines so that the edges meet in the middle.

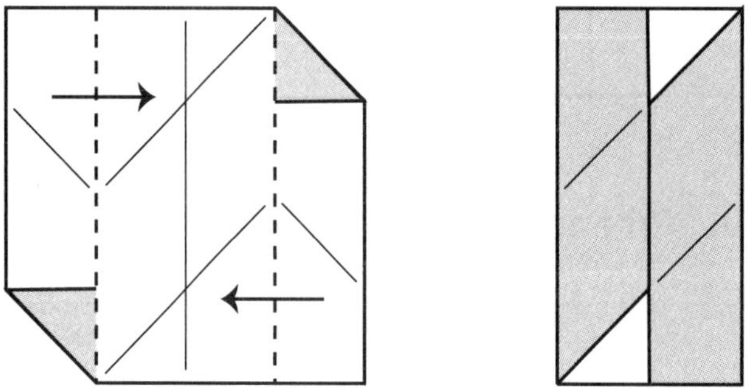

6. Fold the bottom right corner up along the existing crease line, tucking the corner underneath the flap as indicated.

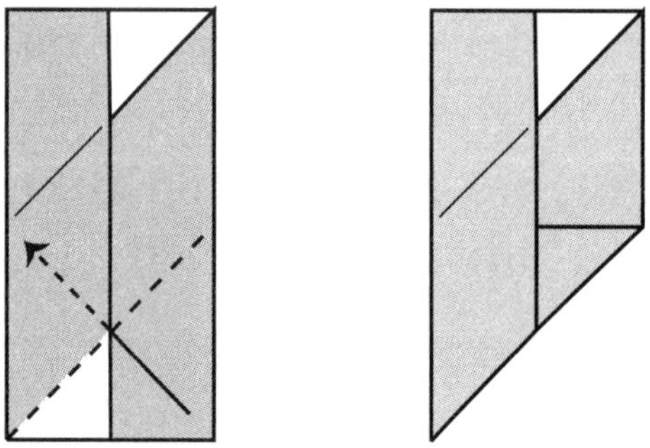

7. Repeat this process with the upper left corner, tucking it under the flap on the right side as indicated.

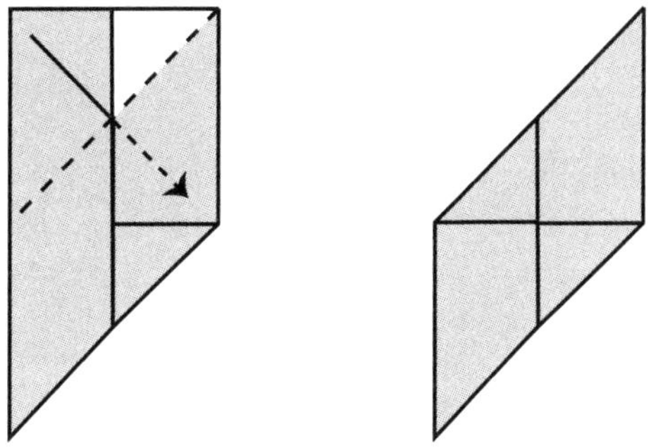

8. Flip the unit over and crease where indicated by the dashed lines. This is the completed Sonobè unit.

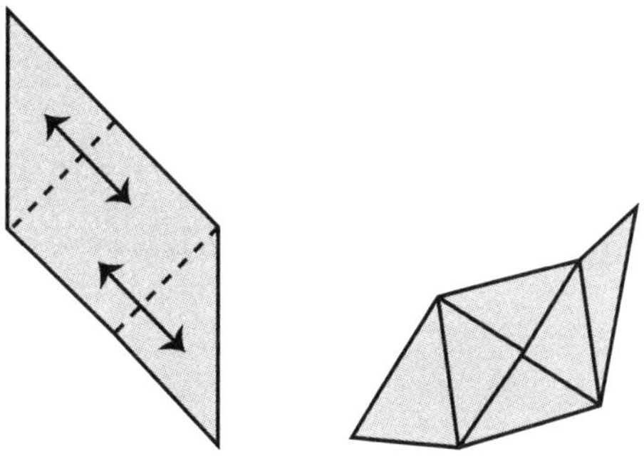

SONOBÈ UNIT Exploration

The following figures in this book can be folded with the Sonobè unit:

- Bird Tetrahedron
- Cube
- 24-Sided Figure
- Stellated Icosahedron

What do all of these figures have in common?

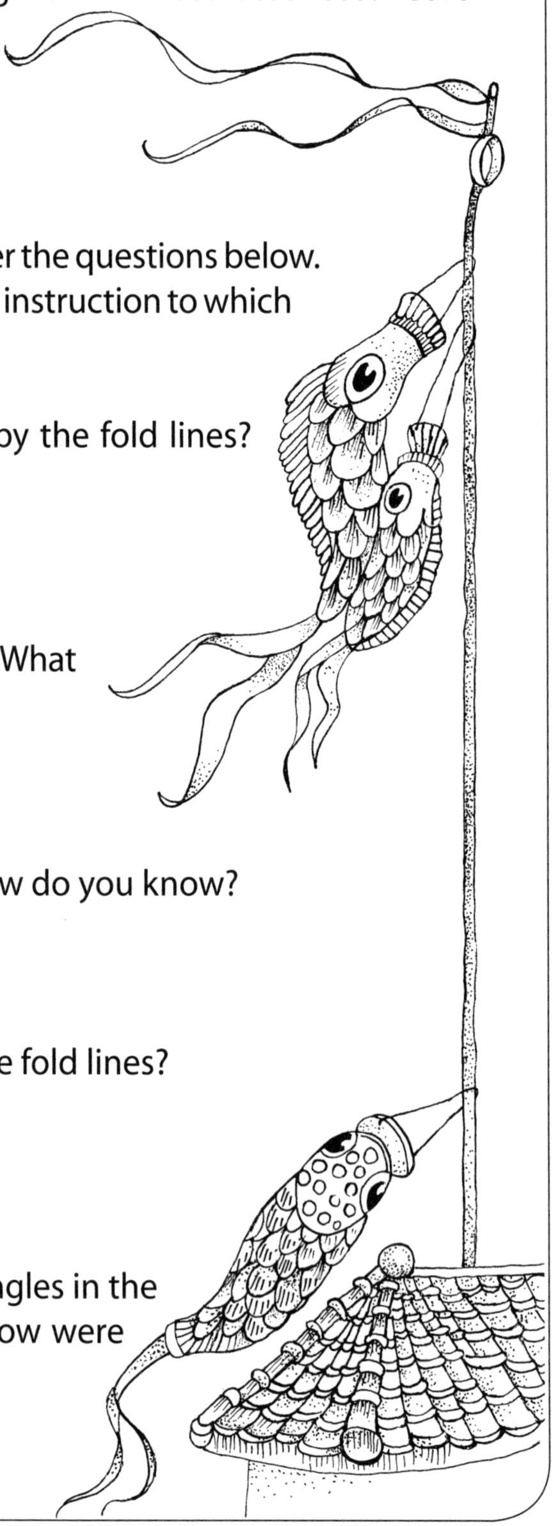

Fold an additional Sonobè unit. As you fold, answer the questions below. Each question is numbered according to the folding instruction to which it corresponds.

2. Into what shapes has the paper been divided by the fold lines? How are these shapes related to each other?

3. What shape is the paper now? How do you know? What are three characteristics of this shape?

4. What shape are the corners that you fold in? How do you know?

5. What angles do you see formed as a result of the fold lines? Justify your response.

8. What is the measure of the two small interior angles in the final shape? ...the two large interior angles? How were you able to determine this?

SONOBÈ UNIT Anatomy

Draw in all of the fold lines on the blank square provided. You will need to use your ruler to determine the exact placement of some of the lines. Beginning with the letter A at the top left corner of the square, label each corner and every place where a fold line intersects the edge of the square. Move in a clockwise direction, coming back to the place where you started. If you have drawn your diagram correctly, you should use the letters A through N.

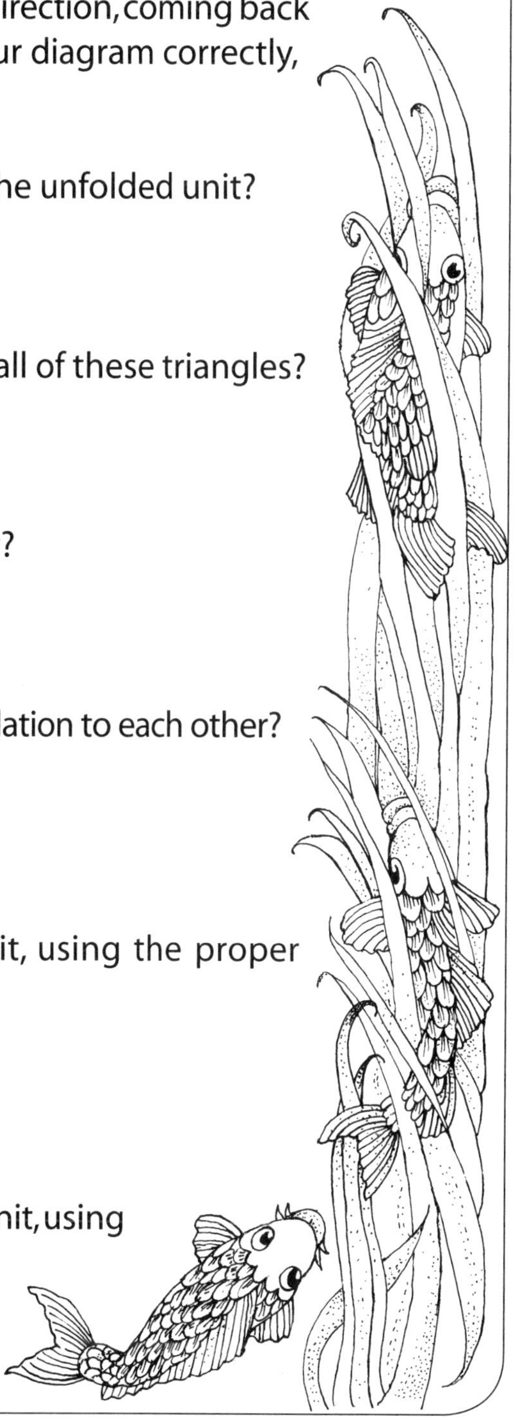

1. How many different sizes of triangles are there in the unfolded unit?

2. What can you say about the relationship between all of these triangles?

3. What angles are the diagonals in the unfolded unit?

4. What are some characteristics of these diagonals in relation to each other?

5. List each set of parallel lines in the unfolded unit, using the proper geometric notation.

6. List each set of perpendicular lines in the unfolded unit, using the proper geometric notation.

SONOBÈ UNIT Anatomy

Use this square to draw in the fold lines of the Sonobè unit.

Sonobè Unit Exploration

2. Into what shapes has the paper been divided by the fold lines? How are these shapes related to each other? [It has been divided into four congruent rectangles.]
3. What shape is the paper now? [parallelogram] How do you know? What are three characteristics of this shape? [two sets of parallel sides, two sets of congruent sides, two sets of congruent angles]
4. What shape are the corners that you fold in? [isosceles right triangles] How do you know? [They have one right angle (the corner of the square) and two congruent sides.]
5. What angles do you see formed as a result of the fold lines? [45°, 135°] Justify your response. [The fold lines bisect the corners. Half of 90° is 45°. The fold lines intersect the edges of the paper at the same angle (45°), which makes the larger angle 135° (180° - 45° = 135°).]
8. What is the measure of the two small interior angles in the final shape? [45°] ...the two large interior angles? [135°] How were you able to determine this?

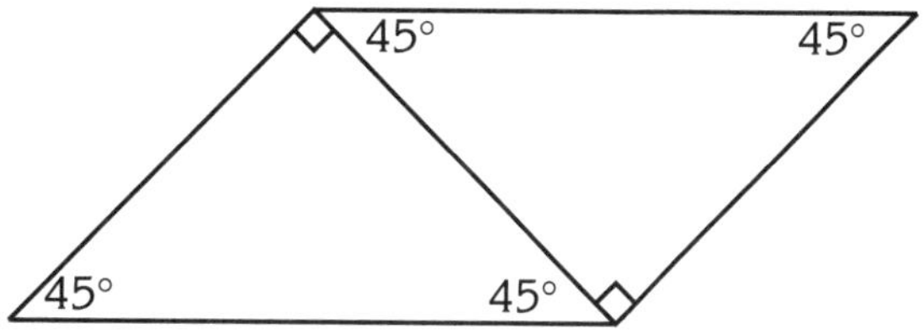

As you can see in the illustration above, the Sonobè unit can be divided into two isocoles right triangles. When the shape is thought of in this manner, the measures of the interior angles can be very quickly determined by using what is already known about isocoles right triangles (45° + 90° = 135°).

Sonobè Unit Anatomy

1. How many different sizes of triangles are there in the unfolded unit? [Five. One example of each size is highlighted in the diagram below.]]
2. What can you say about the relationship between all of these triangles? [They are all similar.]
3. What angles are the diagonals in the unfolded unit? [All of the diagonals are 45° angles.]
4. What are some characteristics of these diagonals in relation to each other? [They are parallel and perpendicular to each other.]
5. List each set of parallel lines in the unfolded unit, using the proper geometric notation. [BK || CJ || DI, BN || DM || FK || GI, DF || BG || NI || MK]
6. List each set of perpendicular lines in the unfolded unit, using the proper geometric notation. [BN $\perp$ BG, BN $\perp$ NI, BG $\perp$ DM, DM $\perp$ DF, DF $\perp$ FK, FK $\perp$ BG, GI $\perp$ NI, NI $\perp$ FK, FK $\perp$ MK, DM $\perp$ NI, DM $\perp$ MK, BG $\perp$ GI]

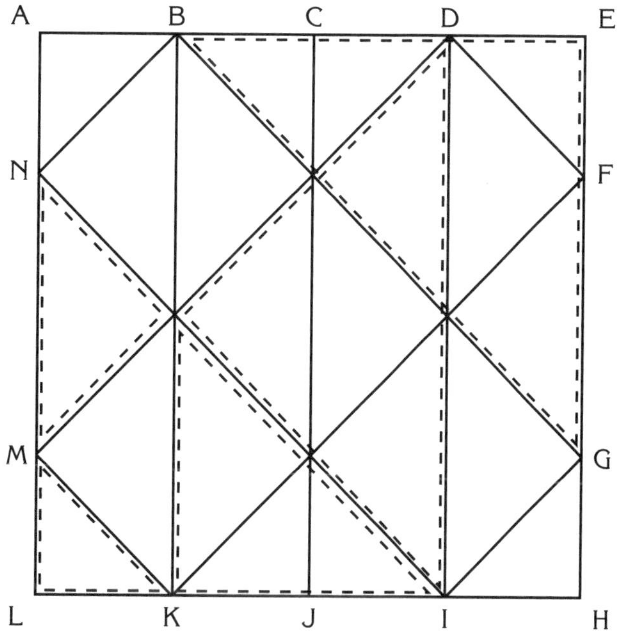

EQUILATERAL TRIANGLE UNIT

Folding Instructions

1. Fold the square in half vertically and unfold.

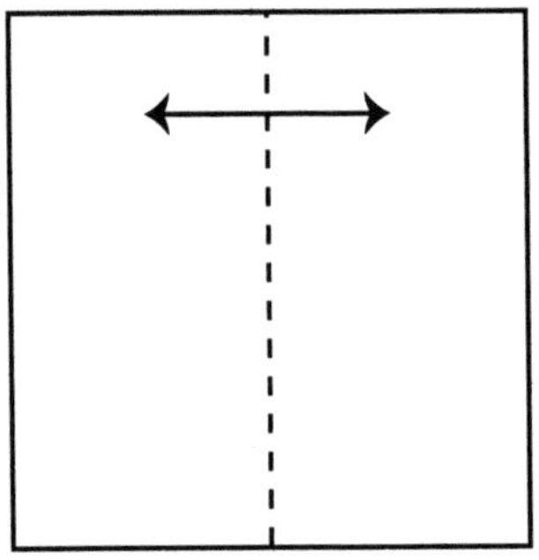

2. Fold from the bottom left corner as indicated by the dashed line so that the bottom right corner touches the midline.

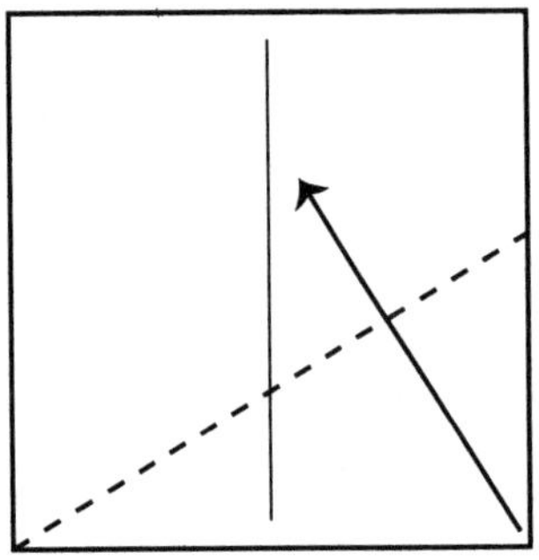

3. Fold the right side over so that the two points marked with dots meet as shown.

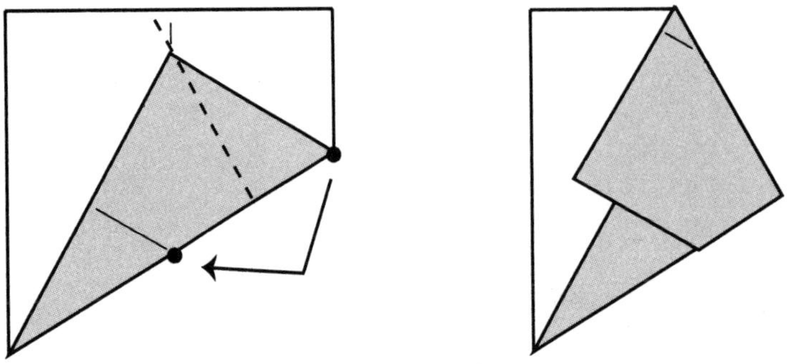

4. Unfold completely and fold the paper horizontally so that the two points marked by dots meet. The horizontal fold should go through the intersection of the two diagonals.

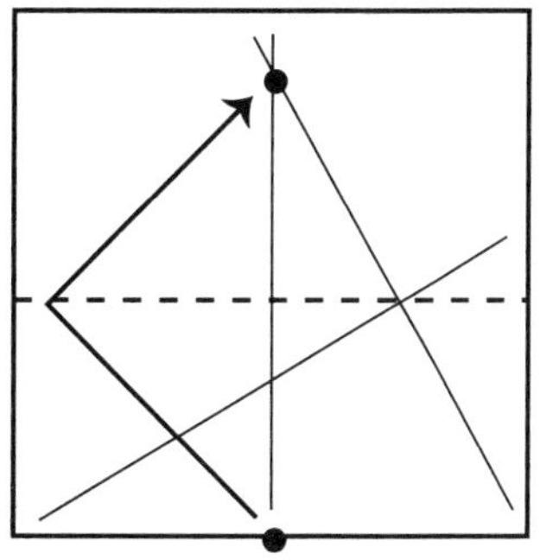

5. a. Fold the top part of the paper down at the point where the bottom edge meets the paper.
   b. Unfold the bottom half, but leave the top part folded down.

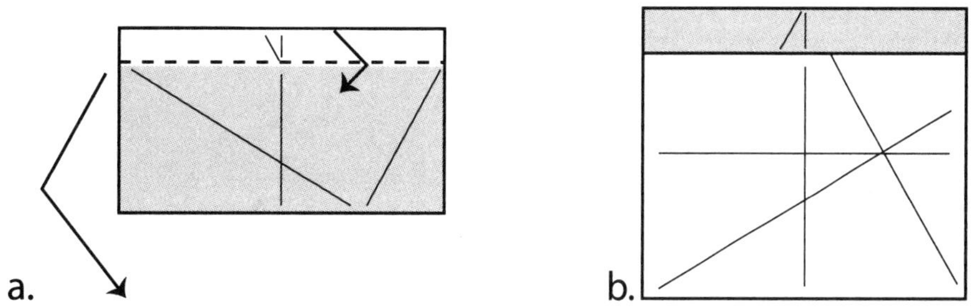

6. Crease as indicated by each of the dashed lines, bringing the corners in to meet the horizontal midline.

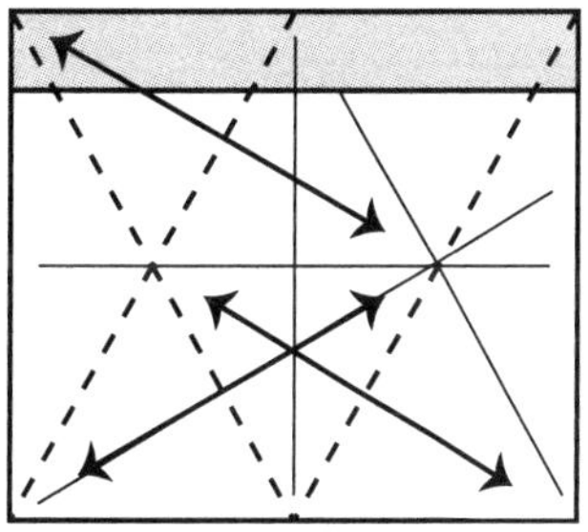

7. Fold the top left and bottom right corners where indicated by the dashed lines so that the corners touch the nearest diagonals. Notice that the two new sides formed are parallel to the nearest diagonals.

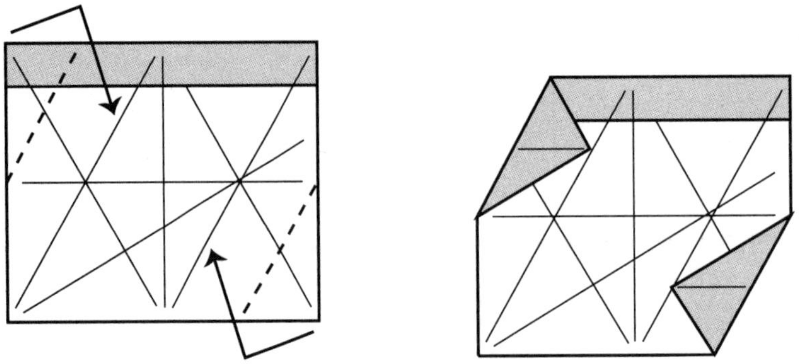

8. Fold again along the diagonals so that the two sides meet in the center.

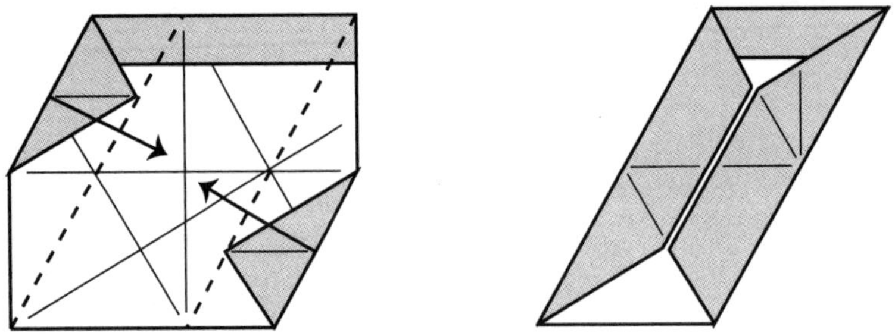

9. Flip the paper over and crease where indicated by the dashed lines. This is your completed equilateral triangle unit.

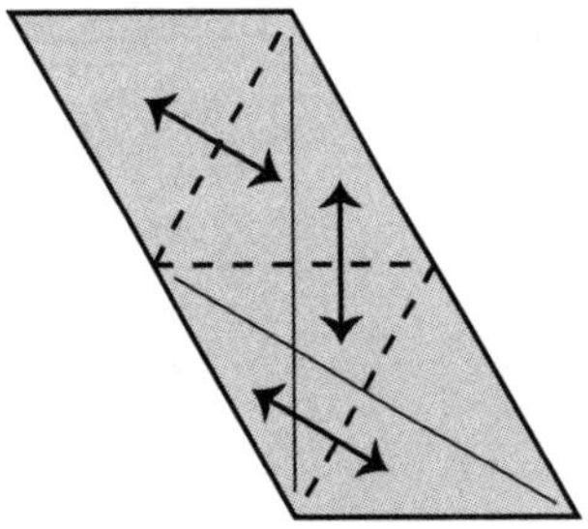

EQUILATERAL TRIANGLE UNIT Exploration

The following figures in this book can be folded with the Equilateral Triangle Unit:

• Tetrahedron • Octahedron • Icosahedron

1. What do all of these figures have in common?

Fold an additional equilateral triangle unit. As you fold, answer the questions below. Each question is numbered according to the folding instruction it corresponds with.

2. Estimate the measure of the angle formed by the bottom left corner of the paper. Explain your thinking.

3. What is the angle of the corner that was created by folding the right side over to meet the crease? How could you verify this?

6. What shapes are formed by these diagonal fold lines?

7. What shape is the paper now? How do you know? What shape are the tabs that you folded over?

8. What shape is the paper now? How do you know?

EQUILATERAL TRIANGLE UNIT Anatomy

Unfold the additional unit you just folded and use it to answer the following questions and complete the diagram on the next page.

1. Draw in the diagonals formed by your folds in step six. What angles do these folds form with the edges of the paper? Justify your response.

2. Label the new intersections created by the lines you drew in with uppercase letters that have not already been used. List all of the equilateral triangles in the diagram.

3. List all of the right triangles in the diagram.

4. How does the number of right triangles compare to the number of equilateral triangles?

5. Are there any similar triangles? List them and show why they are similar.

6. Identify the parallel fold lines in the figure. How do you know that they are parallel?

EQUILATERAL TRIANGLE UNIT

Anatomy

Follow the instructions on the previous sheet to complete the diagram.

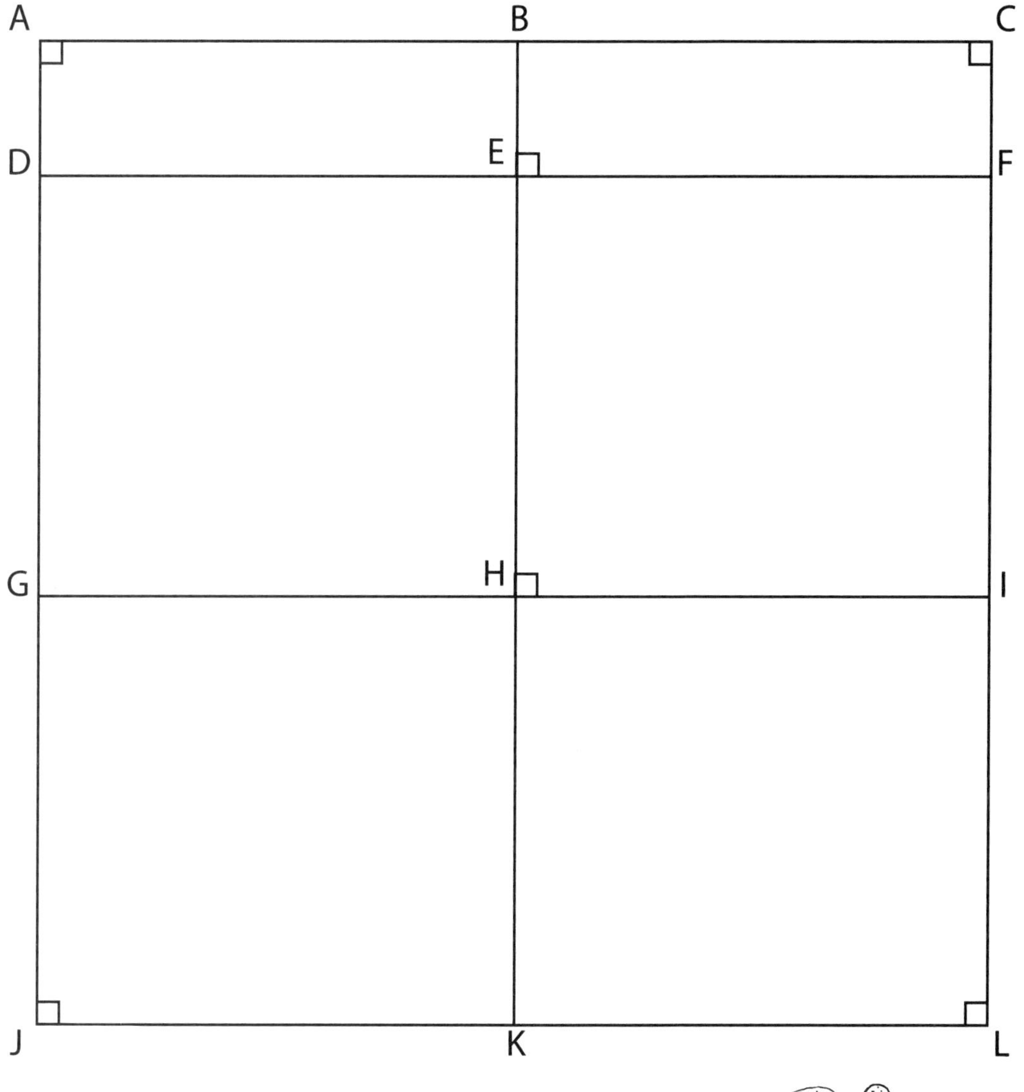

Equilateral Triangle Exploration

2. Estimate the measure of the angle formed by the bottom left corner of the paper. Explain your thinking. [The angle is 60°. Students should be able to recognize that it is greater than 45° but less than 90°.]
3. What is the angle of the corner that was created by folding the right side over to meet the crease? [90°] How could you verify this? [Hold the corner of a piece of paper up to the angle. If it matches, it is 90°.]
6. What shapes are formed by these diagonal fold lines? [equilateral triangles, right triangles, obtuse isosceles triangles]
7. What shape is the paper now? [irregular hexagon] How do you know? [It has six sides, but the angles are not the same and the lengths of the sides are not the same.] What shape are the tabs that you folded over? [right triangles]
8. What shape is the paper now? [parallelogram] How do you know? [It has two sets of parallel sides.]

Equilateral Triangle Anatomy

1. What angles do these folds form with the edges of the paper? [The fold lines form 30° and 60° angles with the edges of the paper. You know this because each diagonal forms the side of an equliateral triangle, and each interior angle of an equilatearal triangle is 60°. The smaller angles formed must be 30° because 90° – 60° = 30°.]
2. List all of the equilateral triangles in the diagram. [The equilateral triangles in this diagram are: ΔMNE, ΔDEO, ΔEPO, ΔEFP, ΔOKJ, ΔOPK, ΔPLK, ΔELJ, and ΔDFK.]
3. List all of the right triangles in the diagram. [The right triangles in this diagram are: ΔMBE, ΔBNE, ΔDOG, ΔEHO, ΔEPH, ΔFIP, ΔGOJ, ΔOHK, ΔHPK, ΔPIL, ΔDEK, ΔEFK, ΔEKJ, ΔELK, ΔDKJ, ΔFLK, ΔDEJ, and ΔEFL.]
4. How does the number of right triangles compare to the number of equilateral triangles? [There are twice as many right triangles as there are equilateral triangles.]
5. Are there any similar triangles? List them and show why they are similar. [There are similar right triangles and similar equilateral triangles in the diagram. The small right triangles ΔMBE and ΔBNE are similar to all of the larger right triangles. The two large equilateral triangles ΔELJ and ΔDFK are similar to all of the smaller equilateral triangles.]
6. Identify the parallel fold lines in the figure. How do you know that they are parallel? [The parallel lines in this diagram are: DF || GI, NJ || FK, DK || ML .] The way in which the additional intersections are labeled may vary from student to student.

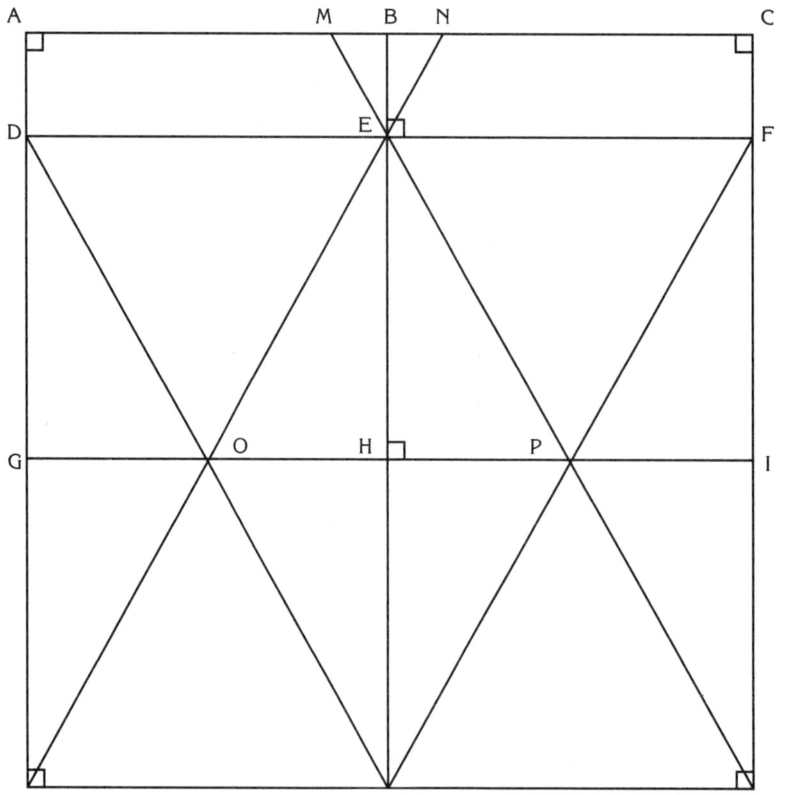

RIGHT TRIANGLE UNIT Folding Instructions

1. Fold the square in half vertically and unfold.

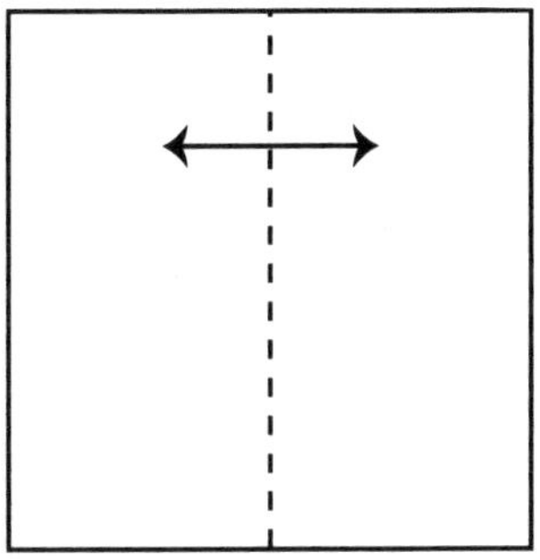

2. Fold the left and right edges in to meet the midline and unfold.

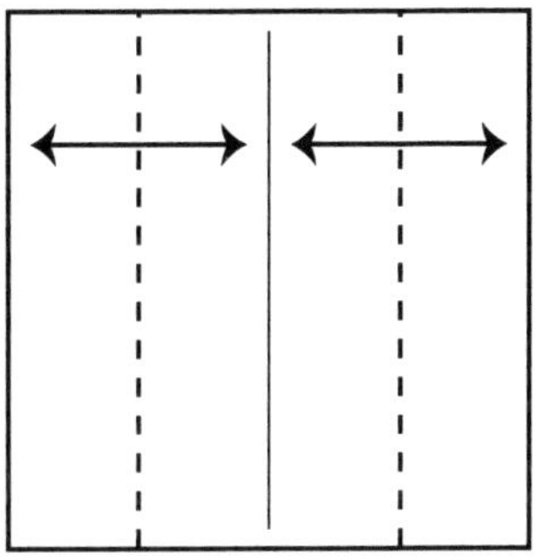

3. Fold the upper right and lower left corners as indicated by the dashed lines so that they lie flush with the nearest fold line.

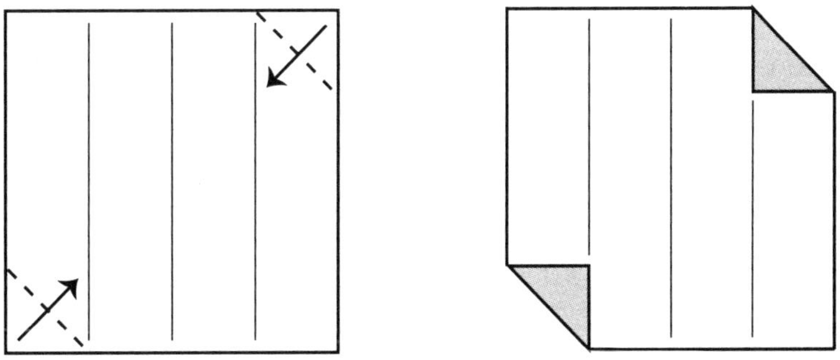

4. Fold the same corners in again as indicated by the dashed lines so that they lie flush with the nearest fold line.

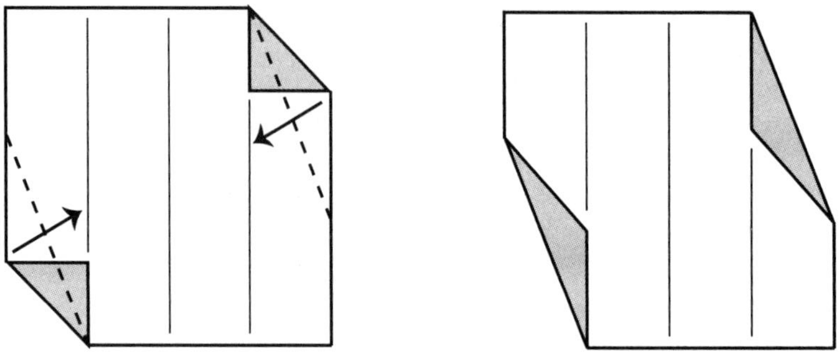

5. Fold the right and left sides in along the vertical folds to meet the midline.

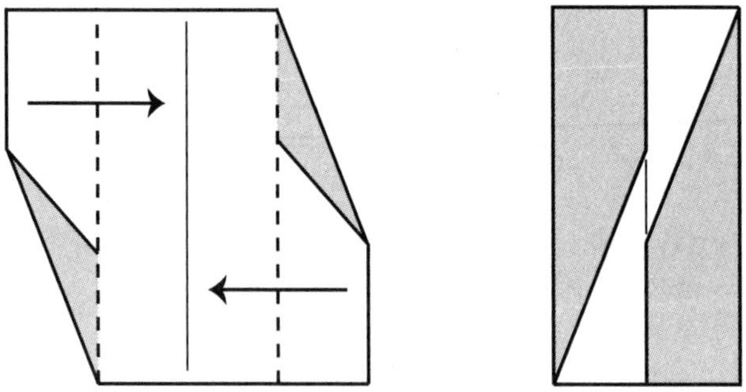

6. Fold the bottom side up so that it is flush with the left side of the paper. Fold the top side down so that it is flush with the right side of the paper.

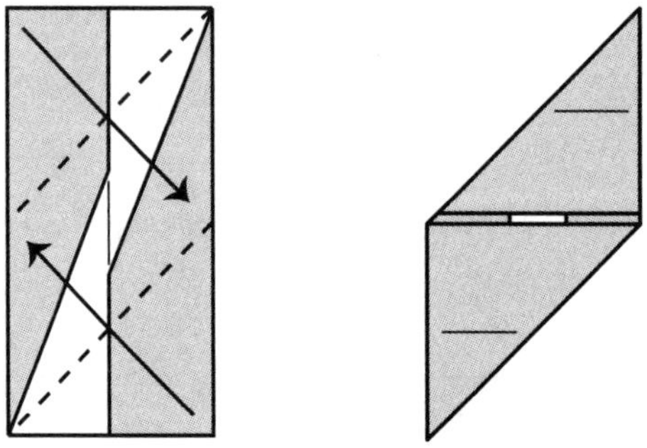

7. Tuck the corner points of each triangle into the pockets directly underneath them.

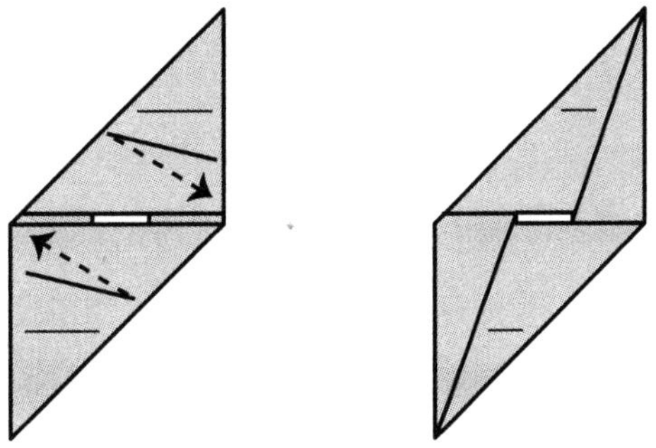

8. Flip the unit over to the back side. Fold as indicated by the dashed lines to form a square-shaped piece with two triangular tabs. This is the completed right triangle unit.

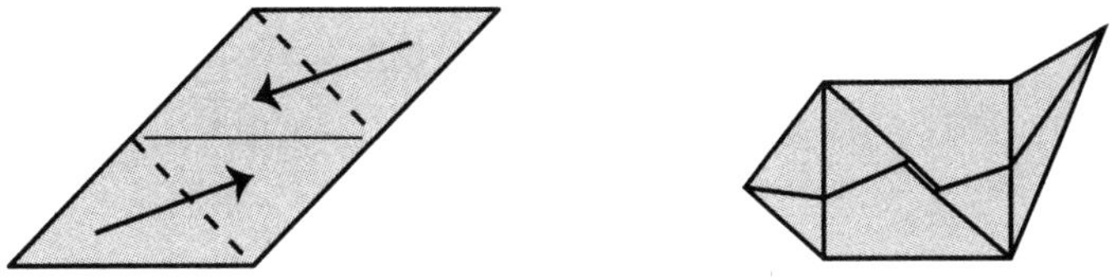

RIGHT TRIANGLE UNIT Exploration

The following figures in this book can be folded with the right triangle unit:

- Bird Tetrahedron • Cube • 24-Sided Figure • Stellated Icosahedron

1. What do all of these figures have in common?

Fold an additional right triangle unit. As you fold, answer the questions below. Each question is numbered according to the folding instruction it corresponds with.

2. What are the characteristics of the fold lines on the square? What shapes do these fold lines create on the paper? How are these shapes related to each other?

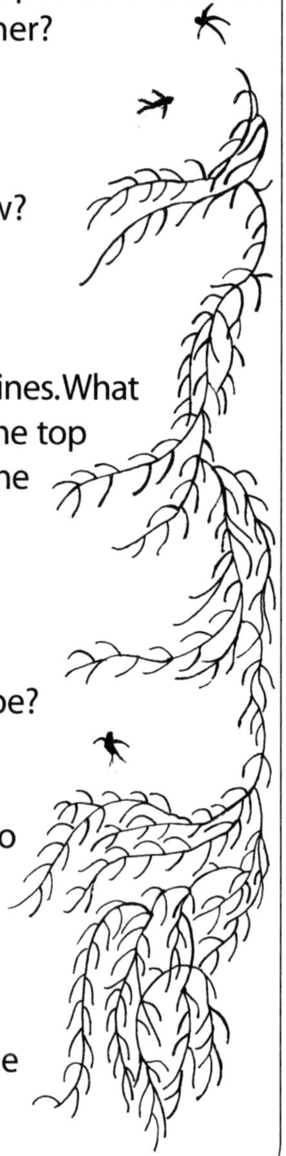

3. What type of triangles were created by this fold? How do you know?

4. Unfold the top right corner of the square and look at the diagonal fold lines. What is the measure of the angle of each of these fold lines in relation to the top edge of the paper, and how do you know? (When you have answered the question refold the top right corner and continue folding.)

6. What shape is the paper now? What are three properties of this shape?

7. What kind of triangles exist before the corner points are tucked in to the pockets? What types of triangles exist after the corner points are tucked in to the pockets? How do you know?

8. Look at the final unit. Into what shapes can this parallelogram be divided?

RIGHT TRIANGLE UNIT Anatomy

Use the additional unit you folded and the diagram on the following page to answer the questions below.

1. How many parallel fold lines are there in the right triangle unit? Label each one using upper case letters and use appropriate geometric notation to record them below.

2. Label and list at least five perpendicular fold lines that exist in the right triangle unit.

3. What shape appears to be in the center of the paper? What other unit has this shape at its center? Why do you think that is?

4. List the different kinds of triangles that exist in the unfolded unit. Highlight one example of each kind on the diagram.

RIGHT TRIANGLE UNIT Anatomy

Use this square to answer the questions on the previous page. Use upper case letters to label the necessary intersections.

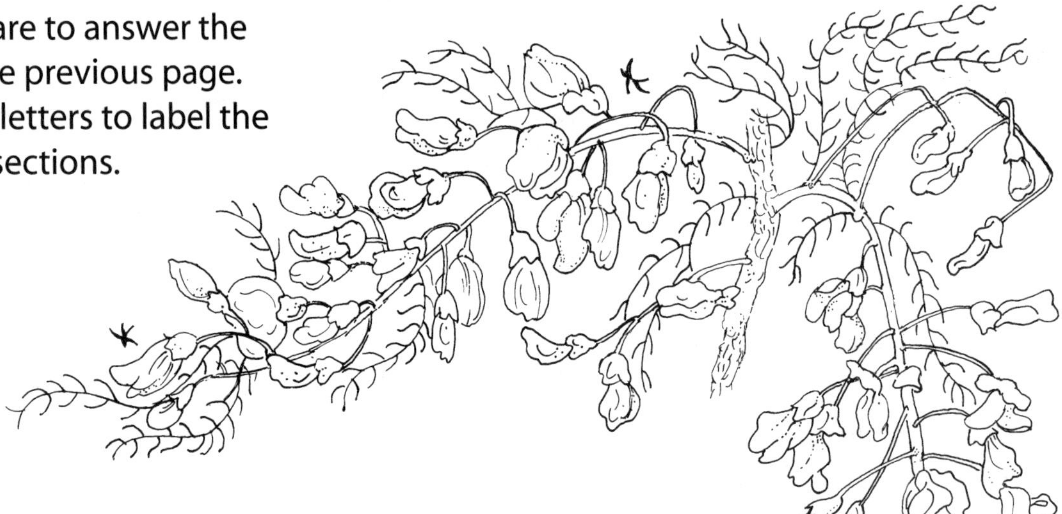

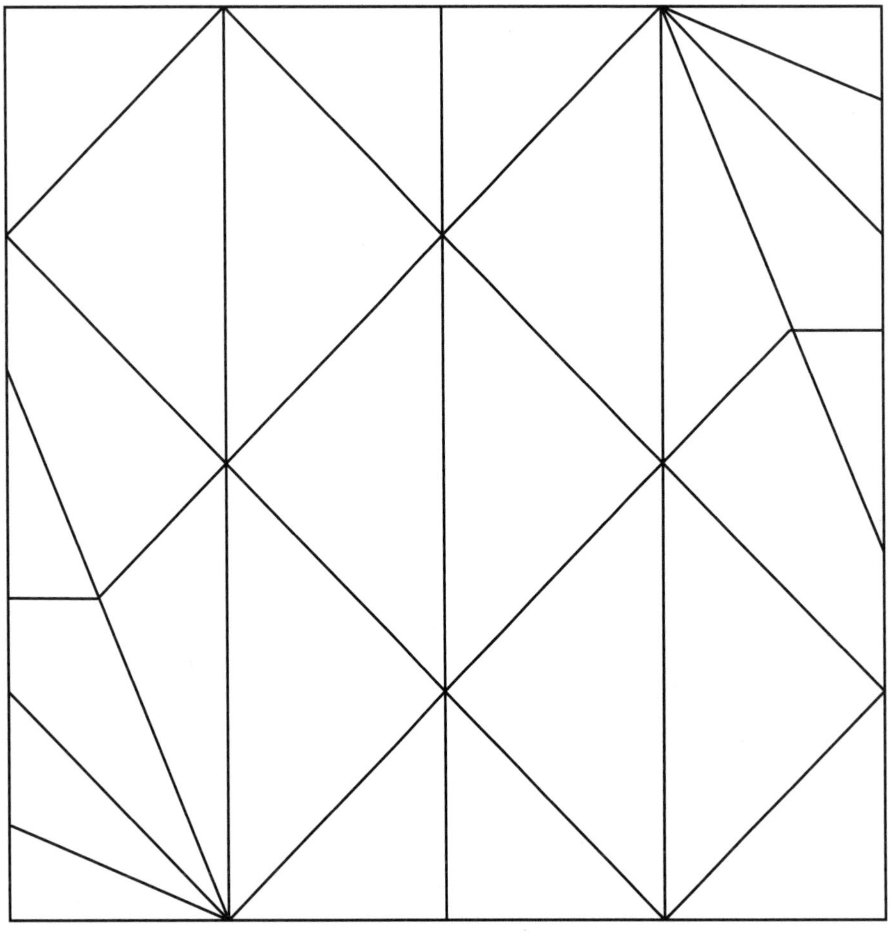

Right Triangle Exploration

2. What are the characteristics of the fold lines on the square? [They are parallel.] What shapes do these fold lines create on the paper? [They divide the paper into four rectangles.] How are these shapes related to each other? [They are congruent.]
3. What type of triangles were created by this fold? [isosceles right triangles] How do you know? [They have one right angle (the corner of the square) and two congruent sides.]
4. What is the measure of the angle of each of these fold lines in relation to the top edge of the paper, and how do you know? [The fold lines divide a 90° angle into even fourths. The first line has a measure of 22.5°, the second 45°, and the third 67.5°.]
6. What shape is the paper now? [parallelogram] What are three properties of this shape? [two sets of parallel sides, two sets of congruent sides, two sets of congruent angles]
7. What kind of triangles exist before the corner points are tucked in to the pockets? [isosceles right triangles] What types of triangles exist after the corner points are tucked in to the pockets? [scalene triangles] How do you know? [None of the sides or angles are congruent.]
8. Look at the final unit. Into what shapes can this parallelogram be divided? [It can be divided into a square and two congruent isosceles right triangles, or four congruent isosceles right triangles.]

Right Triangle Anatomy

1. How many parallel fold lines are there in the right triangle unit? [All sets of parallel fold lines are listed here, but keep in mind that the way students have labeled their diagrams may be different than the way shown below. AP || BQ || CR, GH || KL, AE || CL || GP || NR, CF || AN || ER || MP, CD || OP, CJ || IP.]
2. Label and list at least five perpendicular fold lines in the unit. [AE ⊥ AN, AN ⊥ CL, ER ⊥ CL, ER ⊥ GP, MP ⊥ GP, etc.]
3. What shape appears to be in the center of the paper? [a square] What other unit has this shape at its center? [the Sonobè unit] Why do you think that is? [The Sonobè unit and the right triangle unit can all be used to make shapes with faces that are squares or isosceles right triangles. The square in the center of the unit corresponds to the square face that the folded unit produces.]
4. List the different kinds of triangles that exist in the unit. Highlight one example of each kind on the diagram. [There are three kinds of triangles in the unfolded unit. Each kind has been highlighted with a dashed line. From the top right corner to the bottom left corner they are: right triangle (not isosceles), isosceles right triangle, and obtuse scalene triangle.]

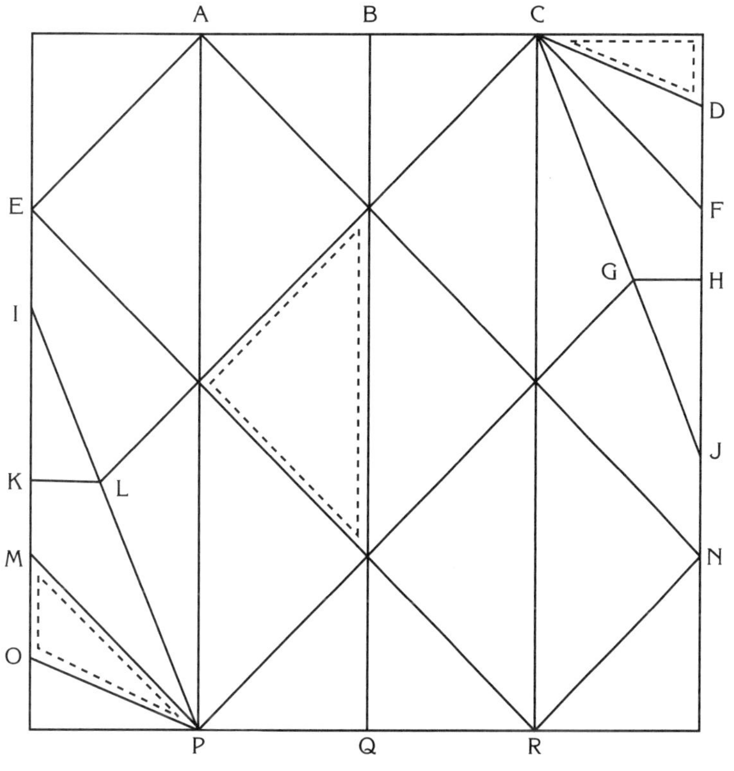

SYMMETRY

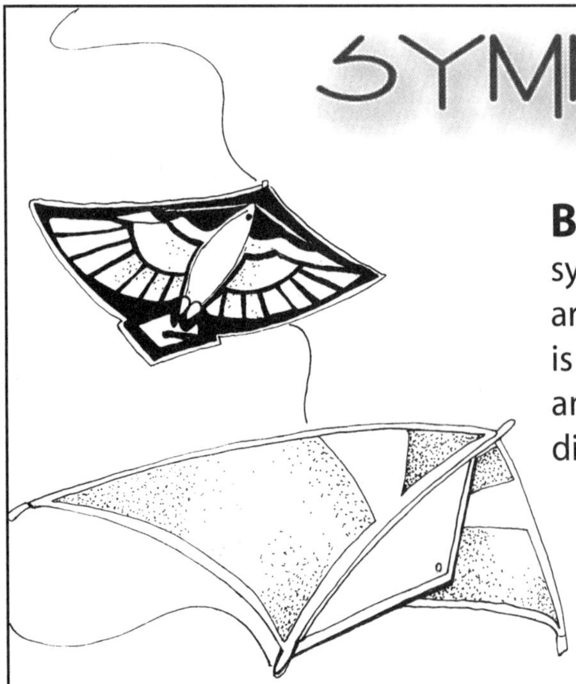

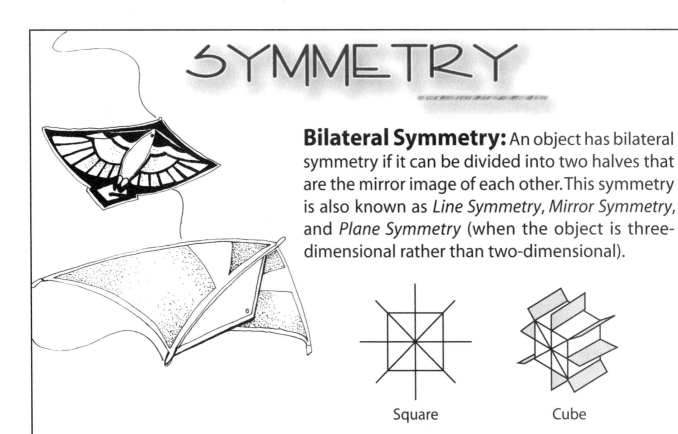

Bilateral Symmetry: An object has bilateral symmetry if it can be divided into two halves that are the mirror image of each other. This symmetry is also known as *Line Symmetry*, *Mirror Symmetry*, and *Plane Symmetry* (when the object is three-dimensional rather than two-dimensional).

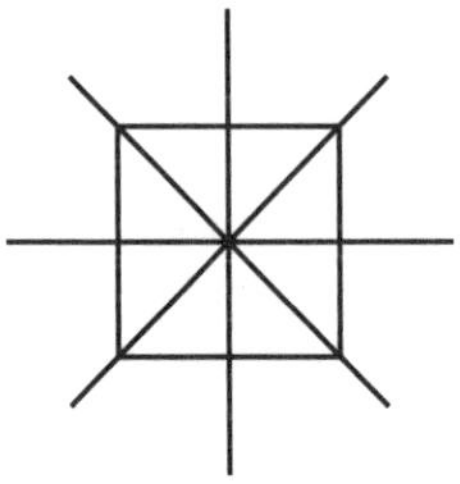

Square

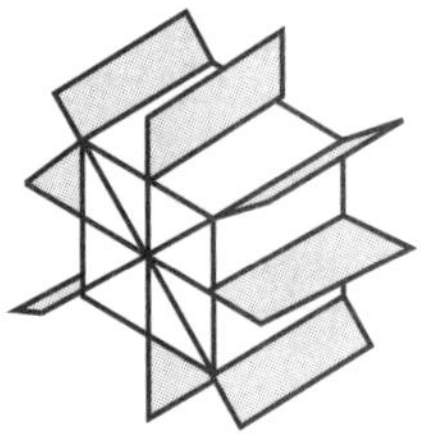

Cube

As you can see in the example above, the square has four lines of bilateral symmetry, meaning that there are exactly four places where it can be divided into two halves which are mirror images of each other. The cube, however, has more than the four planes of bilateral symmetry shown in the picture. How else could you divide a cube so that the two resulting pieces would be mirror images of each other?

Draw the line(s) of bilateral symmetry that exist in each of the figures below.

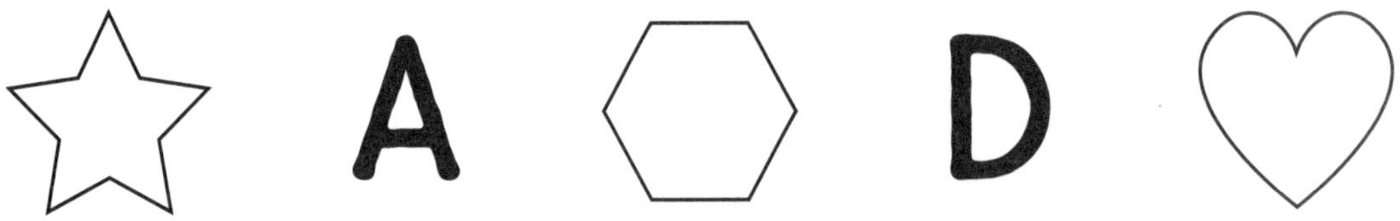

Write your first and last name in all upper case letters. How many letters in your name have bilateral symmetry? Identify each one and show the line(s) of symmetry.

SYMMETRY

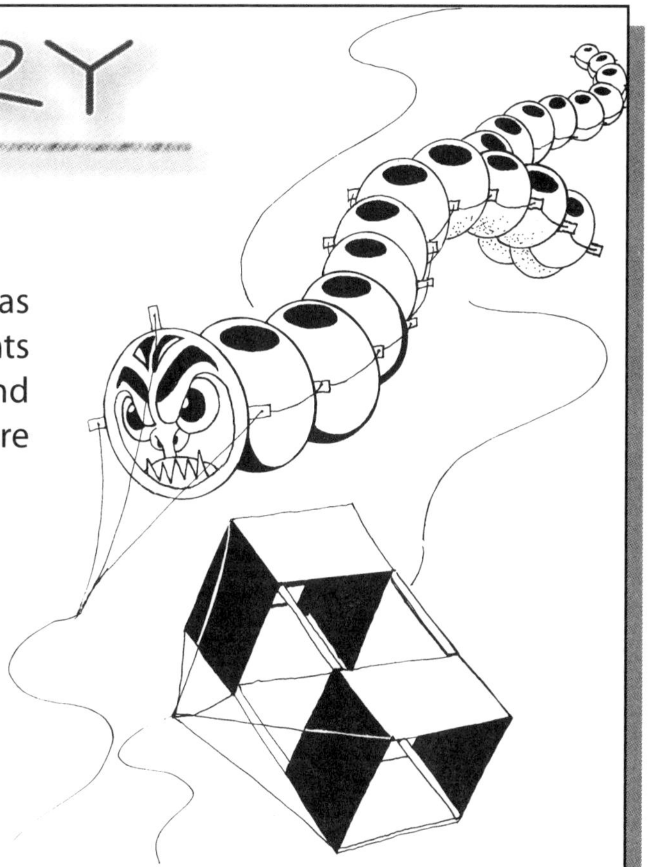

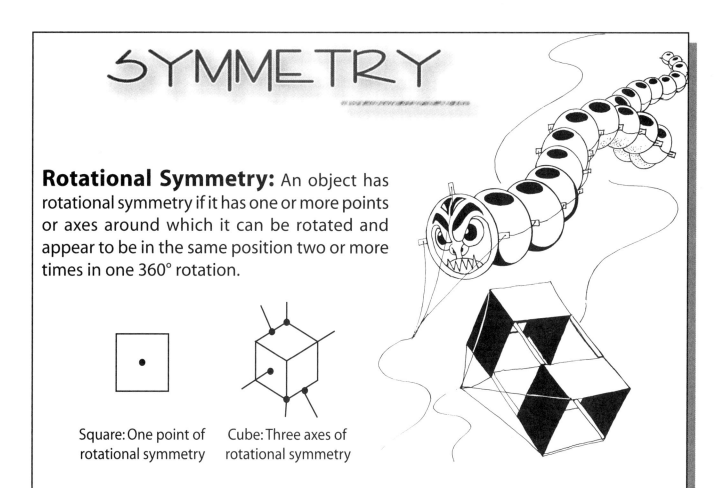

Rotational Symmetry: An object has rotational symmetry if it has one or more points or axes around which it can be rotated and appear to be in the same position two or more times in one 360° rotation.

Square: One point of rotational symmetry

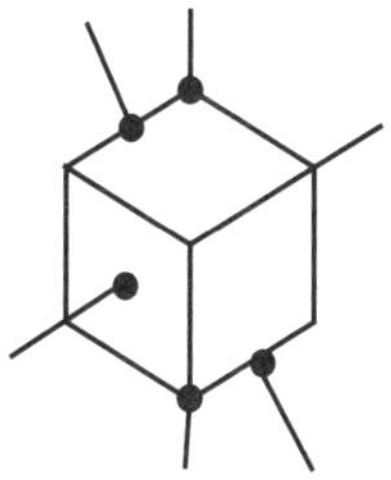

Cube: Three axes of rotational symmetry

Looking at the diagrams above, we can see that the square has one point of rotational symmetry—its center. If the square is rotated around this point, it will appear to be in the same position every 90 degrees it is rotated. The cube, however, has three different types of axes of rotational symmetry, one that goes through the center of one face to the center of the opposite face, one that goes from one vertex to the opposite vertex, and one that goes from the center of one edge to the center of the opposite edge.

Rotational symmetries are classified by the number of times an object appears to be in its original orientation during one 360° rotation. The example below shows a figure that appears to be in the same position each time it is rotated 90°. Because it can be rotated 90° four times during one 360° rotation, we say that it has 4-fold rotational symmetry.

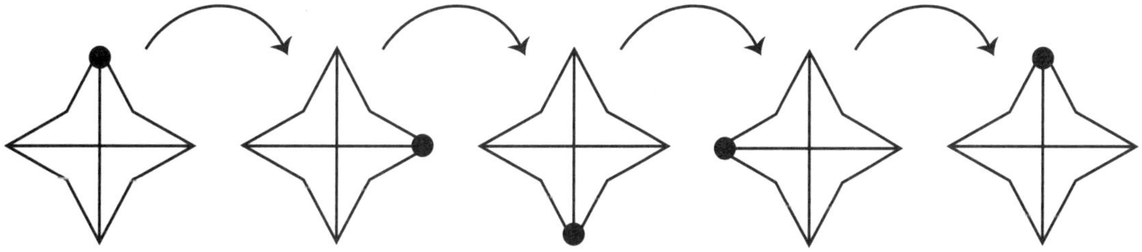

Starting position | Rotated 90° | Rotated 180° | Rotated 270° | Complete rotation

SYMMETRY

Determine the how many times each figure below will appear to be the same position in one rotation and record it in the appropriate space.

____-fold rotational symmetry	____-fold rotational symmetry	____-fold rotational symmetry	____-fold rotational symmetry	____-fold rotational symmetry

Complete the table below by filling in how many degrees you need to rotate an object to have it appear to be the same for the different rotational symmetries.

Rotational Symmetry	Degrees rotated to appear the same
2-fold	
3-fold	
4-fold	90°
5-fold	
6-fold	
7-fold	
8-fold	

RESOURCES

The resources listed here include books, paper sources, and websites. A brief description is given of each, including "best bets" for the most cost-effective option from each paper source. Please note, prices on paper were the most recent at the time of publication. AIMS is not responsible for any changes.

SELECTED ORIGAMI BOOKS

Franco, Betsy. *Unfolding Mathematics with Unit Origami.* Key Curriculum Press. Berkeley. 1999. (Examines the geometry inherent in both two- and three-dimensional folding. Contains 16 activities in blackline master form.)

Fusè, Tomoko. *Unit Origami: Multidimensional Transformations.* Japan Publications, Inc. Tokyo. 1990. (A must for unit origami, this book is one of the most complete on the subject containing many variations on everything from cubes to rhombicuboctahedrons.)

Fusè, Tomoko. *Origami Boxes.* Chikuma Shobo Publishing Co. Tokyo. 1989. (Contains multiple designs for triangular, square, hexagonal, and octagonal boxes and their lids.)

Gurkewitz, Rona and Bennett Arnstein. *3-D Geometric Origami: Modular Polyhedra.* Dover Publications. New York. 1995. (Folding instructions for over 60 different regular and irregular polyhedra.)

Hargittai, István and Magdolna. *Symmetry: A Unifying Concept.* Shelter Publications. Bolinas, CA. 1994. (Explores the different kinds of symmetry in nature, architecture, art, and geometric shapes. Also has information on the Platonic solids and stellations.)

Kasahara, Kunihko and Toshie Takahama. *Origami for the Connoisseur.* Japan Publications, Inc. Tokyo. 1987. (A wonderful well-rounded book for the advanced folder, it moves from geometric shapes to unit sculptures to flowers to intricate animal models requiring almost 50 steps to complete.)

Kenneway, Eric. *Complete Origami.* Books UK Limited. London. 1987. (An A-Z book of facts and folds with step-by-step instructions for over 100 projects. Includes background information and things other than traditional origami.)

Mitchell, David. *Mathematical Origami: Geometric Shapes by Paper Folding.* Tarquin Publications. Norfolk, VA. 1997. (Gives instructions on many regular and irregular geometric shapes including the Platonic solids mostly using A4 paper.)

Pearce, Peter and Susan. *Polyhedra Primer.* Van Nostrand Reinhold Company. New York. 1978. (A comprehensive guide to polygons and polyhedra listing faces, edges, vertices, angles, symmetries, etc.)

Simon, Lewis, Bennett Arnstein, and Rona Gurkewitz. *Modular Origami Polyhedra.* Dover Publications. New York. 1999. (Folding instructions for units to create more than 35 different modular polyhedra, including eight variations of the Sonobè unit.)

Temko, Florence. *Origami Magic.* Scholastic, Inc. New York. 1993. (Contains many simple origami projects for children, including the *Flexastar* model from this publication.)

Wenninger, Magnus J. *Polyhedron Models for the Classroom.* NCTM. Reston, VA. 1966. (A small booklet that contains valuable discussions of the Platonic solids, the Archimedean solids, and stellations, among other topics.)

SELECTED PAPER SOURCES

Please note, all prices were current at the time of publication; AIMS is not responsible for any changes.

1. AIMS Education Foundation
   http://www.aimsedu.org
   P.O. Box 8120
   Fresno, CA 93747
   (888) 733-2467
   (AIMS offers 480 sheets of six-inch squares Fadeless® paper in 20 colors for $17.95. Paper is a good weight for unit origami and is colored on the front and white on the back. Item # 4130.)

2. Key Curriculum Press
   http://www.keypress.com
   1150 65th Street
   Emeryville, CA 94608
   (800) 995-MATH
   Origami paper
   (400 sheets of six-inch squares in 20 assorted colors for $18.95. Colored on one side, white on the other. Item #: 978-1-55953-085-9)
   Patty paper
   (1000 sheets for $6.95. Item #: 978-1-55953-073-6)

3. Shizu: Traditional Japanese Paper and Origami
   http://www.shizu.com
   120 W. Colorado Blvd.
   Pasadena, CA 91105
   (626) 395-7293
   (A wide variety of origami paper in solids and prints available in various sizes and quantities. *Best bet: 100 sheets of 6" x 6" paper in assorted colors for $4.50. Item #: 0630004.*)

4. Origami USA
   http://www.origami-usa.org
   (Many different paper options including foil papers, patterned papers and Chiyogami paper. *Best bet: 100 sheets of Kami paper in six-inch squares, colored on one side, white on the other for $5.00. Item #: P10_7006)*

5. Kim's Crane
   http://www.kimscrane.com
   P.O. Box 222971
   Chantilly, VA 20153
   703-758-0061
   (Very extensive paper selection in many colors, sizes, and styles. *Best bet: "Teachers Pack of Origami Paper" 300 sheets of 150 mm (6") paper for $9.00. Item #: 090006.)*

6. Creased, Inc.
   http://creased.com
   PO Box 3529
   New York, NY 10163
   (866) CREASED
   (Origami greeting card company that sells origami paper and supplies.
   Best bet: "40 Color Tones Economy Variety Pack" 252 sheets of 6" x 6" paper I 40 colors for $8.99. Item #: 021100-1236)

SELECTED ORIGAMI WEBSITES

Due to the constantly changing nature of the Internet, AIMS cannot guarantee the permanence or the location of the pages cited.

Paperfolding.com (http://www.paperfolding.com)
The number of diagrams on this site is limited, however, it contains a very comprehensive set of origami links. It also has nice sections on *origami history* and *origami and math.*

Origami.com (http://www.origami.com)
This site, maintained by Alex Barber, is a great resource for diagrams. It has a database searchable by model, creator, or level of difficulty, a gallery with pictures of origami, and links to other folders and origami related sites on the web.

Fascinating Folds (http://www.fascinating-folds.com)
"World's Largest Supplier of Origami and Paper Arts Products" An extensive site where you can order origami paper, books, supplies, and more. Also has a learning center designed to "help teachers and educators (and parents) explore the world of Origami and the Paper Arts from an educational viewpoint."

OrigamiUSA (http://www.origami-usa.org)
The official website of OrigamiUSA, it contains a few simple diagrams, a searchable model database, information about OrigamiUSA events, and an online catalog with a great selection of origami materials.

Joseph Wu's Origami Page (http://www.origami.vancouver.bc.ca/)
An award winning site that contains countless diagrams for folding models in every category that range from the simple to quite complex. Also has probably the most extensive set of searchable links to other websites that deal with all things origami. A virtual Yellow Pages for origami—if you can't find it here, it probably doesn't exist.

Tom Hull's Origami Math Page (http://www.merrimack.edu/~thull/origamimath.html)
This site has information about origami and mathematics, links to other sites dealing with the mathematics in origami, and a very extensive bibliography of published articles dealing with the mathematical aspects of origami. It also has directions for folding a fascinating model of five intersecting tetrahedra.

The AIMS Program

AIMS is the acronym for "**A**ctivities **I**ntegrating **M**athematics and **S**cience." Such integration enriches learning and makes it meaningful and holistic. AIMS began as a project of Fresno Pacific University to integrate the study of mathematics and science in grades K-9, but has since expanded to include language arts, social studies, and other disciplines.

AIMS is a continuing program of the non-profit AIMS Education Foundation. It had its inception in a National Science Foundation funded program whose purpose was to explore the effectiveness of integrating mathematics and science. The project directors in cooperation with 80 elementary classroom teachers devoted two years to a thorough field-testing of the results and implications of integration.

The approach met with such positive results that the decision was made to launch a program to create instructional materials incorporating this concept. Despite the fact that thoughtful educators have long recommended an integrative approach, very little appropriate material was available in 1981 when the project began. A series of writing projects have ensued, and today the AIMS Education Foundation is committed to continue the creation of new integrated activities on a permanent basis.

The AIMS program is funded through the sale of books, products, and staff development workshops and through proceeds from the Foundation's endowment. All net income from program and products flows into a trust fund administered by the AIMS Education Foundation. Use of these funds is restricted to support of research, development, and publication of new materials. Writers donate all their rights to the Foundation to support its on-going program. No royalties are paid to the writers.

The rationale for integration lies in the fact that science, mathematics, language arts, social studies, etc., are integrally interwoven in the real world from which it follows that they should be similarly treated in the classroom where we are preparing students to live in that world. Teachers who use the AIMS program give enthusiastic endorsement to the effectiveness of this approach.

Science encompasses the art of questioning, investigating, hypothesizing, discovering, and communicating. Mathematics is the language that provides clarity, objectivity, and understanding. The language arts provide us powerful tools of communication. Many of the major contemporary societal issues stem from advancements in science and must be studied in the context of the social sciences. Therefore, it is timely that all of us take seriously a more holistic mode of educating our students. This goal motivates all who are associated with the AIMS Program. We invite you to join us in this effort.

Meaningful integration of knowledge is a major recommendation coming from the nation's professional science and mathematics associations. The American Association for the Advancement of Science in *Science for All Americans* strongly recommends the integration of mathematics, science, and technology. The National Council of Teachers of Mathematics places strong emphasis on applications of mathematics such as are found in science investigations. AIMS is fully aligned with these recommendations.

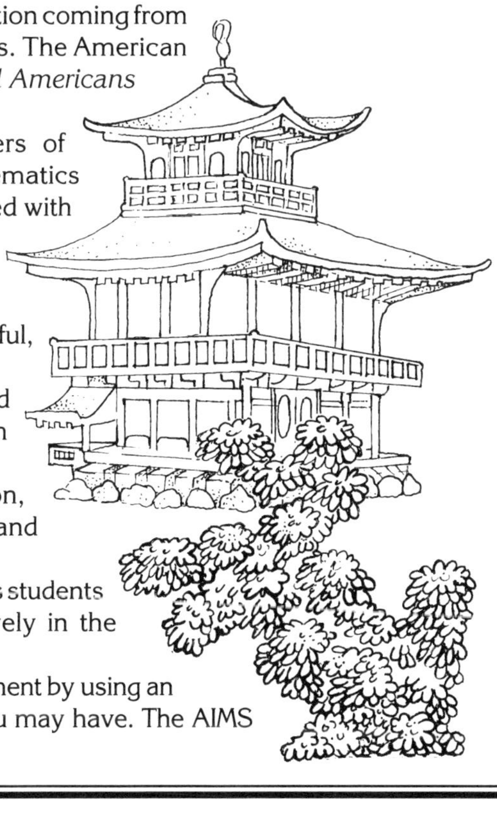

Extensive field testing of AIMS investigations confirms these beneficial results:

1. Mathematics becomes more meaningful, hence more useful, when it is applied to situations that interest students.
2. The extent to which science is studied and understood is increased, with a significant economy of time, when mathematics and science are integrated.
3. There is improved quality of learning and retention, supporting the thesis that learning which is meaningful and relevant is more effective.
4. Motivation and involvement are increased dramatically as students investigate real-world situations and participate actively in the process.

We invite you to become part of this classroom teacher movement by using an integrated approach to learning and sharing any suggestions you may have. The AIMS Program welcomes you!

AIMS Education Foundation Programs

Practical proven strategies to improve student achievement

When you host an AIMS workshop for elementary and middle school educators, you will know your teachers are receiving effective usable training they can apply in their classrooms immediately.

Designed for teachers—AIMS Workshops:

- Correlate to your state standards;
- Address key topic areas, including math content, science content, problem solving, and process skills;
- Teach you how to use AIMS' effective hands-on approach;
- Provide practice of activity-based teaching;
- Address classroom management issues, higher-order thinking skills, and materials;
- Give you AIMS resources; and
- Offer college (graduate-level) credits for many courses.

Aligned to district and administrator needs—AIMS workshops offer:

- Flexible scheduling and grade span options;
- Custom (one-, two-, or three-day) workshops to meet specific schedule, topic and grade-span needs;
- Pre-packaged one-day workshops on most major topics—only $3,900 for up to 30 participants (includes all materials and expenses);
- Prepackaged *week-long* workshops (four- or five-day formats) for in-depth math and science training—only $12,300 for up to 30 participants (includes all materials and expenses);
- Sustained staff development, by scheduling workshops throughout the school year and including follow-up and assessment;
- Eligibility for funding under the Eisenhower Act and No Child Left Behind; and
- Affordable professional development—save when you schedule consecutive-day workshops.

University Credit—Correspondence Courses

AIMS offers correspondence courses through a partnership with Fresno Pacific University.

- Convenient distance-learning courses—you study at your own pace and schedule. No computer or Internet access required!

The tuition for each three-semester unit graduate-level course is $264 plus a materials fee.

The AIMS Instructional Leadership Program

This is an AIMS staff-development program seeking to prepare facilitators for leadership roles in science/math education in their home districts or regions. Upon successful completion of the program, trained facilitators become members of the AIMS Instructional Leadership Network, qualified to conduct AIMS workshops, teach AIMS in-service courses for college credit, and serve as AIMS consultants. Intensive training is provided in mathematics, science, process and thinking skills, workshop management, and other relevant topics.

Introducing AIMS Science Core Curriculum

Developed in alignment with your state standards, AIMS' Science Core Curriculum gives students the opportunity to build content knowledge, thinking skills, and fundamental science processes.

- *Each* grade specific module has been developed to extend the AIMS approach to full-year science programs.
- *Each* standards-based module includes math, reading, hands-on investigations, and assessments.

Like all AIMS resources these core modules are able to serve students at all stages of readiness, making these a great value across the grades served in your school.

For current information regarding the programs described above, please complete the following:

Information Request

Please send current information on the items checked:

_____ *Basic Information Packet* on AIMS materials ____ Hosting information for AIMS workshops
_____ *AIMS Instructional Leadership Program* ____ AIMS Science Core Curriculum

Name ____________________ Phone ____________________

Address ____
Street City State Zip

AIMS Program Publications

Actions with Fractions, 4-9
Awesome Addition and Super Subtraction, 2-3
Bats Incredible! 2-4
Brick Layers II, 4-9
Chemistry Matters, 4-7
Counting on Coins, K-2
Cycles of Knowing and Growing, 1-3
Crazy about Cotton, 3-7
Critters, 2-5
Electrical Connections, 4-9
Exploring Environments, K-6
Fabulous Fractions, 3-6
Fall into Math and Science, K-1
Field Detectives, 3-6
Finding Your Bearings, 4-9
Floaters and Sinkers, 5-9
From Head to Toe, 5-9
Fun with Foods, 5-9
Glide into Winter with Math and Science, K-1
Gravity Rules! 5-12
Hardhatting in a Geo-World, 3-5
It's About Time, K-2
It Must Be A Bird, Pre-K-2
Jaw Breakers and Heart Thumpers, 3-5
Looking at Geometry, 6-9
Looking at Lines, 6-9
Machine Shop, 5-9
Magnificent Microworld Adventures, 5-9
Marvelous Multiplication and Dazzling Division, 4-5
Math + Science, A Solution, 5-9
Mostly Magnets, 2-8
Movie Math Mania, 6-9
Multiplication the Algebra Way, 6-8
Off the Wall Science, 3-9
Out of This World, 4-8
Paper Square Geometry:
The Mathematics of Origami, 5-12
Puzzle Play, 4-8
Pieces and Patterns, 5-9
Popping With Power, 3-5
Positive vs. Negative, 6-9
Primarily Bears, K-6
Primarily Earth, K-3
Primarily Physics, K-3
Primarily Plants, K-3
Problem Solving: Just for the Fun of It! 4-9
Problem Solving: Just for the Fun of It! Book Two, 4-9
Proportional Reasoning, 6-9
Ray's Reflections, 4-8
Sensational Springtime, K-2
Sense-Able Science, K-1
Soap Films and Bubbles, 4-9
Solve It! K-1: Problem-Solving Strategies, K-1
Solve It! 2nd: Problem-Solving Strategies, 2
Solve It! 3rd: Problem-Solving Strategies, 3
Solve It! 4th: Problem-Solving Strategies, 4
Solve It! 5th: Problem-Solving Strategies, 5
Spatial Visualization, 4-9
Spills and Ripples, 5-12
Spring into Math and Science, K-1
The Amazing Circle, 4-9
The Budding Botanist, 3-6
The Sky's the Limit, 5-9
Through the Eyes of the Explorers, 5-9
Under Construction, K-2
Water Precious Water, 2-6
Weather Sense: Temperature, Air Pressure, and Wind, 4-5
Weather Sense: Moisture, 4-5
Winter Wonders, K-2

Spanish Supplements*
Fall Into Math and Science, K-1
Glide Into Winter with Math and Science, K-1
Mostly Magnets, 2-8
Pieces and Patterns, 5-9
Primarily Bears, K-6
Primarily Physics, K-3
Sense-Able Science, K-1
Spring Into Math and Science, K-1

* Spanish supplements are only available as downloads from the AIMS website. The supplements contain only the student pages in Spanish; you will need the English version of the book for the teacher's text.

Spanish Edition
Constructores II: Ingeniería Creativa Con Construcciones LEGO® 4-9
The entire book is written in Spanish. English pages not included.

Other Publications
Historical Connections in Mathematics, Vol. I, 5-9
Historical Connections in Mathematics, Vol. II, 5-9
Historical Connections in Mathematics, Vol. III, 5-9
Mathematicians are People, Too
Mathematicians are People, Too, Vol. II
What's Next, Volume 1, 4-12
What's Next, Volume 2, 4-12
What's Next, Volume 3, 4-12

For further information write to:
AIMS Education Foundation • P.O. Box 8120 • Fresno, California 93747-8120
www.aimsedu.org • 559.255.6396 (fax) • 888.733.2467 (toll free)

Duplication Rights

Standard Duplication Rights

Purchasers of AIMS activities (individually or in books and magazines) may make up to 200 copies of any portion of the purchased activities, provided these copies will be used for educational purposes and only at one school site.

Workshop or conference presenters may make one copy of a purchased activity for each participant, with a limit of five activities per workshop or conference session.

Standard duplication rights apply to activities received at workshops, free sample activities provided by AIMS, and activities received by conference participants.

All copies must bear the AIMS Education Foundation copyright information.

Unlimited Duplication Rights

To ensure compliance with copyright regulations, AIMS users may upgrade from standard to unlimited duplication rights. Such rights permit unlimited duplication of purchased activities (including revisions) for use at a given school site.

Activities received at workshops are eligible for upgrade from standard to unlimited duplication rights.

Free sample activities and activities received as a conference participant are not eligible for upgrade from standard to unlimited duplication rights.

Upgrade Fees

The fees for upgrading from standard to unlimited duplication rights are:
- $5 per activity per site,
- $25 per book per site, and
- $10 per magazine issue per site.

The cost of upgrading is shown in the following examples:
- activity: 5 activities x 5 sites x $5 = $125
- book: 10 books x 5 sites x $25 = $1250
- magazine issue: 1 issue x 5 sites x $10 = $50

Purchasing Unlimited Duplication Rights

To purchase unlimited duplication rights, please provide us the following:
1. The name of the individual responsible for coordinating the purchase of duplication rights.
2. The title of each book, activity, and magazine issue to be covered.
3. The number of school sites and name of each site for which rights are being purchased.
4. Payment (check, purchase order, credit card)

Requested duplication rights are automatically authorized with payment. The individual responsible for coordinating the purchase of duplication rights will be sent a certificate verifying the purchase.

Internet Use

Permission to make AIMS activities available on the Internet is determined on a case-by-case basis.

• P. O. Box 8120, Fresno, CA 93747-8120 •
• aimsed@aimsedu.org • www.aimsedu.org •
• 559.255.6396 (fax) • 888.733.2467 (toll free) •